The Author

Hadhrat Mirza Bashir-ud-din Mahmud Ahmad was the son and second successor of Hadhrat Mirza Ghulam Ahmad, the Promised Messiah and Founder of the Ahmadiyya Movement in Islam. He was born on 12 January 1889, in fulfilment of a prophecy made by the Founder of the Movement in 1886 foretelling some of the attributes of the promised Son, and was elected Head of the Ahmadiyya Movement in 1914 at the early age of twenty-five. He died in 1965. His works cover a wide field, and explain the significance of the cardinal doctrines of Islam such as the Existence and Unity of God, the significance and functions of Angels, the Doctrine of predestination, the Islamic concept of salvation, and the economic order of Islam. He also translated the Holy Quran into Urdu and wrote a detailed commentary on it.

He it is Who has sent His Messenger with the guidance and the true faith that He may make it prevail over all other faiths.

(Al-Quran, 9:33; 48:29; 61:10)

Invitation to Ahmadiyyat

Being a statement of beliefs, a rationale of claims and an invitation, on behalf of the Ahmadiyya Movement for the propagation and rejuvenation of Islam

by

Hadhrat Mirza Bashir-ud-din Mahmud Ahmad
Khalifatul Masih II

ISALAM INTERNATIONAL PUBLICATIONS LTD

INVITATION TO AHMADIYYAT

(Dawatul Amir)

English translation

The original Dawat al-Amir (in Urdu) was published in 1926. A translation into Persian by the late Maulvi Ghulam Ahmad of Ooch was published the same year. Several impressions of the Urdu edition have appeared since. It was translated into English by Qazi Muhammad Aslam, and was published in Pakistan in 1961. First published in UK in 1980 by *Routledge & Kegan Paul Ltd.*

Third edition (UK) 1997
Fourth edition (UK) 2002
Present edition (UK) 2007

Published by:
Islam International Publications Ltd.
Islamabad,
Sheephatch Lane
Tilford, Surrey GU10 2AQ
United Kingdom

Printed in U.K. by:
The Bath Press,
Lower Bristol Road,
Bath, BA2 3BL.

British Library Cataloguing in Publication Data

Ahmad, Mirza Bashir-ud-din Mahmud
Invitation to Ahmadiyyat
1. *Islam* 2. *Ahmadiyya*
I. Title
297 BP163 78-41203

ISBN 0 7100 0119 3
ISBN 1 85372 608 7

Contents

Part III Invitation

Foreword

By Mirza Mubarak Ahmad, Secretary, Tabshir, Jama'at-i-Ahmadiyya

Invitation to Ahmadiyyat is an English translation of *Dawat al-Amir*, an epistle written in Urdu and presented in Persian to a Ruler of Afghanistan, Amanullah Khan. The epistle was in the best tradition of evangelism, which at all times in history has used this medium of exposition for the benefit of earthly rulers and their subjects.

The present epistle acquired special significance from the fact that about two years before its presentation three Afghan Ahmadis were stoned to death by the orders of Amanullah Khan. The tragic events made it necessary that the message, aims, and rationale of the Ahmadiyya Movement should be expounded for the special attention of the then King. The events and the epistle now belong to history, but their significance not only survives but keeps increasing in its impact and influence. No wonder *Dawat al-Amir* has seen several editions since it was first published. The present edition is the first in English. In this the varying forms of address used in the original for the then Ruler of Afghanistan have been dropped; instead, the simple address 'dear reader' has been inserted in appropriate places.

The epistle has become associated with the name of Khan Faqir Muhammad Khan, well known in Peshawar and the districts around, whose conversion to Ahmadiyyat he himself attributed to it. Virtually against his instructions a copy of the *Dawat* had been included in his baggage for a holiday in Europe. In Europe the Khan was overwhelmed by the material prosperity and progress of the West and the dominance over Muslims and the rest of the world which Christian nations had come to have in our time. Will there be a change? the Khan asked himself. Were Muslims to remain down and out, never to rise again as the spiritual leaders of the world? Bewildered, the Khan searched for something in his baggage and found this book. He began to read. In it he found a description of the prosperity and power and other signs of the Christian West, prophesied by the Holy

Prophet. If these signs had come true, he thought, the promise relating to the rebirth of Islam could also be true. The promise of Islamic rebirth, according to prophecies, centred round the Muslim Messiah. He read on and on, and before he had finished, he had become convinced that Ahmadiyyat was the answer to the challenge posed to Islam by the Christian West.

Translator's Note

The translator's grateful thanks are due to all those at the Ahmadiyya Headquarters, Rabwah, who have been concerned in the preparation and publication of this English version of this well-known book by the present Head of the Ahmadiyya Movement. Most of all he is grateful to his friend Sahibzada Mirza Mubarak Ahmad and the Tabshir Staff for the interest they have taken in this venture and the assistance they have provided in seeing it into print and also to Chaudhri Muhammad Ali for special assistance in checking the English of the translation.

Thanks are also due to steno-typists Mirza Rahmatullah and Salim Ahmad and typist Nazir Husain for the pains they took over the type-script; also to the translator's daughter Kausar and her husband Ishaq, under whose roof the corrections of the translation were finalized. This reminds him also of the years he spent at Government College, Lahore, where the translation was prepared during intervals of leisure from the heavy duties of a college professor and principal. The translator owes much to the comforts and conveniences of those days; so he remembers them with gratitude.

The translation itself may be described as a moderately free translation, the major aim of which is to communicate a vital theme of contemporary Islam to readers who prefer to read about it in English. The idiom, vocabulary, and rhapsody of the original Urdu are not easy to turn into English; they certainly could not be presented except by taking a certain amount of freedom with the original; the freedom, however, has been kept to a minimum.

I seek refuge with Allah from
Satan the Accursed

In the name of the Most Gracious,
the Most Merciful

We praise Him and invoke His blessings on
His Noble Prophet

With the grace and mercy of God,
He, the only Helper

Part 1

Preliminaries

On the Reader peace and the Mercy of God and His Blessings!

The following pages contain an account of the beliefs and teachings of the Ahmadiyya Movement in Islam, an elucidation of the claims of its Holy Founder and the arguments on which they are based.

My object in writing these pages, dear reader, is to deliver to you and others the Message which God has addressed to mankind today to bring them again to Islam and its Holy Prophet (on whom be peace and the blessings of God). If you take the trouble to read these through you will not only earn *my* deep gratitude but also the Grace and Approval of *God*.

The names Ahmadi, Ahmadiyyat

A point I wish to make quite clear at the outset is that the names Ahmadi, Ahmadiyyat, etc., do not point to a new religion. Ahmadis are Muslims and their religion is Islam. The slightest deviation from it they consider wrong and degrading. True, Ahmadis have adopted the names Ahmadiyyat, Ahmadiyya Movement, Ahmadiyya Jama'at and so on. But the adoption of a name is not the adoption of a new religion. The name Ahmadiyyat is the name of a reinterpretation or a restatement of the Religion of the Holy Quran. It is a restatement presented under divine guidance by the Founder of the Ahmadiyya Movement. The names Ahmadi, Ahmadiyyat, etc., are meant only to distinguish Ahmadi Muslims from other Muslims, Ahmadi interpretation from other interpretations of Islam.

The name Islam

The name Islam is the name which God Himself gave to the

followers of the Holy Prophet and which long before him had found an honoured place in the prophecies of earlier prophets. Thus the Holy Quran says:

هُوَ سَمّٰىكُمُ الْمُسْلِمِيْنَ مِنْ قَبْلُ وَ فِيْ هٰذَا

'He [God] gave you the name Muslims before, as well as in this [the Quran].'[1]

And in the Bible:

'Thou shalt be called by a new name, which the mouth of the Lord shall name.'[2]

No name can be more blessed than the name which God Himself chose for His servants and which He invested with importance by making other prophets prophesy about it. Who will give up this name?

It is dearer to us than our lives. The religion it connotes is for us the only religion, the only source of spiritual life.

But as in our time different groups of Muslims, out of regard for their special beliefs and outlook, have adopted different names, it became necessary for us to adopt a name to distinguish ourselves from others. The best name we could adopt was the name Ahmadi or Ahmadiyyat. This name has a significance for our time. Ours is the time appointed for the propagation, *all over the world*, of the Universal Message of the Holy Prophet (on whom be peace). It is the time for the diffusion of the Praises of God and for the spread of a knowledge of His Bounty and Beauty, the time for the manifestation of the attribute of *Ahmadiyyat*, the attribute of *Muhammadiyyat* having had its manifestation already. A better name could not have been adopted by us.

We are Muslims heart and soul. We hold the beliefs a true Muslim must hold, and deny the beliefs a true Muslim must deny. If, in spite of our sincere subscribing to the truths of Islam and our conforming to the Commands of God, anybody attributes unbelief, or *Kufr*, to us and describes us as innovators or as believers in a new religion, he is unkind and cruel. He is answerable to God for this. A man may be convicted for what he declares with his mouth, not for

1 *Al Hajj*, 79.

2 Isaiah 62:2.

what he holds in his heart. For who can say what is in a man's heart? If a person accuses another of saying one thing and believing another, he raises himself to the status of God. Only God knows what is in human hearts. Only He can say what a man thinks and believes. The Holy Prophet (on whom be peace) admitted this human limitation. And yet, who could know another man's heart better than he? Says he:

اِنَّكُمْ تَخْتَصِمُوْنَ اِلَيَّ وَ اِنَّمَآ اَنَا بَشَرٌ مِّثْلُكُمْ وَلَعَلَّ بَعْضَكُمْ اَنْ يَّكُوْنَ
اَلْحَنَ بِحُجَّتِهٖ مِنْ بَعْضٍ، فَاِنْ قَضَيْتُ لِاَحَدٍ مِّنْكُمْ بِشَيْءٍ مِّنْ حَقِّ
اَخِيْهِ فَاِنَّمَآ اَقْطَعُ لَهٗ قِطْعَةً مِّنَ النَّارِ فَلَا يَاْخُذْ مِنْهُ شَيْئًا

> 'There are amongst you those who bring their disputes to me. I am a man as much as you. It is possible that some amongst you may espouse their cause better than others. Therefore, if I give to one what is due to another, I give to him a part of the fire. It is for him to refuse.'[3]

We read in the Traditions that Usama bin Zaid was appointed commander of a division by the Holy Prophet (on whom be peace). Usama confronted an unbeliever whom he attacked. When he was about to be killed, this unbeliever recited the *Kalima*, affirming his faith in the truth of Islam. Usama killed him nevertheless. When the Holy Prophet heard of this, he castigated Usama. Usama said in his own defence: 'O Prophet of God, he did so out of fear,' upon which the Holy Prophet said, 'Why? Did you split his heart to see?' Knowledge of what passes in human hearts is not given to ordinary mortals. It was not for Usama to guess whether this man's affirmation of Islam was out of fear or conviction.

Therefore, we may be condemned for what we declare, not for what may be supposed to lie in our hearts. What lies in our hearts is known only to God. He who claims to condemn another for what is in his heart exceeds his limits and is answerable to God for his excess.

So, while we of the Ahmadiyya Jama'at declare ourselves Muslims, nobody has the right to say that our Islam is a pretence; that at heart we deny Islam or deny the Holy Prophet (on whom be

3 Sahi-al-Bukhari, *Kitabul-Ahkam*, chap. *Muuzatul-Iman*.

peace); that we subscribe to a new *Kalima* or turn to a new *Qibla* in our prayers. If it were right for others to attribute such things to us, it would be right for us to attribute such things to others. We could say that *their* declaration of Islam is a pretence, that *they*, God forbid, deny Islam and the Holy Prophet when they repair to their homes. But we cannot be led astray by opposition. We will not say of anyone that he says one thing and believes another; that he has one thing on his lips and another in his heart. In deference to the *Shariyat*, our judgment of others will be based on what they openly affirm and acknowledge.

Beliefs held by Ahmadis

I now proceed to enumerate the beliefs held by our Jama'at so that you can see whether any of them are contrary to Islam:

(1) We believe that God exists; to subscribe to a belief in His existence is to affirm the most important truth; it is not to follow an illusion or superstition.

(2) We believe that God is One. He has no partner here or in Heaven. Everything else is His creation, dependent on His help and sustenance. He is without son or daughter or father or mother or wife or brothers, Unique in His Oneness and in His Individuality.

(3) We believe that God is Holy, free from all defects and full of all perfections. There is no imperfection which may be found in Him, and no perfection which may not be found in Him. His Power is unlimited. So is His Knowledge. He encompasses everything and there is nothing which encompasses Him. He is the First and the Last, the Manifest and the Hidden, the Creator and Master of all creation. His control has never failed in the past, nor is it failing at present, nor will it fail in the future. Free from death, He is the Living, the Enduring. He suffers no defect or decay. His actions are willed, not forced or constrained. He rules over the world today as He ever ruled before. His attributes are eternal, His power always evident.

(4) We believe that angels are a part of God's creation. They follow the law laid down in the Quran – 'they do what they are commanded.' They have been created in His Wisdom for the discharge of determinate duties. Their existence is real and references to them in the Holy Book are not metaphorical. They depend

on God in the same way as men or His other creatures. He is not dependent on them for the manifestation of His power. Had He willed, He would have created the universe without angels, but His perfect wisdom willed their creation. So angels came into being. God created light for the eye and bread for hunger. He created light and bread not because He was in need of them but because man was in need of them. The angels only manifest the Will and Wisdom of God.

(5) We believe that God speaks to His chosen servants and reveals to them His purpose. Revelation from God descends in words. The recipient provides neither the meaning nor the words of revelation. Both come from Him. Revelation provides real sustenance for man. Man lives by it, and through it man comes to have contact with God. The words which embody a revelation of God are unique in their power and majesty. No man can coin such words. They carry treasures of knowledge and wisdom. They are like a mine the stone of which is the more valuable the deeper you dig. Indeed, a mine is nothing compared with revelation. A mine can be exhausted, but not the wisdom of revelation. Revelation is like a sea with a scented surface and a bed strewn with the most precious pearls. Those who turn to the surface enjoy the fragrance of the surface, and those who dive deep find the pearls below. Revelation is of many kinds. Sometimes it consists of ordinances and laws, sometimes of exhortations. Sometimes it brings knowledge of the unseen, sometimes knowledge of spiritual truths. Sometimes it conveys the goodwill and approval of God, sometimes His disapproval and displeasure, sometimes His love and regard, sometimes warnings and rebukes. Sometimes it teaches points of morality, sometimes His insight into secret evils. In short, our belief is that God communicates His Will to His servants. These communications vary according to the circumstances and the spiritual status of the recipient. Of all divine communications, the most perfect, the most complete and comprehensive, is the Holy Quran. The law laid down in the Holy Quran and the spiritual guidance it contains are to last for ever. They cannot be superseded by any future revelation or communication from God.

(6) We also believe that when darkness prevails in the world and human beings sink deep in sin and evil, when without the help of God it becomes difficult for them to release themselves from the hold of Satan, then out of His Mercy and Beneficence, God chooses

from out of His own loving and loyal servants those whom He charges with the duty to guide the world. God says, 'And there are not a people but had had a warner.'[4] This means that God has sent His Messengers to all peoples of the world. Their pure lives and perfect example ever serve as guides for other human beings. Through them God reveals His will and purpose. Those who turn away from them degrade themselves. Those who turn to them earn the love of God. The doors of His blessings are opened to them. His grace and mercy descend on them. They become spiritual preceptors for generations to come and attain greatness in this world and the next.

(7) We also believe that Divine Messengers, who in the past have helped mankind out of darkness and evil, have belonged to different levels of spiritual greatness and have fulfilled in different degrees the divine purpose which determined their advent. The greatest of them was the Holy Prophet (on whom be peace and the blessings of God). God described him as 'the chief of men, a messenger unto all mankind'. God revealed to him the knowledge of good and evil and blessed him with His help. The most powerful earthly rulers trembled in awe of him. The entire earth was as sacred as a mosque to him. The time came when his followers could be seen in every part of the world; in every part there were believers who bowed and prostrated themselves before the One God, the God without an equal. Justice began to reign instead of injustice, kindness instead of cruelty. If the earlier prophets had lived in the time of our Holy Prophet, they would have had to obey and follow him. Truly has the Quran said:

وَإِذْ أَخَذَ اللّٰهُ مِيْثَاقَ النَّبِيّٖنَ لَمَآ اٰتَيْتُكُمْ مِّنْ كِتٰبٍ وَّحِكْمَةٍ
ثُمَّ جَآءَكُمْ رَسُوْلٌ مُّصَدِّقٌ لِّمَا مَعَكُمْ لَتُؤْمِنُنَّ بِهٖ وَلَتَنْصُرُنَّهٗ

'And remember the time when Allah took a covenant from the people through the prophets, saying "whatever I give you of the Book and Wisdom and then there comes to you a Messenger fulfilling what is with you, you shall believe in him and help him."'[5]

Truly has the Holy Prophet himself (on whom be peace and the blessings of God) said:

4 *Al-Fatir*, 25.

5 *Al-Imran*, 82.

لَوْ كَانَ مُوْسٰى وَعِيْسٰى حَيَّيْنِ لَمَا وَسِعَهُمَا إِلَّا اتِّبَاعِيْ

'If Moses and Jesus were alive today, they would have had to believe in me and follow me.'[6]

(8) We also believe that God hears the prayers of His suppliants and servants. He helps them out of difficulties. He is a Living God, His living character being evident in all things, at all times. The guidance that comes from God is not like the scaffold we build when we dig for a well, to be destroyed after the well has been built, being required no more; a hindrance rather than a help. The guidance that comes from the Living God is like the light, but for which we should see nothing; it is like the spirit, but for which everything would become dead. Take away the spirit and we would be only lifeless masses. It is not true that God created the world and then chose to sit by. He continues His beneficent and benevolent interest in His servants and creatures. When they feel humble and weak, He turns to them with His help. If they forget Him, He reminds them of Himself and of His concern and solicitude for them. Then through special Messengers He reassures them, saying:

فَإِنِّيْ قَرِيْبٌ ۖ أُجِيْبُ دَعْوَةَ الدَّاعِ إِذَا دَعَانِ فَلْيَسْتَجِيْبُوْا لِيْ
وَلْيُؤْمِنُوْا بِيْ لَعَلَّهُمْ يَرْشُدُوْنَ ۔

'I am near indeed. I answer the prayer of the suppliant when he prays to Me. So that they should hearken to Me and believe in Me that they may go aright.'[7]

That is, God hears the prayers of His men. It is up to men to believe in Him and pray to Him. If they do so, they will have guidance from Him.

(9) We also believe that from time to time God determines and designs the course of events in special ways. Events of this world are not determined entirely by the laws known as the laws of nature. Besides these laws, there are special laws through which God manifests His might, interest, and purpose. It is these special laws which constitute evidence of the Will and Power and Love of

6 Tafsir Ibn-i-Kasir, vol. 2, p. 246. 7 *Al-Baqarah*, 187.

God, but which many out of ignorance deny. Such men believe in nothing besides the laws of nature. Yet laws of nature may be laws of nature but not laws of God. Laws of God are laws through which God helps His chosen ones, those whom He loves; through them He disgraces and destroys the enemies of His friends. If there were no such laws, could the weak and friendless Moses have triumphed over a cruel and mighty Pharaoh? Could Moses succeed and Pharaoh fail while Moses was weak and Pharaoh strong? If there are no laws other than the laws of nature, how could the Holy Prophet Muhammad have triumphed against an Arabia determined to put an end to him and his mission? In every encounter God helped the Holy Prophet and made him triumph over his enemies. Every attack the enemies made ended in failure, and at last, with ten thousand saints, he re-entered the valley out of which, ten years before, he had had to flee for his life in the company of only one self-sacrificing friend. Can laws of nature account for such events? Can they permit such things? Laws of nature only guarantee the success of the strong against the weak; and conversely, the failure of the weak against the strong.

(10) We also believe that death is not the end of all existence for human beings. Man survives death and has to account for his deeds in the Hereafter. Those who do good deeds merit generous rewards. Those who offend against His teachings and commandments meet the punishment which is their due. Nothing can avert this reckoning. Human beings must survive and face it. A man may be burnt to ashes and the ashes dispersed in the air; he may be eaten by birds or animals or worms or reduced to dust and the dust changed into something else; he will nevertheless live after death and meet his Maker to give an account of his deeds. The Power of God guarantees human survival. It is not necessary that the human body should remain intact in order that the human soul may survive. God has the power to restore a man to life from the meanest particle or atom of his soul or being. That is how it will happen. The body may be reduced to ashes, but the ashes need not disappear into nothing. Nor can the spirit, housed in the body, pass into nothing. Not without the Will of God.

(11) We believe that non-believers in God and enemies of His revealed guidance, unless forgiven out of His infinite mercy, will stay in a place called Hell. Extremes of heat and cold will be the punishments awarded in this place, but the object will not be to

give pain to the inmates, but to reform them. In Hell, unbelievers and enemies of God will spend their days in wailing and woe, in regrets over days spent in evil. They will continue so until the Mercy of God, which encompasses all things, will encompass the evil-doers and their evil also. Then will the Promise of God be fulfilled which the Holy Prophet announced.

يأتي على جهنم زمان ليس فيها احد ونسيم الصبا تحرك ابوابها

> 'A time will come when no one will be left in Hell; winds will blow and the windows and doors of Hell will make a rattling noise on account of the blowing winds.'[8]

(12) We believe that those who believe in God, His prophets, His angels and His books; who affirm with heart and soul the guidance which comes from Him; who walk in humility and abase themselves in His presence; who live like the poor though they be rich; who serve humanity and sacrifice their comfort for others; who abjure excesses of all kinds, hate, cruelty, and transgression; who are models of human goodness – these men will go to a place called Heaven. Peace and pleasure will reign in this place. Pain will not exist. The pleasure and approval of God will have been won by every man. God will be present to all, His Universal Grace enveloping every one. So near will God be and so conscious will everyone become of His existence and presence that everyone will be as a mirror reflecting God and His perfect attributes. All the low desires of men will disappear. The desires of men will be the desires of God. They will have attained everlasting life, every one an image of his Creator.

These are our beliefs. Whether there are any other beliefs which one must accept before one can be said to subscribe to Islam, we do not know. The doctors of Islam point to no other belief. We affirm all the beliefs of Islam and hold these beliefs as our beliefs.

Differences from other Muslims

Now, dear reader, you may be wondering why we are thought to

8 Tafsir-ul-Maalam-ut-tanzil under the verse:
فاما الذين شقوا ففي النار (*Hud*: verse 107).

be so different, when we accept and subscribe whole-heartedly to all the well-known beliefs of Islam. Why is it that the scholars of religion, the *Ulema*, are so violently opposed to us? Why these *Fatwas* of *Kufr* (proclamations of unbelief) against us?

In reply, I can only cite the objections which the *Ulema* have raised against us, because of which we are said to have strayed out of the fold of Islam. May God guard you against evil designs and may He open to you the gates of His Grace!

Jesus died a natural death

The first and the most crucial objection raised against us by our enemies is that we believe that Jesus of Nazareth died a natural death. To believe that Jesus died a natural death is said to be an insult to Jesus, an offence to the Holy Quran and dissent from the teaching of the Holy Prophet. Now, it is true that we believe Jesus to have died a natural death. But it is not true that to believe him to have died is to insult him or to offend the Holy Quran or to dissent from the teaching of the Holy Prophet. For the more one ponders over the subject, the more one becomes convinced that the offences we are charged with do not follow from our belief in the death of Jesus. They follow rather from the belief that Jesus did *not* die but is *alive* in Heaven.

We are Muslims, and as Muslims our first concern is to uphold the Greatness of God and the honour of His Prophet. True, we believe in all the Prophets of God. But our love and our regard for the Holy Prophet are the highest, for he sacrificed himself for our sake; he carried our burdens; he invited his own physical death to save us from spiritual death; he grieved so much for us. He gave up even the slightest comforts for our sake. He abased himself so that we should stand high. He planned for our lasting good and prayed for our eternal welfare. He would let his feet swell through standing long in prayer. Sinless, he prayed to cure us of our sins, to save us from Hell-fire; he would pray till his prayer-mat became wet with tears. He wept till his breast heaved like a boiling pot.

He drew unto us the Mercy of God; he toiled for His pleasure, again for us. He caused us to be wrapped in the mantle of His Grace, the cloak of His Compassion. He strove to find for us ways by which we may also please God; means by which we may also achieve union with Him. What he did for us to make light our journey to God had not been done before by any prophet for his people.

Fatwas of *Kufr* only please us. We would rather have the *Fatwas* than hold Jesus an equal of God, our Creator, Nourisher, Sustainer, and Guardian, One Who gives us our daily bread and the knowledge and guidance on which we depend for our spiritual welfare. *Fatwas* of *Kufr* are more welcome to us than that we should have to believe that Jesus is alive in Heaven without food or drink, even as God lives for ever without food or drink. We hold Jesus in honour. But why? Because he is a prophet of God, because God loved him and he loved God. Our regard for him is due to our regard for God. Can we hold *him* above God and dishonour God for *his* sake? Must we please the *Ulema*, but strengthen the hands of Christian missionaries, whose daily occupation is to find fault with Islam and the Quran? Must we let them think Jesus was God? For if he was not God, how can he be alive in Heaven? If he was man, why did he not die like other men? How can we, with our own mouths, say a thing derogatory to the Unity and Oneness of God? How can we harm the interests of true faith? The *Ulema* are free to do what they like; they may incite people against us, put us to death or stone us. We cannot give up God for Jesus. We would rather die than say that Jesus is alive in heaven as God's equal – Jesus who Christians think is the son of God and for whose sake they detract from the Oneness and Independence of God. If we had remained ignorant, it might have been different. But having had our eyes opened by a Divine Messenger, who has shown us the implications of God's Oneness, Majesty, Power, Greatness, Goodness, we cannot do so. Whatever the consequences, we cannot abandon God for the sake of a human being. If we did so, we cannot say where we should be. Honour belongs to God and comes from Him. When we perceive clearly that to believe Jesus to be alive is to insult God, we cannot regard this belief as true. We do not understand why belief in the death of Jesus entails an insult to Jesus. Prophets greater than Jesus have died and their death brought no humiliation to them. So the death of Jesus cannot be humiliating to him. But if, to suppose the impossible, we are confronted with the alternatives – God or Jesus – and if we must make a choice, certainly we will choose God. We feel certain that Jesus himself, who loved God with his mind, heart and soul, would never have been reconciled to a position which entails honour to Jesus but dishonour to God and His Oneness. The Holy Quran teaches us the same:

لَنْ يَّسْتَنْكِفَ الْمَسِيْحُ اَنْ يَّكُوْنَ عَبْدًا لِّلّٰهِ وَلَا الْمَلٰٓئِكَةُ
الْمُقَرَّبُوْنَ ۔

'Surely, the Messiah will never disdain to be a servant of Allah, nor will the angels near [unto God]'.[9]

Death of Jesus taught by the Holy Quran and Hadith

We are bound by the Word of God. We have in the Quran:

وَكُنْتُ عَلَيْهِمْ شَهِيْدًا مَّا دُمْتُ فِيْهِمْ فَلَمَّا تَوَفَّيْتَنِيْ كُنْتَ
اَنْتَ الرَّقِيْبَ عَلَيْهِمْ وَاَنْتَ عَلٰى كُلِّ شَيْءٍ شَهِيْدٌ ۔

'And I was a witness over them as long as I remained among them, but since Thou didst cause me to die, Thou hast been the Watcher over them and Thou art Witness over all things.'[10]

God in the name of Jesus declares that Christians became corrupt after the death of Jesus. While he lived, they and their beliefs remained uncorrupt. Reading this in the Quran, how can we think Jesus is not dead but alive in Heaven? And we also read in the Holy Quran:

يٰعِيْسٰٓى اِنِّيْ مُتَوَفِّيْكَ وَرَافِعُكَ اِلَيَّ وَمُطَهِّرُكَ مِنَ الَّذِيْنَ كَفَرُوْا
وَجَاعِلُ الَّذِيْنَ اتَّبَعُوْكَ فَوْقَ الَّذِيْنَ كَفَرُوْٓا اِلٰى يَوْمِ الْقِيٰمَةِ

'O Jesus! indeed I will cause thee to die and exalt thee to Myself, and will clear thee of [the charges of] those who disbelieve, and will place those who follow thee above those who deny thee, until the Day of Resurrection.'[11]

Jesus was *exalted* (or *raised*) to God *after* his *death*. The words

9 *Al-Nisa*, 173.
10 *Al-Maidah*, 118.
11 *Al-Imran*, 56.

'exalt thee' or 'raise thee' come after the words 'cause thee to die'. We must observe the ordinary rules of language. What is mentioned first, must take place first. But maybe the *Ulema* know these rules better than God. Maybe they think that although 'raising to God' occurs *later* in the verse, it should have been *earlier*. But God is Wise beyond conception. He knows best how ideas should be expressed. In His speech, there can be no error, no deviation from the correct word order. He is our Creator and we are His creatures. We dare not find errors in His speech. We are ignorant and He is All-Knowing. How can we point to faults in His speech? But the *Ulema* seem to think there could be errors in the speech of God but not in their understanding of it. We cannot say this; for we see only perdition in such a thought. While we have eyes, we cannot fall into a pit. While we know, we must turn away the cup of poison held to our lips.

After God, we love only the Holy Prophet Muhammad (on whom be peace and the blessings of God). He is the greatest of all prophets, the greatest of all benefactors. No other human being, prophet or not, has done even a fraction of what the Holy Prophet has done for us. We can hold no one in greater honour. It is impossible for us to think that Jesus, the Messiah, is alive in Heaven while Muhammad, our Holy Prophet, lies buried in the earth. We cannot think so. We believe that in spiritual rank the Holy Prophet stands much higher than Jesus. How can it be that God raised Jesus to Heaven on the slightest sign of danger to his life, but did not raise the Holy Prophet even as high as the stars when the Holy Prophet was pursued by his enemies from place to place? If it is true that Jesus is alive in Heaven, we cannot feel more dead. We cannot tolerate the thought that our master is dead and buried, while Jesus is alive and in Heaven. We feel humiliated before Christians. But, thank God, this is not so. God cannot have treated and has not, in fact, treated our Prophet in this way. God is the Lord of all lords. He himself called the Holy Prophet the Chief of mankind. Having called the Holy Prophet the Chief of mankind, he could not have taken more care of Jesus. For the sake of the Holy Prophet, God shook the world. Whoever thought of humiliating him, himself met with humiliation. Could God Himself have disgraced the Prophet and given his enemies the chance to gloat over the disgrace? The thought that the Holy Prophet Muhammad is buried in the earth and Jesus of Nazareth is alive in Heaven makes my hair stand on end. I find it both astonishing and depressing, therefore I find myself declaring, 'No, God cannot do such a thing.' He loves the Holy Prophet Muhammad more than He loves anyone else. He could not have let him die and be buried and have let Jesus ascend to Heaven. If any man deserved to remain alive and to ascend to Heaven it was our Holy Prophet. If he died in the usual way, other prophets have died in the same way. Knowing the high rank which the Holy Prophet Muhammad holds in the Sight of God, we cannot think for a moment that he could have received at the hands of God treatment inferior to that which Jesus had had at His hands. We cannot think that at the time of Hijra when the Holy Prophet sought refuge in the cave Thor, to reach which he had to mount the shoulders of Abu Bakr, God sent no angels for his rescue; but when the Jews set out to grapple with Jesus, God raised him to the Fourth Heaven to save him from the murderous designs of the Jews. In the battle of Ohud, the Holy Prophet had only a few friends left around him when the enemy attacked him. God did not send any angel, nor did he create a phantom, so that the enemy could attack this phantom instead of the Prophet, and break the phantom's teeth instead of the Prophet's. God let the enemy attack the Prophet himself and when the Prophet fell down as if dead, the enemy raised cries of joy and declared they had (God forbid) killed Muhammad, the Prophet. But in the case of Jesus, God did not let the slightest pain or discomfort trouble him. As soon as the Jews resolved to lay hold of him, God raised Jesus to Heaven, and in his place caught hold of one of his enemies and, making him the same in appearance as Jesus, had this enemy of Jesus put on the cross instead of Jesus!

We are amazed at what can happen to some people. On the one hand they claim such great love for the Holy Prophet; on the other, they themselves tend to dishonour and disgrace him. And they do not stop at this. They go further and award *Fatwas* of *Kufr* against those who refuse to subscribe to beliefs which amount to ranking another one superior to the Holy Prophet. We wonder what they mean by *Kufr*. To esteem the Holy Prophet higher in rank than others, to attribute to him the spiritual eminence which belongs to him – is it *Kufr*? Those who hold the Holy Prophet the highest in love and esteem, are they *Kafirs* (unbelievers)? If this is *Kufr*, then, God be our witness, we value this *Kufr* many times more than the *Iman* (belief) of those who attribute *Kufr* (unbelief) to us. Very appropriately did Hazrat Mirza Ghulam Ahmad, the Promised Messiah, express this thought when he said:

بعد از خدا بعشقِ محمدؐ مخمّرم ؛ گر کفر ایں بود بخدا سخت کافرم

'Intoxicated am I after God with the love of Muhammad. If this be *Kufr*, then, by God, I am the most hardened *Kafir*.'

Some day we must all die, present ourselves before God, and answer for ourselves. Why should we fear any humans? What harm can come to us from them? We fear only God and we love only Him. After Him, we love and honour the Holy Prophet the most. If for the sake of the Holy Prophet we have to sacrifice the honour, interests and the good things of this world, we will find it easy enough. But dishonour and disrespect to the Holy Prophet we cannot bear. Knowing how very holy he was, what spiritual knowledge and insight he had and how close was his contact with God, we cannot think for a moment that God loved some other man or prophet more than He loved our Holy Prophet. If we entertained such a thought we would be more deserving of punishment than others. We know too well that those who denied the Holy Prophet challenged him and asked him if he could perform the miracle of ascent to Heaven. They said:

اَوْ تَرْقٰى فِي السَّمَآءِ ۚ وَلَنْ نُّؤْمِنَ لِرُقِيِّكَ حَتّٰى تُنَزِّلَ عَلَيْنَا كِتٰبًا نَّقْرَؤُهٗ ۔

'We will not believe except if you ascend to Heaven. And we will not believe in your ascent unless you bring to us from Heaven a Book which we may then read.'[12]

In reply to this challenge, God did not empower the Holy Prophet to show the miracle which those who denied the Prophet asked him to show. Instead, God made the Prophet say: 'Only my God is free from all weaknesses. As for me, I am a mere man.' And yet, as the Maulvis teach, when the enemies of Jesus confronted him with a similar challenge, God raised him to Heaven. When the Holy Prophet is challenged and asked to ascend to Heaven, ascent

12 *Bani-Israil*, 94.

to Heaven is declared by God to be inconsistent with humanity. But when Jesus is similarly challenged, he is raised to Heaven without the least hesitation. If this be true, will it not follow that Jesus was not man but God? We seek refuge with God from this wild thought. Will it not imply that Jesus was spiritually superior to our Holy Prophet and more dearly loved by God? But we know, and it is as evident as the sun, that the Holy Prophet Muhammad is the best, the highest, in the hierarchy of prophets. Knowing this, how can we think that the Holy Prophet should not rise to Heaven but instead die in the normal way and be buried here on this earth, while Jesus should go to Heaven and remain alive for these two thousand years?

Now, it is not merely that our feeling for the Holy Prophet is strong. It is a question also of his truth, the truth of his claims. Did not the Holy Prophet say: 'If Moses and Jesus had been alive, they would have had to believe in me and follow me.'[13]

If Jesus is alive, the claim of the Holy Prophet that in that case Jesus would have had to follow him has to be set down as false. The Holy Prophet's words are significant and clear. *If*, says he, Moses and Jesus were alive. This 'if' means that the two are not alive. Moses is not alive, nor is Jesus. This is an important declaration by the Holy Prophet bearing on the subject. After hearing this declaration, no true follower of the Prophet can think that Jesus is alive in Heaven, because, if Jesus is alive, this declaration of the Holy Prophet turns out to be false, as also his knowledge of the subject. For is not Jesus dead according to him?

There is another important statement by the Holy Prophet. During his last illness, the Holy Prophet said to his daughter Fatima:

اِنَّ جِبْرِيْلَ كَانَ يُعَارِضُنِي الْقُرْاٰنَ فِيْ كُلِّ عَامٍ مَرَّةً فَاِنَّهٗ عَارَضَنِيْ
بِالْقُرْاٰنِ الْعَامَ مَرَّتَيْنِ وَاَخْبَرَنِيْ اَنَّهٗ لَمْ يَكُنْ نَبِيٌّ اِلَّا عَاشَ
نِصْفَ الَّذِيْ قَبْلَهٗ وَاَخْبَرَنِيْ اَنَّ عِيْسَى ابْنَ مَرْيَمَ عَاشَ عِشْرِيْنَ
وَمِائَةَ سَنَةٍ وَلَا اُرَانِيْ اِلَّا ذَاهِبًا عَلٰى رَأْسِ السِّتِّيْنَ ـ

'Once in every year, Gabriel recited the Quran to me. This year he recited twice. He also told me that every succeeding prophet

13 *Zurqani*, vol. VI, p. 54.

> has lived to half the age of his predecessor. He told me that Jesus, son of Mary, lived to a hundred and twenty years. Therefore, I think, I may live to about sixty years.'[14]

The statement is an inspired one. The Holy Prophet does not say anything on his own, but reports what he received from Gabriel, the angel of revelation. The important part of the statement is that Jesus lived to a hundred and twenty years. According to the New Testament records, Jesus was about thirty-two or thirty-three years old when the event of the Cross took place and Jesus 'ascended' to Heaven. If Jesus really did 'ascend', his age up to the time of the Holy Prophet comes to about six hundred years, not a hundred and twenty. If what the Holy Prophet received from Gabriel is true, the Holy Prophet should have lived for at least three hundred years. But he lived only for sixty-three years. Yet, according to Gabriel, Jesus lived for a hundred and twenty years. This important statement by the Holy Prophet proves that to think Jesus alive is against the teaching of the Holy Prophet, against what was revealed to him by God. In view of all this, how can we be persuaded to believe that Jesus is alive? How can we deny anything which the Holy Prophet has taught so clearly?

Companions of the Holy Prophet agreed on the death of Jesus

It is said sarcastically that for thirteen hundred years nobody but ourselves could spot the truth about the death of Jesus. All the doctors and teachers of Islam remained ignorant of it. The suggestion is that the consensus of early Muslims does not favour the view which we teach on the subject. But those who indulge in this sarcasm forget that the first exponents of Islam were the Companions of the Holy Prophet. The Companions first expounded the beliefs and practices of Islam to others. Then these others became the teachers of Islam, spreading to other parts of the world. Now, as far as the Companions are concerned, they were united in teaching what we think today about Jesus. And could they have taught anything else? Could they have taught a belief derogatory to the Holy Prophet? Not only are the Companions one with us; but the first formal affirmation which the Companions of the Holy

14 *Mawahib-ud-duniya* by Qastalani, vol. 1, p. 42.

Prophet collectively resolved on was the truth of the death of Jesus. The first *Ijma* of the Companions set its seal on his death. For in the recorded Traditions we find that when the Holy Prophet died, the Companions were prostrated with grief. They could not move, nor utter a word. Some were so deeply affected that they died a few days later, unable to bear the pangs of separation. Omar, indeed, was so afflicted by grief that he made up his mind not to believe that the Prophet had died. He unsheathed his sword and declared that whoever said the Prophet was dead would lose his head. He began to say that the Holy Prophet had disappeared from their midst temporarily, even as Moses had disappeared on a Call from God. Moses returned to his people after forty days, and so would the Holy Prophet. On his return, the Holy Prophet would call to account all those who had said unworthy things about him and had behaved hypocritically towards him. He would even put them to death or order their crucifixion. Omar was solemn and determined. None of the Companions dared to resist and deny what he said. Some were even persuaded by Omar's declaration. They began to think the Prophet had not died. Because of this, their dejection changed to delight. The signs of it were on their faces. Those who had their heads bowed with grief raised their heads. Others, who were not so overcome by grief and who could also see far into the future, sent out one of their number to fetch Abu Bakr. Abu Bakr was not in Medina when the Holy Prophet died. The Holy Prophet had permitted him to go, because his condition seemed to have improved. This Companion had hardly left the town when he saw Abu Bakr coming. On seeing Abu Bakr, the Companion could not contain himself. Tears rolled down his cheeks. No words were necessary. Abu Bakr understood what had happened. He asked the Companion, 'Has the Prophet died?' In reply, the Companion not only confirmed the sad news but also told Abu Bakr what Omar had been saying, that 'whoever should say the Prophet had died would lose his head!' Abu Bakr heard this and at once made for the place where the Holy Prophet's dead body lay. He lifted the mantle which covered him and knew at once that he had died. The pain of separation from his beloved friend and leader made his eyes wet. He bent low and kissed the Prophet's forehead and said:

> 'By God, you will not suffer more than one death. The loss mankind have suffered by your death is greater than the loss

they suffered by the death of any other prophet. You need no praises, and mourning cannot reduce the pangs of separation. If we could but avert your end, we would have done so, with our lives.'

Abu Bakr said this, and covered the Prophet's face; then he went to the spot where Omar was speaking to the Companions. Omar, of course, was telling them that the Prophet had not died, but had only disappeared temporarily. Abu Bakr asked Omar to stop for a time and let him speak to the assembly. Omar did not stop but went on. Abu Bakr turned to some of the Companions and started telling them that the Holy Prophet had really died. Other Companions turned to Abu Bakr and began to listen to him. Omar also was compelled to listen. Abu Bakr recited from the Holy Quran:

وَمَا مُحَمَّدٌ إِلَّا رَسُولٌ قَدْ خَلَتْ مِنْ قَبْلِهِ الرُّسُلُ أَفَإِنْ مَّاتَ
أَوْ قُتِلَ انْقَلَبْتُمْ عَلَىٰ أَعْقَابِكُمْ ۔

'The Holy Prophet is but a prophet. There have been prophets before him and they had all died. If he also should die or be put to death, would they turn back upon him?'[15]

إِنَّكَ مَيِّتٌ وَّإِنَّهُمْ مَّيِّتُونَ ۔

'Thou (O Muhammad) art surely going to die and they surely are going to die.'[16]

Having recited these verses, he went on to say:

يَا أَيُّهَا النَّاسُ مَنْ كَانَ يَعْبُدُ مُحَمَّدًا فَإِنَّ مُحَمَّدًا قَدْ مَاتَ
وَمَنْ كَانَ يَعْبُدُ اللّٰهَ فَإِنَّ اللّٰهَ حَيٌّ لَا يَمُوتُ ۔

'O ye men, whoever amongst you worshipped Muhammad, let him know that Muhammad is dead, and whoever amongst you worshipped Allah, let him know that Allah is Living,' there is no death for Him.'[17]

15 *Al-Imran*, 145.
16 *Al-Zumar*, 31.
17 Bukhari, vol. 2, chap. *Manaqibe Abu Bakr*.

When Abu Bakr recited the verses of the Holy Quran and pointed to their meaning, the Companions realized what had happened. The Prophet had died. They began to cry. Omar is reported to have said that when Abu Bakr recited the verses out of the Holy Quran, and their meaning suddenly dawned upon him, it seemed as though the verses had been revealed on that day, at that moment. His legs could no longer support him. He staggered and fell down in a paroxysm of grief.

This account of what passed between the Companions at the Holy Prophet's death proves three important things:

Firstly, it proves that the first formal and collective expression of opinion upon which the Companions resolved after the death of the Holy Prophet was that all prophets before the Holy Prophet had died. There was no exception. If the Companions present on this solemn occasion thought that some earlier prophets had not died, they would have stood up and pointed to the exceptions. They could have said that at least Jesus had been alive in Heaven for six hundred years. It was wrong to say that all the earlier prophets had died. If some could remain alive, why not the Holy Prophet?

Secondly, it proves that the Companions' belief that the earlier prophets had died was not a mere matter of opinion: it was a truth recorded in the Holy Quran and taught clearly by the Holy Book. When Abu Bakr recited the verses, the Companions received them without demur. If the truth of the death of the earlier prophets was not contained in these verses, they could have said that, although the earlier prophets had really died, the verses recited by Abu Bakr were not relevant. The fact, therefore, that Abu Bakr recited the verse 'and there had been [other] prophets before him' to prove the death of earlier prophets, and the fact that the Companions, who heard this verse and heard Abu Bakr's argument based upon the verse, not only remained silent but began to rejoice over it and went about the town reciting it, proved beyond doubt that the Companions agreed entirely with Abu Bakr's interpretation of the verse.

Thirdly, it proves that whether or not the Companions believed in the death of other prophets, they certainly did not think that Jesus was alive in Heaven. All accounts of this important incident and the important speeches made on this occasion show that even Omar, in the height of his excitement, threatening to kill those who should say the Prophet had died, could cite the analogy only of

Moses, who disappeared for forty days from amongst his people. Even Omar did not cite the analogy of Jesus. If the Companions had believed that Jesus was alive in Heaven, could not Omar, or the Companions who thought like him, have cited the analogy of Jesus? The fact that they cited only the analogy of Moses proves that they did not believe that Jesus had not died, or that he had even had an experience similar to that of Moses.

Family of the Holy Prophet agreed on the death of Jesus

Besides this unanimity of opinion among the Companions, opinion held in the family of the Holy Prophet also supports the belief that Jesus died in the normal way. Imam Hasan, recounting the events relating to the death of Hazrat Ali, is reported to have said:

أَيُّهَا النَّاسُ قَدْ قُبِضَ اللَّيْلَةَ رَجُلٌ لَمْ يَسْبِقْهُ الْأَوَّلُوْنَ وَلَا يُدْرِكُهُ
الْآخِرُوْنَ۔ قَدْ كَانَ رَسُوْلُ اللهِ يَبْعَثُ الْمَبْعَثَ فَيَكْتَنِفُهُ جِبْرَائِيْلُ
مِنْ يَمِيْنِهِ، وَمِيْكَائِيْلُ مِنْ شِمَالِهِ، فَلَا يَنْثَنِيْ حَتّٰى يَفْتَحَ اللهُ لَهُ،
وَمَا تَرَكَ إِلَّا سَبْعَ مِائَةِ دِرْهَمٍ، أَرَادَ أَنْ يَشْتَرِيَ بِهَا خَادِمًا،
وَلَقَدْ قُبِضَ فِي اللَّيْلَةِ الَّتِيْ عُرِجَ فِيْهَا بِرُوْحِ عِيْسَى ابْنِ مَرْيَمَ لَيْلَةَ
سَبْعٍ وَّعِشْرِيْنَ مِنْ رَمَضَانَ۔

> 'The man who has died today is without an equal in many respects. He had none like him either amongst his predecessors or among his successors. When the Holy Prophet sent him to battle, he had Gabriel on his right and Michael on his left to assist him. He never returned from a battle except as victor. He left seven hundred *Derhams* as a bequest. He had saved this to purchase a slave's freedom. He died during the twenty-seventh night of the month of Ramadhan, the same night that the spirit of Jesus was raised to Heaven.'[18]

From this remark of Imam Hasan it appears that even according to the family of the Holy Prophet Jesus died in the ordinary way. Unless they believed this, Imam Hasan could not have said that

18 Tabaqat Ibn Sa'ad, vol. III.

Hazrat Ali died the same night that Jesus's spirit ascended to Heaven.

Besides the Companions of the Holy Prophet and his family, later doctors of religion have also testified to the death of Jesus. They were devotees of the Holy Quran, of the utterances of the Holy Prophet, of opinions held by the Companions and by the family of the Holy Prophet. It seems that whether or not Jesus had died did not strike them as a very important question. Therefore they did not pronounce on the question as such. Nor have their views on the subject been preserved. But as far as the recorded opinions of the later doctors of Islam go, these leave no doubt that even they believed Jesus had died. It is recorded in *Majma-al-Bahar* that, according to Imam Malik, Jesus died in the natural way.

In short, the Holy Quran, the Traditions, the consensus of opinion among the Companions and the family of the Holy Prophet, and the opinions of the doctors of Islam all support belief in the death of Jesus. All of them teach that Jesus died like all mortals. It is wrong, therefore, to say that by attributing death to Jesus we dishonour Jesus, and that therefore by implication we deny the Holy Quran and the Traditions of the Holy Prophet. We do not dishonour Jesus. Instead of dishonouring Jesus, we have a genuine conception of the Oneness of God and point to the high spiritual rank to which our Holy Prophet belongs. We honour Jesus, because Jesus himself would not have subscribed to a belief which is derogatory to the conception of the Oneness of God; which helps *shirk* (associating others with God), and detracts from the spiritual status of the Holy Prophet.

Now, dear reader, you can see for yourself who is in the right: we or our opponents. Is it for them to be offended by us, or for us to be offended by them? *They* set up a man as the equal of God. *They* propose a belief which entails indignity to the Holy Prophet; it is *they* who lend support to the enemies of Islam, *they* who weaken Islam.

Second coming of the Messiah means coming of a follower of the Holy Prophet

The second objection levelled against us is that, contrary to the accepted Muslim belief, we hold that a follower of the Holy

Prophet has appeared amongst us as the Promised Messiah. To hold this belief, we are told, is contrary to the Traditions of the Holy Prophet, as, according to these Traditions, the Messiah is Jesus, son of Mary, due to return from Heaven when the time comes.

Now, it is quite true that we regard the Founder of the Ahmadiyya Movement, Hazrat Mirza Ghulam Ahmad of Qadian (Gurdaspur, Punjab, India), as the Promised Messiah and Mahdi. And why not? The Holy Quran, the Traditions, and ordinary common sense declare that the first Messiah died in the normal way; so our belief that the Promised Messiah was to come from among the followers of the Holy Prophet cannot be against the Holy Quran and the Traditions. The Holy Quran declares that Jesus is dead. The Traditions say the same thing. If, therefore, the Traditions promise the advent of a Messenger described as the son of Mary, this promised one can only be a follower of the Holy Prophet, not the Messiah of Nazareth who died in the normal way. It is said that even if the Quran and the Traditions declare the death of Jesus, son of Mary, we should continue to expect the second coming of the self-same son of Mary. For is not God All-Powerful? Can He not resuscitate the dead Messiah and send him back to the world? If we did not cherish such a hope and such a thought, we should be denying the Power of God. But our position is very different. We do not deny the Power of God. We believe that God is All-Powerful. Because God is All-Powerful, He has no need to resuscitate the Messiah of Nazareth. He can raise a teacher from among the followers of the Holy Prophet, install him as the Promised Messiah and charge him with the duty of reforming the world. We fail to see how anyone who deliberates over this subject in a proper manner can insist that the Power of God requires God to bring the first Messiah back to life. Such a thing is against all ordinary canons. It is everyday experience that a person who can afford to have a new one hates to have an old coat turned for longer use. If he needs a new coat, he throws away the old one and gets a new one. It is the man who cannot afford one who wants the old coat turned or altered to be used again. It is the poor man who takes excessive care of his things. God is not poor. He is Powerful. If He finds that His servants need someone to guide them, He does not have to put life into a dead prophet. He is able to raise one from amongst His living servants to reform and lead the rest. From

Adam down to the Holy Prophet, not once did God have to restore a dead prophet to life for the purpose of guiding His men. Such a course is quite unnecessary. It might have been necessary if the purification and reformation of a given people at a given time had been beyond the Power of God; if the dominion of God did not extend to all men at all times. God is All-Powerful and His dominion extends to all men at all times. It is senseless to think that for the guidance of a given people at a given time He should have to restore one of the dead prophets to life. God's Power is boundless. He was able to raise a prophet like the Holy Prophet (on whom be peace) from among the Arabs. It is not beyond His Power to raise one in our time similar to Jesus or greater than him from among Muslims.

The fact is, therefore, that we deny the physical second coming of the first Messiah because God, according to us, is All-Powerful and can raise anyone to the status of a guide and prophet, at any time, and from among any people. They are in error who think that God cannot do this, that instead of raising one from amongst us He has to bring back to life a dead prophet. They have not esteemed the Power of Allah as Allah deserves.

The second coming of the first Messiah, therefore, is derogatory to the Power and Wisdom of God. It is also disparaging to the spiritual power of the Holy Prophet. To say that the second coming of the first Messiah is inevitable is to say something very strange. At all times in the past, whenever a people went astray and needed divine guidance, it was one from amongst themselves whom God raised for the purpose. Was this time-honoured divine practice to be dropped when followers of the Holy Prophet went astray and needed divine guidance? Was the *Umma* to be reformed by one of the earlier prophets, the Prophet's own followers failing to provide a reformer from among themselves? This means that Muslims would have to follow Jews and Christians who ever cavil at the spiritual competence of our Holy Prophet. It is strange that Muslims should distrust the regenerative power of the Holy Prophet. If we think that a follower of the Holy Prophet cannot guide his other followers – the *Umma* – in time of need, we support those who underrate the spiritual influence of the Holy Prophet. One lighted torch can light many other torches. It is a dead torch which will not do this. If followers of the Holy Prophet were to become so very corrupt that no one from amongst them would then be able to reform the rest, it must be admitted that at that time the spiritual grace and productiveness of the Holy Prophet's teaching and example would have come to an end. This consequence cannot be accepted by any true Muslim. Every true Muslim knows that the followers of Moses needed to be rejuvenated from time to time, and the rejuvenation was brought about by teachers raised from amongst themselves. It was a follower of Moses who reformed the followers of Moses. The dispensation of Moses lasted for as long as God wanted. At last when the time came for the dispensation to end, God turned away from Moses' followers and turned to the progeny of Ishmael to raise a prophet for the guidance of mankind. If now a prophet belonging to the dispensation of Moses should come to guide the followers of the Holy Prophet, it would mean that God has decided (God forbid) to terminate the dispensation of the Holy Prophet as He terminated the dispensation of Moses, and that in place of this He is going to initiate a new dispensation. It would mean that (God forbid again) the spiritual power of the Holy Prophet is no longer effective, that it fails to inspire even a single follower to receive from the Holy Prophet's teaching and example the illumination necessary for the reformation and guidance of his followers.

Alas! People show intolerance of the slightest offence to conceptions of their own greatness; they cannot accept the imputation of any defect or shortcoming to themselves. Yet they do not hesitate to attribute defects and weaknesses to the Holy Prophet while claiming to love the Holy Prophet. What use is the love which is loud in professions but finds no echo in the heart? What use are professions unsupported by proper performance? If Muslims really did love the Holy Prophet, they would not tolerate the second coming of an Israelite prophet for the rejuvenation of the followers of the Holy Prophet. Who would turn to a neighbour for needs which he can fulfil in his own house? Who would turn to another for help when he can help himself? Mullas, who think and teach that the Holy Prophet's followers would need the second coming of the Messiah of Nazareth at the time of sorest need, have such an excessive idea of their own dignity that in religious debates they would rather lose the argument than accept help from any other. If there is an offer of help they do not feel grateful: they are hurt and say, 'Are we so lacking in learning that others dare offer us help?' But when it comes to the Holy Prophet, how casual they are!

They are quick to believe and teach that when the Prophet's followers need to reform, the reformation will come not from amongst the followers, not from the Prophet's own spiritual influence, but from the good offices of a prophet from an earlier dispensation, owing nothing to the Holy Prophet or his teachings. Have men become so utterly dead and dull? Have they lost all capacity to think or feel? Do they value dignity and self-respect for themselves, but not for God and the Prophet? May anger and annoyance be shown to personal enemies but not to those who offend God and His Prophet?

We are asked why we deny the second coming of an Israelite prophet. But what can we do? We cannot change our hearts. We cannot show our love for the Holy Prophet except in ways which are normal and natural. The honour of the Holy Prophet is dearest to us. We cannot accept that, for the reformation of his followers, the Holy Prophet should need the help of another and become indebted to him. We cannot believe for a minute that when on the Day of Judgment mankind, from the first-born to the last, will assemble before God, and the deeds and achievements of all will be cited, the Holy Prophet would stand burdened by the debt he owed to the Israelite Messiah, the angels making the citation would declare in the hearing and presence of all humankind that when the Holy Prophet's followers became corrupt the Prophet's own spiritual example failed to restore them to spiritual strength and the Israelite Messiah, out of compassion for the Holy Prophet, decided to return to the world to reform the Prophet's followers and rid them of spiritual stagnation! We cannot contemplate such a thought. We would rather have our tongues torn out than attribute such a humiliating proposition to the Holy Prophet. We would rather lose our hands than commit to writing such a thing about the Holy Prophet. The Holy Prophet is God's beloved. His spiritual power can never lapse. He is the Seal of the Prophets. His spiritual grace and munificence can never end. He has no need to be indebted to anyone else. It is other prophets who are indebted to him. There is not a prophet whose truth the Holy Prophet has not proclaimed to those who denied him. It is the Holy Prophet whose teaching has converted millions of human beings to a belief in prophets they had not heard of before. There are about eighty million Muslims in India. A few among them have come from outside. The others belonged to this very land and they had not heard of any prophet.

But since they came to believe in the Holy Prophet Muhammad, they began to believe in Abraham, Moses, Jesus and others (on all of whom be peace). If they had not become Muslims, they would have continued to disown these prophets, even to remain hostile to them. They would have continued to regard them as pretenders, as indeed Hindus in India continue to do to this day. The same is true of Afghanistan, China, and Iran. The inhabitants of these countries did not know, so they did not acknowledge, Moses or Jesus as prophets. The Holy Prophet's message and teaching spread to these countries, and the people of these countries came to believe in the Holy Prophet and whatever he taught. They began to acknowledge other prophets and revere them as true prophets. The Holy Prophet, therefore, has put all earlier prophets in his debt. Their truth was unknown. The Holy Prophet revealed it. The Holy Prophet is in nobody's debt. The grace and beneficence of his teachings must continue for ever. For the reform and resuscitation of his own followers he does not need the assistance of another prophet. Whenever such a need arises, God will raise one of his own followers to lead and guide his other followers. Such a one will owe everything to the Holy Prophet. He will have learnt everything from him. Whatever he is able to do by way of reform and reconstruction will be credited to the Holy Prophet. What one owes to any one teacher, one really owes to the teacher's teacher. A follower cannot be separated from his leader, even as a pupil cannot be separated from his teacher. The follower who leads other followers will owe a debt to the Holy Prophet.

In short, the coming of a former prophet for the purpose of reforming the followers of the Holy Prophet is an insult to the Holy Prophet. Such an event would injure the greatness of the Holy Prophet. It would also contradict the teaching of the Holy Quran, which says:

إِنَّ اللّٰهَ لَا يُغَيِّرُ مَا بِقَوْمٍ حَتّٰى يُغَيِّرُوْا مَا بِاَنْفُسِهِمْ۔

> 'God never withdraws the reward from a people except when the people themselves become undeserving of it.'[19]

In view of this teaching of the Quran, we have to admit either

19 *Al-Ra'd*, 12.

that the Holy Prophet (God forbid) has become undeserving of God's promise, or that God Himself has gone back on that promise. With all others, God's practice has been not to withdraw a reward once made; but with the Holy Prophet, His way is different! To entertain such a thought amounts to unbelief. It amounts to the denial of God. It amounts either to a denial of God or a denial of His Prophet. Because of this grave consequence we shun such beliefs. We believe that the Messiah whose coming was foretold by the Holy Prophet is to arise from amongst the Holy Prophet's followers. It is for God to award this status to whomsoever He likes.

The Messiah and the Mahdi, one and the same person

From the Traditions of the Holy Prophet it is evident also that the Promised Messiah was to be a follower of the Holy Prophet. One Tradition tells us that 'the Mahdi is none other than the Messiah':

لَا مَهْدِیَ اِلَّا عِیْسٰی

Another Tradition says:

كَيْفَ اَنْتُمْ اِذَا نَزَلَ فِيْكُمُ ابْنُ مَرْيَمَ وَ اِمَامُكُمْ مِنْكُمْ ـ

> 'How would it be with you when the son of Mary will descend among you and you will have a leader raised from among you?'[20]

These two Traditions leave no doubt that the Messiah himself would be the Mahdi. He would lead followers of the Holy Prophet and would be one of them, not an outsider. To think that the Messiah and the Mahdi are two different persons is wrong. It is against the clear indication in the Tradition 'The Mahdi is none other than the Messiah.' It behoves good believers to ponder carefully over the utterances of the Holy Prophet. If the utterances seem contradictory, it is for us to try and resolve the contradictions. If the Holy Prophet said, on the one hand, that the Mahdi would appear before the Messiah and the Messiah would then join the Mahdi and his followers in worship, and, on the other, that the

20 Bukhari, Kitabul-Anbiya, chap. *Nazul Isa bin Maryam*.

Messiah himself was the Mahdi, what are we to do – accept one utterance and reject the other? Is it not rather our duty to consider the two utterances carefully and try to reconcile one with the other? The two utterances can be reconciled at once if we use one of them to interpret the other. It seems that the promise of the advent of the Messiah was couched in words which suggested that the Messiah and the Mahdi were two different persons. This suggestion is corrected by the Tradition which says, 'No Mahdi but the Messiah.' This Tradition makes it plain that the other Tradition is metaphorical. It means that a follower of the Holy Prophet will arise for the purpose of revivifying the world, but will not have the rank of a prophet. *Then* the promise relating to the second coming of Jesus will be fulfilled in his person and he will announce himself as the Promised Messiah. The Tradition, therefore, tells us that the Promised One will start his career as a Muslim reformer who will become invested with the office of Messiah. Divine prophecies have to employ metaphors. They would convey very little otherwise.

If our interpretation of these Traditions is not correct, then there are only two alternatives left for a seeker after truth, both of them absurd and dangerous. Either we admit that the Tradition which describes the Messiah and the Mahdi as one and the same person is not a true Tradition, or we admit that the Messiah and the Mahdi are two different persons and that the intention of the Tradition is to point to a difference of spiritual significance in the two. It may mean that the true Mahdi would be the Messiah. The other Mahdi would be insignificant compared with the Messiah. It would be like saying, 'Nobody knows but so and so.' When we say such a thing, we do not mean literally that nobody else knows. What we mean is that the given person knows very much more. However, both interpretations are dangerous. One requires us, without good reasons, to treat as spurious a Tradition which is a well authenticated one, true according to all sound criteria. The other implies that the Mahdi, in comparison with the Messiah, will be as nothing. Such a thought would be contrary to the Traditions which teach that the Mahdi will be the Imam, and the Messiah a follower who stands behind the Imam in a congregation. Both alternatives, therefore, are absurd. The only worthwhile interpretation we can put upon the Traditions is that they foretell the coming of *a* Messenger from among the followers of the Holy Prophet. *This*

Messenger will first present himself as a reformer and later announce himself as the Messiah of the prophecy. The same person will be the Mahdi as well as the Messiah. Except for this interpretation, there can be no plausible interpretation of the Traditions on the subject.

Meaning of nuzul

The fact of the matter is that nearly everybody has been misled by the word *nuzul* in the Tradition. Literally it means 'descent'. Therefore, most people have been misled into thinking that as the Messiah was to have a descent, it can only be the first Messiah. Now, it is quite wrong to think that the word *nuzul* always means 'descent from an eminence'. The word 'descent' only points to how important, significant and far-reaching the thing is which is to descend. It tells us that the thing to *descend* is to be the instrument of the Majesty and Power of God. Such things are said to *descend* from God to a people. This meaning of 'descent' (sending down) is in conformity with usage sanctioned by the Holy Quran in several passages. Thus:

ثُمَّ اَنْزَلَ اللّٰهُ سَكِيْنَتَهٗ عَلٰى رَسُوْلِهٖ

ثُمَّ اَنْزَلَ عَلَيْكُمْ مِّنْ بَعْدِ الْغَمِّ اَمَنَةً نُّعَاسًا۔

وَاَنْزَلَ لَكُمْ مِّنَ الْاَنْعَامِ ثَمٰنِيَةَ اَزْوَاجٍ۔

قَدْ اَنْزَلْنَا عَلَيْكُمْ لِبَاسًا يُّوَارِيْ سَوْاٰتِكُمْ وَرِيْشًا، وَلِبَاسُ
التَّقْوٰى ذٰلِكَ خَيْرٌ ذٰلِكَ مِنْ اٰيٰتِ اللّٰهِ لَعَلَّهُمْ يَذَّكَّرُوْنَ۔

وَاَنْزَلْنَا عَلَيْكُمُ الْمَنَّ وَالسَّلْوٰى

وَاَنْزَلْنَا الْحَدِيْدَ فِيْهِ بَاْسٌ شَدِيْدٌ وَّمَنَافِعُ لِلنَّاسِ وَ
لِيَعْلَمَ اللّٰهُ مَنْ يَّنْصُرُهٗ وَرُسُلَهٗ بِالْغَيْبِ اِنَّ اللّٰهَ قَوِيٌّ عَزِيْزٌ۔

وَلَوْ بَسَطَ اللّٰهُ الرِّزْقَ لِعِبَادِهٖ لَبَغَوْا فِي الْاَرْضِ وَلٰكِنْ يُّنَزِّلُ
بِقَدَرٍ مَّا يَشَآءُ اِنَّهٗ بِعِبَادِهٖ خَبِيْرٌۢ بَصِيْرٌ۔

'Then Allah *sent down* His peace upon His messenger.'[21]

'Then after the sorrow, He *sent down* peace on you, a slumber that overcame a party of you.'[22]

'And He has *sent down* eight head of cattle in pairs.'[23]

'We have indeed *sent down* raiment to you to cover your shame, and to be an elegant dress; but the raiment of righteousness, that is the best. That is one of the Signs of Allah that they may remember.'[24]

'And *sent down* on you *Manna* and *Salwa*.'[25]

'And We *sent down* iron, wherein is material for violent warfare and many benefits for mankind and that Allah may distinguish those who help Him and His Messengers without having seen Him. Surely, Allah is Powerful, Mighty.'[26]

'And if Allah should enlarge the provision for His servants, they would rebel in the earth; but He *sends down* according to a proper measure as He pleases. Indeed, He is All-Aware and All-Seeing with regard to His servants.'[27]

Everybody knows that peace is a quality of the human mind and sleep a function of the human brain. Animals, garments, green fields, quails (*salwa*), iron, and other things grow on the soil or come from under it. They do not descend or drop down from Heaven. Nor is their *descent from Heaven* a description sanctioned by the Holy Quran. The description of the Holy Quran is quite clear. It says:

21 *Al-Tauba*, 26.
22 *Al-Imran*, 155.
23 *Al-Zumar*, 7.
24 *Al-A'raf*, 27.
25 *Al-Baqarah*, 58.
26 *Al-Hadid*, 26.
27 *Al-Shura*, 28.

وَجَعَلَ فِيْهَا رَوَاسِيَ مِنْ فَوْقِهَا وَبَارَكَ فِيْهَا وَقَدَّرَ فِيْهَا أَقْوَاتَهَا
فِيْٓ أَرْبَعَةِ أَيَّامٍ سَوَآءً لِّلسَّآئِلِيْنَ ۔

'And He put therein firm mountains on the surface, and He put blessings therein and measured its foods therein into four periods, alike for all seekers.'[28]

In this verse, God points out that the whole subject of the creation of nature and the creation of different kinds of wealth needs for its comprehension a knowledge of the different sciences. This knowledge God reveals in pieces. Some of it has been revealed already, some will be revealed in days to come. Ever new questions will be raised and they will receive their answers. But, says God, We have described the creation of nature and the creation of the wealth of nature in such a way that all men at all times (according to their capacity) will find in them a description which will be both satisfying and true.

From the Holy Quran, therefore, it appears that all things in nature *descend* from God – are gifts of God – and yet they do not drop from Heaven. Their creation takes place in and on and through this very earth. They grow on it or show themselves from under its surface. Therefore, the word *nuzul* (descent), when used for the coming of the Messiah, can have no other meaning. It can only point to the importance, the blessedness and the spiritual significance of the Promised Messiah. It is not in the least intended to suggest that he would physically drop from Heaven to earth. Most people forget that the word 'descent' has been used in the Holy Quran for the Holy Prophet also. All commentators of the Holy Book take this expression to point to the greatness of the Holy Prophet and to the importance of his advent. And they are right; for, as all the world knows, the Holy Prophet was born in the house of honourable Quraish parents. The name of his father was Abdullah and the name of his mother Amina. The verse which describes the advent of the Holy Prophet as *descent* is this:

قَدْ أَنْزَلَ اللّٰهُ إِلَيْكُمْ ذِكْرًا ۔ رَّسُوْلًا يَّتْلُوْا عَلَيْكُمْ اٰيٰتِ اللّٰهِ مُبَيِّنٰتٍ
لِّيُخْرِجَ الَّذِيْنَ اٰمَنُوْا وَعَمِلُوا الصّٰلِحٰتِ مِنَ الظُّلُمٰتِ إِلَى النُّوْرِ ۔

28 Ha Mim Sajdah, 11.

> 'Allah has indeed *sent down* to you a Reminder, a Messenger, who recites unto you the clear Signs of Allah, that he may bring those who believe and do good deeds out of every kind of darkness into light.'[29]

Now it is amazing that the same word *nuzul* is used about the Holy Prophet and the Messiah. Yet that same word is interpreted one way for the Holy Prophet and quite another way for the Messiah. The Holy Prophet was born like any other human being on this earth and grew up to be a prophet. The event was described as *nuzul* (literally, descent). Why not mean the same thing when the same word is used for the Messiah? Why not let even the Messiah *descend* in the ordinary way, that is, be born on this earth and grow up to be a prophet?

Why the Promised Messiah is called Isa Ibn Maryam (Jesus, son of Mary)

A third difficulty is raised about the prophecy with regard to the second coming of the Messiah. In the Traditions the Promised One is called Isa Ibn Maryam (Jesus, son of Mary). The prophecy, therefore, relates literally to the first Messiah, the Jesus of history. If it is to be fulfilled, it must be through the advent of Jesus in the flesh. The fact that metaphors abound in all languages is forgotten. The name Jesus is freely applied to persons other than Jesus. No difficulty is raised then. But if in the speech of God a person is given the name of Jesus, they begin to wonder about its meaning. Do they forget that a person who excels in the virtue of charity is metaphorically called Hatam of Tai, a person with a philosophical bent of mind is called Tusi, a person who displays a capacity for dialectical reasoning is called Razi? Why then make any difficulty about the name Ibn Maryam? If the name Ibn Maryam is the name of a known individual, are not Hatam, Tusi, and Razi names of known individuals? If by giving these names to other persons nobody is misled into thinking that these persons are the original Hatam, Tusi, or Razi, need anybody think that, when the Promised One is named Isa Ibn Maryam, or Jesus, son of Mary, it must mean

29 *Al-Talaq*, 11.

the self-same Jesus, son of Mary, who appeared in the world nineteen hundred years ago? And yet there is a difference between the names Hatam, Tusi, and Razi and the name 'Son of Mary'. The former have each come to have one definite meaning, but the name Maryam has been used to describe a spiritual condition by the Holy Quran itself:

وَضَرَبَ اللّٰهُ مَثَلًا لِّلَّذِيْنَ اٰمَنُوا امْرَاَتَ فِرْعَوْنَ اِذْ قَالَتْ رَبِّ ابْنِ لِيْ
عِنْدَكَ بَيْتًا فِي الْجَنَّةِ وَنَجِّنِيْ مِنْ فِرْعَوْنَ وَعَمَلِهٖ وَ نَجِّنِيْ مِنَ
الْقَوْمِ الظّٰلِمِيْنَ ـ وَمَرْيَمَ ابْنَتَ عِمْرٰنَ الَّتِيْٓ اَحْصَنَتْ فَرْجَهَا
فَنَفَخْنَا فِيْهِ مِنْ رُّوْحِنَا وَصَدَّقَتْ بِكَلِمٰتِ رَبِّهَا وَكُتُبِهٖ وَكَانَتْ
مِنَ الْقٰنِتِيْنَ ـ

> 'And Allah sets forth for those who believe the example of the wife of Pharaoh when she said, "My Lord! build for me a house with Thee in the Garden and deliver me from Pharaoh and his work and deliver me from the wrong-doing people."
>
> 'And *the example* of Mary, the daughter of Imran, who guarded her chastity; so We breathed into her of Our Spirit and she fulfilled in *her person* the Words of her Lord and His Books, for she was one of the obedient.'[30]

In this passage believers are *likened* to the wife of the Egyptian Pharaoh who persecuted Moses. She sought her end in Heaven, in the nearness of God, and she asked for release from Pharaoh and his machinations and from participating in his cruel deeds. Believers are also *likened* to Mary, the daughter of Imran. She guarded her chastity and she received the revelation of God and affirmed the truth of God's teaching and His Books. She proved to be one of the most loyal servants of God. Here, believers are described as being of two types: the type which is like the wife of Pharaoh, and the type which is like Mary. It is obvious that at least one type of believer is Mary-like. If, therefore, the Promised One is called son of Mary, it might mean that this Promised One will have his origin in a Mary-like condition, and that growing out of this, he will attain a Jesus-like condition. It might mean that the earlier life of the

30 *Al-Tahrim*, 12–13.

Promised One will be holy and spotless even as Mary was holy and spotless, his later life being akin to that of Jesus. Jesus received sustenance and support from the Holy Spirit; so will the Promised One. Jesus devoted his life to the service of truth and goodness; so will the Promised One.

It is a pity that the *Ulema* of our time do not ponder over the words of the Holy Quran. They have forbidden themselves to go deeply into its meaning. Small wonder that they miss the beauty and the significance which lie beneath the surface of the Holy Text. But if our *Ulema* had read the writings of the early doctors of Islam (writings based on the Holy Quran and on the lives and experiences of early prophets), they would have found the truth. Shaikh Shahab al-Din Suhrawardy, to cite one example of a Muslim saint who has written relevantly on this subject, says in his book *Awarifa'l-Maarif* that birth is of two kinds: ordinary physical birth and metaphorical birth. In support of this statement, the great saint goes on to quote no other person than Jesus himself. The Shaikh writes:

يَصِيْرُ الْمُرِيْدُ جُزْءَ الشَّيْخِ كَمَا اَنَّ الْوَلَدَ جُزْءُ الْوَالِدِ فِي الْوِلَادَةِ
الطَّبْعِيَّةِ، وَتَصِيْرُ هٰذِهِ الْوِلَادَةُ اٰنِفًا وِلَادَةً مَّعْنَوِيَّةً، كَمَا وَرَدَ
عَنْ عِيْسٰى صَلَوٰتُ اللهِ عَلَيْهِ: لَنْ يَّلِجَ مَلَكُوْتَ السَّمَآءِ مَنْ لَّمْ
يُوْلَدْ مَرَّتَيْنِ، فَبِالْوِلَادَةِ الْاُوْلٰى يَصِيْرُ لَهٗ ارْتِبَاطٌ بِعَالَمِ الْمُلْكِ
وَبِهٰذِهِ الْوِلَادَةِ يَصِيْرُ لَهٗ ارْتِبَاطٌ بِالْمَلَكُوْتِ -

'The *Murid* [disciple] is part of the Shaikh [preceptor], even as in physical birth the son is part of the father. The *Murid* comes to birth in a metaphorical manner in the sense which Jesus described when he said that no man will enter the Kingdom of Heaven unless he is born twice over.'

The first birth, according to the saint, links the person with the physical world, the second links him with the spiritual world. This theme is also in the Quran:

وَكَذٰلِكَ نُرِيْٓ اِبْرٰهِيْمَ مَلَكُوْتَ السَّمٰوٰتِ
وَالْاَرْضِ وَلِيَكُوْنَ مِنَ الْمُوْقِنِيْنَ -

'And thus did We show Abraham the Kingdom of the Heavens and the earth that he might be rightly guided, that he might be of those who have certainty of faith.'[31]

According to Shaikh Shahab al-Din Suhrawardy, therefore, every human being experiences a spiritual birth. In support of this view he cites a verse of the Holy Quran and a saying of Jesus according to whom the experience of spiritual birth is necessary for the spiritual development of an individual. Why should such a spiritual birth be impossible or difficult in the case of the Promised Messiah?

Briefly, then, the thought that the first Messiah should come to life again and appear today for the guidance of mankind impugns the Greatness of God and His teaching, and the high spiritual status of our Holy Prophet. It also contradicts the recorded Saying of the Holy Prophet. The thought is ill-conceived, a result of parochial thinking. The truth is that the second coming of the Messiah was to take place in and through a follower of the Holy Prophet. This follower was to rise in the spirit and character of the first Messiah. According to us the second Messiah has already come. His teaching has provided guidance for many. Many who had strayed away from God have found Him again.

Continuity of revelation and the coming of prophets

The fourth major objection raised against us is that, according to us, the institution of revelation and of the coming of prophets continues after the Holy Prophet (on whom be peace). This objection also results from lack of deliberation, or through sheer hostility and prejudice. The truth is that we do not care so much for words as for their meaning. We prefer to believe whatever helps to glorify God and His Prophet. We cannot even for a moment believe in the coming of one whose coming implies the superseding of the Holy Prophet, who should give the world a new *Kalima* (creed) and a new *Qibla* (direction of the face in worship) and give the world a new religious law or alter any part of the law of the Holy Quran; or who should wean people away from obedience to the Holy

31 *Al-An'am*, 76.

Prophet and ask them to obey him instead of the Holy Prophet; or who should arise from outside the circle of the Holy Prophet's servants and devotees, or should have achieved even a part of his spiritual status without owing it to the Holy Prophet. The coming of such a one, in our view, would be the end of Islam. It would mean that the promises made by God to the Holy Prophet are proved untrue. Such a thing is impossible and we hate to think of it. At the same time we think it wrong to believe that with the advent of the Holy Prophet the graces and blessings which human beings have ever received in the past have come to an end. We do not think the Holy Prophet came and closed off the known avenues of spiritual progress. We think instead that the advent of the Holy Prophet provided expanded opportunities and means for spiritual advancement. We do not think the Holy Prophet came to stop human beings from attaining nearness to God. Just as we hate to think that any revealed teacher can now supersede the Holy Prophet, we also hate to think that the coming of the Holy Prophet is the end of revelation and of the blessings which revelation brings. Both beliefs are derogatory to the Holy Prophet and subversive of his teaching. We accept neither the one nor the other. We are certain that the Holy Prophet was a blessing for mankind. We know that the blessings and beneficence of the Holy Prophet continue. His coming has not prevented mankind from earning spiritual benefits. Instead, the spiritual benefits and graces which God has ever granted to human beings have begun to flow more copiously than before. If before they were a stream, they have since become a mighty river. Before the Holy Prophet, knowledge of spiritual matters had not advanced very far. With the coming of the Holy Prophet it attained perfection; and only spiritual knowledge can bring spiritual wisdom.

The Holy Quran teaches what had not been taught before by any Heavenly Book. The Holy Prophet, therefore, was gifted with a deeper insight into spiritual matters than had been granted to anyone before. Increase of spiritual insight enables believers today to attain spiritual heights which could not be attained before. But for such blessings, what superiority can the Holy Prophet have over other prophets? The attainment of prophethood independently of the Holy Prophet is not possible now. That is why we deny that the Messiah of Nazareth can return to guide the followers of the Holy Prophet. His coming would be without the spiritual guardianship of the Holy Prophet. But prophethood which comes through the Holy Prophet and which, therefore, is glory to him, we cannot deny.

May God illumine the reader's heart with spiritual light and open wide his mind. A prophet who supersedes an earlier prophet is one who brings a new law and who attains his rank without the tutelage of the earlier prophet. But a prophet who attains his rank through dependence on the earlier prophet, through the grace and influence of his example and teaching, and through obedience to him, does not and cannot supersede the earlier prophet. Far from being derogatory to him, this sort of prophethood glorifies the earlier prophet, his teaching and example. This way to prophethood, it appears from the Holy Quran, is open to attainment by the followers of the Holy Prophet. Ordinary human reason also supports such a view. For if such a prophethood is not attainable by the followers of the Holy Prophet, then the followers of the Holy Prophet can have no superiority over the followers of other prophets.

The Holy Prophet has said that among the followers of Moses there were persons who attained the status of *Muhaddath*, a spiritual rank lower than that of a prophet. Therefore, if the spiritual example and influence of the Holy Prophet can result in raising persons to a status no higher than that of *Muhaddath*, then the Holy Prophet cannot be superior to other prophets and yet he is 'the best of mankind' and 'the best of prophets'. To be 'the best of prophets', it is necessary for the Holy Prophet to possess merits not possessed by earlier prophets. This distinctive merit, according to us, is that the followers of earlier prophets could attain at most the status of *Muhaddath*. The spiritual power of earlier prophets could achieve no more. But the followers of the Holy Prophet can attain the status of prophets, and this is due to the superior spiritual influence of the Holy Prophet's example and teaching. Thanks to this, a believer has his heart full of love for the Holy Prophet and of devotion to his person and example.

If the advent of the Holy Prophet put an end to the attainment of this sort of prophethood, then his advent has to be accounted not as a blessing but as a bane. The Holy Quran has to be dismissed as a useless book. For if the followers of this Prophet and this Book cannot attain the status of prophets, we have to admit that before his advent it was possible for believers to rise to this spiritual station, but that it has become impossible after his advent. Books revealed before the Holy Quran had the power to raise their readers and followers to the status of prophets (that is, to enable them to reach that degree of divine grace); but the Holy Quran does not have this power! If this were really true, the hearts of true believers would bleed and their spirits would cool. The coming of the Holy Prophet, the promised 'mercy unto all the worlds', 'the chief of all prophets', was to open new ways to spiritual advancement; by following him they were to come closer to their Lord than ever before. But, instead, even the doors open before are to be closed to them. No true believer can for a moment entertain such a thought about the Holy Prophet. No one who loves the Holy Prophet can believe such a thing. God be our witness, the Holy Prophet was an ocean of spiritual blessings and spiritual possibilities which no mortal may measure. The doors to spiritual blessings and spiritual progress have not been closed by him. They have instead been thrown wide open. This is the difference between him and the earlier prophets. The followers of earlier prophets could reach the rank of *Muhaddath*. To reach the rank of *Nabuwwat* (prophethood), they had to have further training and tuition. It is different with the followers of the Holy Prophet. Obedience to him and imitation of his example can raise a man to the rank of prophet; even as prophet, however, the follower remains a follower. However high his rank, he cannot go out of the fold. He remains the Holy Prophet's slave and servant. He may attain high rank but the height of his rank cannot alter his status as a follower of the Holy Prophet. For, in fact, the higher his rank, the greater is his indebtedness to the Holy Prophet. In respect of nearness to God, the Holy Prophet has reached a point which no mortal has ever reached. He has attained a height which others cannot think of attaining. At the same time, the greatness of his status continues to increase at a pace swifter than thought. But as the Holy Prophet advances, so do his followers. As the Holy Prophet steps forward, his followers behind him do likewise.

This conception of the spiritual status of the Holy Prophet means that the gift of prophethood should be open to the followers of the Holy Prophet. If such a gift is open to the followers, it will redound to the glory and greatness of the Holy Prophet. If such a gift is abolished, it means detraction and defeat for him. Who does not know that an able teacher who will have his ability proved must have able pupils. A great king must have other kings as his vassals. If an able teacher does not produce able pupils, he cannot be very able. A great king who does not have kings below him cannot be very great. An emperor is a king of kings. To be an emperor is an honour. Similarly, a prophet whose followers can be prophets is a greater prophet than prophets whose followers remain followers but cannot become prophets.

How this erroneous conception of prophethood became current among Muslims of the present day is an important question. I speak of Muslims of the present day because earlier doctors of the faith have views quite contrary to the conception accepted by the present-day Muslims. Saints and scholars like Mohyal-Din Ibnal-Arabi, Ibn-i-Qayim, Maulana Rumi, and Hazrat Sheikh Ahmad of Sirhind can be cited among the great doctors of the Muslim faith who have expressed views contrary to the views held by Muslims of the present day on this subject. The erroneous conception arose because Muslims began to interpret the term *Nabuwwat* in a wrong manner. Somehow they began to think that a prophet *must* be a law-giver also. He must either bring a new law, or he must abrogate parts of an older law, or he must be free from the obligation to obey an earlier prophet. The fact of the matter is that these conditions are not necessary in order for a prophet to be a prophet. A prophet may or may not fulfil these conditions. A person may fulfil none of these conditions and yet be a prophet. Though he does not bring a new law, does not abrogate any part of an earlier law, and is not free from the obligation to follow an earlier prophet, he may still be a prophet. For prophethood is a spiritual state, a degree of nearness to God. A person who attains this state, this degree of nearness, is appointed to lead mankind to God. He is charged with the duty of revivifying the spiritually dead and of making green the hearts which have become dry through a spiritual drought. It is his duty to tell mankind of the revelation he has received from God, to gather those who believe in him and his revelation, and to make of them a Jama'at willing to devote their lives to the propagation of Truth. His example should have the effect of cleansing people's hearts and of raising the quality and level of their everyday actions.

In short, people have begun to deny or to doubt the continuity of the gift of prophethood, because they have failed to grasp the meaning of this spiritual state. Some states of prophethood are such that their continuity among the followers of the Holy Prophet only raises his status instead of lowering it.

Meaning of Khatam al-Nabiyyin

It is said that the Holy Quran teaches the discontinuity of prophets of all kinds, because it says:

مَا كَانَ مُحَمَّدٌ اَبَآ اَحَدٍ مِّنْ رِّجَالِكُمْ وَلٰكِنْ رَّسُوْلَ اللّٰهِ وَ خَاتَمَ النَّبِيّٖنَ ۔

> 'Muhammad is not the father of any male amongst you, but he is a Messenger of God and *Khatam al-Nabiyyin*.'[32]

In the translation of the verse the Arabic appellation *Khatam al-Nabiyyin* is retained because on it hangs the meaning of the verse. It is argued from this that, according to the Holy Quran, there can be no prophets now, even from among the followers of the Holy Prophet. But many seem to forget that in the divine text the word *khatam* is used by God with a *fatha*, that is, a stroke above *t*, not with a *kasra*, a stroke below *t*. *Khatam* means 'seal'. *Khatim* would mean 'the last person' or 'the last one'. Now 'seal' has the function of attestation. The verse in question would, therefore, mean the Muhammad, the Holy Prophet (on whom be peace), is the Seal of the Prophets. The great doctor of *Hadith*, Imam Bukhari, has interpreted the divine title, *Khatam al-Nabiyyin*, as 'Seal of the Prophets'. Imam Bukhari in commenting upon this verse has cited the Traditions which speak of a mark on the Prophet's holy person which has been called by traditionists the seal of prophecy.

Alas! people do not ponder over the beautiful words of the Holy Book, so they miss its true significance. If they would ponder first over the general context, then over the verses and words, they would not miss the significance of the verse. For without grasping the context, nobody can understand the meaning of individual verses. Now, the passage begins by saying that the Holy Prophet is not the father of any male; that is, he has no physical son. The verse then goes on to assert that although the Holy Prophet is without

32 *Al-Ahzab*, 41 (33:41).

male issue, he is a prophet; and not only a prophet but the Seal of all Prophets. It should be evident that what is asserted in the second part of the verse is in extenuation of what is conceded in the first. The first part concedes an apparent defect, the second part asserts something in extenuation of that defect. However, Muslims who read the Holy Book know that to admit that the Holy Prophet had no male issue is to contradict what is asserted in another well-known verse of the Holy Quran:

إِنَّ شَانِئَكَ هُوَ الْأَبْتَرُ۔

'Verily, not you, but your enemy is without issue."[33]

An admission contradictory to an assertion needs some explanation. One verse (108:4) describes the Holy Prophet's *enemy* as issueless; the other (33:41) describes the Prophet *himself* as issueless. To resolve this contradiction, God makes an important claim on behalf of the Holy Prophet in verse 33:41. The claim is to repel the doubt or difficulty which the admission of this contradiction may easily raise. The claim is this: True, the Holy Prophet has no physical son. But this is no disgrace. It does not mean that he is really without offspring or progeny. Why? *Because* he is a Prophet of God. As a Prophet of God, he would have his followers; his spiritual progeny would more than compensate for any lack of physical progeny. But he is more than a prophet. He is the Seal of the Prophets. The expression 'Seal of the Prophets' asserts something further. It asserts that not only will the Prophet have followers and believers of the usual order: as Seal of the Prophets he will have the further power of raising others to the spiritual rank of prophet. He will be the progenitor not only of ordinary believers but even of prophets. In the verse cited against continuity of prophethood, we really have an affirmation of such a continuity; the continuity of an order of prophethood which has been mentioned and defined already, a prophethood which does not entail the instituting of a new law or dissociation from an earlier law. The continuity of prophethood which entails the revelation of a new law, or even partial abrogation of an older law, or the independent, unmediated realization of prophetic status, is offensive to the

33 *Al-Kauthar*, 4 (108:4).

spiritual fatherhood of the Holy Prophet. It is the possibility of such prophethood only which is denied in verse 33:41.

The Traditions 'I am the last of the Prophets', 'There is no prophet after me', and 'My mosque is the last of the mosques'

It is also asserted that some Sayings of the Holy Prophet are contrary to a belief in the continuity of prophethood. For instance, he said, 'I am the last of the prophets,' and again: 'There is no prophet after me.' From these Sayings, it follows that there can be no prophet of any kind after the Holy Prophet! It is a pity that those who cite these Sayings of the Holy Prophet forget that the words 'I am the last of the prophets' are followed by the important words 'and my mosque is the last of the mosques.' The whole Saying is: 'I am the last of the prophets and my mosque is the last of the mosques.' If, therefore, the Holy Prophet is literally the last of the prophets, then the mosque which he built in Medina is literally the last of the mosques. It would be wrong to build any mosque after the Holy Prophet's mosque at Medina. But nobody sees any contradiction between the meaning put today on the first part of the Saying and the meaning put on the second part of the same Saying. The first part is taken to mean the termination of every kind of prophethood with the advent of the Holy Prophet. But the second part is not likewise taken to mean the end of mosque-building. Those very people who believe in the termination of prophethood see no harm in building more mosques. In fact, their zeal for building mosques is excessive. There are towns which contain more mosques than are really required; many, therefore, remain without worshippers. In many towns mosques are to be found at short distances from each other, so that their superfluity is evident. If the expression 'the last of the prophets' entails the abolition of prophethood, the expression 'last of the mosques' must entail the abolition of mosque-building after the Prophet's mosque.

To be sure, solutions of this difficulty are attempted. It is said that mosques built by Muslims after the Holy Prophet's time are mosques devoted to the form of worship instituted by the Holy Prophet. They are built for the same purpose as the Holy Prophet built the first mosque. Mosques built by Muslims, therefore, are the Prophet's own mosques. They cannot be separated from the model which they imitate. Such mosques cannot and do not contradict the fact that the Prophet's mosque is the last. The solution is a valid one. But it is equally valid to say that the expression 'the last prophet' does not prohibit the coming of prophets who imitate the life and example of the Holy Prophet, teach nothing new, and only follow him and his teaching; who are charged with the duty of spreading the Holy Prophet's teaching; who attribute their spiritual acquisitions including prophethood to the spiritual example and influence of their preceptor and master, the Holy Prophet. The coming of such prophets does not offend against the Holy Prophet's prerogative as the 'Last Prophet', in the same way and for the same reason that the building of mosques today does not offend against the status of the Prophet's mosque as the 'Last Mosque'.

Now, let us turn to the Saying 'There is no prophet after me.' This Saying also cannot mean that there is to be literally no prophet after the Holy Prophet. This Saying also means only this: that no prophet can now come who would abrogate the teaching of the Holy Prophet. The Prophet's Saying turns on the word 'after'. One thing comes *after* another only when the first thing is over and the second thing takes its place. The prophet who appears in order to propagate, promulgate, and in every way to support and promote the prophethood of the Holy Prophet and all it stood and stands for cannot be said to have appeared *after* the Holy Prophet. The prophethood of the Holy Prophet would be extant still. The prophet who comes to serve this prophethood is a part of the Holy Prophet's dispensation. Such a prophet could be said to have appeared *after* the Holy Prophet if he had proposed the abrogation of any part of the Holy Prophet's teaching. A wise man tries to ponder over every important subject and to reach the depth of meaning which every single word and every single text contains. No wonder Ayesha (God be pleased with her), the holy consort of the Holy Prophet, fearing that Muslims in time to come should miss the meaning of the Holy Prophet's Sayings on the subject of prophethood, warned people, saying:

قُوْلُوْا اِنَّهٗ خَاتَمُ الْاَنْبِيَآءِ، وَلَا تَقُوْلُوْا لَا نَبِيَّ بَعْدَهٗ۔

'Certainly, do say, he [the Holy Prophet] is the Seal of all Prophets, but do not say, there is no prophet after him'.[34]

34 Takmala Majma-ul Bahar, p. 15.

If in Ayesha's view, in her knowledge, the coming of prophets was literally over, why did she warn people against saying there was to be no prophet after the Holy Prophet? If when she sounded this warning she was wrong, and what she said was against the teaching of the Holy Prophet, why did not the Holy Prophet's Companions contradict her? Her warning against the casual repetition of the Saying 'There is no prophet after me' shows clearly that, according to her, the coming of a prophet after the Holy Prophet was possible. Only such a prophet could not be a law-giving prophet, or a prophet independent of the Holy Prophet. The fact that the Companions of the Holy Prophet received Ayesha's warning without question or criticism shows that the Companions of the Holy Prophet understood what she said and believed what she believed.

The Holy Quran and the institution of prophets

Woe to those who do not ponder over the Words of the Holy Book: misled, they seek to mislead others. Woe to those who show their wrath against us who refuse to be misled. They call us irreligious and *Kafirs*. But a believer is not afraid of other people's threats. He is afraid only of God. What harm can one man do to another? Kill, at the most? But a believer is not afraid of being killed. For him, death opens the door to the Vision of God. If only those who decry us knew what a treasure the Holy Quran is. It is a treasure which cannot be exhausted; it is to continue to meet human needs for all time. It contains teaching about the spiritual advancement of human beings such that other books do not contain even a fraction of it. If people had any idea of the value of the Holy Quran, they would not be content with the little knowledge they have gleaned. They would delve deep into the meaning and seek ways to please God more and more, and acquire nearness to Him. If they had known the value of purity of heart as against outward conformity, if they had cared for the spirit and not merely for the letter of the Holy Prophet's teaching, they would have tried to know the ways into which the Holy Quran invites them for their spiritual advance. Had they done so, they would have discovered that they care more for the shell than for the kernel, that they hope to enjoy a drink by holding an empty cup to their lips. Do they not read the *Surah Fatiha*, the first chapter of the Holy Quran? Does not the prayer in this chapter teach believers to ask God for spiritual rewards? Do they not repeat about fifty times a day the prayer 'Show us the straight path, the path of those on whom Thou hast bestowed Thy rewards'? If they do so, do they ever ponder over the meaning of rewards for which believers pray in the *Surah Fatiha* in their daily prayers? Had they even once prayed with their inward eye on the meaning of the prayer, they would have asked themselves again and again: 'What is this straight path? What are the rewards which following the straight path is supposed to bring?' And had they asked these questions, their attention would have been drawn to the important verse contained in chapter 4, which says:

وَلَوْ أَنَّهُمْ فَعَلُوا مَا يُوعَظُونَ بِهِ لَكَانَ خَيْرًا لَّهُمْ وَأَشَدَّ تَثْبِيتًا
وَّإِذًا لَّآتَيْنَاهُم مِّن لَّدُنَّا أَجْرًا عَظِيمًا ۝ وَلَهَدَيْنَاهُمْ صِرَاطًا مُّسْتَقِيمًا ۝
وَمَن يُطِعِ اللَّهَ وَالرَّسُولَ فَأُولَٰئِكَ مَعَ الَّذِينَ أَنْعَمَ اللَّهُ عَلَيْهِم
مِّنَ النَّبِيِّينَ وَالصِّدِّيقِينَ وَالشُّهَدَاءِ وَالصَّالِحِينَ ۚ وَحَسُنَ أُولَٰئِكَ
رَفِيقًا ۝ ذَٰلِكَ الْفَضْلُ مِنَ اللَّهِ ۚ وَكَفَىٰ بِاللَّهِ عَلِيمًا ۝

> 'And if they do as they are told, it would certainly be better for them and more effective in establishing their faith: and in that case We would certainly have given them a great reward from Ourself, and We would surely have guided them to the right path. And he who obeys God and the Prophet, then such a one is of those whom God has rewarded, namely, the Prophets and the Truthful and the Martyrs and the Virtuous: and what a good company are these. This is the grace from God: and sufficient is God as One Who knows.'[35]

It is evident from this passage that when a believer prays for the path of those who have been rewarded by God's blessings, he prays for the company of prophets, the truthful, the martyrs, and the virtuous. Therefore, as God has taught us this prayer through His Prophet, a prayer we repeat about fifty times every day, and as the straight path for which we pray has been explained by God Himself as the path at the end of which believers find themselves in the

35 *Al-Nisa*, 70–1.

company of prophets, the truthful, the martyrs and the virtuous, who can assert and how can it be possible that, for the followers of the Holy Prophet, the door to every kind of prophethood is closed? Would not such a thought be ridiculous? Can God teach anything ridiculous? Is it possible that He should, on the one hand, exhort us to pray for our inclusion among the prophets, the truthful, the martyrs and the virtuous and, on the other, tell us that the reward of prophethood is now banned for the followers of the Holy Prophet and banned for ever? God forbid that this should be so. God is Holy and Pure, free from all faults and all evil. If, for some reason, He had really banned the reward 'prophethood', then He would not have taught us to pray for the path which leads to those rewarded by God. Nor would He have declared so clearly that obedience to the Holy Prophet makes a follower blessed, and to be blessed in the highest sense is to become a prophet.

It is said that the crucial verse in the passage contains the word *ma'a* (lit. 'with') and not *min* (lit. 'of' or 'from'). Therefore, it is asserted, the prayer only entails the possibility of a believer joining the company of prophets, of being *with* them, not *of* them. But those who assert this forget that the verse does not speak of prophets only. It speaks also of the truthful, the martyrs and the virtuous. If *ma'a* (lit. 'with') in the verse implies that a believer is banned from rising to the status of a prophet, then we have to admit that he would be banned also from rising to the status of the truthful, or the martyrs, or the virtuous. It is not discontinuity of prophets only, but also the discontinuity of the blessed ones of lower degree that we must accept and become reconciled to. A believer who prays for inclusion with the rewarded must be content only to join their company. He cannot be one of them. A believer may join the company of the truthful, but may not be one of the truthful. He may join the company of the martyrs, but may not be a martyr. He may join the company of the virtuous, but may not be one of the virtuous. It means that all spiritual rewards and ranks are banned for the followers of the Holy Prophet. The most they may expect, in response to their prayers and their exertions for spiritual merit, is that they may *join the company* of one spiritual galaxy or another. They may not expect to acquire the status of others in any such galaxy. Each galaxy would consist of the followers of earlier prophets. The followers of the Holy Prophet can only aspire to join them as onlookers, not as equals. No true

Muslim can entertain such a thought. Such a thought is derogatory to the dignity of Islam, the Quran and the Holy Prophet. It implies that the followers of the Holy Prophet cannot aspire even to the status of virtuous believers. They can only aspire to the privilege of their company. The word *ma'a* or 'with', therefore, cannot be taken in its superficial or literal sense. In that sense, the verse makes no sense whatever. It may serve the purpose of the *Ulema* by banning the gift of prophethood for the followers of the Holy Prophet. But if *ma'a* is to be interpreted in this way, not only prophethood but the other categories of blessedness, namely, truthfulness, martyrdom and virtue, will be banned likewise.

The truth, however, is that the word *ma'a* (lit. 'with') is not used only in the sense of simultaneity in time or place. It does not merely mean that two things or persons are found together. It often means also similarity or community of status. We have examples of it in the Holy Quran. Thus:

إِنَّ الْمُنَافِقِينَ فِي الدَّرْكِ الْأَسْفَلِ مِنَ النَّارِ وَلَنْ تَجِدَ لَهُمْ نَصِيرًا
إِلَّا الَّذِينَ تَابُوا وَأَصْلَحُوا وَاعْتَصَمُوا بِاللّٰهِ وَأَخْلَصُوا دِينَهُمْ
لِلّٰهِ فَأُولٰئِكَ مَعَ الْمُؤْمِنِينَ وَسَوْفَ يُؤْتِ اللّٰهُ الْمُؤْمِنِينَ
أَجْرًا عَظِيمًا

> 'Surely the hypocrites are in the lowest depth of the fire and thou shalt not find for them a helper. Except those who repent and amend and hold fast to Allah, and are sincere in their obedience to Allah. These then are among [or with?] the believers. And Allah will soon bestow upon believers a great reward.'[36]

In this verse those who repent and do good deeds and are devotees of God and are sincere in their obedience are described as those who will be *with* the believers. If 'being *with* the believers' is taken literally, it would mean that in spite of being penitent, doing good deeds, being devoted to God, and being sincere in obedience to Him, those who practise these virtues will not attain the *status* of believers, but will only be *with* the believers. They will only acquire the right of company, but not be their equals and among them. Such a consequence is absurd in the extreme. Therefore we have to

36 *Al-Nisa*, 146–7.

admit that *ma'a* (lit. 'with') often means similarity or equality of status. It is similarity of status which is asserted in the words 'they are *with* those whom God has blessed' in the verse in question.

From other places in the Holy Quran too it appears that the door to one kind of prophethood remains open for the followers of the Holy Prophet. This prophethood is an image of the prophethood of the Holy Prophet, and its purpose is to promote and propagate the truth of his teachings. Such prophethood will accrue from obedience and loyalty to the Holy Prophet. Thus in the chapter *Al A 'raaf*, God says about the Holy Prophet and his followers:

قُلْ إِنَّمَا حَرَّمَ رَبِّيَ الْفَوَاحِشَ مَا ظَهَرَ مِنْهَا وَمَا بَطَنَ وَالْإِثْمَ
وَالْبَغْيَ بِغَيْرِ الْحَقِّ وَأَنْ تُشْرِكُوا بِاللَّهِ مَا لَمْ يُنَزِّلْ بِهِ سُلْطَانًا
وَأَنْ تَقُولُوا عَلَى اللَّهِ مَا لَا تَعْلَمُونَ - وَلِكُلِّ أُمَّةٍ أَجَلٌ فَإِذَا
جَاءَ أَجَلُهُمْ لَا يَسْتَأْخِرُونَ سَاعَةً وَلَا يَسْتَقْدِمُونَ - يَا بَنِي
آدَمَ إِمَّا يَأْتِيَنَّكُمْ رُسُلٌ مِنْكُمْ يَقُصُّونَ عَلَيْكُمْ آيَاتِي فَمَنِ اتَّقَى
وَأَصْلَحَ وَلَا خَوْفٌ عَلَيْهِمْ وَلَا هُمْ يَحْزَنُونَ -

'Say: This is what my Lord has forbidden, indecencies which are evident and which are hidden, and sin, and revolting without just cause, and that you join with Allah that for which He has sent down no warrant and that you say of Allah what you know not.

'And for every people there is a term, so that when their term is come, they cannot remain behind for an hour, nor can they precede it.

'O children of Adam, if or when My Messengers come to you from amongst you, relating My Signs to you, then as to him who is reverent and does good, there is then no fear of such, nor shall they grieve.'[37]

From this it is evident that prophets will appear from amongst the followers of the Holy Prophet. The context relates to the followers of the Holy Prophet and it is in relation to them that God speaks of the coming of prophets and reminds them of their duty to

37 *Al-A'raaf*, 34–6.

accept such prophets. If they do not accept them, they will suffer. If anybody wishes to suggest that there is an 'if' in the Quranic text and that this 'if' makes the coming of prophets conditional and uncertain, it will not serve his purpose; because such an expression has been used in the Holy Quran in the description of the exit of Adam from Heaven. But even if we take the 'if' in the verse to denote a condition, it is evident that, according to God, prophetic revelation has not come to an end. A phenomenon which is avowed and which is no longer to be observed or experienced cannot be mentioned by God even in a conditional manner. To mention the impossible even in such a manner would be against the Dignity of God.

Besides the evidence of the Holy Quran, the Sayings of the Holy Prophet also support the view that prophetic revelation has not come to an end. It is not completely and absolutely prohibited. The Holy Prophet has described the Promised Messiah as a Prophet. If, according to the Holy Prophet, no prophet of any kind was possible after him, why did he describe the Promised Messiah as a Prophet of God?[38]

Ahmadis believe in Jehad

The fifth big objection raised against us is that we deny the Muslim institution of Jehad. I have always wondered how such a false charge could be made against us, for to say that we deny Jehad is a lie. Without Jehad, according to us, belief cannot be made perfect. The weakness of Islam and of Muslims, the decay or the disappearance of belief, that we observe today on all sides, are due to casualness in the matter of Jehad. To say that we deny Jehad, therefore, is a fabrication. The teaching about Jehad occurs in several places in the Holy Quran, and we as Muslims and as devotees of the Holy Book cannot possibly deny it. What we deny and resist vehemently is the view which makes it right to shed blood, to spread disorder and disloyalty, and to disrupt civil peace in the name of Islam. To do so is to soil the fair name of Islam. We cannot be persuaded that the teachings of Islam may be distorted so as to serve our own designs and desires. We are not against Jehad.

38 *Muslim*, Zikre Dadjjal.

We are only against the tendency to label any kind of aggrandizement as Jehad.

And, dear reader, you can well understand that if an attempt is made to find fault in a beloved, how great is the offence which the attempt causes to the lover. How angry he would be at the fault-finder. Likewise we are angered by those who defame Islam by their words or deeds. The world at large regards Islam as a barbaric religion, and the Prophet of Islam as a savage militarist monarch. Have they found anything in the life of the Holy Prophet which warrants such a description, anything against the canons of piety and virtue? No. Muslims themselves by their deeds have prejudiced the world at large against Islam, so that it is no longer very easy to make them take a different view. Among the wrongs done to the Holy Prophet is the wrong which Muslims themselves have done to him by misrepresenting the Holy Prophet – by holding up a wrong image of him before others. The Holy Prophet was an embodiment of compassion and forgiveness. He did not want to harm even the meanest of God's creatures. Yet he has been described in such a way as to repel people and to prejudice their minds against him.

The cry of Jehad is heard again and again and from many different quarters. But what was the Jehad to which God and His Prophet invited Muslims? And what is the Jehad to which we are invited today? The Jehad to which God invites us in the Holy Quran is described in the verse:

وَلَا تُطِعِ الْكٰفِرِيْنَ وَجَاهِدْهُمْ بِهٖ جِهَادًا كَبِيْرًا -

'So obey not the disbelievers and strive by means of it [i.e. the Quran] a great striving.'[39]

The highest Jehad, therefore, is Jehad with the help of the Quran. Is it such a Jehad to which Muslims are invited today? How many are there who turn out to strive against disbelievers with only the Quran in their hands? Are Islam and the Quran so utterly devoid of inherent merit and attractiveness? If Islam and the Quran cannot attract people today by their intrinsic beauty, what evidence have we for the truth of Islam? Human speech can change hearts. Can

39 *Al-Furqan*, 53.

the speech of God change no hearts? Can it bring about no change in the world except with the help of the sword? Long human experience shows that the sword cannot effect a change of heart, and, according to Islam, it is a sin to try and convert a people through fear or favour. Has not God clearly said in the Holy Quran:

إِذَا جَاءَكَ الْمُنٰفِقُوْنَ قَالُوْا نَشْهَدُ إِنَّكَ لَرَسُوْلُ اللّٰهِ ۘ وَاللّٰهُ
يَعْلَمُ إِنَّكَ لَرَسُوْلُهٗ ۗ وَاللّٰهُ يَشْهَدُ إِنَّ الْمُنٰفِقِيْنَ لَكٰذِبُوْنَ -

'When the hypocrites come to thee, they say: "We bear witness that thou art indeed the Messenger of Allah." And Allah knows that thou art indeed His Messenger, but Allah bears witness that the hypocrites are most surely liars.'[40]

Here is a description of the hypocritical believers. If it were correct to spread Islam by the sword, then would it be meet or necessary to describe in this way those who had accepted Islam outwardly but were inwardly unbelievers still? If it were correct to convert people to Islam by force, then even such converts as did not believe in their hearts would have been true converts, according to the Holy Quran. Nobody can hope to win sincere converts by the sword. It is wrong, therefore, to think that Islam teaches the use of the sword for the conversion of non-Muslims. On the other hand, Islam is the first religion which lays down the principle of freedom in religious matters in clear and unambiguous terms. The teaching of Islam is:

لَآ إِكْرَاهَ فِي الدِّيْنِ قَدْ تَبَيَّنَ الرُّشْدُ مِنَ الْغَيِّ -

'There shall be no compulsion in religion. Surely, right has become distinct from wrong.'[41]

According to Islam, every human individual is free to believe or not to believe. He is free to follow reason. Islam also teaches:

40 *Al-Munafiqun*, 2.

41 *Al-Baqarah*, 257.

وَقَاتِلُوْا فِي سَبِيْلِ اللّٰهِ الَّذِيْنَ يُقَاتِلُوْنَكُمْ وَلَا تَعْتَدُوْا ۚ إِنَّ اللّٰهَ
لَا يُحِبُّ الْمُعْتَدِيْنَ ۔

'And fight in the cause of Allah against those who fight against you, but do not transgress. Surely, Allah loves not the transgressors.'[42]

Here the law of religious wars is laid down clearly. A religious war is to be waged against those who make war on Muslims because of religion; who seek by force to convert Muslims. Even in such a war Islam forbids the transgression of limits. If non-Muslims seeking to convert Muslims by force withdraw from such an attempt, then Muslims must stop fighting. In the face of such a teaching, nobody can say that Islam teaches the waging of war for its expansion. If Islam sanctions war, it is not in order to destroy or harm any religion. It is to promote religious freedom, to protect places of religious worship. It is clearly laid down in the Holy Quran:

أُذِنَ لِلَّذِيْنَ يُقَاتَلُوْنَ بِأَنَّهُمْ ظُلِمُوْا ۚ وَإِنَّ اللّٰهَ عَلٰى نَصْرِهِمْ لَقَدِيْرٌ ۔
الَّذِيْنَ أُخْرِجُوْا مِنْ دِيَارِهِمْ بِغَيْرِ حَقٍّ إِلَّآ أَنْ يَّقُوْلُوْا رَبُّنَا اللّٰهُ ۚ
وَلَوْلَا دَفْعُ اللّٰهِ النَّاسَ بَعْضَهُمْ بِبَعْضٍ لَّهُدِّمَتْ صَوَامِعُ وَبِيَعٌ
وَّصَلَوٰتٌ وَّمَسَاجِدُ يُذْكَرُ فِيْهَا اسْمُ اللّٰهِ كَثِيْرًا ۚ وَلَيَنْصُرَنَّ اللّٰهُ
مَنْ يَّنْصُرُهٗ ۚ إِنَّ اللّٰهَ لَقَوِيٌّ عَزِيْزٌ ۔

'Permission to fight is given to those against whom war is made, because they have been wronged. And Allah indeed has power to help those who have been driven out of their homes unjustly only for saying "Our Lord is Allah." And if Allah did not repel some men by means of others, cloisters and churches and synagogues and mosques would have been pulled down wherein the name of Allah is oft remembered. And Allah will surely help him who helps Allah. Allah is indeed Powerful, Mighty.'[43]

42 *Al-Baqarah*, 191.

43 *Al-Hajj*, 40–1.

This passage from the Holy Quran leaves no doubt whatever that a religious war is not permitted by Islam unless it is against a people who force another people to abjure their religion; unless, for instance, Muslims are forced to abjure Islam. A religious war may be justified when there is interference in religion. But even when permitted, a religious war is not intended to force a people to give up their faith, nor is its purpose to desecrate or destroy places of worship, or to kill. The purpose of religious wars is to protect religion, to protect every religion, and to save from disgrace and destruction all places of worship, irrespective of the denomination to which they belong. Only such a religious war is permitted by Islam. Islam is a witness of other religions and their protector. Islam is no party to violence or cruelty or unfreedom.

In short, the Jehad sanctioned by Islam is to make war against a people who prevent others by force from accepting Islam, or who wish to force people to deny Islam. It may be made against a people who kill others because of Islam. Only against such a people is the making of war permissible in Islam. Against any other people, Jehad is wrong and contrary to Islam. War not sanctioned by these conditions may be a political war, a war between country and country or people and people. It may be a war between two Muslim peoples. But it will not be a religious war.

The current view of Jehad, which is nothing but violence and lawlessness, has been borrowed by Muslims from others. There is no sanction for it in Islam. It is not even known in Islam. Strange as it may seem, the responsibility for the spread of this view among Muslims lies with Christians, who are loudest in their condemnation of Islam for its supposed teaching of Jehad. In the Middle Ages, religious wars were the order of the day. The whole of Europe took part in them. Christian warriors and crusaders attacked the borders of Muslim countries in the same way as semi-independent trans-border tribesmen attack the border of India. At the same time they attacked those European peoples who were holding back from Christianity. Christians who took part in these wars did so to earn the pleasure of God. It seems that, under the violent and unprovoked attacks of Christians, Muslims lost their balance. Following the example of Christians, they too started attacking the borders of other peoples and countries. They forgot the teaching of their own religion. So completely do they seem to have assimilated the

Christian example that Christians themselves have started raising objections. In spite of the fact that objections now come from Christians, Muslims fail to see through the Christian game. All over the world today this objection is directed against Islam. Everywhere it is used as a weapon against Islam; but Muslims do not realize it. Unwittingly they continue to supply the enemies of Islam with texts and arguments to use against Islam. The enemy is able to attack Islam with weapons forged by Muslims. The wars which they call Jehad have not helped Islam. They have only done it harm. Muslims have lost sight of the moral conditions of victory. Victory comes not from weapons or numbers, but from skill, organization, education, equipment, morale and the goodwill of other nations. A very small nation can sometimes score a victory over a big nation, because the smaller nation happens to have the moral conditions of victory on its side. Without these conditions the largest armies may prove useless. It would have been infinitely better had Muslims sought their prosperity not in misconceived Jehad, but in the virtues and skills which make for the success of nations. By subscribing to a misconceived Jehad they defame Islam and harm their interests. If a nation indulges in political warfare in the guise of religion, it only drives other nations into united hostility against it. The other nations begin to feel insecure. When international conflicts are stimulated by religious differences, the state with the largest amount of goodwill for others is not immune from attack by an external enemy. When states are divided over religion, each is afraid of the others. Good behaviour and goodwill are then of no avail. These virtues may avert a political war but not a religious war.

In short, we do not deny but affirm, the importance of Jehad. We deny only a wrong interpretation of it, which has done incalculable harm to Islam. The future of Muslims, in our view, depends on how far they succeed in understanding the true meaning of Jehad. If they are able to realize that the best form of Jehad is Jehad with the Quran (25:53), and not Jehad with the sword, if they recognize that difference of religion provides no sanction for violence against the lives or property or honour of others (Quran, 4:91, 2:191, 60:90), their minds and outlook will undergo a wholesome change, a change which will take them nearer to the right path. Then they will be acting on a verse of the Holy Quran which says:

لَيْسَ الْبِرُّ بِأَنْ تَأْتُوا الْبُيُوتَ مِنْ ظُهُورِهَا وَلٰكِنَّ الْبِرَّ مَنِ اتَّقٰى
وَأْتُوا الْبُيُوتَ مِنْ أَبْوَابِهَا وَاتَّقُوا اللّٰهَ لَعَلَّكُمْ تُفْلِحُونَ۔

> 'And it is not righteousness that you come into houses by the backs thereof; but truly righteous is he who fears Allah. And you should come into houses by the doors thereof and fear Allah that you may prosper.'[44]

Then will they go from success to success.

I have briefly described the beliefs of the Ahmadiyya Jama'at. I have also described the objections raised against those beliefs and our answers to those objections. I now proceed to give a brief account of the claim of the founder of the Ahmadiyya Movement and of the arguments on which the claim is based. I do so in order that I should stand absolved before God; that it may be said that I have delivered the message, and that you, dear reader, may become acquainted with the purpose of God, and make an effort to act in accordance with that purpose, and inherit the grace of God and receive the gift of His love.

The claim of Hazrat Mirza Ghulam Ahmad

The claim of Hazrat Mirza Ghulam Ahmad (upon whom be peace) is that God has raised him for the guidance and direction of mankind; that he is the Messiah foretold in the Traditions of our Holy Prophet and the Mahdi promised in his Sayings; that the prophecies contained in the different religious books about the advent of a Divine Messenger in the latter days have also been fulfilled in his person; that God has raised him for the advocacy and promulgation of Islam in our time; that God has granted him insight into the Holy Quran, and revealed to him its innermost meaning and truth; that He has revealed to him the secrets of a virtuous life. By his work, his message, and his example, he has glorified the Holy Prophet and demonstrated the superiority of Islam over other religions. The purpose of his advent was that God's love and concern for Islam should become manifest, that it

44 *Al-Baqarah*, 190.

should become clear how improper it is to neglect God and to keep at a distance from Him. He claimed also that his coming had been foretold by almost all the prophets and founders of religions in the past. This, because the Holy Prophet of Islam had been sent by God as a teacher of all mankind. He was to collect mankind in one fold, to unite them in one faith. If this design was to be fulfilled, it was necessary that national and traditional divisions and hatreds should be swept out of the way, so that the Holy Prophet could be accepted as the Seal of Prophets by all the peoples of the world. Therefore, under God's design, the prophets and religious teachers of the past had each foretold his own second coming in the latter days. These prophecies pertained to a follower of the Holy Prophet, who was to be commanded by God to affirm and propagate the truth of the Holy Prophet, and was to unite the followers of different religions into an acceptance of Islam. He was to do so by declaring himself to be the Promised One of each religion. The prophecies in the books of other religions which foretold the coming of a teacher all met their fulfilment in him. He was the Messiah for Christians and Jews, the Masiodarbahmi for the Zoroastrians, and Krishna for the Hindus. His coming in fulfilment of prophecies contained in the ancient books is evidence of his truth. As he himself is a witness of the religion of Islam, his coming is an invitation to the followers of other religions to come and enter the universal brotherhood of Islam.

Having briefly described the claim of the Promised Messiah, the Founder of the Ahmadiyya Movement, I wish, in Part II, to enumerate the major criteria by which the truth of such a claimant can be judged. When it is proved that a certain person is divinely commissioned as a Messenger of God, it becomes incumbent upon everyone to accept his claim. If a person is a divinely appointed leader, it is inconceivable that he should try to mislead or misguide. If a divine leader could mislead, it would be to the discredit of Divine Knowledge. It would mean that, God forbid, God has made an error in selecting a Messenger or leader, that He has appointed as His vicegerent a person who is impure of heart, who seeks honour and fame for himself and not the propagation of truth, who holds himself above God.

Not only does such a thought contradict common sense and reason; the Holy Quran explicitly denies it. The Holy Quran says:

مَا كَانَ لِبَشَرٍ أَنْ يُّؤْتِيَهُ اللّٰهُ الْكِتٰبَ وَالْحُكْمَ وَالنُّبُوَّةَ ثُمَّ يَقُوْلَ
لِلنَّاسِ كُوْنُوْا عِبَادًا لِّيْ مِنْ دُوْنِ اللّٰهِ وَلٰكِنْ كُوْنُوْا رَبّٰنِيّٖنَ بِمَا كُنْتُمْ
تُعَلِّمُوْنَ الْكِتٰبَ وَبِمَا كُنْتُمْ تَدْرُسُوْنَ - وَلَا يَأْمُرَكُمْ أَنْ تَتَّخِذُوا
الْمَلٰٓئِكَةَ وَالنَّبِيّٖنَ أَرْبَابًا ۔ أَيَأْمُرُكُمْ بِالْكُفْرِ بَعْدَ إِذْ أَنْتُمْ مُّسْلِمُوْنَ -

> 'It is not possible for a man that Allah should give him the Book and dominion and prophethood, and then he should say to mankind. "Be ye my servants and not servants of Allah"; but he would say, "Be solely devoted to the Lord because you teach the Book and because you study it." Nor is it possible for him that he should bid you take the angels and the Prophets for Lords. Would he enjoin you to disbelieve after you have submitted to God?'[45]

It is impossible, that is to say, that God should grant a man a Book, give him wisdom and the rank of a prophet, and yet that such a person should teach men to abandon God and to obey him instead. Such a Messenger cannot but teach people to obey God. Nor can such a person teach people to take the angels and prophets as Gods. It is impossible for anyone to persuade people to believe and yet make them disbelieve.

The central question, therefore, when we are confronted with the fact of a claimant to divine leadership, is whether the leader's claim is true. If his claim is found to be true, then all his teaching is true. If his claim is not found to be true, it is futile to examine his teaching in detail. Following this golden principle, I wish to examine the claim of the Founder of the Ahmadiyya Movement, so that my readers should become acquainted with the grounds on which the claim stands, and because of which hundreds of thousands of persons have already accepted him.

45 *Al-Imran*, 80.

Part II

Arguments

Argument 1
The Need of the Hour

The first argument bearing on the truth or falsehood of a claimant to divine leadership is based on the need of the hour. A well-established divine law tells us that an act of God is neither out of place nor out of time. A new idea does not descend from God unless the world is in need of it. On the other hand, when the need for an idea has become clear, it can be withheld no longer. The law holds good in the physical world. There is no physical need that God has left unprovided for. The smallest need is included in the divine design. What is true of the physical needs of man must also be true of his spiritual needs. It would be against the beneficence and bounty of God were it not so. It is inconceivable that He should provide for the body of man but not for his spirit. The body is mortal. Its needs are short-lived. Its function and purpose are limited. In contrast the spirit is destined for eternal life. The aspirations of the spirit are without limit. The ends which the spirit seeks and the means by which it seeks them can be infinite.

Guidance of man, the special concern of God

If one ponders over the attributes of God in the light of the Holy Quran, one cannot think for a moment that when the spiritual condition of mankind cries for a spiritual reformer nothing should be done by God for the raising of such a reformer. If this were so, there would be no meaning in human life; and yet God teaches in the Holy Quran that the heavens and the earth and whatever is in them have not been created in sport, have not been made except with truth:

وَمَا خَلَقْنَا السَّمٰوٰتِ وَالْاَرْضَ وَمَا بَيْنَهُمَا لٰعِبِيْنَ وَ مَا خَلَقْنٰهُمَا
اِلَّا بِالْحَقِّ وَلٰكِنَّ اَكْثَرَهُمْ لَا يَعْلَمُوْنَ ۔

> 'And We have not made the heavens and the earth and what is between them in sport. We did not make them except with truth, but most people know not.'[1]

According to the Holy Quran, the heavens and the earth, with all they contain, have been created as part of a grand purpose. They are not without meaning, nor merely for sport. Their creation is the expression of eternal and everlasting truths. Most people do not know this, however.

It follows, therefore, that when mankind begins to suffer from spiritual decline and to need a spiritual reformer, one must be sent by God. This reformer brings men back to the true path and relieves them of inner weakness, and puts them again on the road to truth.

Divine attributes therefore forbid the thought that God should do nothing while His creatures need His Help and Guidance. But in addition, we have in the Holy Quran a clear assurance of God's Help whenever help is needed. God says:

وَإِن مِّن شَيْءٍ إِلَّا عِندَنَا خَزَائِنُهُ وَمَا نُنَزِّلُهُ إِلَّا بِقَدَرٍ مَّعْلُومٍ

> 'And there is nothing of which there are no large treasures with Us. But We send them not down except in a known measure.'[2]

The sources of all things are in the possession of God. Man receives them as gifts; but they are always carefully measured. These gifts are linked with human needs. They do not descend except when needed, but neither are they kept back when the need has become evident.

Similarly:

وَآتَاكُم مِّن كُلِّ مَا سَأَلْتُمُوهُ وَإِن تَعُدُّوا نِعْمَتَ اللَّهِ لَا تُحْصُوهَا

> 'And He gives you of everything that you ask Him for: and if you were to count the blessings of God, you would not be able to number them.'[3]

1 *Al-Dukhan*, 39.
2 *Al-Hijr*, 22.
3 *Ibrahim*, 35.

God gives man everything he needs. God gives it as a gift. These gifts cannot be counted. What a man *asks for* is what he *really* needs. Man asks for many things, but he does not receive everything he asks for. The verse therefore means that the *real* needs of man, the ends for which man yearns by nature, ends which are relevant to his everlasting life, are guaranteed by God.

We have thus a general assurance that human needs, physical or spiritual, cannot go unprovided for. On the subject of guidance, however, we have special assurances from God. When human beings need guidance God must provide it. In fact, the provision of guidance is God's Own responsibility, a responsibility unshared by anyone else. God says:

إِنَّ عَلَيْنَا لَلْهُدٰى ـ

'Verily, it is for Us to guide.'[4]

The guidance of man is God's Own duty, a duty He has appointed exclusively to Himself.

In the Holy Quran we are told that the provision of divine guidance from time to time is not only desirable but necessary. Had not God made the provision, on the Day of Judgment human beings would have answered Him by saying that because they had no guides from God, He had no right to hold them answerable for their omissions and commissions, no right to punish them. We read in the Holy Quran:

وَلَوْ اَنَّا اَهْلَكْنٰهُمْ بِعَذَابٍ مِّنْ قَبْلِهٖ لَقَالُوْا رَبَّنَا لَوْلَآ اَرْسَلْتَ
اِلَيْنَا رَسُوْلًا فَنَتَّبِعَ اٰيٰتِكَ مِنْ قَبْلِ اَنْ نَّذِلَّ وَ نَخْزٰى ـ

'And had We destroyed them with a punishment before his coming, they would have said: "Our Lord, wherefore didst Thou not send us a Messenger, that we might have followed Thy Commands before we were humbled and disgraced."'[5]

That is to say, if God had sent His punishment before He sent His Messenger to a people, they would have objected, saying: 'Why did

4 *Al-Lail*, 13.

5 *Taha*, 135.

not God guide us when we needed His guidance? Why did He not send us a Messenger whom we could have accepted and followed before degrading ourselves?' God does not refute the objection: He accepts it. God's duty to guide is stressed elsewhere in the Holy Quran.

The Quran goes further. It thinks it unjust to send punishment unless, in time of need, a people have had someone to guide them. Says the Holy Quran:

يٰمَعْشَرَ الْجِنِّ وَالْاِنْسِ اَلَمْ يَاْتِكُمْ رُسُلٌ مِّنْكُمْ يَقُصُّوْنَ عَلَيْكُمْ
اٰيٰتِيْ وَيُنْذِرُوْنَكُمْ لِقَآءَ يَوْمِكُمْ هٰذَا قَالُوْا شَهِدْنَا عَلٰٓى اَنْفُسِنَا
وَغَرَّتْهُمُ الْحَيٰوةُ الدُّنْيَا وَشَهِدُوْا عَلٰٓى اَنْفُسِهِمْ اَنَّهُمْ كَانُوْا كٰفِرِيْنَ ۔
ذٰلِكَ اَنْ لَّمْ يَكُنْ رَّبُّكَ مُهْلِكَ الْقُرٰى بِظُلْمٍ وَّ اَهْلُهَا غٰفِلُوْنَ ۔

'O Company of Djinn and men! Did not Messengers come to you from among you, who related to you My Signs and who warned you of the meeting of this your day? They will say, "We bear witness against ourselves." And the life of this world deceived them. And they will bear witness against themselves that they were disbelievers. This is because thy Lord would not destroy towns unjustly, while their people were unwarned.'[6]

Addressing the Djinn and men, God asks if they did not receive His Messengers and if they had not been warned of the day which now confronts them. In reply the Djinn and the men plead guilty and admit that they did have the warning, but they were misled by the life of the world. They affirm their own disbelief. Thus God warns before He destroys; for destroying without warning would be cruel, unjust, and uncharacteristic of God.

These verses of the Holy Quran make it clear that to declare that a people deserve punishment and to treat them as though truth and falsehood had been made plain to them, while they have had no warning whatever, is cruel in the extreme. In other words, if a people need guidance but receive no guidance from God, and if, in spite of this, God were to punish them for their misguidedness on the Day of Judgment, it would be wanton cruelty. But God is not

6 *Al-An'am*, 131–2.

cruel. It is impossible, therefore, that if a people need His guidance God would not provide it.

Guidance for Muslims specially promised in the Holy Quran

It appears, therefore, that according to Islam when a people need guidance, guidance is provided. It further appears from the Holy Quran that, quite apart from the general law of guidance in time of need, the followers of the Holy Prophet, the *Unmat-i-Muhammadiyya*, have had a special promise of divine guidance. This promise is contained in the verse

إِنَّا نَحْنُ نَزَّلْنَا الذِّكْرَ وَإِنَّا لَهُ لَحٰفِظُوْنَ ۔

> 'Verily, We Ourself have sent down this Exhortation and most surely We will be its Guardian.'[7]

That is to say, God is both the Revealer and the Protector of the Holy Quran.

Now, protection is of two kinds. One protection is external – the protection of the text of the Holy Quran. The other is internal – the protection of its meaning and message. Both kinds of protection are important. Unless both letter and spirit are protected, the ends of protection are not served. If we save the skin, beak and legs of a bird and stuff the skin with straw, we will have saved the external appearance of the bird, not the bird itself. The bird no longer lives. Similarly, if the bird damages its beak or its feet, if it loses its feathers, it cannot be said to be protected. A book that suffers interpolations or extrapolations, a book whose language is dead so that nobody can understand it, a book which no longer serves the purpose for which it was revealed, is a dead book. It is not protected. Maybe its words are intact, but its meaning has disappeared. A book is what it means. If the words of a book need protection, it is for the sake of the meaning. Therefore the protection of the Holy Quran is protection of both words and meaning.

7 *Al-Hijr*, 10.

The different ways in which God has guarded the text of the Holy Quran and thus fulfilled one part of the promise of protection fill one with wonder. Until the revelation of the Holy Quran, the Arabic language had not been systematized, its grammar, its diction and its idiom had not been fixed. The forms of speech and other linguistic criteria had not been formulated. Even the art of writing was in its infancy. As soon as the Holy Quran was revealed, however, God stimulated the believers to organize these studies. Only to serve the Holy Quran and to protect it from the ravages of time, early Muslims founded many linguistic sciences: the science of Arabic verbs and the Arabic sentence, the science of rhetoric, the science of *Tajwid* or phonetics, diction and idiom, the science of history, the science of *Fiqh* or law. These studies advanced in proportion to their importance for the protection of the Holy Quran. The science of Arabic verbs and the Arabic sentence and the science of diction were the most important for the protection of the Holy Quran. Small wonder that these sciences are the most advanced among the Islamic sciences. Even according to European scholars, Arabic grammar and Arabic dictionaries are the most systematized of all grammars and dictionaries.

Not only did we have these linguistic sciences; we also had hundreds of thousands of persons who were inspired to commit the Holy Quran to memory. On the other hand, the text of the Holy Quran being neither prose nor poetry, but something in between, committing it to memory became very easy. Those who have any experience of memorizing texts of some size know that the text easiest to memorize is the text of the Holy Quran. Not only is the Quran easy to memorize, we also have hundreds of thousands of persons who are eager to memorize it. Besides, every Muslim is obliged to recite portions of the Holy Quran in his daily prayers, so that even ordinary Muslims know parts of the Quran by heart. If, God forbid, all existing copies of the Holy Quran were to disappear, it would not mean the disappearance of the Holy Quran. The Holy Quran would survive in the memory of Muslims.

It seems, therefore, that God has provided fully for the outer protection of the Holy Quran. In view of these provisions it is next to impossible that we should lose any part of the Holy Text.

The point, however, is that the guarding of words is not half as important as the guarding of meaning. Words are for meaning, not meaning for words. If God has done so much for the protection of the Words of the Holy Quran, He cannot have done less for the protection of their meaning. Everybody who wishes to exercise his reason and understanding will admit that it is impossible that God should not protect the meaning of the Holy Quran when He has done so much to protect its Words. If God has done anything for the outer protection of the Holy Quran, how much more must He have done for its inner protection. The plain truth is in the verse

إِنَّا نَحْنُ نَزَّلْنَا الذِّكْرَ وَإِنَّا لَهُ لَحٰفِظُوْنَ۔

'We Ourself have sent down the Exhortation and We Ourself are its Protector.'[8]

We have the promise of both outer and inner protection. The inner protection of the Holy Quran at least means that when the followers of the Holy Book deviate very far from the Holy Quran, so that the Book becomes reduced to mere words, and the minds and hearts of men become sealed against it, God will restore the original power and influence of the Holy Book, make its meaning plain once again and restore to the dead book all its life and freshness. This promise by God is corroborated by the Traditions of the Holy Prophet – one has reached us through Abu Huraira, according to whom the Holy Prophet once declared:

إِنَّ اللّٰهَ يَبْعَثُ لِهٰذِهِ الْأُمَّةِ عَلٰى رَأْسِ كُلِّ مِائَةِ سَنَةٍ مَّنْ يُّجَدِّدُ لَهَا دِيْنَهَا۔

'Verily God will continue for ever to raise for this *Ummat* in the beginning of every century one who will restore for it its faith.'[9]

This Tradition of the Holy Prophet is an amplification of verse 15:10 of the Holy Quran. It presents more simply the meaning of this grand verse. It is possible that those who take a superficial view of everything and pin their faith on the letter of a text, ignoring its spirit and meaning, might think that this verse of the Quran promises protection only of its Words. The Holy Prophet, pointing to the coming of spiritual reformers at the turn of every century, has

8 *Al-Hijr*, 10 (ch. 15:10).

9 Abu Daud – Kitabul-Fitan.

warned Muslims not to forget the real meaning of protection. It is up to them now not to mislead themselves or others.

Protection of the Holy Quran means protection of Islam

The Tradition brings out another point, however. Spiritual reformers, promised in the Tradition, were to rise at the turn of each century. The evils which they would fight – evils arising from a failure to understand the meaning of the Holy Quran – would abound at the beginning of every century. A reformer every hundred years assures a continuity of divine protection. Islam was to be guarded by the advent of a reformer every one hundred years. It was to be served by these reformers or by others who came under their influence. It was to be protected from the danger of misinterpretation.

In short, the teaching of the Holy Quran may be summarized as follows:

1 Both the physical and the spiritual needs of man have been promised fulfilment; spiritual needs in particular have been promised fulfilment because their scope is more extensive and their importance much greater. But for such a promise, the whole drama of creation would be without meaning.
2 There is a definite promise of divine guidance whenever such guidance is needed by man.
3 If such guidance does not come, man will have the right to find fault with God.
4 If guidance does not come in time of need, those who suffer for want of guidance cannot be punished; to punish them would be an act of cruelty and God cannot be cruel.
5 There is an unambiguous promise for the raising of reformers to interpret afresh the meaning of the Holy Quran.
6 Such reformers will appear every one hundred years.

Present condition of Muslims

Now, dear reader, may God open your heart to the acceptance of

His truth! It is up to you to see whether the present is not the time for the advent of a divine reformer. It appears from the Traditions that the need for such a reformer recurs every hundred years. Every hundred years we are to have a reformer to interpret the Holy Quran and Islam to all and sundry. But now it is not the beginning but the middle of a century. Even if we ignore the Prophet's Tradition, we cannot ignore facts as we find them. Looking at facts, we are persuaded at once that a reformer is surely needed at this time. If Muslims and other nations were spiritually as well off as they might be, if they could be trusted to go on without divine guidance, we would not have needed to pay any attention to any claimant to spiritual office. But if the spiritual condition of Muslims demands a reformer and if the enemies of Islam have exceeded all previous records of enmity, we have to admit that the present is the time for a divine reformer to come, to teach Islam again, to fight its enemies, to bring Muslims back to the true Islam, to re-create in their hearts the old love of religion; in short, to demonstrate once again the living power of Islam.

On the general condition of Muslims today and the aims of the enemies of Islam, there can be no two opinions. Everyone who has no cause to hide the truth, everyone who can discriminate between good and evil, will admit that intellectually as well as spiritually, in belief as well as in action, Muslims have strayed far from Islam. A verse of the Holy Quran says:

يَا رَبِّ إِنَّ قَوْمِي اتَّخَذُوْا هٰذَا الْقُرْاٰنَ مَهْجُوْرًا۔

> 'O my Lord, my people indeed treated this Quran as a thing abandoned.'[10]

This is the stark truth about Muslims today. The question no longer is: How many Islamic things have they abandoned. The question rather is: How many have they not abandoned? True it is today: 'You may meet Muslims in a graveyard and Islam in its books.' Islam today can be found in the pages of the Holy Quran, the books of *Hadith*, and the books of the Imams, but not in the lives of Muslims. In the first place, Muslims are hardly aware of the teachings of Islam. If they seek such awareness, they soon find that access

10 *Al-Furqan*, 31.

to the meaning and spirit of Islam has become nearly impossible. Everything relating to Islam has become distorted. The conception of God presented in the name of Islam today is so hideous that spontaneous praise of God has become impossible for an honest person. The conception of angels is similarly ugly in the extreme. Of angels, God taught: 'They do as they are commanded' (16:50). Yet interpreters of Islam present them as critics of God, base creatures in human form, who indulge in the love of bad women. The Prophets of God are described as liars and sinners, so that the love and reverence which they should receive as favourites of God cannot be given to them. We are also told that divine revelation is not free from the influence of Satan; the only source of security is thus taken away. The metaphors of wine, and Heaven and Hell, are pushed to extremes, so that what is presented in the name of Islam seems either absurd or mere moonshine.

As well as attacking other prophets, the 'interpreters' of Islam have not spared even the Holy Prophet. Falsely and indiscriminately they have attributed to him a love affair with Zainab, or secret relations with a slave girl, or other inconceivable things. In this way they have detracted from the matchless beauty of character which is the Holy Prophet's. 'The Holy Prophet was a picture of the Holy Quran,' said Hazrat Ayesha, who knew him best. Yet the commentators have a different picture to paint.

A theory of abrogation has been invented, and a perfect book like the Holy Quran has been put in doubt. Not being able to understand parts of the Holy Quran, the commentators have condemned them as abrogated. They have done so without authority from the Holy Quran or from the Holy Prophet. They forget that by doing this they cast doubt not on parts of the Holy Quran but on the whole of it.

Then it is taught that a dead prophet, himself a follower of Moses, will come and rejuvenate Islam in our time, the followers of the Holy Prophet and his example of influence being unable to do so.

So much for the beliefs of Muslims. Their practical lives are no less deplorable. About seventy-five out of one hundred do not observe the daily prayers or the annual fasts. Nobody pays *Zakat*, or the obligatory alms. Of those who pay, very few, hardly two per cent, do so willingly. Few of those whose obligation to perform the pilgrimage to Mecca is obvious ever think of it. Those for whom the pilgrimage is not only not obligatory but possibly forbidden go on pilgrimage. They only bring dishonour to Islam. The few who observe the ordinances of Islam do so in such a manner that the purpose for which the ordinances have been prescribed is completely lost. The meaning of the Arabic words used in the daily prayers is hardly known to those outside the Arab countries. Those who say their prayers without understanding them do not say them willingly, but as an unpleasant obligation. The prostrations are carried out with such indecent haste that an observer cannot distinguish between one prostration and another. To pray in one's own language during pauses between prescribed prayers is branded as *Kufr*, or unbelief. Fasting, instead of bringing spiritual benefit, has become a cause of divine punishment.

The Islamic laws of inheritance are being ignored altogether. The taking of interest, described in the Quran as making war on God, is now an almost universal vice. Thanks to the *Ulema*, many interpretations and many amplifications enable ordinary Muslims today to accept interest on their capital wealth without thinking it a sin; and in spite of this, Muslims remain poor, far behind others in economic prosperity.

Moral grace, once the birth-right of all Muslims, now seems as remote as *Kufr* is from Islam. Time was when a Muslim's word was received as a promise set down in black and white, and a Muslim's written promise as unalterable law. But today nothing seems more unreliable than a Muslim's word, nothing more empty than a Muslim's undertaking. Loyalty has disappeared. Truth-speaking has become scarce, courage a thing of the past, disloyalty, lying, dishonesty, cowardice, and foolhardiness having taken their place. The result of this moral deterioration is that the whole world is set against Muslims. Their economic enterprise has ended. Their great name is gone. Science and intellect, once their handmaids and constant companions, seem like strangers to them.

Muslim mystics have also degenerated. They have converted religion into irreligion and religious law into lawlessness. Muslim clergy promote disaffection and mutual hostility. They sponsor their own opinions as the teaching of God and His Prophet. They thus strike at the root of Islam and the power of Muslims. Rich Muslims, not so rich compared with the rich of other nations, are yet so proud that associating themselves with religion seems dishonourable to them. As well as participating in religious duties, they have little regard left for them in their hearts. We may find missionaries amongst the rich of European nations, but amongst the Muslim rich it will be difficult to find many possessing even an elementary knowledge of religion. The ruling classes amongst Muslims are corrupt. Exploiting the poor and the ignorant is their daily business. The opportunity to rule is for them not an opportunity to serve, but an opportunity to dominate and dictate. Muslim kings revel in the pursuit of pleasure. Their ministers plan disloyalty and dishonesty. The Muslim masses are worse than savages. Hundreds of thousands among them cannot even recite the *Kalima*, and to be able to tell its meaning is completely out of the question. Islam, once the scourge of other religions, is today a carcass, being eaten by worms and vultures. Money and means can be found by Muslims for all their needs but not for the defence and dissemination of Islam. Time can be found for scandal-mongering, for gossip and for the entertainment of friends, but not for learning or teaching the Holy Book. Everybody knows how great was the importance of the daily prayers in the eyes of the Holy Prophet. Not the habitual defaulter or the habitual absentee, but the absentee only from the early morning and the late evening congregations, was condemned by the Holy Prophet as a hypocrite. Though the embodiment of forgiveness and generosity, he declared:

وَالَّذِي نَفْسِي بِيَدِهٖ لَقَدْ هَمَمْتُ اَنْ اٰمُرَ بِحَطَبٍ فَيُحْطَبَ ثُمَّ
اٰمُرَ بِالصَّلٰوةِ فَيُؤَذَّنَ لَهَا ثُمَّ اٰمُرَ رَجُلًا فَيَؤُمَّ النَّاسَ ثُمَّ اُخَالِفَ
اِلٰى رِجَالٍ فَاُحَرِّقَ عَلَيْهِمْ بُيُوْتَهُمْ۔

> 'Verily, by God in Whose possession is my life, sometimes when men have congregated for prayer, I wish to have enough dry wood with me, then appoint someone else as Imam and go out myself to set fire to the houses where people have stayed away from the congregation.'[11]

Today to join congregational prayers is too much trouble. Excepting the two *Ids*, millions of Muslims cannot find the few minutes needed for the daily prayers. Those who join in the daily prayers do not observe all the rules and proprieties. Often they join in only for show. They omit even the preliminary of ablutions.

11 Tajridul Bukhari, vol. 1, p. 2.

In one word, Islam today is friendless. Everybody has a friend but not Islam. This condition of Islam is depicted by the Promised Messiah and Mahdi, the Founder of the Ahmadiyya Movement (on whom be peace). I quote from his Persian verse:

می سزد گر خوں ببارد دیدۂ ہر اہلِ دیں
بر پریشاں حالئِ اسلام و قحط المسلمیں

دینِ حق را گردش آمد صعب ناک و سہمگیں
سخت شورے اوفتاد اندر جہاں از کفر و کیں

آنکہ نفسِ اوست از ہر خیر و خوبی بے نصیب
می تراشد عیب ہا در ذاتِ خیر المرسلیں

آنکہ در زندانِ ناپاکی است محبوس و اسیر
ہست در شانِ امامِ پاکبازاں نکتہ چیں

تیر بر معصوم می بارد خبیثِ بدگہر
آسماں را می سزد گر سنگ بارد بر زمیں

پیشِ چشمانِ شما اسلام در خاک اوفتاد
چیست عذرے پیشِ حق اے مجمع المتنعّمیں

ہر طرف کفر است جوشاں ہمچو افواجِ یزید
دینِ حق بیمار و بے کس ہمچو زین العابدیں

مردمِ ذی مقدرت مشغولِ عشرتہائے خویش
خرّم و خنداں نشستہ با بُتانِ نازنیں

عالماں را روز و شب باہم فساد از جوشِ نفس
زاہداں غافل سراسر از ضرورت ہائے دیں

ہر کسے از بہرِ نفسِ دُونِ خود طرفے گرفت
طرفِ دیں خالی شد و ہر دشمنے جست از کمیں

ایں زمانے آں چناں آمد کہ ہر ابنُ الجہول
از سفاہت میکند تکذیبِ ایں دینِ متیں

صد ہزاراں ابلہاں از دیں بروں بُردند رخت
صد ہزاراں جاہلاں گشتند صیدُ الماکریں

بر مسلماناں ہمہ ادبار زیں راہ اوفتاد
کز پئے دیں ہمّتِ شاں نیست با غیرت قریں

گر بگردد عالمے از راہِ دینِ مصطفےٰ
از رہِ غیرت نمی جنبند ہم مثلِ جنیں

فکرِ ایشاں غرق ہر دم در رہِ دُنیائے دُوں
مالِ ایشاں غارت اندر راہِ نسوان و بنیں

ہر کجا در مجلسے فسق است ایشاں صدرِ شاں
ہر کجا ہست از معاصی حلقۂ ایشاں نگیں

با خرابات آشناء بیگانہ از کوئے ہُدیٰ
نفرت از اربابِ دیں بامَے پرستاں ہمنشیں

ایں دو فکرِ دینِ احمدؐ مغزِ جانِ ما گداخت
کثرتِ اعدائے ملّت، قلّتِ انصارِ دیں

اے خدا زود آ و بر ما آبِ نصرت ہا ببار
یا مرا بردار یا رب زیں مقامِ آتشیں

اے خدا نورِ ہُدیٰ از مشرقِ رحمت بر آر
گمرہاں را چشم کن روشن ز آیاتِ مبیں

چوں مرا بخشیدۂ صدق اندریں سوز و گداز
نیست امیدم کہ ناکامم بہ میرانی دریں

کاروبارِ صادقاں ہرگز نماند ناتمام
صادقاں را دستِ حق باشد نہاں در آستیں

Meet is it if the faithful shed tears of blood
Over the plight of Islam and the disappearance of Muslims.

The true faith has suffered a shaking big and dreadful,
Unbelief and hatred have made a great noise in the world.

Those without the least virtue themselves
Find fault with the greatest of all divine teachers.

He who lives himself in a cell of vice
Is ready to detract from the greatness of the most pious among men.

The most vicious among men aims his arrows at the most innocent,
Just is it if, therefore, heaven rains stones on earth.

Islam is being thrown into the dust before your very eyes,
You who live in luxury, what defence will avail you before God?

On all sides unbelief is storming like the armies of Yazid,
The faith of God all alone is prostrate like Zain-ul-Abidin.

Men of means are lost in the pursuit of private pleasures,
Happy and hilarious in the company of sweet-hearts.

Doctors and divines busy day and night in personal quarrels,
Ascetics and mediators sit aside ignorant of the needs of faith.

Everyone has gone to care for his own mean interests, faith is alone,
So enemies have leapt out of their hidden places to attack.

The time has emboldened every stupid person
To use his stupidity to find fault with this established faith.

Millions of fools have left the faith with their bag and baggage,
Millions of the ignorant have submitted to charlatans and cheats. cheats.

Not a misfortune which has not befallen Muslims in their path,
Their shame and valour stand not together.

Even if the whole world turns away from the faith of Mustafa,
Muslims, much as the embryo in the womb, will not make the slightest movement.

They are drowned the whole time in low thoughts about the world,
Their wealth is all squandered on their wives and children.

They adorn gatherings of vice and wickedness,
Become centres in circles of sinners.

Friendly and familiar in the tavern, they know not the path to the righteous,
Strangers to the faithful, hot companions of worshippers of wine.

Two anxieties about the faith of Ahmad have consumed my life,
Abundance of enemies and lack of friends.

O God, rush to our side and rain on us your help,
Or remove me from near this blazing fire.

O God, send the light of guidance from the sun of Thy beneficence,
And illumine the eyes of those who have strayed away from Thy clearest Signs.

As thou hast granted truth and reality to my feelings and passions,
I fear not that I will fail or die a failure.

The duties which lovers of truth set themselves do not remain undone,
The lovers of truth have the Hand of God helping them in secret.

It seems, therefore, that the general conditions obtaining today are such that we must have not just a reformer but a great reformer from God; one who will put Islam on its feet again, meet unbelief on every front, and subjugate it again with unanswerable arguments, the weapons of reason. At the beginning of this century, only one man had come forward with the claim that he had been appointed by God for the defence of Islam, and he was the Founder of the Ahmadiyya Movement. It behoves all wise and rational men and women to ponder over this claim, not to turn away without giving it sufficient thought. If they turn away, they turn away from a major obligation and they will have to answer for it.

A doubt resolved

May God help you, reader, with His special help! Many at this point will whisper a doubt. They will say that the Holy Prophet of Islam (peace be on him) was a perfect prophet. After a perfect prophet we need no reformer or restorer. The Holy Quran is our reformer and the spiritual power of the Holy Quran will restore us to faith and wisdom. This is a beautiful thought. But when examined closely, it is found to be contrary to the teaching of the Holy Quran and *Hadith* and contrary also to reason and past experience. The thought is contrary to the Holy Quran and *Hadith* because in both we have a clear promise of the advent of divine leaders and reformers. If the coming of a *Mujaddid* (reformer) or a *Mamur* (divine leader) was derogatory to the Holy Prophet's perfection, why did God promise the advent of such reformers and leaders after He had made the Holy Prophet, the chief and the best of all prophets and the most perfect of all men? Would God contradict Himself? Would He do and undo a thing Himself? And why did the Holy Prophet predict the coming of reformers and leaders? Do we know more than he did himself? What did his perfection as man and prophet mean? Is it not strange that the Holy Prophet himself should tell us about the coming of reformers and we should think it contrary to his greatness?

The thought is also contrary to reason, because if after the Holy Prophet there were to be no reformers or spiritual leaders, then the spiritual condition of Muslims should not have suffered the least deterioration. Muslims should have maintained themselves in virtue and purity. But facts are against this. Reason cannot bring itself to think that Muslims should deteriorate spiritually and become worse and worse and that no reformer should come from God to reform them. If Islam is to be left uncared for like this, it will not prove the Holy Prophet to be the most perfect among men and prophets. It will prove rather that God wishes to end Islam. If reformers and spiritual leaders were to cease, the cessation should have been accompanied by a visible assurance to Muslims against being misled and going astray. Muslims today should have been spiritually as strong and healthy as they were in early Islam, in the time of the Companions of the Holy Prophet. If there is spiritual decay, we must have the means of spiritual regeneration.

Another consideration makes the thought contrary to reason, namely that if the perfection of the Holy Prophet means the cessation of spiritual leaders, who represent the Holy Prophet and imitate his qualities and character, then why do we have in the world vicegerents of God the Source of all Perfection, Ever-living, Ever-present? The truth seems to be that when a thing is hidden from ordinary human view, we need something to remind us of it and to enable us to experience something of the influence of which that thing was capable. The Holy Prophet, therefore, is the most perfect among men and among prophets. Nevertheless, after him, we need men who will portray his qualities, will imitate his spirit and follow his example. These men should remind us of him and re-establish his influence in the world.

The thought is contrary also to experience. During the thirteen hundred years which have passed since the time of the Holy Prophet (on whom be peace), many spiritual reformers have appeared amongst Muslims. They received the gift of revelation from God and claimed to have been raised for the restoration of Islam. These reformers were distinguished examples of Islam, and played a very important part in spreading and establishing Islam – Hazrat Junaid of Baghdad, Syed Abdul Qadir Jilani, Shaikh Shahab-ud-Din Suhrawardy, Hazrat Mohy-ud-Din Ibnal-Arabi, Hazrat Baha-ud-Din Naqshbandi, Shaikh Ahmad Sirhindi, Khawaja Moin-ud-Din Chishty, Hazrat Shah Wali Ullah of Delhi and others (on all of whom we invoke the mercy of God). Remembering them all, and not forgetting what they did for Islam and Muslims, how can we believe that after the Holy Prophet (on whom be peace) we can have no reformer or spiritual leader appointed by God for the rejuvenation of Islam? The plain truth, therefore, is that even after the Holy Prophet we should have reformers and restorers. We have had them in the past and must continue to have them in the future. The present condition of Muslims cries out for one, and a great one. The fact that Hazrat Mirza Ghulam Ahmad is the only one today who has claimed to be such a reformer constitutes a strong argument in his support.

Argument 2
Testimony of the Holy Prophet

The first argument was that the present is the time for a reformer and, as no one else had claimed to have been appointed by God to the office, we are obliged to consider seriously the claim of the Founder of the Ahmadiyya Movement, the only one who has made the claim. However, the claim of the Founder of Ahmadiyyat is not merely that he is a divine reformer, but that he is the divine reformer promised to Muslims long ago. He is the Messiah and Mahdi of ancient prophecies. In support of this claim I now present the powerful testimony of the Holy Prophet of Islam, Chief of mankind, Elect of God (on whom be peace and the blessings of God). Greater testimony cannot be found.

Second coming of the Messiah, important Islamic belief

Belief in the second coming of the Messiah has been held from before the time of Islam. It existed centuries before the advent of the Holy Prophet Muhammad, as part of the Mosaic tradition. But in Islam the second coming of the Messiah has been taught so systematically and determinately that we are obliged to regard it as one of the important beliefs of Islam. Factors which have strengthened and systematized the Islamic belief are the following:

1 The Promised Messiah, according to Islamic teaching, was to come at a time marked also by the advent of a Mahdi. True, in other Traditions, we are told that the Mahdi is none other than the Messiah. But belief in the simultaneous appearance of the Mahdi and the Messiah led Muslims as a people to regard the coming of the Messiah as the coming of a great fellow-believer not the coming of a stranger.

2 The advent of the Messiah is described in Muslim Traditions as the advent of a new era in the advancement of Islam. The conquest of other faiths by Islam was to wait on the coming of the Messiah. It was to be initiated by the Messiah.
3 The Messiah and the Mahdi being one and the same person, the coming of the Messiah has seemed like the coming of the Holy Prophet himself, the first believers in the Messiah like the first believers in the Holy Prophet. Descriptions of this kind created a great longing for the second coming in the hearts of the Holy Prophet's devotees.
4 The Promised Messiah was to render Islam a great service at a time of great difficulty. The time is described in the most fearful terms in the *Hadith*. A time of unparalleled danger, it was to shake Islam to its very foundations; then was the Promised Messiah to come and make Islam secure against its enemies. These descriptions led Muslims to await the advent of the Promised Messiah as an angel of mercy. Had not the Holy Prophet said, 'Nothing can avail against a community which has me at one end and the Messiah at the other'? Such powerful words invested the advent of the Promised Messiah with special importance and filled the hearts of Muslims with great expectations. The coming of the Messiah was to strengthen Islam on all sides and make it proof against attacks.

These factors have combined to make the advent of the Messiah a great event in the later history of Islam. This event was to help Muslims to witness again an image or imitation of the Holy Prophet himself. It was also to mark the restoration of Islam to safety. It was impossible to promise such an event without pointing to the signs which would show when it was to take place.

The coming of reformers and messengers is often described in religious books. Such descriptions are always metaphorical, literal descriptions being useless for the promotion of spiritual merit. If the signs indicating the time of a reformer are described in minute detail and the detail is to be taken literally, there can be no distinction between a believer and a non-believer. In the presence of such descriptions, the question whether a claimant is genuine or not makes little sense. Descriptions of coming reformers have to be veiled so as to rouse men of faith and goodwill to honest curiosity. They ponder over the signs and are able to reach the truth. The mischievous and the ill-intentioned are able to find excuses for their refusal to believe. When the sun is at the zenith, nobody thinks it a merit to believe in its presence. Such belief has no reward. In the matter of reformers and messengers the way of God has been not to guide beyond a certain point. A thin veil hangs over prophetic descriptions so that their truth is as easily denied as affirmed.

When we consider prophecies about the time of the Promised Messiah, we must keep this principle in view. These prophecies are couched in language in which prophecies of the appearance of reformers and messengers have always been couched in religious books. This does not in any way reduce the value of those descriptions for seekers after truth. The signs mentioned in the prophetic literature are nevertheless illuminating. He who believes in a single prophet on the basis of reason, and whose faith in that prophet is not the result of family or community prejudice, can obtain all the guidance he needs from these signs. Those who apparently believe in many hundreds of prophets, but do not believe in a single one on the basis of reason, will find it difficult to believe in any true messenger of God, though he should appear with endless signs. Such persons do not believe of their own accord. Their belief is given to them by their *Ulema*, or religious teachers, by parents or grandparents. Since they have never seen a prophet in the flesh and have never believed in one on the basis of reason, they find it difficult to recognize a new prophet and to believe in him through a free consideration of his claims. Such persons cannot see the truth of a prophet unless they rub their eyes first. They must clear their eyes of dust and rise above man-made beliefs and prejudices if they wish to perceive the truth of a true prophet.

Signs of the Promised Messiah and Mahdi

After this explanation, I shall now give an account of the signs of the Promised Messiah as narrated by the Holy Prophet. Anybody who looks at these signs with an open mind will have no difficulty in identifying the time appointed for the advent of the Promised Messiah. It is important, however, to remind ourselves that when the Muslim Community became divided into sects many people began to fabricate Traditions to serve their respective interests. The fabrications were made to promote sectarian beliefs. We meet with many so-called Traditions which tell of the coming of the Mahdi and describe the signs of his advent. But the words employed in these Traditions make it quite clear that they have been designed to favour some sectional or sectarian belief. Some of these Traditions may be true or may contain elements of truth. Even so, a seeker after truth must exercise great care in using them. Such Traditions should not be allowed to become decisive in the discovery of truth. To cite an example: many Traditions recorded during the Abbaside times apparently speak of the Mahdi and his time. But their net effect is the suggestion that the pro-Abbaside disturbances in Khurasan were sanctioned and supported by God. That those Traditions were fabricated is proved by subsequent history. A thousand years have passed since those Traditions were recorded, but a Mahdi answering their description has not appeared in the world. Similarly, there are Traditions in which the signs announcing the time of the Mahdi have been mixed up with descriptions of past events. Unless the two are disentangled from each other, unless the past events which figure as signs of the future are clearly distinguished from the true signs of the future, we cannot reach the truth. Those who were ignorant of the main currents of Islamic history have been misled by such fabrications. They treated these Traditions as descriptions of the future and waited in vain for events which had occurred long before. The fabrications, as I have said, were designed to further sectarian ends. Therefore, while considering the signs of the coming of the Mahdi, it is imperative that we should eliminate, out of the traditional descriptions, those which do not point to any definite events. Only thus can we guard against falling into a pit dug by interested people for the furtherance of their own ends.

The Holy Prophet of Islam (may he receive unlimited mercy and blessings from God) took care to narrate the signs of the coming of the Messiah and the Mahdi as one continuous chain. If we remember this, we can guard against many a mistake and many a mischief created deliberately by interested persons. A chain of signs has to hang together. Any interpolation not fitting into the chain as a whole can be spotted at once as something foreign and false. For instance, if the Holy Prophet had said that the Promised One would have such and such a name, his father such and such a one and so on, many persons would have assumed those names and then claimed that they answered the Prophet's description of the Promised One. No wonder the Holy Prophet avoided descriptions of this sort; it was too easy for interested persons to copy them. Instead, the Holy Prophet pointed to signs which it was not possible for anyone to bring together.

These are signs which have to wait on cosmic changes spread over hundreds of years. These signs no human beings, or groups of human beings working together for generations, could create. Another precaution which the Holy Prophet observed in narrating the signs of the Mahdi is that many of those signs have been marked out by him as signs *peculiar* to the time of the Mahdi. They are signs which were not to appear at any time before the advent of the Mahdi. We should be guided by these rational and useful pointers. If in the course of our consideration of signs narrated in the Traditions of the Holy Prophet we come upon cosmic events and changes which it is not in the power of man to produce, and those changes and events are said to mark the time of the Mahdi, then we cannot but think that when they occur the time appointed for the advent of the Messiah and the Mahdi has come. If, at such a time, we are told of other signs of the Mahdi which have not yet appeared, we have to admit either that those signs are not signs but fabrications mixed up with the signs by unscrupulous individuals, or that the meaning of those signs lies below the surface and that they are symbols needing interpretation.

After this, I wish to stress the point that the signs narrated by the Holy Prophet of the advent of the Messiah and the Mahdi have to be taken together. They cannot be taken singly. It is the many-sided picture, the whole, which is to be treated as the picture of the time of the Promised Messiah and Mahdi. For example, it is said in the Traditions that one sign of the Mahdi is the disappearance of honest dealings, another, the disappearance of knowledge. Now, if these signs are taken separately and each treated as the sign of the Messiah and the Mahdi, we may think that when honest dealings disappear from the world, we should expect the Mahdi and the Messiah, and when knowledge disappears and ignorance takes its place, again we should expect the Mahdi and the Messiah. This would be absurd. During the last thirteen hundred years Muslims have suffered many fluctuations in their history. Sometimes they have lost the virtue of knowledge, sometimes the virtue of honest dealings, but the Mahdi or the Messiah did not appear. It follows, therefore, that such signs are not to be applied singly. What we have to do is to put together all the signs enumerated by the Holy Prophet (on whom be peace) and treat the total picture as the picture of the appointed time. Taken singly, these signs can apply to other times, but taken together they cannot apply to any but the time of the Messiah and Mahdi.

To identify a time we have to use the same methods which we use to identify a human individual. When we wish to describe an unknown person, one who has not been seen by others, what do we do? We describe his face, his height, his complexion, his habits and other qualities, his friends, relations, and so on. We may even describe the house in which he lives. We may say the man is tall, fair, of medium weight, with a broad forehead, a sharp nose, large eyes, large lips, a big chin. We might say further that he knows Arabic, is Muslim by faith, that his community is against him and that he is a man of high character. We might even describe his house and the houses close by. A man so fully described can be identified by anybody. Nobody who goes in search of such a man will miss him even though efforts are made to defeat the search. Now what signs can possibly serve to identify a time? If we can point to the condition of heavenly bodies, changes in the earth, political and social conditions, the state of religion, of knowledge, of morals, if we can add to this a description of relations between nations, of economic facts, of methods of transport and travel, then whoever looks about with these signs in his mind will be able to identify the time to which the signs apply. As soon as he enters such a time, he will be able to say that the time (which had been foretold) has come. He will have no difficulty. The total description given to him will leave no doubt in his mind.

This is why the Holy Prophet has given an exhaustive description of the time of the Promised Messiah and the Mahdi. He did so in order that sectarian rivalries should not result in the invention of Traditions making difficult the identification of the time of the Messiah and the Mahdi. There is no doubt that there has been fabrication of Traditions, but the fabricators had little idea of the signs described by the Holy Prophet. Therefore, their fabrications did not result in any mischief. Anybody today who has considered the signs as a whole will certainly have felt that the present is the time of the Promised Messiah and the Mahdi.

I shall now narrate the signs told by the Holy Prophet. It will become clear as I proceed that the Messiah could not have come at any other time.

General state of religion

The first sign I wish to describe relates to the state of religion. The state of religion at any given time can be described either in terms of statistics (how many persons belong to one religion or the other?); or it can be described in terms of the influence which religious teaching has on its followers. The Holy Prophet has used both methods in describing the state of religion at the time of the Promised Messiah.

The statistical part of the Holy Prophet's description is very clear. The Holy Prophet (on whom be peace) said that at the time of the second coming Christianity would be in the ascendant. In the book of Traditions called *Muslim*, it is said that on the Day of Judgment most people would be Romans, which in Islamic vocabulary means Christians. In the time of the Holy Prophet, Romans were the votaries of Christianity, the instruments of its progress. The sign is full of significance. The Holy Prophet also said:

إذا هلك كسرى فلا كسرى بعده وإذا هلك قيصر فلا قيصر بعده
والذي نفسي بيده لتنفقن كنوزهما في سبيل الله -

> 'When Chosroes dies, there will be no Chosroes after him. Similarly, when Caesar dies, there will be no Caesar after him. Then will you expend the treasures of both in the way of God.'[1]

Here the Holy Prophet prophesied about the fall of the Roman Empire and the disappearance of the official name of its emperors. If after the destruction of the Roman Empire Christians were to rise again and become a world power, it must be a most unusual development in history. Yet it is this development which is pointed out as a sign of the promised time. The dominance of Christianity after its earlier destruction, improbable as it was, happens to have been clearly foretold. The prophecy was duly fulfilled. The empire of Caesar disappeared according to the prophecy. For a time the

1 *Tirmidhi*—Abwabul Fitan.

nominal title of Caesar continued. The last rulers of Constantinople called themselves Caesars. On the fall of Constantinople this nominal title also disappeared. Islam displaced Christianity in all parts of the then known world. From the tenth century of the Hijra began the decline of Islam. Christianity began to re-assert itself in countries in which it was completely unknown at the time of the Holy Prophet's prophecy. Now for the last hundred years or so Christian nations have become so completely dominant in the world that the Holy Prophet's prophecy 'the earth will be under the Romans' can be said to have been fulfilled to its very letter.

This prophecy is important for another reason. Some doctors of Islam have said that this sign – the ascendancy of Christianity – will be the last to appear among the signs of the appointed time. Thus Nawab Siddiq Hasan Khan in his book *Hujajul Kiramah*, citing another book, *Risala-i-Hashriya*, writes:

چوں جملہ علامات حاصل شود قوم نصاریٰ غلبہ کنند و بر ملک ہائے بسیار متصرف شوند

'When all the Signs have appeared, then will the Christian people rise and establish their dominion over most parts of the world.'[2]

Therefore it seems that the sign of Christian dominance is not only a sign among signs but a sign of special importance. It is the sign which, in the view of some Muslim *Ulema*, was to complete the picture of the time of the Promised Messiah.

General state of Muslims

What was to be the state of Islam in comparison? In the words of the Holy Prophet, 'Islam at the time will be very weak and poor.' It was to become a religion of the poor. In the prophecy relating to the *Dadjjal* (the anti-Christ), the Holy Prophet says that many Muslims would become followers of the Dadjjal. This part of the prophecy has been literally fulfilled. Muslims had their great days. There was a time when they were the only power in the world. Today they are like helpless orphans. Unless some Christian or other power comes to their help, Muslim nations cannot ensure

2 *Hujajul Kiramah*, p. 344.

their existence. Hundreds of thousands of Muslims have turned Christian and the process continues.

The inner state of religion is clearly described in the prophecies of the Holy Prophet. The inner state of Muslims, the professed believers of Islam, is described in detail. It is said, for instance, that Muslims at the time would no longer believe in *Qadr*, the law of determination by divine design. According to Hazrat Ali, the Holy Prophet said that the Day of Judgment would be marked by general lack of belief in *Qadr*. This certainly means lack of belief by Muslims. The followers of other religions already denied this important divine law. The denial of *Qadr* is now widespread among Muslims. The influence of the new sciences has been the strongest in this regard. Even third-rate European authors are able to overawe Muslim readers, who seem ready to deny the importance of *Qadr*. Muslims as a people have become confused over the question. The importance of it has become lost to them.

A second sign of the inner state of religion is the 'practical indifference of Muslims to the institution of *Zakat*'. This part of the prophecy has been narrated by Hazrat Ali and reported by Albazar, and it has been literally fulfilled. At the present time Muslims are in dire straits. They are the victims of all sorts of difficulties. At such a time it is their duty to practise voluntary charity to promote the interests of the community. Leaving aside voluntary charity however, they are chary of practising *Zakat*, which for Muslims is obligatory charity. In some Muslim countires *Zakat* is carried out under the law of Islam. Many Muslims in those countries pay *Zakat*, but not willingly. Where *Zakat* is not state-sponsored very few Muslims practise it. Some sections of Muslims practise it voluntarily, but not in the correct way. They practise it as though it were not a holy duty but a burden to be endured by some for the sake of others.

An important change in the moral condition of Muslims which the Holy Prophet has mentioned is their love of the world. A people who were able to sacrifice things most dear to them, in whose eyes things of the world were not more than shining stones, were to change so as to be ready to sell their religion for the sake of the world. This change which the Holy Prophet prophesied is now apparent: so apparent that those who have any love of Islam still left in them cannot view it with equanimity. The change seems to have involved all classes of Muslims: *Ulema*, mystics, the rich, the poor. All seem to put worldly interests above their religion. For insignificant worldly benefits, they are prepared to ignore the interests of their religion and their community.

Another change predicted by the Holy Prophet was (as reported by Ibn Abbas according to Ibn Mard'waih) the disappearance of *Namaz*, the institution of the five daily prayers. The change is now visible. If a statistical estimate is made, one could say that hardly one in a hundred Muslims observes the five daily prayers, and yet the daily prayers constitute the first among the obligatory observances of Islam. According to some doctors of Islam, those who habitually omit the daily prayers are *Kafirs*. Today mosques are in abundance, but few Muslims repair to them for their daily prayers. Mosques have been used as stables and desecrated. Muslims generally are indifferent to the duty of using mosques as houses of worship.

Another change predicted by the Holy Prophet is the *speed* with which worshippers would go through their obligatory prayers. According to a report by Ibn Masud, the Holy Prophet said (as recorded by Abul Shaikh in Ishaat) that a time would come when fifty persons would congregate for prayers and not one of them would have his prayers accepted by God. They would observe their external form and go through them with unbecoming speed. Whether a prayer is acceptable or not, nobody can tell. However, one external sign which makes prayers unacceptable is excessive speed. A man went through his prayer quickly. The Holy Prophet, who observed him, told him to say it again. Muslims who observe the daily prayers today do so with indecent haste. The prostrations, in rapid succession, seem like the pecking of a hen. After the prescribed prayer, they sit a long time repeating some formulary prayers.

A sign predicted by the Holy Prophet is the 'disappearance' of the Holy Quran. It was to be a disappearance in spirit. The words of the Holy Book were to remain intact. This sign is fully visible today. The Holy Book is to be found in every house. It is even read, but few read it with the intention to go deeply into its meaning. It is strange as well as true that, except among the followers of the Promised Messiah (on whom be peace), the Holy Quran is not read with this intention by Muslims. Maulvis, learned in the sciences of *Fiqh* and *Hadith*, are not interested in the study and interpretation of the Holy Quran. They think it forbidden to reflect on the meaning of the Holy Book and think it wrong to try and apply its teaching to new situations. In their view, the last word has been said by the commentators, and the Holy Book contains nothing more than what has been brought out already by the commentators. This is amazing, for the interpretation of the Holy Quran has gone on even after the Holy Prophet. There is no reason why it should not go on for ever. The Holy Quran is capable of an infinite variety of meanings and applications. To say that the door to its understanding is already closed is only to say how useless the Holy Book has become.

Another sign foretold by the Holy Prophet (on whom be peace) (Ibn Mard'waih on the authority of Ibn-i-Abbas) is that at the time of the Promised Messiah external reverence shown to the Holy Book would be in inverse ratio to the attention paid to its meaning and teaching. The Holy Book would be wrapped in gold and silver. This sign is almost too apparent today. Muslims are indifferent to the Holy Quran. They hardly ever open it to read, but they take care to wrap it in gold and satin and put it away securely on some shelf. The external deference shown to the Holy Book was not much in evidence among the early Muslims, yet the early Muslims were infinitely superior to the Muslims of today.

Another change indicated by the Holy Prophet (on whom be peace) is the exaggerated devotion to the outer decoration of mosques. Again, the change is visible. In imitation of other people, especially Christians, Muslims take enormous pains over decorating and beautifying their mosques. They provide floral and other embellishments for the walls and put up chandeliers and other expensive fittings for the ceilings. They also install curtains. All this makes Muslim mosques seem more like temples for idol worship than houses of Islamic worship.

A change indicated for the time relates to the people of Arabia. According to it, Arabs were to deviate far from true Islam, and this may seem very strange. It is true that the religion of Islam was revealed to Arabs. Its earliest followers were Arabs. It was taken to the outside world by Arabs. Its book was revealed in the language of the Arabs. It is still written and read in that very language, and that language lives because it is the language of the Book of Islam. Who could think that of all peoples the Arabs would give up Islam, and notwithstanding their knowledge of Arabic they would become as ignorant of the Arabic Quran as non-Arabs unable to read the Arabic Quran? According to *Dailmy*, Hazrat Ali has reported the Holy Prophet as saying that in the latter days Arabs would speak Arabic but their mind and spirit would be as the mind and spirit of non-Arabs. The religion of Arabia would not be in their hearts. This change is visible. Arabs as a people are today as much strangers to Islam as non-Arabs who cannot read and understand the Arabic Quran.

A great change predicted by the Holy Prophet in the condition of Muslims relates to freedom of religion in Arabia. According to this prediction Arabia was to become a difficult country for any well-meaning person to initiate a movement for reform in. According to Hazrat Ali (reported by *Dailmy*), the Holy Prophet said that in Arabia men of good intentions and sound ideas would keep themselves in the background. This amazing change can be seen today in Arabia. Religious tolerance has disappeared from that country. Love of their own traditional beliefs and customs has become strong again. Those who believe in God and the Holy Prophet and wish to interpret their teaching independently are not safe. The disease is common to other Muslim countries, but it is of special significance for Arabia because Arabia is the centre of Islam. The annual pilgrimage enjoined upon Muslims has to be performed to Arabia. Intolerance in Arabia reacts upon the freedom of Muslims in other countries. It is bound to have an adverse effect on the interests of religious truth. Muslims of different persuasions still go to Arabia to perform the pilgrimage, but if they hold minority beliefs or beliefs unacceptable to Arabs they have to perform the pilgrimage in silence and return. Would that the people of Arabia realized their special responsibility! Would that they held aloft the banner of Islam as they did thirteen hundred years ago!

State of morals

After the state of religion I come to the state of morals as predicted by the Holy Prophet (on whom be peace). One sign relating to the state of morals in the time of the Promised Messiah is the increase in sexual immorality. So great was to be this increase that instead of being ashamed, people would take pride in being sexually immoral. According to Ibn Abi Shaiba, one of the signs of the eve of Doomsday is a visible increase in sexual immorality. Similarly, according to Anas Ibn Malik, as reported in *Muslim*, one of the signs of the latter days is an increase in adultery. Ibn Mard'waih has reported from Abu Huraira that one of the prophecies of the Holy Prophet about the latter days relates to the increase in illegitimate births. Sexual immorality is evident today. Sexual sins are more abundant. Acts which Islam condemns as immoral now seem like good manners. Ballroom dancing, praising the beauty of women, spending holidays with strange women, are common practices today. Until the present time these things were inconceivable everywhere. They were inconceivable in Arabia as in other countries. India had no conception of One God, but it was free from sexual immorality. Iran was a pleasure-loving country, but Iran was free from the public display of laxity in sexual behaviour. The early Romans (greatly increasing the strength for Christianity) were morally primitive, but they practised due restraint in sexual-behaviour. But what do we find today? If a picture of what is true today had been painted earlier, nobody would have believed it possible. Nobody would have thought that sexual laxity could be practised on such a scale in the name of civilization. Dancing and entertainment existed in the past, but nobody would have thought that women of good families – families which constitute the backbone of civilized society – would take to dancing on such a scale. Nobody could imagine that dancing would be treated as the accomplishment of a lady, a source of social prestige and not of disrepute. The worst of all sexual sins – adultery – is on the increase. It has spread on such a large scale (and mostly in Christian countries) that it is hardly regarded as a sin. It is thought to be a natural activity and is taken for granted. There were prostitutes before. But nobody could imagine that they would be employed at high rates and maintained at army centres to entertain the soldiers and to satiate their sexual appetites, so that they did not have to leave their camps for the purpose. Nobody could think that friendly relations between men and women would grow so much that a strange woman living with a strange man would not seem strange at all, but that such behaviour would begin to seem an essential part of human freedom. On the other hand, marriage would begin to be described as slavery. Hundreds of thousands of persons in Europe and America seem to think in these terms. Until today, who could even think that a time would come when people would seriously debate whether the contract of marriage is a wholesome human institution at all, or whether promiscuity is not as good or even better? After all, woman's function is to bear children. Whether children are born in or out of marriage is a matter of secondary importance!

This being the state of sexual laxity, one can estimate how large must be the number of illegitimate children. Where sexual relations outside marriage are thought to be sinful, people do not like to have children tainted with sin. But when society becomes insensitive to sin, when marriage is regarded as an incomprehensible interference on the part of religion, there can be no shame in producing and acknowledging illegitimate children. In fact, when things come to such a pass, legitimacy becomes the exception rather than the rule. Those who are insensitive to the vice of adultery do not hesitate to produce children by it.

However, many voices are raised in support of the marital relationship. But there is also morbid sympathy for illegitimate children. Philosophers and social scientists write on behalf of them and describe them as part of the wealth of each country and the means of its defence. Or else they try and persuade each state to regard illegitimate children as its own. From this scale of sexual sin, one can see how large must be the number of illegitimate children in the world. We cannot find a parallel for this in earlier history. Nobody could think of such a state of affairs.

A moral change relating to the time of the Promised Messiah and prophesied by the Holy Prophet is an increase in the use of alcoholic drinks. According to Anas bin Malik (as recorded in *Muslim*), one of the signs of the latter days is the excessive use of drink. Similarly Abu Naim has reported on the authority of Hozaifa bin al-Yaman that one of the signs of the time, according to the Holy Prophet, would be the public drinking of wine. The abundance with which wine is used in our time needs no proof. In European countries more wine is drunk than water. Wine was used in the past, but only as a source of pleasure or as medicine. But now in a large part of the world it is used as an ordinary drink at meals or at other times. The sign stressed by the Holy Prophet that wine would be drunk in public distinguishes the present from all other times. At other times, wine was a luxury and a pleasure for the few. Not in demand by everybody, it was provided only at special places. But now it has become a common drink, so it has to be provided in all places and made accessible to all and sundry. In

European countries wine shops are found at short distances from each other so that people do not have to go a long way to find a place where they can buy wine to drink. Dining cars on railway trains are stocked with wine. In places like London wine and water are sometimes sold at the same price. Nobody needs water for drinking. It is needed only for other uses. I am reminded here of the experience of one of our missionaries in England. This missionary had made a very favourable impression on his landlord by his courteous manner and straight dealings. One day the landlord said to him: 'Remember my advice—it will help you to keep fit. Drink no water at all while you are in this country. My father drank water only once in his life and he died soon after. I am being wise. I have not touched water up to now.' When told that his tenant did not drink wine but only water, the landlord was taken aback and found it hard to believe!

Another great moral change relating to the promised time and predicted by the Holy Prophet is excessive gambling. It has been reported by Hazrat Ali and recorded by *Dailmy* that one of the signs of the Doomsday eve is excessive gambling as a sport. This great change is also apparent. In Europe and America gambling is not merely a sport. It is part and parcel of the life of the great cities. In every walk of life gambling has a place. It is common enough to play for stakes after dinner parties, but this is not all. Lotteries are so widespread that it may be said that about a quarter of the money which by rights should be used in trade is used in gambling. People of all classes, poor as well as rich, indulge in it, and they do so not occasionally but almost daily. The most prosperous clubs are those where gambling is a feature. In Monte Carlo sometimes many millions of pounds change hands in a single night. So widespread is the evil of gambling that it is impossible to conceive of modern civilization without it. True, gambling existed even in the past, but there is no comparison between then and now. Perhaps a year of gambling in the past would be little compared with a day's gambling today. Many forms of insurance, life, fire, theft etc., have been invented. In the past people did not know even their names, but today they have become a necessity.

A great moral change predicted by the Holy Prophet for the time is the disappearance of men of conscience as reported by Naim bin Himad from Imar bin Yasir. It is disastrous but true. Some people have tried to explain this away, but it remains an important sign. It means that at the time of the Promised Messiah men of good intentions, those who are ready to obey their consciences, will become the exception rather than the rule. We can readily see that change already. Outside the ranks of the followers of the Promised Messiah, men of conscience, men who follow the inner voice, have become rare. There was a time when Muslim communities everywhere contained hundreds of thousands of persons who could be described as godly men. But if we look for them today, when our need for these men is so much greater, we will find hardly any. No doubt we have our hereditary saints, scholars, dignitaries and sufis. Their followers run into millions, but not one of them has any real contact with God. They spend long hours reciting their special formulae and performing other ostensibly religious exercises. But repeating formulae and performing such exercises is not inner purity. The sign of inner purity is absorption in the love of God, which should result in an open return of love by God. We should find God coming to the help of those whom He loves. We should find Him standing by them for their triumph, opening secrets of the Holy Book to them, bestowing on them an abundance of spiritual knowledge. Those who love God and are loved by Him in return should then fight the battles of Islam, try and resolve the difficulties which confront Muslims, and cure the spiritual maladies from which they suffer. But the whole tribe of doctors, mystics, saints, savants and scholars cannot produce one man of this description. In short, human conscience is as good as dead. In its place, we have the reign of low desires. Our saints and scholars pursue their desires rather than their consciences.

A change pointed out by the Holy Prophet is the disappearance of honest dealings. Hazrat Ali had reported (as recorded in *Dailmy*) that one sign of the eve of Doomsday is the disappearance of honest dealings. The general replacement of honest dealings by dishonest ones is apparent everywhere. It needs no elaboration and no proving. Today every street, every town, and every household can furnish examples of dishonest dealings.

Another moral change predicted by the Holy Prophet is that regard for parents will decline and regard for friends will increase (reported by Abu Naim in *Hilyia*, on the authority of Hozaifa bin Al-Yaman). The time of which the prophecy speaks was to be marked by increasing disobeying of parents by their children. Correspondingly regard for friends was to increase. This change also is so acutely apparent that all decent men are distressed by what they see. Fond of Western manners and trained in Western sciences and literature, the young men of today look upon their elderly relations as primitive and foolish. They hate their company and love to spend their time instead in the company of friends who also follow Western ways. Lewd talk and immoral entertainment are their pastimes. Young men hold receptions and are ready to pay for the amusement of their friends while forgetting the needs of their poor parents. In our country thousands of cases can be found of parents living on very little. They worked and saved to complete the education of their children. When the children grew up and began to earn money, however, they treated their parents with contempt, thinking it beneath their dignity to treat them even as their equals but treating them as though they were their servants. Examples of such ill-treatment of parents can be found by the thousand. In the past they were very rare.

Religious knowledge and the Ulema

The Holy Prophet has also described the intellectual conditions of the time of the Promised Messiah. It is recorded in *Tirmidhi* (on the authority of Anas bin Malik) that the Holy Prophet said that one of the signs of the time would be the disappearance of knowledge and the appearance of ignorance. Without the slightest variation this report is contained in the collection of *Bukhari* also. This change – the replacement of knowledge (obviously knowledge of religion) by ignorance – is also visible. There was a time when even women discharged the functions of jurists, so deep was their knowledge of Muslim Law. Omar once said that the women of Medina were more learned than Omar in their knowledge of the Holy Quran. Women and children knew the Holy Quran so well that they were able to criticize the judgments of scholars. And they criticized their *Fatwas*, not out of ignorance or bad manners, but on the basis of sound understanding and out of regard for public interests. Hazrat Ayesha was one of the most learned persons who ever lived. Her knowledge and her judgment were of a high order. These facts have never been questioned. But today knowledge of religion is acquired only by those who, for lack of means or lack of intelligence, cannot acquire worldly knowledge. Religious knowledge is today acquired by those who cannot afford the conventional type of education, who acquire it because to do so entails no expense or fees, etc., and because the acquisition of a little knowledge enables them to maintain themselves as Mullas. Knowledge of this kind is of little avail and those who seek it are of little use to the world.

This Tradition which predicts the disappearance of knowledge is supported by other Traditions. 'Knowledge' in these Traditions means religious knowledge. Knowledge of ordinary sciences and skills is a different thing altogether. In the books of *Hadith* we have prophecies about the increase of such knowledge. Thus *Tirmidhi* has recorded, on the authority of Abu Huraira, that in the latter days people will acquire knowledge and take pains over it: not, however, in order to promote their duty to religion but for other purposes. This is exactly what is happening today. Secular sciences and studies have advanced so much that everybody is filled with wonder. On the other hand, religious sciences and studies have declined so much that the ignorant and the uninitiated pass for scholars and learned men.

Social conditions and the condition of women

The Holy Prophet has also described the social conditions of the time. He has pointed to signs which taken together afford us a fairly complete picture of social conditions at the time of the Promised Messiah's coming. One of the social changes pointed out by the Holy Prophet is a change in the method of salutation taught to Muslims. According to a report by Imam Ahmad Muaz bin Anas, one important sign of the degradation and decay of the Muslim peoples was to be the replacement of the Muslim salutation *al-salamu alaikum* by forms of salutation common amongst non-Muslims. The Tradition on this point describes the non-Muslim salutation as a form of cursing each other. Commentators of *Hadith* think that this change relates to the lower classes among Muslims. Individuals belonging to these classes, when they meet, will curse each other instead of using the Islamic salutation, 'Peace.' But the change does not seem to be limited to any one class. In fact, it is more evident among gentlemen than among other classes. Muslim gentlemen in many parts of India say *Bandgi* or *Taslim* or *Adab* instead of *Salam*. They feel embarrassed at having to use the Muslim salutation. Now *Bandgi* is a Hindu salutation which means the offer of subjection amounting to slavery. This is against the dignity of man, and certainly contrary in letter and spirit to the Muslim salutation – *Salam*. The Hindu forms of salutation current among Muslims entail treating human beings as equals of God and using forms of address which should be reserved for God. They amount to pronouncing curses upon one another. The apparently polite salutation *Adab* makes little difference. Such an expression only avoids the more obviously Hindu salutations *Bandgi* or *Taslim*. Its function is to lessen the sense of guilt arising from the use of an un-Islamic salutation.

A great change predicted by the Holy Prophet is that at the time public esteem will be enjoyed by those who have high financial or political status, not status based on knowledge or the practice of religion. Ibn Mard'waih has reported, on the authority of Ibn Abbas, that the Holy Prophet said that one of the signs of the time would be excessive deference shown to the rich. The change is quite evident. There was a time when old families were greatly esteemed, but respect for old families has gone. Social status is measured by one criterion only and that is, 'How rich?' There was a time when the wealthy thought it an honour to go and meet the scholars of religion. Now the time has come when scholars of religion – the *Ulema* – think it an honour to go to the rich. To have access to the porch of some rich man is considered by them a great thing.

Huzaifa bin al-Yaman has also reported the coming of a time when men will be praised for virtues which they do not possess. A man will be described as brave or courteous or wise without meriting it in the least. This condition is quite evident. The most irreligious man can become a leader of Muslims today if he can only raise an impressive slogan. Nobody questions whether the man possesses any Islamic virtues. Without Islamic virtues, how can he become an exponent of Islam? If he can address a public meeting, if he has the capacity to outwit or outbid his political rivals, that is quite enough.

Another social change mentioned by the Holy Prophet is that believers will be degraded and will try to keep in the background for want of social status. According to another authority, the Holy Prophet said that a believer will be more degraded than a woman slave. A woman slave can expect love and marriage, but a believer cannot expect even this. Ali has reported, on the authority of *Dailmy*, that at the time of the Promised Messiah good men will become obscure. The change has become even more evident since the advent of the Promised Messiah. Those who follow the Quran and the Holy Prophet are more hated and avoided than women of ill fame and men who cut the daily prayers and offer insult to God and the Holy Prophet. Those who choose to respond to the Voice of God are treated with obvious contempt.

Yet another change described by the Holy Prophet is the decline in the vogue of Arabic among Muslims. According to Ibn Mard'waih, Ibn Abbas reported that at that time the lines of worshippers would be long but voices too many. The change can be seen during the days of Haj. One purpose of the institution of Haj was that Muslims from different parts of the world should assemble and discuss their common problems. But this has become impossible because Muslims in countries other than Arabia have abandoned the use of Arabic; so, for want of a common language, they can have no exchange of ideas at the Haj. They cannot use the great gathering for the promotion of common religious, social, or cultural ends. Had Muslims kept up their knowledge of Arabic, it would have served as a binding force between Muslims from different parts of the world. It would have welded them into a unity which the strongest could not have challenged.

Another change described by the Holy Prophet relates to women's dress. Women of the time would seem undressed in spite of being dressed. The change has come about in two ways. Firstly, silks and other light fabrics are now produced in large quantities. The flimsiest of them are now available for all and sundry. In the past they were only for the rich. The cloth manufactured is finer. So the dresses made are thinner. This may satisfy fantastic notions of feminine beauty, but must offend against modesty and sobriety. Secondly, the change has come through fashions which prevail in Europe and America. In these countries women tend more and more to expose parts which it was thought indecent to show in the past. The breast tends to be exposed. Arms are bared at least up to the elbows, and so on. The prophetic description of women's dress, therefore, is true – women today seem undressed even though dressed. The change has come about among Muslims through the use of flimsy silks, and among Christians through fashions which expose the breast, head, arms, and so on.

Another change relating to women describes the mode of dressing their hair. According to the description given by the Holy Prophet, women were to coil up their hair so as to produce a hump-like effect on the head. In Europe, women today do not braid their hair as they used to do in the past. Now they keep their hair puffed, giving the impression that something sits neatly on the head. In imitation of European women, women in other parts of the world also dress their hair in the same way. The tendency to imitate is general. People in Asia imitate the fashions of Europe. A European fashion is treated with more respect than a message from God. Asians seem honour-bound to follow Europe. Imitation of Europe seems like progress.

Yet another change described by the Holy Prophet and reported by Ibn Abbas is the entry of women into business life as companions of their husbands or their men-folk. The change has become quite apparent; so much so, in fact, that shops and business places cannot be said to prosper unless they contain women. Pretty women are employed in shops to attract customers and encourage purchases.

Yet another change described by the Holy Prophet relates to the increased freedom of women. Women would become more and more free. They would dress like men, ride horses, and so on. Altogether, women would rule over men. The change has already taken place. In America and other Christian countries an exaggerated conception of the freedom of women has taken root. In imitation of the Christian West the same conception is spreading to other countries. This conception of freedom has changed the social scene.

More and more women join men in hunting on horseback, and racing. More and more women now work as circus artistes. The vogue of masculine dress among women is also widespread in Christian countries. The change became very evident after World War I. Hundreds of thousands of women started dressing like men. Many women would wear a short jacket over a pair of breeches. The use of masculine dress by women has become a fashion.

The general domination of men by women which is mentioned in the prophecy is also unique. Consequently the general living conditions in European countries and, under their influence, the living conditions of other countries have undergone a tremendous change. These conditions entail dangerous consequences unless God, out of His Grace, wills otherwise. This deterioration in the functions of men and women may mean a major disaster. There may be a big social upheaval or the institution of marriage may receive a rude shock and the social progress of man suffer an irreversible setback.

Another change described by the Holy Prophet is that men would take pains over their appearance and tend to look like women. The change is already apparent. Shaving of chin and lips is now the fashion and this has made men look more like women. Time was when the beard was thought to be a male's glory. For Muslims, it was a thing of merit, because it was an imitation of the Holy Prophet, a sign of deference to his wish. The beard has disappeared amongst Muslims. Muslim scholars and philosophers held in great esteem in the Muslim world prefer to shave their chins. Further evidence for the change is to be found in forms of entertainment in which men artists dress like women and women like men. Men in Europe and America lavish an excessive amount of attention on the cleansing and dressing of their hair. The attention men devote to the dressing of their hair is not more than the attention women devote to it today, but it is certainly more than the attention women gave to their hair in the past.

Pestilences

The Holy Prophet has included a description of the physical conditions of the people at the time of the Promised Messiah. For instance, Anas has reported (according to *Tirmidhi*) that when the Dadjjal appeared and turned to Medina, a plague epidemic would appear in the world. God would protect Medina from both the Dadjjal and the plague however. The prophecy has been fulfilled. For many years now plague has played havoc in the world. It has ravaged several hundred thousand homes, and has ruined hundreds of villages. But the holy places of Islam have been immune from any considerable attack. Preventive measures have been invented which help to protect the holy places. Among them are quarantine restrictions which keep the plague away from the holy places of Islam. The appearance of plague was predicted by the Holy Prophet in different ways. On occasion he described it as *Daba* (literally, a worm). The description is true because plague is the result of being bitten by a flea. The flea rises from the ground and bites the human body. The Holy Quran uses the same name. This is no ordinary disease. It is a world disease which has brought death and destruction to many parts of the world. In the Indian sub-continent it has prevailed for many years.

The appearance of *Daba*, as described in the prophecy, does not indicate the coming of plague only. It indicates the appearance of many epidemics which owe their fatal effects to bacteria. No wonder we have today diseases, unknown in former times, which are caused by micro-organisms. In the past, such diseases were either unknown or they did not spread and did not cause death on the scale they do now. The prophecy relating to plague and plague-like diseases made by the Holy Quran and the Holy Prophet foretells by implication the invention of the microscope and the discovery of bacteria as causes and carriers of disease. At the time of the Holy Prophet nothing was known about bacteria. In his time, medical science still talked in terms of bile, black-bile, blood, and phlegm.

The Holy Prophet has mentioned some other signs relating to health and disease. One such sign is an increase in the number of sudden deaths due to heart failure and so on. One reason for the rise in the number of such deaths is the excessive use of alcohol. Another is increased mental stress and the fact that more people suffer from stress. Alcohol weakens the heart and the brain; and excessive stress or study has a deleterious effect on the nerves. Both these causes are on the increase. The result is an increase in the number of sudden deaths. Among nations given to alcohol, sudden death is rampant. One shudders at its frequency. Thousands of persons die every year of heart failure. They collapse standing or working, in their chairs or in their beds. This sort of thing was not known before.

Among diseases the Holy Prophet has mentioned is a disease connected with the nose which was to claim a very large number of lives. This disease appeared soon after the end of hostilities in World War I and has since been named influenza. In 1918 the influenza epidemic claimed twenty million lives, while the war claimed only six million. Therefore influenza destroyed 1.5 per cent of the population of the whole world. When influenza was raging in the world, it brought the fear of God into many hearts. Everybody could see that life and security depended on the Will of God.

Sex ratio in the general population

The Holy Prophet has also mentioned the ratio between the sexes as an important sign of the time of the Messiah. The prophecy says that at that time women would outnumber men, so much so that fifty women would have one man to look after them. The prophecy has come true. There are more women in the world today than men. In European countries the number of men has been depleted by wars. In fact, the situation is grave enough to have led social scientists to consider the Islamic provision of polygamy as a remedy for the excess of women. Those who used to criticize Islam for this provision are being forced to give serious thought to it. There can be no doubt that Islamic polygamy is the remedy for this increase in the proportion of women. Many social philosophers seem convinced that the only alternative to social chaos is the legalization of plural wives. The other alternative is the acceptance of adultery as a necessary social evil. Small wonder that today they treat bigamy lightly. They are not now so eager to drag bigamists into court. This change of attitude is new and it has been brought about by the excess of women in European society. Not so long ago, bigamy ranked as a social sin in Europe. No Christian or European could talk of it with equanimity. So great was the European horror of bigamy that, in imitation of Europeans, educated Muslims also felt embarrassed over its provision in Islam and were apologetic about it.

Transport, communications, and international contact

The Holy Prophet gave a picture of the general conditions of transport and communications at the appointed time. He said that the old methods of transport would disappear and their place would be taken by swifter vehicles and methods. The swifter means would be used over both land and sea. To quote the words of the Tradition:

لَيُتْرَكَنَّ الْقِلَاصُ فَلَا يُسْعٰى عَلَيْهَا۔

'The camel as a means of transport will be abandoned and people will not look to the camel with this intent.'[3]

The change has established itself completely. All the old methods of transport have disappeared in most countries. First we had the railway. Those who did not then travel by rail travelled by other means. They rode camels or other animals. But since the discovery of the motor car even road travel has become mechanized. As new and mechanical methods of transport advance, the use of animals disappears.

The Holy Prophet also prophesied the appearance of both steamships and the railway. The Holy Prophet said:

'The Dadjjal's donkey will travel on water as on land. Travelling on land it will have clouds both in front and behind.'[4]

Clearly this is a description of the railway and the steamship. Vehicles propelled by steam can go over both land and water. Incidentally, these new methods of transport are at the special disposal of the Dadjjal. The prophecy hints at the extensive use which Christian missionaries would make of the new methods. No other class has made such tremendous use of the new means of transport. Thanks to the railway and the steamship, Christian missionaries have travelled to different parts of the world to spread knowledge of the Bible. Their teaching is the teaching of the Dadjjal. The clouds mentioned in the prophecy are the clouds of smoke which seem now in front of the steam-driven vehicle and now behind. Smoke and steam seem to be the inevitable accompaniment of these vehicles. The fuel used in both is coal. This is the food of the Dadjjal's donkey mentioned in the books of *Hadith*. The new means of transport have completely transformed relations between different parts of the world.

Economic conditions

About economic conditions, the Holy Prophet (as reported by

3 Sahih Muslim—Kitabul Iman.

4 Kanzul-Ummal, vol. VII, p. 267.

Hozaifa bin al-Yaman) said that at the time of the Promised Messiah gold and silver would become abundant. The description is true. There is so much gold and silver in the world today that we did not have even one-tenth of it before. Every town is full of people dealing in gold and silver. New and more efficient methods of mining gold and silver have been invented. This has led to an abundance of these precious metals. England alone possesses more gold than was possessed by the whole world in the past. As a result trade has become very brisk, for trade advances with the help of gold and silver. In the ancient past, the medium of exchange was copper pieces or cowries. Today cowries have disappeared altogether and even copper pieces are not much used. In England the smallest coin is a penny, in America a cent. The greater part of the business in these countries is transacted through gold coins.

Among economic practices mentioned by the Holy Prophet is the taking and giving of interest. Hazrat Ali has reported, according to *Dailmy*, that one of the signs of the eve of Doomsday is an increase in transactions of interest. The description is true. So universal is the practice of interest today that in the past it was less than a millionth part of what it is now. So inevitable does the institution of interest seem to most people that it is said that trade and commerce cannot go on without it. Commercial banks have multiplied to such an extent that thousands exist even in small countries. Governments give and take interest. Traders give and take interest. Artisans and industrialists do the same. The rich do the same. All classes of all nations practise interest. It seems that everybody has determined to lend on interest to others and to borrow on interest from them. Out of, say, ten million, a few thousands' worth of trade may be free from interest. The rest involves interest. Muslims were told in their Holy Book to desist from interest. If they did not they should

فَأْذَنُوْا بِحَرْبٍ مِّنَ اللّٰهِ -

'beware of war from Allah and His Messenger.'[5]

But what are Muslims doing today? They practise interest and call it 'profit'. Many among them admit interest to be forbidden,

5 *Al-Baqarah*, 280.

but they still practise it, though with a sense of guilt. Muslim doctors of religion have invented strange definitions of 'interest' and profit, and have issued *Fatwas* legalizing the acceptance of bank interest. They have legalized interest in countries ruled by non-Muslims, so that even Muslims do not desist from interest. They forget that the Law of Islam is the last law for man. They have, in effect, invented a new law. All this shows that the practice of interest has spread enormously. Nobody can now resist it, unless it is with the special grace and help of God.

Among economic signs of the time of the Promised Messiah, an important sign stated by the Holy Prophet is that Christians will constitute the richest classes in the world. All others will count as poor. In *Tirmidhi*, Nawas bin Saman has reported that the Holy Prophet said that the Dadjjal will say to the people, 'Accept me and my leadership.' Those who refuse will become economic slaves of the Dadjjal. Those who accept will become rich and prosperous. The Dadjjal will undertake to rain goods upon them from the sky and produce for them from out of the earth. The description is quite true. Christian nations are advancing economically, and nations suffering from political subjection are becoming poorer and poorer. During the last hundred years the change has pushed itself more and more.

Political conditions

Among the political conditions mentioned by the Holy Prophet are conditions which taken together seem to present a complete picture of the present time. Among those mentioned by the Holy Prophet (according to Hozaifa bin al-Yaman and Abu Naim) are the political misfortunes of Muslims. The description of the Holy Prophet is summed up in the words 'Muslims will become like Jews'. The analogy with Jews implies loss of political power and political prestige. Like Jews they will be reduced to political subjection and will have to live at the mercy of others. How true this description is! The political power of Muslims has declined steadily. Very little of it is now left. There was a time when Muslim flags flew in all parts of the world, but today we can point to only a few countries where Muslim flags can be seen flying. Muslims enjoy political independence here and there, but they find it difficult to maintain this independence except with the help of Christian powers. Allah help us! 'To Him we belong and to Him we return.'

Another political sign of the time of the Promised Messiah, according to the Holy Prophet, was that Syria, Iraq, and Egypt were to rebel against their Muslim kings and Arabs would be divided into several different kingdoms. According to Abu Huraira, as recorded in *Muslim*, the Holy Prophet said, apparently addressing the Arab peoples:

عَنْ اَبِیْ ھُرَیْرَۃَ قَالَ قَالَ رَسُوْلُ اللّٰہِ صَلَّی اللّٰہُ عَلَیْہِ وَسَلَّمَ مَنَعَتِ
الْعِرَاقُ دِرْھَمَھَا وَقَفِیْزَھَا وَمَنَعَتِ الشَّامُ مُدَّھَا وَدِیْنَارَھَا
وَمَنَعَتْ مِصْرُ اِرْدَبَّھَا وَدِیْنَارَھَا وَعُدْتُمْ مِنْ حَیْثُ بَدَاْتُمْ۔

'Iraq will refuse to share her produce and her prosperity. So will Syria, so will Egypt. And you [meaning the Arab peoples] will become as divided and disunited as you were once.'[6]

This prophecy has been fulfilled. Iraq, Syria and Egypt are independent countries, no longer owing allegiance to Turkey and refusing to share their produce and wealth with the leading Muslim power. Arabs have become divided again. True, Hejaz has an Arab government. But it has many enemies and is economically poor and primitive. Other parts of Arabia are without stable administrations. Their governments cannot compare with other governments of today. Another political change predicted by the Holy Prophet was that two peoples mentioned in ancient prophecies, Gog and Magog, would assume such tremendous power that other nations of the world would be as nothing compared with them. The books of *Hadith, Muslim* and *Tirmidhi* report Nawaz bin Saman as saying that, according to the Holy Prophet, God would command the Promised Messiah, saying:

حَرِّزْ عِبَادِیْ اِلَی الطُّوْرِ فَاِنِّیْ قَدْ اَنْزَلْتُ عِبَادًا لِّیْ لَا یَدَانِ لِاَحَدٍ
لِقِتَالِھِمْ قَالَ وَیَبْعَثُ اللّٰہُ یَاْجُوْجَ وَمَاْجُوْجَ۔

'Lead my servants to Sinai. I have sent some men into the world whom no one can fight in battle.'[7]

6 Sahih Muslim—Kitabul Fitan wa Ashraat-ut-Saat.
7 Muslim wa Tirmidhi.

The Holy Prophet also said that God would raise Gog and Magog in the world. These signs have been fulfilled. Gog and Magog have appeared already. They are the Eastern and the Western nations whom no nations can fight in battle. The Eastern nations are aligned with Russia, the Western nations with England and America. We have a reference to it in the Bible:

> 'Gog, the chief prince of Meshech and Tubal, and Magog, and among them that dwell carelessly in the isles.' (Ezekiel 39)

Both these nations and their respective allies have reached the zenith of their power. As predicted in the *Hadith*, the rise of these blocs was to take place after the advent of the Promised Messiah. The rise of Gog and Magog, therefore, shows that the Promised Messiah has already come.

A political change of great importance, mentioned by the Holy Prophet, relates to the rise of the labouring classes. As narrated by Hozaifa bin al-Yaman, an important sign of the coming of the Promised Messiah would be the rise of poor, ill-clad persons as rulers. The word used in the *Hadith* is 'naked', and this is to be understood in a relative sense. Compared to the rich, the poor are naked and unclothed. For want of variety and quality which the rich can afford, the poor are often described as naked. The sign has been fulfilled. As governments have become more and more representative, political power has gone to the poor. The poor, therefore, have become kings. So powerful is labour now that the kings of the world quail before the labour leaders. Other political parties also think it necessary to remain at peace with labour. In countries like Russia and Switzerland, they are the ruling class. In parts of Australia, they are steadily gaining strength.

Another sign of the time of the Promised Messiah, narrated by the Holy Prophet, according to Hozaifa bin al-Yaman, is the expansion and elaboration of the ruling hierarchy. The expression used in the *Hadith* is *Shurt*, and *Shurt* means 'Assistants' and 'Deputies' of the ruler. The sign has been fulfilled. In state administration before, we did not have the large number of deputy-under- and assistant-secretaries that we have today. Most territorial units had one ruler, who functioned by himself. But now administrative organizations have become so large that the number of assistants and deputies has increased many times over. There is a long list of departments and divisions into which state administration is divided – police, public health, registration, public works, post office, communications (such as railway, telegraph, telephone), irrigation, excise, audit, etc., etc. The actual number of divisions and departments is much larger than this. Every state has to appoint experts for the administration of departments or divisions. Each expert has to have a number of assistants. So each government today consists of a very complete and very elaborate organization of secretaries and their staffs.

A change connected with the time of the Promised Messiah, and mentioned by the Holy Prophet, is the abrogation of penalties prescribed by the criminal law of Islam. Hazrat Ali has narrated, according to *Dailmy*, that one sign of the latter days would be the abrogation of statutory penalties. The sign has been fulfilled. In all Islamic governments today Islamic penalties have disappeared. In Turkey, Arabia, Egypt, and Iran, and even in Afghanistan, 'stoning for adultery' and 'cutting off the hand for theft' are no longer recognized punishments. Some Muslim governments have agreed to their abrogation under treaty agreements with other countries. This is a clear and a significant sign. When Muslim governments were prosperous and Islamic ideas prevailed, nobody could think that Islamic penalties would ever be set aside. Nobody could imagine that there would arise such a general prejudice against the use of Islamic penalties that even those Islamic governments who wished to retain these penalties would be unable to do so.

The conditions and signs so far described relate to the general state of religion, to morals, and to culture. They also relate to health and disease, to political and social conditions, and to the relation of the sexes in the general population. But the signs of the time narrated by the Holy Prophet also include signs of a cosmic character. They include signs which relate to the earth as a whole and to other heavenly bodies. Some of these I shall now describe.

On the surface of the earth

About the state of our planet, the earth, Hozaifa bin al-Yaman relates that the Holy Prophet narrated to his Companions a number of important signs which he said were the signs of the time of the Promised Messiah. Having done so, he said:

> 'When these signs have been fulfilled, you should be ready to face some afflictions.'

One affliction was *Khasf*. And *Khasf* means the rising of tides. Physical science tells us that the rising of tides is connected with the shaking of the earth. So when the Holy Prophet mentioned *Khasf*, he meant earthquakes, which were to mark the advent of the Promised Messiah. The sign has been fulfilled. In our time so many earthquakes have come that the total number of earthquakes during the previous three hundred years pales into insignificance. So many lives have been lost in the earthquakes of our few years that the number who died in earthquakes during the centuries before is nothing by comparison.

Important heavenly events

Besides these earthly changes, the Holy Prophet has mentioned important heavenly events which were to mark the advent of the Promised Messiah. For instance, the Holy Prophet said that at the time of the Promised Messiah there would be eclipses of the sun and the moon on certain dates of the month of Ramadhan. The Holy Prophet regarded this as a very important and significant sign. In fact, he said that since the creation of the heavens and the earth, these two signs – eclipses of the sun and the moon in the month of Ramadhan – had not been shown in support of any prophet. The words of the *Hadith* are:

إِنَّ لِمَهْدِيِّنَا آيَتَيْنِ لَمْ تَكُوْنَا مُنْذُ خَلْقِ السَّمٰوٰتِ وَالْأَرْضِ، يَنْخَسِفُ
الْقَمَرُ لِأَوَّلِ لَيْلَةٍ مِّنْ رَمَضَانَ وَتَنْكَسِفُ الشَّمْسُ فِي النِّصْفِ مِنْهُ
وَلَمْ تَكُوْنَا مُنْذُ خَلَقَ اللّٰهُ السَّمٰوٰتِ وَالْأَرْضَ -

> 'As reported by Muhammad bin Ali, the advent of our Mahdi will be marked by two important signs. These signs have never appeared before, not since the creation of Heaven and earth. One is the eclipse of the moon on the first of Ramadhan, and the other is the eclipse of the sun in the middle of Ramadhan, and

these two signs have not appeared since the creation of the Heaven and earth.'[8]

This sign is of very great importance. The Tradition makes it clear that the sign has not appeared before as the sign of the coming of any other teacher or divinely appointed reformer. The sign is accepted as the sign of the time of the Promised Messiah by both Sunni and Shia authorities and is mentioned in the books of both. Sunni and Shia collections of *Hadith* mention these signs. It cannot be said, therefore, that the sign is reported by some and not by other authorities. Thirdly, the sign becomes important because it is mentioned even in earlier books as a sign of the second coming of Jesus. In the New Testament, Jesus, narrating the signs of his second coming, said:

> 'Immediately after the tribulation of those days shall the sun be darkened, and the moon shall not give her light.'[9]

The sign clearly refers to the eclipses of the sun and the moon.

Though I am concerned at present with recounting the signs mentioned in the *Hadith*, it does not seem out of place to say that even in the Holy Quran the eclipses of the sun and the moon are mentioned as important signs of the latter days. In the chapter *Qiyamah* we have:

يَسْـَٔلُ اَيَّانَ يَوْمُ الْقِيٰمَةِ ـ فَاِذَا بَرِقَ الْبَصَرُ ـ وَخَسَفَ الْقَمَرُ ـ
وَجُمِعَ الشَّمْسُ وَالْقَمَرُ ـ

> 'He asks, "When is the Day of the Awakening?" But when the sight is dazzled and the moon is eclipsed and the sun and the moon are in conjunction.'[10]

The verses embody a significant description of the present time. The question is posed, 'When is the Day of Awakening due?' The answer is, 'When certain signs appear.' Among the signs are the dazzling of sight, meaning the occurrence of strange events and changes, also eclipses of the moon and the sun and the occurrence

8 Dar Qutani, p. 188.
9 Matthew 24:29.
10 *Al-Qiyamah*, 7–10.

of the two eclipses in the same month. The coming of the Promised Messiah marks the eve of the end of the world. The Holy Quran, therefore, supports the prophetic description given in the *Hadith*.

The prophecy is of great importance and its fulfilment an event of unusual cosmic and spiritual significance. In 1311 A.H. (1894 A.D.) the prophecies were literally fulfilled. In the month of Ramadhan of this year, the moon suffered an eclipse on the first of the three dates, (i.e. the 13th) on which the lunar eclipse could be expected. The sun suffered an eclipse on the middle date, i.e. the 28th. This conjunction of the two eclipses in the same month took place in the lifetime of a person who claimed to be the Mahdi as promised in the prophecies.

Two courses, therefore, seem open to thoughtful Muslims. Either (1) accept as true the prophecies of the Holy Prophet, the Holy Quran, and the earlier books – all of which declare that the time of the Messenger of the latter days will be marked by the conjunction of the lunar and the solar eclipses, the lunar eclipse occurring on the first, the solar on the second of the three dates on which they can be expected. If these prophecies are accepted as true, and if they have also been fulfilled in the lifetime of a claimant, then the authenticity of that claimant must needs be accepted also. The prophecy said that the conjunction of the two eclipses would not take place except in the time of the Mahdi. Or, (2) if they are not prepared to accept these prophecies or the Mahdi to whom they relate, then they must admit that the prophecies point to a sign which is no sign at all, which can give no help in identifying a claimant to spiritual office; which is, therefore, a useless sign.

Some people object, saying that the prophecy speaks of the lunar eclipse on the 1st and of the solar eclipse in the middle of Ramadhan. But the eclipses said by us to have fulfilled the prophecy took place on the 13th and the 28th respectively. The objection is ill-founded and is seen to be of no consequence if we consider the phenomenon of eclipses and the words of *Hadith* which carry the prophecy. We should not forget that the eclipses, lunar and solar, are bound to take place on certain dates. There can be no deviation from these unless the whole cosmic system, the laws governing the movement of the heavenly bodies, are overhauled and ordered on a new basis altogether. A new cosmic system may entail the destruction of the present one. So, if the words of the prophecy are taken superficially, the prophecy may point to Doomsday, to its eve, or the time of the Mahdi.

Those who raise this objection no doubt pin their faith on the first date and the middle date mentioned in the prophecy, but they forget that the word used for *moon* in the prophetic text is *Qamar*. If the prophecy relates strictly to the first of the lunar month of Ramadhan, then in strict Arabic the word *Hilal* should have been used and not *Qamar*. The moon is not called *Qamar* until it has advanced into the fourth night. We have the authority of the dictionary:

وَهُوَ قَمَرٌ بَعْدَ ثَلَاثِ لَيَالٍ إِلَىٰ اٰخِرِ الشَّهْرِ وَاَمَّا قَبْلَ ذٰلِكَ فَهُوَ هِلَالٌ۔

> 'The Moon is called *Qamar* after the first three nights and remains *Qamar* up to the end of the month. On the first three nights, the moon is called *Hilal*.'[11]

We therefore have two important considerations. (1) The *Hadith* uses the word *Qamar*, which, in any case, cannot mean the moon of the first, second or third night; (2) the lunar eclipse, according to known cosmic laws, can take place on the 13th, 14th or 15th of a lunar month, not on the 1st. Therefore the 1st of Ramadhan mentioned in the prophecy means the first of the three nights on which the lunar eclipse is possible, that is to say the 13th. To insist that the lunar eclipse should have occurred on the first night of Ramadhan, as the prophecy apparently does, is quite unwarranted. Only persons deliberately ignoring the Word of God and the prophecy of the Holy Prophet would do so. Only persons who, by fair means or foul, wish to dissuade people from accepting the Promised Messenger would say so.

A variety of signs

In short, the Holy Prophet laid down a large number of signs for the identification of the time of the Promised Messiah. Some of

11 Aqrab ul-Muwarid, vol. II.

these signs are significant and important, even taken singly. But the Holy Prophet intended that they should be taken collectively and treated as a total picture of the time of the Promised Messiah. When so many signs appear together, they must constitute a time of great importance. With such a comprehensive picture nobody can have any difficulty in identifying the appointed time when it comes. There is no doubt that we have had plagues in the past, also earthquakes, also an excess of gambling. No doubt people became degraded from time to time, even in the past. Also Christian nations have had their great days, their political power. But the question is, have all these signs, which the Holy Prophet said are the signs of the Promised Messiah, occurred together in the past, or are they likely to occur together in the future? The answer is no. Such a large variety of signs cannot come together again and again. Let us imagine a person who does not know the different conditions, social, moral, religious, etc., which obtain in the world at the present time. Let us narrate to such a person the signs of the time of the Promised Messiah as narrated by the Holy Prophet (on whom be peace). Then let us ask him to study the history of the world and tell us at what time in history the Promised Messiah could have come. This imaginary person will study the time of Adam, then the time of the next prophet, then the time of the next, and so on. None of these times will he identify as the time of the Promised Messiah. But as soon as he reaches our time and begins to read about the signs and conditions that obtain today, he will declare that if the Holy Prophet was a true prophet, if he really did prophesy what he is said to have prophesied, then the present and no other is the time of the Promised Messiah. Our imaginary person will note the indifference to religion which is so evident. He will see the great advance which natural sciences have made. He will see how very weak Muslim states have become after their days of power. He will see Christianity stepping forward to progress after recovering from its earlier decline. He will see Christian nations in possession of the greater part of the wealth of the world. He will see other nations reduced to poverty. He will also see plague and influenza wreaking havoc in the world, the progress of medicine and science notwithstanding. He will see that the great discovery of the time is that disease is caused by bacteria. He will also see a great many old superstitions and customs cramping the intelligence of mankind. He will see the railway and the steamer and an abundance of banks.

He will observe the frequency of earthquakes, the advent of Gog and Magog and their dominion over the whole world. He will note the lunar and the solar eclipses. He will see the increase of wealth. He will also see the labouring classes come up and become rulers in the world. In short, a description of contemporary conditions will convince him that the present is the time for the coming of the Muslim Messiah. Our imaginary observer will not observe the signs singly but as a total picture. As soon as he has gone over the scene, he will find himself trembling, his heart full. He will close the book of signs, lay it aside, and declare that his search is over, that further pursuit of the subject is futile. According to the signs, the Promised Messiah has already come. If he has not come by now, he will not come at all.

Appendix to Argument 2
A Note on the Dadjjal

A difficulty is often raised about the prophecy relating to the Dadjjal. It is said that the Dadjjal was to appear before the Promised Messiah. Therefore, as the Dadjjal has not yet appeared, the time of the Promised Messiah has not yet come.

It must be remembered that the prophecy relating to the Dadjjal, like all prophecies, is subject to interpretation. We read in the Holy Quran:

وَالشَّمْسَ وَالْقَمَرَ رَأَيْتُهُمْ لِي سٰجِدِيْنَ ۔

اِنِّيْ اَرٰى فِي الْمَنَامِ اَنِّيْ اَذْبَحُكَ ۔

> 'And the sun and the moon, I saw them making obeisance to me'.[1]
>
> 'And I have seen in a dream that I am slaughtering thee.'[2]

The references are to the dreams of Joseph and Abraham respectively. Both dreams are well known. Both are symbolic of events which they prophesied. It is not fitting for Muslims to treat prophecies as anything other than symbolic descriptions of the future.

The prophecy about the Dadjjal cannot be understood except in the light of other Traditions and in the light of the general laws of God. If it is true, as the Traditions say, that the Promised Messiah is to be preceded by the Dadjjal, and if it is true that the advent of the Promised Messiah is to be marked by the dominance of Christianity, does it not follow that the prophecy about the Dadjjal relates to the power and overlordship of Christianity in our time? The prophecies are saying in effect that the Dadjjal and Christianity will

1 *Yusuf*, 5.

2 *Al-Saffat*, 103.

be powerful forces and that both will appear some time before the Promised Messiah. Two powerful forces due to appear simultaneously could easily be one and the same. Two different forces cannot acquire dominance at the same time. The difficulty can be solved by assuming that the two names are two different names for the same thing.

A very important consideration which leads to this conclusion is that the Holy Prophet (on whom be peace and the blessings of God) instructed his followers to turn to the first ten verses of *Surah Kahf*, (chapter 18), when they confront the menace of the Dadjjal. The first ten verses of this chapter contain a refutation of Christianity. One of the verses says:

وَيُنْذِرَ الَّذِيْنَ قَالُوا اتَّخَذَ اللّٰهُ وَلَدًا۔

> 'And that it may warn those who say, Allah has taken unto Himself a son.'[3]

The object of the revelation of the Holy Quran is to warn mankind. Among other things, the purpose of the Holy Book is to warn those who attribute a physical son to God. The verses, according to the Holy Prophet, provide guidance for Muslims to meet the menace of the Dadjjal. But they contain a refutation of Christianity. Does this not prove that the Dadjjal and Christianity are one and the same thing? Treatment of a disease must be relevant to the disease. If the Dadjjal and Christianity were two different things, the Holy Prophet would not have recommended the reading of verses of the Holy Book which relate not to the Dadjjal but to Christianity. The reading of these verses would have been next to useless if they did not relate to the Dadjjal. This proves, therefore, that even according to the Holy Prophet, the appearance of the Dadjjal is the appearance of Christian propagandists.

The greatest obstacle to a true understanding of the subject of the Dadjjal is the preconception, from which most people seem to suffer, that the Dadjjal is one powerful individual, a kind of superman. This he is not, even according to Arabic dictionaries. To quote two authorities:

3 *Al Kahf*, 5.

اَوْ مِنَ الدَّجَّالِ بِالتَّشْدِيْدِ لِلرِّفْقَةِ الْعَظِيْمَةِ تُغَطِّي الْاَرْضَ
بِكَثْرَةِ اَهْلِهَا وَ قِيْلَ هِيَ الرِّفْقَةُ تَحْمِلُ الْمَتَاعَ لِلتِّجَارَةِ
اَلدَّجَّالُ اَلرِّفْقَةُ الْعَظِيْمَةُ ـ

> 'The Dadjjal is the name of a large party which, through force of numbers, will spread over the whole earth, and according to some authorities, it is the name of a party which keeps moving from one part of the world to another the goods and material in which it trades.'[4]
>
> 'The Dadjjal is a large party.'[5]

These descriptions apply to Christian propagandists today. They transport their books from one part of the world to another, together with other forms of entertainment; they also promote business activities of various kinds wherever they go. One meaning of the word *Dadjjal* is 'pretender'. To whom is this description more applicable than to the Christian propagandists of our time? They present the man Jesus so that he should seem like God.

True, the Dadjjal has other signs. He was to be one-eyed and was to have with him a donkey of inordinate size. Clouds of smoke were to be seen in front of the animal and behind it. These descriptions are symbolic. The one-eyed Dadjjal is a group or party of men devoid of spiritual vision. The right side in spiritual symbolism indicates religion and virtue. If the Dadjjal is without his right eye, he symbolizes men incapable of spiritual understanding and a spiritual view of things. The donkey of the Dadjjal symbolizes the railway, the most typical of modern means of transport. It was invented by Christians in Christian countries. When the railway whistles, the sound resembles the braying of a donkey. It uses fire and water as fuel, and clouds of smoke are before and behind it. Christian propagandists use it for transporting themselves to different parts of the world.

Nobody can take exception to the interpretation of symbols and prophecies. We have for this the authority of the Holy Prophet himself. In the *Hadith* we read that one day the Holy Prophet went to see Ibn Sayyad, a man credited with strange experiences. He was

4 *Taj.*

5 *Aqrab.*

with him for some time and asked him questions. From the answers to the questions it appeared that Ibn Sayyad had some Satanic or self-caused intuitions. Omar, who accompanied the Holy Prophet, drew his sword, saying on oath that Ibn Sayyad was the Dadjjal of the prophecy. The Holy Prophet (on whom be peace) stopped Omar:

قَالَ عُمَرُ يَا رَسُوْلَ اللّٰهِ أَتَأْذَنُ لِيْ فِيْهِ أَنْ أَضْرِبَ عُنُقَهٗ؟ قَالَ
رَسُوْلُ اللّٰهِ صَلَّى اللّٰهُ عَلَيْهِ وَسَلَّمَ: إِنْ يَّكُنْ هُوَ لَا تُسَلَّطُ عَلَيْهِ
وَإِنْ لَّمْ يَكُنْ هُوَ فَلَا خَيْرَ لَكَ فِيْ قَتْلِهٖ۔

> 'Hazrat Omar asked the Messenger of Allah (peace be on him), "Permit me to strike his head with my sword."
> The Messenger of Allah (peace be on him) replied:
> ' "If he is not the Dadjjal, it is wrong to kill him. If he is, it is not for you but for the Messiah to kill him." '[6]

The incident proves that the signs of the Dadjjal mentioned in earlier prophecies are symbolic and can stand interpretation. When Omar declared Ibn Sayyad to be the Dadjjal, the Holy Prophet did not contradict him. He could have cited the signs which he himself had narrated about the Dadjjal: that the Dadjjal would have KFR written on his forehead, that he would have one eye, that he would fail to reach Medina, and so on. These signs were not present in Ibn Sayyad. He did not have one eye, he did not have KFR written on his forehead. (This important inscription was not visible even to the Holy Prophet, let alone to others.) And he was present in Medina. The question is, if the signs about the Dadjjal are not symbols, if they have to be taken literally, why did not the Holy Prophet contradict Omar straight away? Why did he hesitate? Why did he not tell Omar that the Dadjjal was to have one eye, he was to have KFR written on his forehead and was not to be seen in Medina? So, it was futile to call Ibn Sayyad the Dadjjal of prophecy. The fact that the Holy Prophet did not contradict Omar at once, that he at least thought it possible that Ibn Sayyad was the Dadjjal, proves that, according to the Holy Prophet, signs about the Dadjjal were capable of interpretation, that they were not to be taken literally but

6 *Mishquat*, under Ibn Sayyad.

could have a meaning very different from their surface meaning. If, even the Holy Prophet believed that the signs of the Dadjjal can stand interpretation, nobody else has the right to turn his back upon the facts of contemporary history and demand a literal fulfilment of those signs, ignoring their obvious symbolic significance.

Argument 3
Personal Purity

'The proof of the sun is the sun'

I have shown that the present is the time for the coming of a reformer. I have also shown that, according to the testimony of the Holy Prophet of Islam (on whom be peace), the reformer indicated at the present time is none other than the Promised Messiah and Mahdi. The Founder of the Ahmadiyya Movement is the only claimant to this office. To deny him and his claim is to deny an ancient law of God, to ignore the prophecies of the Holy Prophet.

I now proceed to enumerate arguments which go to prove (apart from the need of the time and apart from the earlier prophecies), that the claim of Mirza Ghulam Ahmad (peace be on him) that he is the Messenger appointed by God for our time is just and true.

The first argument I wish to submit is the testimony of his personal purity.

Personal purity, proof of the authenticity of Divine Messengers

Personal purity is universally admitted as one of the strongest possible proofs of the general truthfulness of a person. In the present context, however, I wish to draw on the argument as stated in the Holy Quran.

In the *Surah 'Yunus'* (chapter 10) of the Holy Quran we have the following:

وَاِذَا تُتْلٰى عَلَيْهِمْ اٰيٰتُنَا بَيِّنٰتٍ قَالَ الَّذِيْنَ لَا يَرْجُوْنَ لِقَآءَنَا ائْتِ
بِقُرْاٰنٍ غَيْرِ هٰذَآ اَوْ بَدِّلْهُ قُلْ مَا يَكُوْنُ لِيْٓ اَنْ اُبَدِّلَهٗ مِنْ تِلْقَآئِ
نَفْسِيْ اِنْ اَتَّبِعُ اِلَّا مَا يُوْحٰٓى اِلَيَّ اِنِّيْٓ اَخَافُ اِنْ عَصَيْتُ رَبِّيْ
عَذَابَ يَوْمٍ عَظِيْمٍ - قُلْ لَّوْ شَآءَ اللّٰهُ مَا تَلَوْتُهٗ عَلَيْكُمْ وَلَآ اَدْرٰىكُمْ
بِهٖ فَقَدْ لَبِثْتُ فِيْكُمْ عُمُرًا مِّنْ قَبْلِهٖ اَفَلَا تَعْقِلُوْنَ -

> 'And when Our clear Signs are recited to them, those who look not for the meeting with Us, say, "Bring a Quran other than this or change it"; say, "It is not for me to change it of my own accord. I only follow what is revealed to me. Indeed, I fear, if I disobey my Lord, the punishment of an awful day." Say, "If Allah had so willed, I should not have recited it to you nor would He have made it known to you. *I have indeed lived among you a* whole *life-time before this*. Will you not then understand?" '[1]

The passage reproduces a dispute between the Holy Prophet and those who denied him. It ends up with a challenge which says that the Holy Prophet has had until now an unimpeachable reputation of personal purity. This being so, he cannot suddenly begin to be different.

This important argument laid down by the Holy Quran for the truth of the Holy Prophet (peace be on him) can be used as a criterion for the truth or falsehood of every claimant to the divine office. Proof of the presence of the sun lies in the sun, in the light and heat which it sheds over us. Similarly evidence of the truth of a truthful person lies in his personal purity, which speaks with an eloquence all its own. It speaks to friend and foe, to strangers and confidants, to those who are near to him and those who are not so near. It says to them all: 'Think twice before you brand me a liar. For you have known me as a truthful person and have judged me as such. If you now declare me a liar, you will have no means left to discriminate between truth and error. You will have no criterion for judging between one man and another.' Everything is bound by continuity. It grows. It cannot jump from one stage to another

1 *Yunus*, 16–17.

without going through the stages which lie in between. A good man becomes good and attains goodness by stages. So a bad man becomes bad and drops to a depth of evil by stages. A man who has been running westward will not suddenly find himself at the eastern horizon. A man who has been running southward will not find himself at the northern horizon. To all those who had decided to deny and to decry him, the Holy Prophet seems to say:

> I have spent a lifetime among you. I was a child and I grew up in your midst. I became an adult and I lived among you. I arrived at middle age and I am among you. You have seen me in public and in private. Whatever I have said or done is known to you. There is none amongst you who imputed to me before this any lies, excesses, intrigues, fabrications, transgressions, any attempt to seek power or dominion over others. You have observed me in many different contexts and have tested and tried me in many different ways. In every context and in every way you found me stable and steadfast in my regard for truth and honesty. You found me free from every evil, every impurity. My friends as well as my present enemies knew and addressed me as the 'trusted' or the truthful one. I could be trusted for honesty and truthfulness until yesterday. I could not lie about anything. I would sacrifice myself for the sake of truth. My life, in fact, was an honour and embellishment for truth. You trusted me in all things, great and small. You accepted anything I told you. But now suddenly you turn on me and tell me I am the worst of human beings, the most hardened liar, and so on. I did not lie about men, but now suddenly have I started lying about God? Is such a sudden change in one's character possible? Does human experience offer any example of it? If I had been truthful and trustworthy for a day or so or even for a year or so, you could have said I had put on an appearance, had adopted an external bearing, to mislead and to misguide others. But I could not have maintained such an appearance for a lifetime. You have seen me as child and as man. Can a child put on an appearance of good conduct? The years of childhood are the years of innocence. No child can put on an appearance of conduct which is not natural to him. Then during adolescence when one is subject to impulses and passions, how could I conceal my real character behind a facade? You must think and tell me how I could possibly

fabricate a character which was not my own. If on thinking about it you find all my earlier life spotless and clean, an embodiment, in fact, of integrity and honesty, then you have no right to brand me a liar and a dishonest person today. Seeing the sun you cannot deny that it is day. Seeing its light you cannot complain of darkness. Do you need evidence of my truth? My life until today lies open before you. What more evidence do you need? My character is my witness. My life is my evidence. Consult your conscience, hear your own inner voice. You will hear it say to you that my life is truth personified. I am the truth and the truth is me. I honour truth and truth honours me. To prove my truth I need no argument, because I am my own argument. If you want the proof of the sun, you have to look at the sun. The proof of the sun is the sun.

Appeal for early believers

This is the argument by which Abu Bakr, the first believer, was consciously and unconsciously converted. This is the argument which has ever brought about the conversion of honest seekers after truth. It is well known that when the Holy Prophet (on whom be peace and the blessings of God) made known his claim, Abu Bakr, his bosom friend, was at a friend's house. A woman servant of his happened to see him there and told him about it: 'The wife of your friend Muhammad tells her friends that her husband has become a prophet, just like Moses.' Abu Bakr said not a word, but rising at once he made for the Holy Prophet's house. He asked if it was true that he had claimed to be a prophet. The Holy Prophet said yes and Abu Bakr believed. The Holy Prophet said, 'I never invited anyone to Islam without his hesitating or stopping to think about it. But when I mentioned it to Abu Bakr, he did not hesitate for a moment and believed at once.' Abu Bakr did not ask for signs or evidence. He found himself constrained to believe as soon as he heard the Holy Prophet's claim. How was Abu Bakr persuaded? He was persuaded by the eloquence of the Holy Prophet's character. A man's character is his evidence.

Khadija the Holy Prophet's wife, Ali his young cousin, Zaid bin Harith his freed slave, believed in the same way and by the same argument. Khadija has narrated the story of her conversion. When the Holy Prophet (on whom be peace) saw Gabriel in the cave Hira and received through him the first divine revelation commanding him to proclaim his prophethood, he came home to tell Khadija about it. 'I am afraid for myself,' he said. Khadija in reply comforted the Holy Prophet. 'No, no,' said she, 'Allah will not disgrace you. You are kind to your relations. You help the helpless. You have the virtues we had forgotten. You entertain your guests and help those in trouble.'

The first proof of the authenticity of a claimant to spiritual office is his own self or character. This self is as eloquent as anything which can be seen or heard. As proof it is self-sufficient. It needs no further support, no miracles or signs. This proof is today provided by God to establish the authenticity of Hazrat Mirza Ghulam Ahmad. Hazrat Mirza Sahib lived at Qadian, the population of which consists of Hindus, Sikhs and Muslims. He grew up, therefore, under the eyes of three of India's most important religious communities. His family's relations with these communities were not as happy as they might have been. The British had taken possession of the Punjab when Hazrat Mirza Sahib was a child. Until then, the inhabitants of Qadian and its environs had lived as tenants and serfs of his family. With the coming of the British a great change had taken place. The old inhabitants of Qadian were determined to make the most of this change. They had started working for their release from old contracts and commitments. The result was that almost the whole village had entered into litigation with the father of Hazrat Mirza Sahib.

Under his father's orders he had to take part in the resulting court proceedings. Left to himself he would have led a life of study and seclusion, but his situation, for some time at least, demanded that he should confront people from his own village and appear in court as one against many.

The Sikh inhabitants of the village were especially hostile to his family. This was because some time before the Sikhs had driven Mirza Sahib's family out of the place and had taken possession of their lands. The returning prosperity of the family of Hazrat Mirza Sahib was not welcome to the Sikhs. They were rivals of his family.

From early life Hazrat Mirza Sahib had been deeply interested in the study and service of Islam. Often he met Christians, Hindus and Sikhs in public debate and spoke and wrote against them. This made all religious communities interested in him.

Hazrat Mirza Sahib was well known to the leaders of all religious communities. He lived and moved among his rivals. But all of them, Hindu, Sikh, Christian, Muslim, agreed that Mirza Sahib had always led a blameless life, had shown the utmost kindness and consideration to others, and had been consistently truthful and honest in all his dealings. He was universally trusted. In disputes with his family, the litigants often offered to accept arbitration by Hazrat Mirza Sahib. In short, those who knew him, knew him as a most honourable and trustworthy person, one who would never compromise with truth and justice. Christians, Hindus and Sikhs, though strongly disagreeing with him on religious matters, testified to the purity of his personal life and character.

Testimony of Maulvi Muhammad Husain of Batala

How greatly esteemed Hazrat Mirza Sahib was by those who knew him (and he was well known in the circles in which he moved) may be gauged from the writing of a Muslim leader and scholar who later became one of his worst enemies; who, in fact, led the hostility which was to grow later against Mirza Sahib and his claim – the first to issue the *Fatwa* of *Kufr* against Mirza Sahib. This Muslim leader was no ordinary person. He was Maulvi Muhammad Husain of Batala the acknowledged chief of the Ahl-i-Hadith sect. He wrote a review of *Barahin-i-Ahmadiyya*, the first big book by Hazrat Mirza Sahib. Writing in his journal, *Ishaat al-Sunnah*, he testified to the character and purity of life of Hazrat Mirza Sahib in the following words:

”مؤلّف براہین احمدیّہ کے حالات وخیالات سے جس قدر ہم واقف ہیں ہمارے معاصرین سے ایسے واقف کم نکلیں گے۔ مؤلّف صاحب ہمارے ہم وطن ہیں۔ بلکہ اوائل عمر کے (جب ہم قطبی وشرح مُلّا پڑھتے تھے) ہمارے ہم مکتب۔ اس زمانہ سے آج تک ہم میں ان میں خط وکتابت وملاقات ومراسلت برابر جاری رہی ہے۔ اس لئے ہمارا یہ کہنا کہ ہم ان کے حالات سے بہت واقف ہیں، مبالغہ قرار نہ دیئے جانے کے لائق ہے۔“

'The author of *Barahin-i-Ahmadiyya* is well known to us. In fact, few know more about his thoughts, aspirations, and circumstances etc., than we do. He belongs to our district and

> when young, attended the same courses and the same instruction as we did. We read *Qutabi* and *Sharah Mulla* together. Since those days we have corresponded, communicated and conferred regularly. Nobody, therefore, should think it an exaggeration if we say that we know the author and his circumstances rather well.'[2]

So far, the reviewer affirms that his testimony is not based on hearsay, but on long, intimate personal association with the author. But look at the testimony itself:

> This book, in our opinion [referring to the *Barahin-i-Ahmadiyya*], is without parallel in our time, and in view of the circumstances and needs of our time there has not been another one like it in the entire history of Islam. About the future no one can say. 'Only Allah will reveal the truth after this.' As for the author, we can say there have been few Muslims, if any, who have been so constant in their service to Islam, service by purse and pen, by personal character, and by speech and silence. If we are accused of exaggeration common in Asia, we should be told at least of one book written in our time, which answers the objections of the enemies of Islam, such as the Arya Sect and the Brahmo Samaj, with the same energy and earnestness. We should also be told of two or more friends of Islam who have resolved to serve Islam in the same way, with purse and pen and with speech and silence; whose lives are similarly devoted; who are able manfully to challenge the enemies of Islam and the deniers of revelation to come and witness these experiences and have their doubts removed; and who have made non-Muslims taste the truth of Islam. (*Ishaat al-Sunnah*, VI, 7)

Opposition and accusations after the announcement of the claim

The writer of this review, Maulvi Muhammad Husain of Batala, later led the opposition to the Promised Messiah's claim and spent the rest of his life denouncing him as a *Kafir* and a liar, much like

2 *Ishaat-al-Sunnah*, vi:7.

the Meccan deniers of the Holy Prophet (peace be on him), who before the declaration of the Prophet's claim had proclaimed him as Muhammad, the trustworthy, the truthful. The opposition and hostility which arises *after* the announcement of one's claim cannot have much meaning. We know from the Holy Quran that it is impossible for a person, proved virtuous and true in the eyes of friend and foe alike and through all kinds of trials, suddenly to turn round and begin to lie about God. Against such sudden metamorphosis God Himself is the surest safeguard. God is not a tyrant. If a man's life has been known to be blameless even by his enemies, God will not reward him by changing him all at once into the worst of human beings. A man who remains steadfast through the worst temptations cannot suddenly begin to lie about God and himself.

The Holy Prophet (on whom be peace and the blessings of God) challenged his enemies again and again and asked them to point to the slightest moral lapse in his early life. Did they not, instead, think him the best of human beings? Nobody accepted the challenge. Similarly, the Promised Messiah (on whom be peace) declared that he had been assured that his opponents would not be able to point to any lapse of a personal character in his life (*Nazul al-Masih*, p. 212). Supported by this assurance he challenged his opponents again and again and asked them to point to a single lapse in his earlier life and dealings. Had they not observed him as boy and man? Had they not found him always an example of personal goodness? He invited his enemies again and again to deny this and make a declaration to the contrary. Those who had known him when he was young were still alive. They might have become his worst opponents, but they could not hide the truth about his earlier life. This, according to universal testimony, was the very best one can imagine. His was a godly life, according to the declared testimony of the many Hindus, Sikhs and Muslims who knew him as a child and continued to know him as a man.

In short, personal purity is one of the strongest arguments which can be urged in support of any claimant to divine office. It is rightly urged in the Holy Quran on behalf of the Holy Prophet. It may be rightly urged on behalf of the Promised Messiah. The truth of his claim is upheld by the acknowledged purity of his life before his claim. This is not denied by his enemies. His personal character, therefore, is proof of his authenticity.

Argument 4
Triumph of Islam over Other Religions

The fourth argument or the fourth group of arguments relates to a prophecy contained in the Holy Quran which assigns to the Promised Messiah the important task of leading Islam again to triumph over other religions. The Promised Messiah did this by proving Islam's superiority over other religions. He could do this only with the help and grace of God, and the fact constitutes an important argument in support of his claim. The Holy Quran says:

هُوَ الَّذِيْٓ اَرْسَلَ رَسُوْلَهٗ بِالْهُدٰى وَ دِيْنِ الْحَقِّ لِيُظْهِرَهٗ
عَلَى الدِّيْنِ كُلِّهٖ

'He it is Who has sent His Messenger, with guidance and the religion of truth, that He may make it prevail over all other religions.'[1]

From the Sayings of the Holy Prophet (peace be on him), it appears that the triumph of Islam over other religions which is promised in this verse was due to take place in the time of the Promised Messiah. The liquidation of the Dadjjal, the destruction of Gog and Magog and the defeat of Christianity are tasks appointed for the Promised Messiah according to the Holy Prophet (peace be on him). These dangers have been described as the gravest in the history of Islam. We are also told that the Dadjjal or Missionary Christianity would succeed in dominating all other religions. The defeat of Christianity by Islam would, therefore, mean the defeat of all other rivals as well.

1 *Al-Taubah*, 33; *Al-Fath*, 29; *Al-Saff*, 10.

Time of universal victory

The words 'make it [Islam] prevail over all other religions' relate to the time of the Promised Messiah. On this point almost all Muslim commentators seem to agree. For instance, in the well-known *Jami al-Bayan*, vol. 29, under the verse in question we have:

وَ ذٰلِكَ عِنْدَ نُزُوْلِ عِيْسَى ابْنِ مَرْيَمَ

> 'The time of which this verse speaks is appointed for the coming of Isa bin Maryam [i.e. his second coming].'[2]

On rational considerations also, the view seems to be sound. The variety of religions found today in the world did not exist before. Contacts between religions and between peoples have increased beyond all expectations. The invention of the printing press has immeasurably facilitated the printing and circulation of books. There is also a spirit of competition between religions. The number of competing religious groups has much increased. In the time of the Holy Prophet (peace be on him), there were only four religions which rose against Islam. They were the idol-worshippers of Mecca, Christians, Jews and Magians. The many other religions and religious and ideological groups which have since appeared in the world were then unknown. Therefore at that time the triumph of Islam over all other religions could not be contemplated in a full sense of the term. That is possible today. Today all religions have come out into the open. New methods of transport and communication have intensified the struggle between religions and ideologies.

It seems therefore that, according to the Holy Quran, the *Hadith*, and rational considerations, the visible triumph of Islam over other religions was destined to take place in the time of the Promised Messiah, this being the most important of the objects of his advent. If a claimant to the office of Promised Messiah is able to accomplish the grand task, no doubt will be left as to the truth of his claim. Facts which I shall now enumerate will show that Hazrat Mirza Ghulam Ahmad has accomplished the appointed triumph of Islam. Therefore he is the Promised Messiah.

2 *Tafsir Jami al-Bayan*, vol. 29.

Before Hazrat Mirza Ghulam Ahmad announced his claim, the condition of Islam had so deteriorated that Muslims themselves had begun to despair. Some did not hesitate to announce the doom of Islam. The general situation of Islam also pointed to an inevitable end. Missionary Christianity was busy driving Islam out of all its strongholds. It was felt that in less than a hundred years Islam would disappear from the world. So dismayed had Muslims become under the Christian attack that even the physical descendants of the Holy Prophet (on whom be peace), the Syeds, had abandoned Islam and joined Christianity in their thousands, to say nothing of other Muslims. These converts were not just nominal Christians. They played a vital part in the preparation and publication of vituperative literature against Islam and its Holy Founder (peace be on him). They would mount public rostrums and make foul attacks on the Holy Prophet (peace and the blessings of God be upon him). Some of these attacks were so heart-rending that Muslims were becoming demoralized. Indeed, so great was their demoralization that even the Hindus, whose religion has long since ceased to be a living force, who had never ventured into the missionary field, and who had ever been occupied in a futile defence of their religion, decided to come out and attack Islam and claim converts from Islam to Hinduism. The well-known Hindu sect of Aryas set themselves the task of converting Muslims to Hinduism and launched a campaign for this purpose. The scene was pitiful. It was as though a brave man who had been dreaded by all when he was alive, now lay dead and was preyed upon by vultures. When the man was alive, these birds dared not even come near him, but now they were tearing his flesh and feeding on him. Muslims who wrote in defence of Islam would do so apologetically. They would say, for instance, that the laws of Islam were meant for an earlier time; that time had gone, so the laws were not relevant today. It was wrong, therefore, to find fault with them. At this time of despair and disaster came Hazrat Mirza Ghulam Ahmad (on whom be peace) and started his defence of Islam. His first attack on behalf of Islam proved stupefying for the enemy. He wrote his famous book, *Barahin-i-Ahmadiyya*, which contained an exposition of the rational foundations of Islam. In this he also included a challenge to the detractors of Islam to produce on behalf of their religions even a fifth of the arguments contained in the *Barahin-i-Ahmadiyya*. If any non-Muslim exponent should succeed in doing so, he could claim a reward of Rs 10,000. Many tried to take up the challenge and reply to the book, but none succeeded. The country resounded with the book's fame. The enemies of Islam were dumb-founded. Islam, which until then had been powerless to defend itself, had now launched an offensive against enemy faiths. The sword of Islam had fallen on them all. They were routed.

The claim to the office of Messiah had not yet been announced. The hostility which the announcement of the claim later produced had not yet arisen. The *Barahin-i-Ahmadiyya* and its challenge were well received by Muslims. Thousands of them declared openly that the writer was the *Mujaddid* (reformer) of the century. A saint and scholar of Ludhiana wrote:

ہم مریضوں کی ہے تمہیں پہ نظر
تم مسیحا بنو خدا کے لئے

'We the sick look to you; for God's sake come and be our Messiah.'

The publication of *Barahin-i-Ahmadiyya* initiated a movement for the defence and support of Islam. At last the enemies of Islam had to admit that Islam was not dead but as alive as ever. Uncertainty and lack of confidence overwhelmed them. They began to fear for their future. The most powerful among the enemy religions, which was full of pride over its universal success and regarded Islam as its prey, has suffered such a blow that its votaries take to their heels as soon as they hear of the approach of an Ahmadi exponent. A Christian missionary cannot stand before an Ahmadi. Through the efforts of Hazrat Mirza Ghulam Ahmad, Islam has again become dominant over other religions. The weapons of Islam are Islam's arguments; and arguments may be slow in their effects, but the effects they produce endure.

Even though Christianity still holds a very strong position in the world as a whole and other religions also continue as before, their death-knell has been sounded and their back is broken. Traditional loyalty and social conformity prevent large numbers of adherents of other religions from joining Islam openly. Therefore, to superficial observers, the triumph of Islam is not so evident. But the deeper signs are there.

A keen observer can judge the future from small beginnings. The tree can be seen in the seed. Hazrat Mirza Sahib has attacked non-Muslim faiths so effectively that they cannot now escape their fate. Sooner or later they will lie dead at the feet of Islam.

Let us now proceed to recount in some detail how Hazrat Mirza Sahib attacked the enemy faiths.

Victory over Christianity

The success which Christianity has achieved over a long period of history is based on the Christian belief that Jesus died on the cross and so atoned for the sins of his followers. Resurrected from death on the cross he now sits in Heaven on the right hand of God. This story has had a tremendous effect on many generations of human beings. The death of Jesus 'for others' roused tender emotions in those who heard the account. His Resurrection and his ascent to Heaven to the right hand of God inspired awe and made people revere him as God. These two beliefs, death on the cross and Resurrection, Hazrat Mirza Sahib disproved with the help of the New Testament itself. He proved that Jesus could not have died on the cross. It was known that even if a man remained nailed to a cross for three days, he did not necessarily die. Jesus remained on the cross for only three or four hours. It is also recorded in the New Testament that when he was taken down, a spear thrust in his side brought out warm blood (John 19:31–4). One cannot extract warm blood from a dead body. Moreover, Jesus had prophesied (and this prophecy remains in the New Testament records) that he would come down alive from the cross. Did he not say:

> 'An evil and adulterous generation seeketh after a sign; and there shall no sign be given to it, but the sign of the prophet Jonas: For as Jonas was three days and three nights in the whale's belly; so shall the Son of man be three days and three nights in the heart of the earth.'[3]

It is known that the prophet Jonas had been devoured alive by a whale but had come out alive. Jesus was to show a sign similar to this sign. So he was to enter the tomb alive and come out alive after three days and three nights. Arguments advanced by Hazrat Mirza Sahib were based on the New Testament records. So Christians

3 Matthew 12:39–40.

were dumb-founded. They could not meet the attack. They are unable to do so even today. The whole theory of the death of Jesus on the cross for the atonement of the sins of others fell to the ground. The main attraction of Christianity for credulous believers disappeared. Christianity lost one of its legs.

Jesus buried in Srinagar, Kashmir

The other leg on which Christianity stood was the belief in the Resurrection of Jesus and his ascent to Heaven to a seat on the right hand of God. By arguments again drawn from the New Testament, Hazrat Mirza Sahib broke this second leg too, as he had broken the first. Hazrat Mirza Sahib proved from the New Testament records that after the event of the cross Jesus did not ascend to Heaven but journeyed to the East, going into Iran, Afghanistan and India in search of the lost tribes of Israel. We know from the New Testament that Jesus ever reminded his audiences that he had come to gather the lost sheep of Israel:

> 'And other sheep I have, which are not of this fold: them also I must bring.'[4]

It is known from history that Nebuchadnezzar, a Babylonian king, had taken prisoner ten out of the twelve tribes of Israel and had driven them into exile in Afghanistan. As Jesus had to gather the lost tribes, it was necessary for him to journey to Afghanistan and Kashmir that they might receive his message. If he had not journeyed to that part of the world, his coming would have failed.

Besides the New Testament, Hazrat Mirza Sahib drew on the evidence of history and geography to support his views. He quoted ancient history to prove that the early followers of Jesus came to India. In Tibet had been found a book similar in content to the books of the New Testament. This book contains an account of the life of Jesus. Evidence of this kind shows that Jesus travelled in these parts. Hazrat Mirza Sahib pointed to evidence visible today in Afghanistan and Kashmir in the names of towns, villages, rivers, and tribes, to show that these regions were peopled by Jews. The most outstanding evidence lies in the name Kashmir itself, which is

4 John 10:16.

a modification of *Kashir*. The original inhabitants of Kashmir called their country *Kashir*, literally 'Like Shir' or 'Like Syria', *Shir* being Syria. Similarly, Kabul and other geographical names in Afghanistan are imitations of names in Syria. The physiognomy, facial features, shape of head, etc., of the people of Afghanistan and Kashmir resemble those common in Israel. Hazrat Mirza Sahib's crowning triumph, however, was his discovery of the tomb of Jesus. He traced it in Khanyar Street, Srinagar. From the ancient history of Kashmir it appears that this tomb has long been described as the tomb of a 'prince prophet' who came from the West nineteen hundred years ago. The old inhabitants of Kashmir described the tomb as the tomb of Isa Sahib.

In short, on evidence drawn from different directions, Hazrat Mirza Sahib proved that Jesus died a natural death and was buried in Kashmir, and the promise of God contained in the Holy Quran:

وَاٰوَيْنٰهُمَآ اِلٰى رَبْوَةٍ ذَاتِ قَرَارٍ وَّمَعِيْنٍ -

> 'and We gave them [Jesus and Mary] refuge on an elevated land of green with streams of running water,'[5]

was literally fulfilled. The description in the verse is a description of Kashmir. This account of the life and death of Jesus, including an account of his tomb, made belief in Jesus as God no longer possible. The God Jesus was dead. Belief in him will never live again.

The Promised Messiah, the Promised One of all religions

Christianity in our time occupies a distinct position because of its political power, its territorial expansion, its missionary activities, and the scientific and intellectual progress made by its followers. Therefore to prove the superiority of Islam over this leading world religion God provided Hazrat Mirza Sahib with special weapons. To deal with other religions he was provided with another master weapon. This one weapon was enough to defeat all of them. The weapon relates to the prophecies contained in the books of all

5 *Al-Muminun*, 51.

religions which foretell the coming of a great reformer in the latter days. In expectation of these prophecies being fulfilled, followers of all religions waited or wait for the coming of a prophet, an *Avatar*, or whatever. With the coming of such a reformer is linked the hope of revival fostered by followers of different religions. Such prophecies exist in the books of Hindus and Zoroastrians. Other religious groups, large and small, also have such prophecies recorded in their holy books. In all of them there is a description of the Promised One and his time. The signs of the appointed time enumerated by different sources are very similar. If in some sources more signs are related than in others, the additional signs also point to the same time. Hazrat Mirza Sahib concluded that the prophecies of all religions which foretell the coming of a reformer in the latter days relate to the same time.

Prophecies which foretell events many thousands of years before they occur must have a divine origin. They cannot have been the concoction of either man or Satan. We have the clear teaching of the Holy Quran on the subject:

فَلَا يُظْهِرُ عَلٰى غَيْبِهٖٓ اَحَدًا - اِلَّا مَنِ ارْتَضٰى مِنْ رَّسُوْلٍ -

'. . . and He reveals not His secrets to anyone except him whom He chooses, namely a Messenger of His.'[6]

Knowledge of the unseen or knowledge of the future is revealed only to true Messengers of God. At the same time it seemed contrary to reason that at one and the same time every religious community, every group, should have a *Rasul, Nabi* or *Avatar* sent to it to effect its domination over all the others. This would mean Messengers of God in conflict and competition with one another. It also seemed absurd that at some time every religious community or group should triumph over every other. In short, while these prophecies are true and divine, they cannot apply to different persons for if they did, it would mean conflict and confusion. It would be against any rational arrangement. The only conclusion we can draw, therefore, is that these prophecies, recorded in religious books and handed down to our time by different religious communities, really relate to one and the same person. The purpose

6 *Jinn*, 27–8.

of God in transmitting these prophecies was that the different religious communities of the world should each look forward to the coming of a teacher. The Promised One would then come in the fullness of time, proclaim the truth of Islam, and invite the followers of all religions to the fold of the one true religion. Thus would he effect the triumph of Islam over all religions. We can say, therefore, that the Mahdi was none other than the Messiah; Krishna none other than the Messiah; the Promised One of the Zoroastrians, Maisodarbahmi, none other than the Krishna, the Mahdi, or the Messiah of early prophecies. So the different religious communities should look forward to one and the same teacher. The coming of this one was prophesied under different names, each familiar to one or other community, and each community looked eagerly for his appearance. Thus the different groups in the world would think of the Promised One as the Promised One of prophecies described in their own books, and in their own language. He would seem to them one of their kin, not a stranger. When, at last, he did appear and the signs of his time and the truth of his claim became evident, they would on his testimony and invitation accept Islam and become Muslims.

The divine plan seems analogous to a dispute between many groups, to effect a settlement among whom someone proposes that each appoint an arbiter. After each group has named its arbiter, it is found that they have each named the same person, only giving him each their own favoured name. Peace, under these circumstances, is irresistible.

Hazrat Mirza Sahib, therefore, said that the prophecies contained in different religions about the coming of a reformer related to the present time, and it was futile to expect more than one Messenger of God at a time, each trying to spread his version of truth and to push the interests of his own group in the world. It was evident that the different religions, under different names, were looking forward to one and the same person. The Promised One was none other than the Promised Messiah of Islam. A prophet or messenger does not belong to any one community. He is of God. Whoever is willing to join him for the sake of God, can claim him as his prophet or messenger. The Promised Messiah, therefore, belongs to all. The followers of all religions can claim him as their own. Their spiritual advancement is linked with him. They have to accept him as their leader and preceptor. They can do so only by accepting Islam and becoming Muslims. They will thus fulfil the grand prophecy which promises the triumph of Islam over other religions.

This approach to other religions was so vital and so effective that the other religions were unable to resist it. Every religion contains a prophecy about a reformer in the latter days. The signs relating to the reformer relate to the present time. All those signs have been fulfilled. There is only one claimant to spiritual office and this one is the Promised Messiah, the Founder of the Ahmadiyya Movement. Followers of religions which teach these prophecies can choose one of two courses: they can deny the prophecies handed down to them; or they must admit that the Promised One of Islam is also the Promised One of their own prophecies, and they must then accept him and accept Islam. A third course does not exist. Either of the two courses which are open would lead to the triumph of Islam. If the followers of other religions deny the prophecies contained in their respective religions, they deny the truth of those religions. This would be a clear triumph for Islam. If they do accept these prophecies and accept the only claimant to spiritual office who answers to their descriptions, they enter the fold of Islam. Again, it would be a triumph for Islam.

This powerful approach by Hazrat Mirza Sahib must produce great results. As time goes on, followers of other religions must turn more and more to Islam, so that the time must come when the only dominant religion in the world will be Islam. The Promised Messiah has sown the seed. This is what messengers and prophets do. The tree grows out of the seed and yields its fruit, but in God's own time. The people of the world taste the fruit and enjoy its sweetness and its flavour and rest under its shade, but only when the time comes.

Guru Nanak, Founder of the Sikhs

One religious group seems to have escaped Hazrat Mirza Sahib's vital and irresistible approach to the religions of the world. This group is the Sikhs. The Founder of the Sikhs, Guru Nanak, came long after the Holy Prophet (on whom be peace and the blessings of God). However, even the Sikh Holy Book contains the prophecy about a messenger in the latter days. It is clearly written in the Sikh records that the Promised Reformer will appear in Batala (Batala is the Tehsil in which the village of Qadian is situated); the Sikh prophecy, therefore, has been literally fulfilled in the person of Hazrat Mirza Sahib. The difficulty which the Sikh religion raises is that the Holy Prophet (on whom be peace and the blessings of God) was *Khatam al-Nabiyyin*, the Seal of the Prophets, the source and sanction of all prophets. How could a religious group, even one as small as the Sikhs, arise after the Holy Prophet (peace be on him)? Hazrat Mirza Sahib received special guidance from God in dealing with the Sikh religion. He saw in a vision that Guru Nanak (the mercy of God be on him) was not the founder of any religion. He was a follower of Islam and a true Muslim.

Hazrat Mirza Sahib started investigating. He found that the Granth Sahib, the Sikh scripture, which is a collection of sermons and speeches by Bawa Guru Nanak (the mercy of God be on him), contains exhortations for the five daily prayers, the annual fasts, *Zakat,* and the Haj. Those who fail to observe these fundamental religious duties are severely warned. From other Sikh books it appears that Bawa Sahib was wont to live in the company of Muslim saints. He visited the tombs of Muslim saints and there spent his time in meditation. He joined them in congregational prayers. He went to the Hedjaz for Hajj, and visited Baghdad and the other holy places of Islam. The most important discovery, however, was a cloak (*Chola*) which the Sikhs guard and adore as a relic. On this cloak are written chapters and verses of the Holy Quran – chapter 112, for instance, the famous verse of the 'Throne', and the verse 'Surely the true religion with Allah is Islam' (3:20). The *Kalima* of Islam, 'There is no God but Allah and Muhammad is His Prophet,' is written in a bold hand. As the Sikh devotees did not know Arabic, they revered these writings as divine mysteries. They did not realize that the writings were a declaration of Islam by Bawa Sahib. By arguments based on the Sikh books and connected with the relics held sacred by them, Hazrat Mirza Sahib began to tell the Sikh community that their great founder was a Muslim. The impact on the Sikh community was very real. They already show a tendency to be sympathetic to Islam, and as the true meaning of these discoveries dawns upon them they will realize that they have only strayed from the faith of their founder. The faith of the early Sikhs was Islam. They gradually dissociated themselves from it because of political controversies. These controversies, as historical research tends to prove, were due to Hindus, not Muslims. They have made the relations between Sikhs and Muslims very bitter. But the Sikhs are a brave people. One can hope that they will put truth above politics, forget the past, and join Islam. When they do so, the air will resound with the cry *Sat Sri Akal* ('Hail, the One True God'). The reformer promised in their scripture has appeared according to the promise in the Tahsil of Batala. It is up to them to accept and join him and join the effort he has initiated on behalf of Islam.

A grand conception

The third method of attack which Hazrat Mirza Sahib employed to bring about the triumph of Islam over other religions was his exposition of a grand conception taught by Islam. This conception relates to the attitude of each religion towards other religions. Before Hazrat Mirza Sahib's time, it was common; in fact, it was thought just and right for each religion to regard other religions and their followers as false. Excepting some individuals and some groups, all Jews believed Jesus to be a liar; all Christians believed the Holy Prophet (peace be on him) of Islam to be so; Zoroastrians regarded the prophets of the other faiths in the same way; and the other religions in their turn treated the Zoroastrian prophet similarly. Followers of each of the four faiths regarded the other religious teachers as false, and the followers of these religions regarded the founders of the four as false and so on. Disputes between religion and religion had become most degrading. Each religious community was at war with every other, and yet sensible persons could spot evidence of truth in all religions. In any case, it seemed cruel to regard the founders of religious traditions as false. One could not easily persuade oneself to think so. But was there a solution?

The result of these disputes was the increase of rancour and religious antagonism. Hindus read about their own religious teachers and were moved by their great moral and spiritual qualities, yet they heard others say that those teachers were liars and pretenders. This surprised them as much as it annoyed them. Naturally they thought the detractors were actuated by malice and by unwillingness to understand. Similarly, the followers of other religions read about their own founders and were persuaded of their spiritual qualities, and when they heard them abused they were enraged. An insuperable difficulty had arisen. How could respect and reverence for religious teachers be established? Those who examined the question without prejudice and without preconceptions could not think that the Universal God would choose one people for His favours and forget all the others. Nobody dared say so, however. Each religious group thought that to accept the founders of other religious groups amounted to a repudiation of their own religious position.

Liberal Hindus invented a solution. They began to teach that all religions are from God: different religions are like different routes leading to the same goal, and the Hindu religion was the best of these routes. This ingenious solution was open to two serious objections and these seemed unanswerable. The first objection was that if all religions, as we find them today, are from God and lead ultimately to Him, why do their teachings differ on vital and important matters? There could be differences on matters of detail, but there should be no difference on fundamentals. Many roads may lead to a mansion, but it would be absurd to think that roads coming from the east should reach it via the west or the north or the south. They can suffer small divergences, but their general direction should be the same. In fundamental and abiding truths there can be no great disagreement or difference. There can be differences, for instance, in modes of worship, in details of religious duty, and so on; but it is difficult to imagine that to the Jews and the Muslims God said 'I am One,' while to the Zoroastrians he said 'I am two,' to the Christians 'I am three,' to the Hindus 'I am many,' to the Chinese 'I am everywhere and everything.' Nor is it possible that to one group (the Muslims) God should declare that He transcends all things and is far from incarnating Himself even in human frame; to another (the Christians) that He could certainly incarnate Himself in the human frame; and to yet another (the Hindus) even in the frames of lower animals. Nor can it be that to the Muslims He should teach that life after death is inevitable, and to the Jews that it is not; nor that He should say at one time (to Islam) that the dead cannot return to life, at another (to Hindus) that they can and that after death human beings pass into a series of lives. In short, it is possible that teachings which come from God may show slight variations depending upon the people addressed (their time, surroundings, and so on); but there can be no vital difference, no disagreement in the description of historical events, for instance, or in the content of the basic propositions. Religious teachings as we find them today differ from one another not just in detail but also in fundamentals. Differences of a fundamental character cannot be attributed to a Universal God, and religious teachings which are so very different from one another cannot all lead to Him.

The second objection to this liberal Hindu conception is that in some sense Hindus regard their own religion as superior to others (even though those others may also lead eventually to God). The Hindu religion is the best, the oldest, and so on. This is a very difficult position. If God had revealed the best religion in the beginning, what need was there to reveal after it religions that were less than the best? If mankind were capable of receiving and benefiting from a perfect religion in the very beginning, there was no point in sending inferior religions in subsequent times. It seems contrary to reason to think that the best religion should have come in the infancy of the human race, and that later on, when human sciences and arts had become more advanced, we should have inferior religions. It is more reasonable to think that the later religions should be more perfect, more advanced than the earlier ones, or if not more, at least as perfect, as good.

These two difficulties were insuperable. For those who proposed to reconcile religions in the Hindu way, the important question was: What exactly was God's arrangement for the guidance of mankind from the earliest times to today?

The Christians also presented a solution to the problem of conflicting religions. They said that God invited the whole of mankind to His guidance. He did this through Jesus Christ. God had no favourites; for Him all sections of humanity were equally deserving of His help and guidance. But even this solution did not solve the difficulty. The question still remained: What had God done for the guidance of mankind before He sent down Jesus? From the Bible we learn that the message of Jesus Christ was meant for Israel, not for others. However, even if it is true that Christian teachers later on addressed the Christian message to all peoples of the world, the question remains: What did God do for the many millions of human beings who had gone before Jesus? Had they gone without divine guidance? The message of Jesus could not reach those who had lived and died before his time.

The question had no satisfactory answer, therefore. The status of different religious messages had to be defined. Without a just definition of status, the different religions found themselves involved in unending war with one another. Hazrat Mirza Sahib turned to the Holy Quran for an answer to this question and presented a new outlook, a new standpoint. The Holy Quran says:

وَاِنْ مِّنْ اُمَّةٍ اِلَّا خَلَا فِيْهَا نَذِيْرٌ۔

'. . . and there is no people to whom a warner has not come.'[7]

According to this teaching there has not been a single people at any time in history or anywhere in the world who have not had a warner from God, a teacher, a prophet. According to the Holy Quran there have been prophets at all times and in all countries. India, China, Russia, Afghanistan, parts of Africa, Europe, America – all had prophets according to the theory of divine guidance taught by the Holy Quran. When, therefore, Muslims hear about prophets of other peoples or other countries, they do not deny them. They do not brand them as liars. Muslims believe that other peoples have had their teachers. If other peoples have had prophets, books, and laws, these constitute no difficulty for Islam. They only confirm the universalistic conception Islam has taught. However, Islam teaches that the earlier teachings were commensurate with the needs and capacities of earlier peoples. The perfect teaching which God eventually sent through the Holy Prophet (peace and the blessings of God be on him) came at a time when mankind was sufficiently advanced to receive and to benefit from such a teaching. The Holy Prophet was sent to all mankind. This conception of divine teaching is the most comprehensive we can have. No people are left out of the plan of divine guidance. Today Islam is the only way, the only guide, because it is the last and the most perfect. With the arrival of the most perfect teaching, earlier teachings must be superseded. Their supersession is not only inevitable according to the Islamic teaching: it is also a patent fact of history. The books of earlier religions have been without divine

7 *Al-Fatir*, 25.

protection. They have suffered from human interpolation and extrapolation. They have become distorted. They are still true because of their divine origin, but they are also false because of the distortions they have suffered since. This conception of divine teaching over the ages which Hazrat Mirza Sahib expounded out of the Holy Quran proved irresistible. Should anyone choose to reject this conception, he will have to admit that God gives guidance to some people but not to others, an idea no man with sound common sense can accept. If, however, it is admitted that God's guidance has been received everywhere, at all times, then the truth of Islam cannot be questioned, because Islam is the last religion and it is Islam which teaches how God's guidance reached different peoples in different times.

This view of God's guidance has a peculiar appeal. Men of education and wide sympathies, subscribing to any religious views, are impressed and persuaded by it. They find that the conception is not easy to deny. The denial of it entails denial of God. If they cannot deny God, nor the Islamic conception of God's guidance, they have to accept Islam. They have no other alternative. The narrow and confused view of divine guidance which prevailed before was changed into a genuinely liberal, clearly formulated view of divine guidance by the Promised Messiah. This, among other things, made for the victory of Islam in our time.

A new outlook in religious debates

The fourth method of approach which Hazrat Mirza Sahib employed for a demonstration of the superiority of Islam consisted of a new conception of religious controversies. This conception also proved irresistible and unanswerable; and again, the conception was defined under divine guidance. Its formulation changed all current conceptions and methods of religious debates. Hazrat Mirza Sahib proposed rational and equitable criteria for the assessment of religious claims. The enemies of Islam could find no fault with them; nor if they accepted them, could they hold their own against Islam. If they rejected the criteria, they were defeated. If they accepted them, they were likewise defeated. The enemies of Islam had no chance in the conflict and no escape from it.

What was this new conception of religious debate? Before the time of Hazrat Mirza Sahib religious debates were of unlimited scope. One side in a debate could raise any objections it liked against the other side. At the same time it could make any claim it liked on its own behalf. With such unlimited scope, there was no end to religious debating and no end to the bitterness it produced; and all this, without any benefit to the human quest for truth. If a race is to have a result, it must be run according to some rules. Without rules we cannot spot the winner. For instance, if no direction is appointed for the participants, we can never name the winner. So it was with religious disputants. Even they must have a direction set for them. Before Hazrat Mirza Sahib's time, a religious disputant could attribute any conception he liked to his books. That conception could have been borrowed from some other book or from some other teaching. But a religious exponent could say it belonged to his religion, his book. The ensuing debate was not about any existing religious conception but about imaginary conceptions: at the most, conceptions entertained by individual disputants, not by the religions they disputed about. Seekers after truth derived no help from such debates. After the fullest discussion they stood just where they did before. Hazrat Mirza Sahib showed the futility of this sort of debating. He laid down the principle that if a divine book is divine and meant for the guidance of mankind, it must speak for itself. It must lay down its teaching in its own clear words. It must also lay down the arguments which it wishes to urge for its teaching. If a divine book fails to state its teaching and its arguments clearly, that divine book is of little use to anyone. If the teaching and the arguments for the teaching are to be formulated by the votaries, what use is the divine book? Can the religion which such a book teaches be divine? No, it must be a man-made religion. For it we owe nothing to God. Instead, God owes something to us, because we formulate both the teaching and the arguments for Him. Hazrat Mirza Sahib taught that for the successful conclusion of religious debates and discussions, it was necessary that votaries of revealed books should not attribute any teaching to those books unless they could cite the teaching from the books, and unless they could also cite from them the arguments for that teaching. The criterion of the merit of religious arguments proved a mighty one. The advocates of other religions could not object to it, for objecting to it would have meant that the teachings attributed to particular religious books did not exist in those books.

If they did exist, they should be found and quoted. Further, if any teachings could be quoted, it should be possible also to quote from the books themselves the arguments on which the teachings were based. Certainly it was not too much to ask this. The human mind fashioned by God is rational, and it refused to acccept a proposition not based on rational grounds. It is impossible that God should invite men to accept propositions without citing any reasons in support of them. Advocates of religious books, therefore, could not take exception to this criterion; it would have been an admission of weakness. But neither did they find it easy to accept the criterion. Many people will be surprised to learn that when the claims of other religions were examined in the light of this criterion, it was found that nine out of ten claims made on their behalf were not supported by the revealed books to which they were attributed. When teaching attributed to the books could be quoted from the books, it was seldom or never supported by arguments provided by the books themselves, as if God was able to put forward large propositions but had to depend upon others for the arguments.

Hazrat Mirza Sahib in this way demonstrated that advocates of different religions invented high-sounding principles or borrowed beautiful thoughts from others and attributed them to their respective religions. They then confronted the advocates of rival religions with these inventions. Futile debates ensued. If such propositions could be proved superior and strong, they would prove only their own superiority and strength or the superiority and strength of the minds of their authors. It would not prove the superiority of their religions if the propositions which had been proved superior and strong were not to be found in the religious books to which they were attributed. Against all this, Hazrat Mirza Sahib showed that all the teachings and claims which Islam put forward could be quoted from its book, the Holy Quran. The arguments for those teachings can also be quoted from the book. Hazrat Mirza Sahib illustrated this in many different ways and on many different occasions. The enemies of Islam were defeated. They found it impossible to meet the challenge or to escape its fatal results. The challenge is and will remain unanswered. It invites religious disputants to a criterion which it is impossible not to accept and which, if accepted, makes impossible the dissemination of false claims or the application of false standards in religious debates. The more Muslims insist on this criterion, the more the advocates of false religions will withdraw from the field. The weakness of their position will become more and more clear to their followers, and the triumph of Islam over other religions will become more and more evident.

Nearness to God, the measure of religious truth

The fifth method of approach which Hazrat Mirza Sahib (peace be on him) employed in his controversy with other religions proved completely fatal for them. It brought Islam a victory which nobody could question. Hazrat Mirza Sahib reminded the enemies of Islam that the ultimate object of religion was to enable man to establish contact with God. Therefore, an important criterion of truth among religions was the degree and quality of contact which each religion succeeded in promoting between God and man. Such contact connoted the degree of truth present in each religion. With it we could determine how far a given religion was acceptable to God. Contact between man and God should have visible signs. We know from ordinary experience that when two things come into contact with each other, each has some effect on the other. When we go near a fire we burn or at least experience the heat, and when we drink water we slake our thirst and become bright and braced up. Good food adds to our weight. Exercise tones the muscles and lends beauty and form to the body. Similarly, drugs have their effects, helping or hampering the normal functions of the body. It would be the strangest thing in the world if contact with God were found to have no effect whatever – if we were to prostrate ourselves in prayer for incredibly long periods, fast almost unto death, give to charity to the end of our resources, and yet experience no change in ourselves or in the conditions in which we live. If all our religious works, our penances and our sacrifices are to end in nothing, why should we seek any nearness to God? What good is it to us? When we establish nearness to an earthly ruler and prove ourselves deserving of his attention and favour, we experience the results of nearness. We receive honour and esteem. Our petitions are heard, our troubles removed. Others who observe us from afar feel that we enjoy the favour and attention of the ruler. But nothing can be known or seen of the results of a man's contact with God. No effects can be observed in terms of self-improvement or in terms of our relations with others. We continue as we were.

Living religion

Hazrat Mirza Sahib insisted that a religion which claims to be a living religion produces visible results for those who act upon its teachings and its provisions. A true follower of such a religion should find God and enjoy His favour. Such nearness between God and man should also have some signs. Advocates of different religions, therefore, should desist from attacking one another, from making large claims on their own religion's behalf, and from pointing to the weaknesses of other religions. Instead they should provide evidence of spiritual life and vitality which they have derived from the practical observance of their religion. They should show what degree of nearness to God they have acquired through their religion. They should present examples of individuals who have practised their religions and reaped the spiritual benefits which the religions promise. A religion which proves its worth by criteria of this kind should be accepted as living and true. A religion which cannot prove its worth in this way should be rejected as dead and false. It burdens its followers instead of bearing their burdens. It does harm rather than good. Association with it brings disgrace in this world and punishment in the next. This criterion of a living religion could not be questioned. As soon as it was proposed, it fell like lightning on other religions. They began to look about for a method of saving themselves from disgrace. The Promised Messiah proclaimed that evidence of life was to be found only in Islam. Other religions were wholly devoid of it. Did anybody wish to question this? If so, he had only to enter into a trial of strength with the Promised Messiah. Nobody dared, and there was nothing to wonder at in this. No religion had any life left in it. Loud and vociferous advocacy of one's religion is easy. To put forward evidence of God's love and concern is difficult. Did God love a given religion? Was He interested in it? The current religions could offer no evidence of even fleeting attention by God. How could they offer evidence of his love and interest?

A Bishop challenged

The Promised Messiah's challenge was addressed to Hindus, Christians, Jews, everybody. But nobody came forward. In different ways and on different occasions he invited leaders of other religions to test the quality of contact with God. But to no avail. He invited the Bishop of Lahore, the head of the large diocese of North India, to have a trial with him over the efficacy of prayer. Had not the New Testament promised that if Christians had faith equal to a mustard seed, they would be able to move mountains? Muslims, likewise, had been told in their books that true believers could rely on the help and support of God and on the success of their prayers. It was fitting for the Bishop, therefore, to join in prayer to God and find out whose prayer was heard – a Christian's or a Muslim's. The Bishop turned a deaf ear. He found it safe to ignore the Promised Messiah's challenge. The Bishop's silence proved exasperating. Some English-edited newspapers attacked the Bishop. Bishops drew fat salaries and made loud claims, they said, but when it came to a contest or trial of some sort, they withdrew from the field. The Bishop was not to be moved. In spite of criticism, in spite of ridicule, he kept putting off the challenge.

The Promised Messiah repeated the challenge again and again. But nobody dared accept it. This approach on behalf of Islam proved as unanswerable as all the others. Every right-thinking person must acknowledge its importance and relevance. Its result was victory for Islam. Non-Muslims must become more and more aware of the lack of life in their respective religions. At the same time, they must also become aware of the visible life in Islam. The superiority of the truth of Islam must become more and more evident. In theoretical discussions one can feel undefeated to the end, but when an issue is a practical and a factual one, the truth must be found on one side or the other. This approach proposed and used by the Promised Messiah must show its deadly effects as time goes on. In the view of the right-thinking men, Islam has already won. No other religion can claim to be alive. The victory of Islam is already apparent.

The five types of approach employed by the Promised Messiah on behalf of Islam led Islam to victory over other religions. The work of the Promised Messiah is therefore done. If Hazrat Mirza

Sahib is not the Promised Messiah, then the question is: What more will the true Messiah do when he comes? Will he convert people to Islam at the point of the sword? What use will forcible conversions be to Islam, or to the converts? Consider a little: if Christians were to start converting Muslims by force, what should all of us and other decent men think and say of them? Should we not say this was wicked and foolish? Should we not then condemn the true Messiah in the same way for doing the same thing? No, no, no. Forcible accessions to Islam would be a menace. They would harm Islam immeasurably and would turn all decent and freedom-loving men against it. The 'Promised' Messiah should have no use for the sword. His method must be the method of argument. By argument by rational approach, by appeal to observation and experience, Hazrat Mirza Sahib has already proved Islam victorious. Hazrat Mirza Sahib, therefore, is the Promised Messiah. He has done what the Promised Messiah was to do.

Sometimes it is said that the arguments used by Hazrat Mirza Sahib were not his own arguments, but ones that existed already, so how can the victory of Islam brought about by such arguments be attributed to him? The objection is futile. A sword without a swordsman can accomplish very little. It can do its work only when someone can be found who can wield it. The situation of Islam at the time of the Promised Messiah was that the sword of argument which Islam had always used was present, but Muslims were not only not able to use it but were not even aware of its existence. The Promised Messiah received from God a fresh insight into the meaning of the Holy Quran. He deduced anew the truths of Islam and restated the arguments on which they were based. He then used those arguments in the defence of Islam and in Islam's battle against other religions. He taught the use of those arguments to his followers and others. The victory of Islam, therefore, is due to him. The Holy Quran, instead of helping Muslims and Islam, had become an encumbrance, a source of embarrassment for them. But for the Promised Messiah, it would have remained so. A gun without a gunner becomes a menace not for the enemy but for the owner. For want of understanding, the Holy Quran had become a burden, a liability. Hazrat Mirza Sahib announced his claim and created a new faith, a new hope. The blessings and benefits of the Holy Quran began to show. He met the enemies of Islam with arguments which they were powerless to resist. They first found themselves defending and later found even defence difficult. Some addressed memorials to the Government, praying it to stop Mirza Sahib's work on behalf of Islam. This was manifest defeat. The victory of Islam became certain. Nothing could now prevent its triumph over other religions.

Argument 5
Rejuvenation of Islam

The fifth argument for the truth of the claims of Hazrat Mirza Ghulam Ahmad (on whom be peace) is that he has rejuvenated Islam. He has restored Islam to purity and power. As this was the task appointed for the Promised Messiah and Mahdi, there can be no doubt that he is the Promised Messiah and Mahdi.

Un-Islamic conceptions current among Muslims

All thoughtful persons agree that Islam today is not the Islam which the Holy Prophet (on whom be peace and the blessings of God) taught to his Companions. The only people who disagree are the Maulvis, who have become insensitive to facts because of incessant religious discussions. There seems little doubt that something is wanting in the Islam of today. Of the Islam of the Holy Prophet's time we are told in the Holy Quran:

رُبَمَا يَوَدُّ الَّذِيْنَ كَفَرُوْا لَوْ كَانُوْا مُسْلِمِيْنَ۔

'Often will the disbelievers of Islam wish they were Muslims.'[1]

Is this the thought and sentiment of non-Muslims today? No, on the contrary, Islam is the object of derision and doubt. To say nothing of non-Muslims, Muslims themselves entertain doubts about many of the teachings of Islam. Some find fault with its basic teachings, others with its moral conceptions, still others with its regulations for daily life. The certainty and conviction which it once produced in the minds of its followers it no longer inspires today. Muslims today are not prepared to make the sacrifices they

1 *Al-Hijr*, 3.

were prepared to make at one time. This being so, we have to concede one of three possibilities. Either we must admit that the electrifying power of Islam of which we read in history is only fiction, an exaggeration by later generations of the second-rate achievements of their ancestors. Or we must admit that nobody tries to practise Islam today. Or we must admit that the Islam we practise is not the true Islam and thus Islam no longer produces the results which it should. It is the third alternative which seems true to the facts. The purifying power of Islam and its practical effectiveness are proved not only by the recorded Traditions of Islam but also by evidence to be found in all parts of the world. When Muslims understood and practised Islam correctly, they were progressive and dominant. Nor can it be said that nobody practises Islam today. Muslims of different persuasions and different conceptions practise the Islam in which they believe. There are Muslims who appoint for themselves the most difficult religious exercises and do not hesitate even to give their lives; yet they achieve nothing for themselves or for Islam. The conclusion is inevitable, therefore, that the conception of Islam present in the minds of Muslims today is not the true one. The Holy Prophet (on whom be peace and the blessings of God) said:

لَايَبْقَى مِنَ الْاِسْلَامِ اِلَّا اِسْمُهٗ -

'A time will come when nothing will be left of Islam except its name.'[2]

It seems that that time has come. Nothing is left of Islam except its name, that is, its superficial and external observances; the substance, the inner significance, is gone. The sort of Islam which is believed and practised today cannot produce the results which it produced at one time. Nor can this sort of Islam impress the followers of other religions as it once did. No doubt individuals belonging to other religions are attracted even today by its faded glory. But they are few, and they must be extraordinarily good at heart. Generally speaking, Islam no longer makes the appeal which it made at one time. The recorded Sayings of the Holy Prophet point to the same conclusion. On one occasion the Holy Prophet said:

2 Mishquat, Kitabul Ilm.

تَفْتَرِقُ اُمَّتِیْ عَلٰی ثَلَاثٍ وَّسَبْعِیْنَ مِلَّةً كُلُّهُمْ فِی النَّارِ اِلَّا مِلَّةً وَّاحِدَةً

'A time will come when my followers will become divided into seventy-three sects. All of them except one will deserve the fire.'[3]

Some in the audience asked who the Muslims were who would be on the side of the true Islam. The Holy Prophet answered:

قَالَ: مَا اَنَا عَلَیْهِ وَاَصْحَابِیْ۔

'. . . those who follow my example and the example of my Companions.'

On another occasion he said:

یَا اَیُّهَا النَّاسُ خُذُوْا مِنَ الْعِلْمِ قَبْلَ اَنْ یُّقْبَضَ الْعِلْمُ وَقَبْلَ اَنْ یُّرْفَعَ الْعِلْمُ

'O men, acquire knowledge before knowledge disappears.'

Those who heard him asked:

قِیْلَ: یَا رَسُوْلَ اللّٰهِ كَیْفَ یُرْفَعُ الْعِلْمُ وَهٰذَا الْقُرْاٰنُ بَیْنَ اَظْهُرِنَا۔

'O Prophet of God, how will knowledge disappear while we have the Holy Quran in our possession?'

The Holy Prophet replied:

فَقَالَ: اَیْ ثَكِلَتْكَ اُمُّكَ وَهٰذَا الْیَهُوْدُ وَالنَّصَارٰی بَیْنَ اَظْهُرِهِمُ الْمَصَاحِفُ
لَمْ یُصْبِحُوْا یَتَعَلَّقُوْنَ بِالْحَرْفِ مِمَّا جَاءَتْ بِهٖ اَنْبِیَاؤُهُمْ اَلَا وَاِنَّ
ذَهَابَ الْعِلْمِ اَنْ یَّذْهَبَ حَمَلَتُهٗ ثَلَاثَ مَرَّاتٍ۔

'In the same way in which it happened before. Your mother may have mercy on you. Do you not see that the Jews and the Christians possess their books? But they have not the least

3 *Tirmidhi*.

regard for the teachings contained in the books, which their prophets brought to them from God. Knowledge disappears from the earth when those who have knowledge disappear from the earth.'[4]

The last sentence the Holy Prophet repeated three times. It appears from the *Hadith* that a most critical time lay ahead for the Muslim community, the *Ummat* of the Holy Prophet. This critical time was the time when knowledge was to disappear from this world. At the same time it seems that when this time arrived a party would be found among Muslims which still adhered to the true Islam. This party was to be the party which would imitate the example of the Companions of the Holy Prophet. This party is none other than the party of the Promised Messiah, for the Holy Prophet (on whom be peace) has also said:

مَثَلُ اُمَّتِیْ مِثْلَ الْمَطَرِ لَا يُدْرٰی اَوَّلُهٗ خَيْرٌ اَمْ اٰخِرُهٗ

'My *Ummat* is like the rain. I do not know whether the better part of it is the earlier one or the later.'[5]

Therefore the Holy Prophet's words 'those who follow my example and the example of my Companions' refer to the followers of the Promised Messiah. In truth, no other party or group can answer to this description. No Muslim group can imitate the example of the Companions of the Holy Prophet unless they have seen a Messenger of God in the flesh, unless they have come under his spiritual influence.

Rejuvenation of Islam, a solemn divine promise

From the Tradition just quoted it follows that the rejuvenation of Islam, after the disappearance of true knowledge and true religion from among its followers, is God's solemn promise. It is therefore necessary that he who claims the office of the Promised Messiah should re-establish the true teaching of Islam and present to the

4 Mishquat, Babul Iatasam bis Sunnah.

5 Mishquat, chap. Sawab, Hazi-hil Ummat.

world the true meaning of the Holy Quran. If he fails in this, he cannot be the Promised Messiah. If, on the other hand, in the difficult days of which the Holy Prophet warned us, he manages to save Islam from the distortions introduced by ignorant followers, then he is the Promised Messiah. He and his followers answer to the description contained in the Holy Prophet's prophecy – 'those who follow my example and the example of my Companions'. It follows that we have in the rejuvenation of Islam a very important criterion for testing the truth of anyone who claims to be the Messiah. We have to see whether Islam, as understood and practised today, has deviated far from its authentic form. Having done this we have to see whether a given claimant to the office of Messiah has or has not restored Islam to that form.

That current Islam has deviated far from the original is admitted on all hands. It is admitted by all thoughtful persons. If there are persons, who deny this, they must be oblivious to practical realities. The Islam as practised today does not produce the old results. Islam as understood today fails to satisfy the conscience even of Muslims. These things prove that the Islam of today is very different from what it used to be. The only question that remains is whether or not Hazrat Mirza Ghulam Ahmad has presented to the world the pure and true Islam which, because of its genuine appeal and attractiveness, is able to draw all and sundry to itself. Has he not separated from the gold the dross which ungodly, ignorant and selfish Mullas had mixed up with it? To answer these questions, I proceed to give some examples of how Islam had become distorted and how it has been restored to its original beauty by Hazrat Mirza Ghulam Ahmad.

Conceptions contrary to *Tawhid*

The central teaching of religion is belief in God. For Islam, belief in God serves as the root from which other beliefs and obligations shoot out as branches and leaves. Belief in God is fundamental. Other beliefs are in the nature of elaborations or corollaries of this fundamental belief. The principal element of belief in God is belief in the Oneness of God. The Holy Prophet (on whom be peace and the blessings of God), from the announcement of his office as prophet right up to his death, kept on teaching the important and basic truth, 'There is no god but Allah.' He suffered all manner of physical and mental tortures but did not give up teaching this truth. When he was dying the only thought occupying his mind was this conception of the Unity and Oneness of God. He was afraid lest this important teaching should decline after he was gone; he had suffered so much for its establishment. Muslims read in the books of *Hadith* and history about the last moments of the Holy Prophet, lying ill with a fatal sickness, weak and exhausted and perspiring profusely. The sickness was growing worse. Thoughts of what might happen to his teaching now that he was going caused him much anxiety. Would Muslims forget what he had taught them for so long? Would they begin to set up equals with God? The anxiety was not about himself or his family, but about his followers, his *Ummat*. Oppressed by these thoughts, he turned over and over in bed, and as he turned he said:

لَعَنَ اللّٰهُ الْيَهُوْدَ وَالنَّصَارٰى اِتَّخَذُوْا قُبُوْرَ اَنْبِيَآئِهِمْ مَسَاجِدَ

> 'Curse of God on the Jews and the Christians! They turned the graves of their prophets into objects of worship.'[6]

In saying this he clearly meant to warn his followers against the tendency to raise human teachers to the status of God, Who is the One, and the Only One. Prophets are only men. In the last moments of his earthly life, no other thought troubled him. He wanted his followers to remember and to worship only God. So persuasive and full of pathos are these words that, on hearing them, those who felt the least love for the Holy Prophet resolved never even to think of *shirk* (of compromising the Oneness of God). They wished to repudiate the least tendency to set up anything or anyone as being in any way equal to God. But, reader, you are well aware that Muslims today – a very large number of them – indulge in open denunciation of a teaching which the Holy Prophet thought it necessary to warn Muslims about on his deathbed. Who could imagine that Muslims, who thirteen hundred years earlier had laid down their lives for the defence of the pure conception of *Tawhid*, would begin to worship their saints and turn towards their graves, even for daily prayers; that they would attribute knowledge of the

6 Bukhari, chap. Miraj-un-Nabi *Sallallaho Alai-hi-Wassalam*.

unseen to mortal human beings; that they would endow their holy men with privilege over the Power of God; that they would address prayers to the dead and would make offerings over their graves; that they would credit their preceptors with the power to persuade God; that they would credit them with miraculous presence in any place at any time; that they would sacrifice animals in the name of those other than God! Worst of all, they would do all this and say it is the teaching of the Holy Quran and the Holy Prophet! But, God be thanked, while the teaching of the Holy Prophet about the One God is being dishonoured by Muslims everywhere, while the greater number of them are indulging in un-Islamic beliefs and actions, the grave of the Holy Prophet himself is safe from such desecration. Out of His regard for the dying thought of His Prophet, God made his grave immune to such evil use. But the graves of the other great ones of Islam are not so immune. They are the scene of idolatrous activities hardly different from the activities of Hindus in their temples. If the Holy Prophet (on whom be peace and the blessings of God) were to come and see his followers today, he would not think they were Muslims, but maybe followers of some pagan faith.

It may be said that those idolatrous beliefs and practices are confined only to the ignorant and the illiterate, that the educated classes are sick of them. But the general condition of a people is judged from the condition of its rank and file. If the common run of Muslims are victims of such thoughts and practices, we have to admit that Muslims have gone back on the *Tawhid* which the Holy Prophet taught them. The thought 'No God but Allah' is the soul and spirit of Islam. This soul and spirit Muslims have forgotten. Nor is it only common Muslims who hold these beliefs and indulge in these practices. Religious leaders and Maulvis also indulge in them and are at one with their followers in this. If at heart they do not approve of these beliefs and practices, why do they not denounce them by their words? It is obvious that they have no self-confidence. They are afraid of alienating their followers. All this is evidence of the general decadence of faith in the Unity and Oneness of God.

True, there are puritanical sects among Muslims who think they are free from the least tendency to compromise with the Oneness of God. They protest against other Muslims and think they damage Islam by indulging in *shirk*. But the amazing thing is that the puritans themselves commit *shirk*. The difference between them and common Muslims is that whereas common Muslims set up many a saint and religious precepter as equal to God, the elect among Muslim *Ulema* set up only Jesus Christ as His equal. Like common Muslims they believe that Jesus is alive in heaven. The Holy Prophet (peace and the blessings of God be on him), the best of all Prophets and their Chief, is buried in the earth; but Jesus Christ has been alive in Heaven now for two thousand years. The time of his death is not yet come. They read clearly in the Holy Quran that the saints and the holy ones who are worshipped besides God are dead. Nobody even knows when they will be raised to life again. As the Holy Quran says,

اَمْوَاتٌ غَيْرُ اَحْيَآءٍ ۚ وَمَا يَشْعُرُوْنَ اَيَّانَ يُبْعَثُوْنَ ۔

'. . . they are dead, not living; and they know not when they will be raised.'[7]

They also know that Christians worship Jesus Christ besides God. Reading this verse in the Holy Quran and knowing that Christians worship Jesus besides God, they still cannot give up the belief that Jesus is alive in Heaven. And holding this belief, they still think that they believe in the Oneness and Unity of God.

Similarly, they protest against other people committing *shirk*, but themselves believe that Jesus Christ could restore the dead to life. They read in the Holy Quran:

وَحَرَامٌ عَلٰى قَرْيَةٍ اَهْلَكْنٰهَا اَنَّهُمْ لَا يَرْجِعُوْنَ ۔

'And it is an inviolable law for those whom We have destroyed that they shall not return.'[8]

This is God's unalterable way. The dead ones do not return to life here. We read elsewhere:

وَمِنْ وَّرَآئِهِمْ بَرْزَخٌ اِلٰى يَوْمِ يُبْعَثُوْنَ ۔

7 *Al-Nahl*, 22.

8 *Al-Anbiya*, 96.

> 'And behind them is a barrier until the day on which they shall be raised again.'[9]

From this also it is clear that those who are dead are, as it were, on the other side of a barrier. They will remain there until the Day of Judgment and will not come back to life before then.

The above sect of Islam is the Ahl-i-Hadith sect. They attach great importance to *Hadith*, the recorded Sayings of the Holy Prophet, but they forget what the Holy Prophet has said about the dead returning to life. When Jabir's father, Abdullah, was dying, God asked whether he had a dying wish. Abdullah said he wished to live so that he might join the Holy Prophet in Jehad and die in the way of God, that he might live again and die again in the way of God, and so on. At this God said:

إِنَّهُ قَدْ سَبَقَ مِنِّيْ أَنَّهُمْ لَا يَرْجِعُوْنَ

> 'Had I not promised to Myself never to do so, I would have given you life. As I have bound Myself to this, I shall not do so.'[10]

People do not seem to remember that restoring the dead to life is not permitted by God in this world. It is His fundamental obligation not to do so. How could Jesus Christ expect otherwise? True, the Holy Quran uses the words:

أُحْيِ الْمَوْتٰى

> 'I will quicken the dead'

and the words are applied to Jesus, but the same words have been used in the Holy Quran about the Holy Prophet. But no Maulvi attributes to the Holy Prophet the power to give life to the dead.

The Holy Quran says:

يٰٓاَيُّهَا الَّذِيْنَ اٰمَنُوا اسْتَجِيْبُوْا لِلّٰهِ وَلِلرَّسُوْلِ اِذَا دَعَاكُمْ لِمَا يُحْيِيْكُمْ

9 *Al-Muminun*, 101.
10 Tirmidhi Kitabut-Tafsir, Surah Al-Imran.

'O ye who believe, respond to Allah and the Messenger, when he calls you that he may give you life.'[11]

'Giving life', when the expression is used in relation to the Holy Prophet, means giving spiritual life to those who are spiritually dead. When such a meaning of *Ihya* (giving life) is possible and when we know that only God can restore the dead to life, when we know also that those who are dead will not be restored to life in this world, why can we not put a spiritual interpretation on the word *Ihya* when it is used about Jesus Christ? Why do we attribute to these verses of the Holy Quran a meaning inconsistent with the rest of the Holy Book a meaning which clearly lands us in *shirk*?

These votaries of the Oneness of God believe, and believe firmly, that Jesus Christ was able to create birds. Yet they read in the Holy Quran that God is the Only Creator. The Holy Quran says:

وَالَّذِيْنَ يَدْعُوْنَ مِنْ دُوْنِ اللّٰهِ لَا يَخْلُقُوْنَ شَيْئًا وَّهُمْ يُخْلَقُوْنَ۔

'And those on whom they call beside Allah create not anything but they are themselves created.'[12]

Again it says:

اَمْ جَعَلُوْا لِلّٰهِ شُرَكَآءَ خَلَقُوْا كَخَلْقِهٖ فَتَشَابَهَ الْخَلْقُ عَلَيْهِمْ قُلِ اللّٰهُ
خَالِقُ كُلِّ شَيْءٍ وَّهُوَ الْوَاحِدُ الْقَهَّارُ۔

'Or, do they assign to Allah partners who have created the like of His creation, so that the *two* creations appear similar to them? Say, "Allah *alone* is the Creator of all things, and He is the One, the Most Supreme."'[13]

And again it says:

اِنَّ الَّذِيْنَ تَدْعُوْنَ مِنْ دُوْنِ اللّٰهِ لَنْ يَّخْلُقُوْا ذُبَابًا وَّلَوِ اجْتَمَعُوْا لَهٗ

11 *Al-Anfal*, 25.
12 *Al-Nahl*, 21.
13 *Al-Ra'd*, 17.

> 'Surely, those on whom you call instead of Allah cannot create even a fly though they were to combine together for the purpose.'[14]

They read these verses of the Holy Quran and yet attribute the power of creation to Jesus Christ, and he is one of those on whom people call instead of Allah.

In short, the Holy Quran unambiguously teaches that only God creates. If anybody else were able to do so, then he also would be worthy of worship. Yet when they come upon verses like 'I will fashion out in you a creation out of clay after the manner of a bird' (3:50), they think that it proves that Jesus Christ could create birds out of clay. They do not remember that a given word can have many meanings. Why attribute to a given word in a given place a meaning which is inappropriate to man or God? Why should they lend that word a meaning contrary to the fundamental teaching of God elsewhere, a meaning which detracts from the Oneness and Glory of God? Why should they profess pure belief in the Oneness of God and yet set up equals with Him? These are dangerous deviations from pure belief in *Tawhid* (Oneness) to which Muslims, learned or ignorant, Sunnis or Shias, of one sect or another, are committed. In the face of these deviations nobody can say that Muslims still believe in 'No God but Allah'. No doubt Muslims still profess belief in this and they still recite this part of the *Kalima*. But they also entertain beliefs contrary to Divine Oneness; so Muslims have moved as far from the true teaching of God as the nations and peoples who hold pagan beliefs. To correct these deviations and to bring Muslims back to the true conception of the Oneness of God, Hazrat Mirza Ghulam Ahmad (on whom be peace) re-stated and re-asserted the true Islamic conception. His exposition of this conception is so true to the original spirit of Islam, and so attractive, that anyone who accepts it finds anew the old love of God as well as the old abhorrence of *shirk*, once a distinctive feature of Muslims. It restores belief in the One God and saves us from the danger of compromising with this belief. One re-acquires the conception of *Tawhid* held by the Companions of the Holy Prophet. Hazrat Mirza Sahib refuted these un-Islamic beliefs by strong arguments. He re-affirmed the Oneness of God.

14 *Al-Hajj*, 74.

God is One and the Only One. To call upon any dead person, to make offerings at the graves of the dead, to make obeisance to anyone alive or dead, to attribute distinctive divine powers or divine knowledge even to a prophet of God, to slaughter animals in the name of anyone other than God, to offer anything else to achieve the pleasure of that one, to think that any man, however holy, can persuade God to grant anything – such beliefs, or tendencies to such beliefs, are compromises with the pure conception of the Oneness of God which Islam has taught.

Hazrat Mirza Sahib also proved that Jesus Christ like other prophets died a natural death and was buried underground somewhere in this world. He gave spiritual life to the spiritually dead, not physical life to the physically dead. He created as any man can create. But restoring the physically dead to physical life was not for him. He could not create life out of death, with or without the permission of God. God is jealous about His special attributes. He does not share them with anyone. The teaching of the Holy Quran is against any such thought. The special divine powers are special to God. They cannot be shared by Jesus Christ or any other human being. Those who compromise with the Oneness of God in different degrees, use this very defence, namely, that the divine powers they attribute to certain men have been bestowed on them by God Himself, that those men have not become deities independent of the One God.

Hazrat Mirza Sahib re-stated the Islamic teaching – the teaching which is true to human conscience and human understanding. He dispelled the darkness of pagan beliefs which had crept into the minds of Muslims and showed again the true path which had been abandoned. He did what the Messiah of the Prophecy was to do.

Strange conceptions about angels

Among the fundamental beliefs of Islam, belief in angels is next to belief in God. This belief also has become distorted in various ways. According to some, angels could sin. They could criticize God. In accounts of Adam, angels are represented as critics standing before God, urging objections of one kind or another against His scheme of creation. It is forgotten that the account of Adam in the Holy Quran puts the highest praises of God in the mouths of the angels:

نَحْنُ نُسَبِّحُ بِحَمْدِكَ وَنُقَدِّسُ لَكَ-

'We glorify Thee with Thy praise and extol Thy Holiness.'[15]

The angels affirm that they only praise God and extol His Wisdom, Power and Holiness. The story of Harut and Marut, a complete invention, has found currency in Muslim theology. It is said that God sent two angels masquerading as men. They fell in love with an evil woman. For punishment they were hung in a well, head downwards (God save us). It is also said, God forbid, that Iblis or Satan was a leader among angels. Another belief about angels which has crept into the Muslim mind is that angels are physical beings engaged in crude physical activities. They run hither and thither on errands of different kinds. The angel Izrael has to run here and there. Being the angel of death he has to take now this man's life, now that man's.

Against such primitive conceptions we have, at the other extreme, a complete denial of angels. According to some modernists angels are imaginary beings. The teaching of the Holy Quran on the subject of angels is interpreted by them in naturalistic ways. Angels, it is said, represent different kinds of physical forces. Some among Muslims deny outright the teaching of the Holy Quran and *Hadith*. They do not think that the message of the Quran was brought by Gabriel. They raise other objections to the Quranic teaching about angels. Belief in angels, they say, is derogatory to the Power of God.

Hazrat Mirza Sahib corrected these misconceptions, taught the true teaching of Islam on the subject, and removed the objections and difficulties raised by some classes of Muslims over this delicate subject. He proved that angels do not commit sins. Nor do they criticize God's plans. We have the clear teaching of God in the Holy Quran:

لَا يَعْصُوْنَ اللّٰهَ مَآ اَمَرَهُمْ وَيَفْعَلُوْنَ مَا يُؤْمَرُوْنَ-

'They disobey not Allah in what He commands them, and do as they are commanded.'[16]

15 *Al-Baqarah*, 31.

16 *Al-Tahrim*, 7.

Angels are a special kind of creation. They are set to do certain things in certain ways. Their essence is complete and perfect submission, without the freedom to do otherwise. Can such creatures sin? The very nature bestowed on them by God forbids such a thought. To make love to evil women is impossible for them. They cannot forget God and involve themselves in divine punishment. If angels can sin, why have we been asked to believe in them? Belief indicates obedience, and God cannot ask us to obey beings capable of error and disobedience. To obey beings who can disobey is unthinkable.

Hazrat Mirza Sahib also taught that angels are spiritual beings. They do not have to move about to go from one place to another. Their powers and functions are exercised from their own positions. They are like the sun, whose light and heat are emitted from a certain centre, and like the sun they carry out the commands of God. In executing divine commands they use the powers with which they are endowed. They do what they are told.

Hazrat Mirza Sahib also refuted the idea that Satan was one of the angels or a leader among angels. Satan, according to the teaching of Islam, was an evil spirit. God says about him: 'And he [Satan] was one of the disbelievers' (2:35), a born disbeliever.

Hazrat Mirza Sahib also corrected the belief which had crept among modern educated Muslims that angels are only imaginary beings or symbols of certain physical forces. He quoted his own experience and observation in support of his belief in angels. He argued against those who said that a belief in angels was derogatory to a belief in the Power of God. God gave us eyes; but He also made light and colours to enable us to see. He gave us ears; but He also made air and other media to enable us to hear. Belief in light and in air and other media is not derogatory to a belief in the Power of God. So how can belief in angels be derogatory to His Power? It seems that God works with means and media; they are a part of His eternal wisdom. He uses them in His spiritual creation. He brings about physical changes through them and also spiritual changes. Hazrat Mirza Sahib showed that means and media do not connote defects in the Power of God. They are provided so that finite human beings with limited sensibility can become aware of what goes on around them. Angels as the spiritual means and media with which God works in the realm of spirit are meant to help the limited understanding of ordinary human beings. In this way

Hazrat Mirza Sahib explained the true meaning of belief in angels. He presented angels as God and His Prophet would have presented them.

Misconceptions about the Holy Quran

The third fundamental belief, according to Islam, is belief in the revealed books. Belief in revealed books underwent curious changes. Muslims had come to entertain strange thoughts about revealed books, in particular about the Holy Quran. We are not concerned with other revealed books; we are concerned first and last with the Holy Quran. For us, Muslim belief in other revealed books is secondary, belief in the Holy Quran primary. Other books do not exist in their original form, nor are we obliged to act upon their distorted teachings.

The thoughts which Muslims had come to entertain about the Holy Quran were very strange indeed. They seem more strange to me because I have learnt the truth about the Holy Book from the Promised Messiah. Indeed, but for him, even I would have accepted many a fable about the Holy Quran. The strangest thing taught and believed about the Holy Quran is that after the death of the Holy Prophet (on whom be peace and the blessings of God), the contents of the Holy Quran disappeared, if not *in toto* at least a large part did. According to some Muslim authorities even the present text of the Holy Quran contains evidence of human interference. Other authorities contradict thoughts of this kind. They even brand them as *Kufr*. But they teach other things about the Holy Quran which are no less obnoxious. For instance, they teach that parts of the Quran have become abrogated. The basis of abrogation is apparent inconsistency between parts. If a verse or a passage is found 'contradicted' by another, it must be considered abrogated. Emboldened by this, other Muslims, pointing to other 'inconsistencies' in the Holy Text, started applying the theory of abrogation to other parts of the Book. Verses said—by different authorities—to have been abrogated add up to a very considerable number. According to the standard theory, a large part of the Holy Quran stands abrogated and Muslims are no longer obliged to believe in or act upon it. (God, save us from such evil thoughts.)

The evil results of this theory of abrogation go very far. Not only have some parts of the Holy Quran become abrogated, according to some authorities; the trust and reliance which early Muslims placed in every part of the Holy Quran is now gone. Thoughtful Muslims are perturbed by the situation. Some parts stand abrogated, some not, but there is no certainty as to which is which. God and the Holy Prophet have not told them about it. How then can they rely on such a book? Apparently Muslims can treat their Holy Book as they like. Parts they do not favour, they can dismiss as abrogated. Parts they favour they can accept as not abrogated.

A misconception about revealed books, especially the Holy Quran, is that no revealed book is completely free from the evil influence of Satan. It is said that Satan mixes up his own speech with the speech of God as it descends to a human recipient. The authority of the Holy Quran is cited in support of this fantastic belief. Verse 22:53 is the supposed authority:

وَمَآ اَرْسَلْنَا مِنْ قَبْلِكَ مِنْ رَّسُوْلٍ وَّلَا نَبِيٍّ اِلَّآ اِذَا تَمَنّٰٓى اَلْقَى
الشَّيْطٰنُ فِيْٓ اُمْنِيَّتِهٖ۔

It is usually translated as follows:

> 'And We have not sent before thee any Messenger or Prophet but when he had any messages, Satan mixed up with them his own messages.'[17]

The crucial word in the verse is *Umniyah*. In the context of the verse the translation of this word is 'plan' rather than 'message'. The Arabic language permits both meanings, but Muslim commentators somehow preferred the wrong meaning. *Umniyah* translated as 'plan' would make the verse perfectly intelligible. The verse would then mean that whenever prophets have sought to carry out their plans, Satan has put obstacles in the way. Muslim commentators have not been content with this fairy tale alone. They have gone further. They have cited examples of verses revealed to the Holy Prophet with which Satan mixed up certain words invented by himself. It is said that the Holy Prophet was reciting verses of *Surah Najm*. When he reached the words 'Now tell me about Lat and Uzza; And Manat, the third one, another goddess' (53:20, 21),

17 *Al-Hajj*, 53.

Satan mixed up with the revealed words the words 'these goddesses with artistic long necks can serve as intercessors'. These words which, it is said, came from Satan were also recited by the Holy Prophet as part of the revealed passage. Among the audience were some non-believers. When they heard this unexpected praise of their goddesses, they prostrated themselves. The Holy Prophet was surprised. Later he realized that the words in praise of the pagan goddesses had been introduced by Satan. The Holy Prophet was embarrassed at the realization.

The whole incident is a fabrication, but how easily Muslim commentators have accepted it.

Some commentators have produced another account. Finding the common version of it utterly nonsensical, they suggest that the words attributed to Satan were not introduced by Satan into the Prophet's recitation but were added by Satan in his own voice modulated like the Prophet's. The audience thought that the words came from the Prophet's lips. This second account is as silly as the first. With either, the Holy Quran as a revealed book remains no longer the indubitable and absolutely reliable revelation which Muslims believe it to be. If Satan is capable of introducing his own speech into any revealed speech, no prophetic revelation can be treated as a pure divine communication. However, Muslim commentators point to a solution of this difficulty. It is in the verse which follows and which says:

فَيَنْسَخُ اللّٰهُ مَا يُلْقِي الشَّيْطٰنُ ثُمَّ يُحْكِمُ اللّٰهُ اٰيَاتِهٖ وَاللّٰهُ عَلِيْمٌ حَكِيْمٌ

> 'But Allah removes the contamination due to Satan and re-establishes His own communications and Allah is Knowing, Wise.'[18]

This is no solution of the difficulty. Once it is admitted that Satan is capable of interpolating his own words into the divine communications, we cannot say whether a given text is free from such interpolation or not. Supposing it is said that the verse which promises the expurgation of the Satanic admixture is itself a Satanic interpolation: we then have no guarantee that the Holy Quran is a pure revelation of God.

18 *Al-Hajj*, 53.

Relative authority of the Holy Quran and the Hadith

Many have reduced the authority of the Holy Quran *vis-à-vis* the *Hadith* (the Traditions of the Holy Prophet). Weak and even fabricated Traditions have been raised to a level higher than that of the Holy Quran. In the name of loyalty to the Holy Prophet, communications of the Mighty God have been dishonoured by selfish and low-minded theologians. The Holy Quran may deny a thing most clearly; but if a weak *Hadith* can be found which deals with the same subject it will be set above the text of the Holy Quran. Similarly, the Holy Quran may assert a thing most clearly; but if a weak *Hadith* can be found contrary to the same thing, the *Hadith* will be set above the Holy Quran.

Some Muslims think that the Holy Quran is not the speech of God but the speech of the Holy Prophet himself. They describe the Holy Book as divine, even as the Word of God. But their view is that thoughts and ideas which emerged in the clean and clear mind of the Holy Prophet were stimulated and supported by God. The speech of the Holy Quran thus becomes the speech of God. More strictly, the thoughts and ideas come from God, but the words in which they are clothed come from the Holy Prophet. God does not communicate the words. The communication of words entails a vocal apparatus which one cannot attribute to God! Therefore the thoughts come from God, the words from the Holy Prophet!

Some Muslims think that the Holy Quran cannot be translated. But ordinary Muslims can understand the Quran only through translations. So a ban on translations has prevented Muslims in general from understanding the Holy Book. What can come of such a ban except ignorance, reaction, and irreligion?

Some think that the Holy Quran is a book containing broad philosophical principles. Determinate teaching here and there does not mean the book can give us detailed guidance.

Some think that the words of the Holy Quran need not always be read in the order in which they are recorded, that they are subject to what is called *Taqdim* and *Takhir*, because of which the apparent order of words may be altered to reach the meaning.

Some have collected all the fictitious stories they could find, whether they have a bearing or not. They may be repugnant to common understanding or conscience, they may be contrary to the plain teaching of the Holy Quran, but they have been admitted into commentaries as Israelite material. The stories are attributed to saints and holy men who lived long ago and who can have no knowledge of what has since been attributed to them.

Some deny that there is any rational order or sequence of meaning between parts of the Holy Quran, between verse and verse, chapter and chapter. They openly declare that the contents of the Holy Book are a disjointed assortment, more like the utterances of a man who is not aware of what he is talking about. Subjects entirely unconnected with one another are introduced in succession. There is no rational connection.

A very general and very widespread view among Muslims is that somehow, for some reason, God no longer speaks to human beings. The divine attribute of *Takallum* (speech) has become suspended. God now sees and hears but does not speak.

In short, different sections of Muslims have proposed different views about the Holy Quran. The result is a dismemberment of the Holy Book. The beauty, grandeur, and living character of the Book have been destroyed, all in the name of service of the Holy Book! This is not service but disservice. The effect has been to alienate people from the Holy Book and make them indifferent to its influence.

Hazrat Mirza Sahib removed all these misconceptions. By powerful arguments he proved that the Holy Quran is the Last Message, the Last Law of God for man. No part of it is abrogated. It is immune to all abrogation. Whatever it teaches can be practised. No part of it really contradicts any other, so that no part stands in need of abrogation. Those who spot contradiction or inconsistency in it are ignorant or feeble of understanding. They project their own lack of understanding onto the Holy Book. The Holy Book, Hazrat Mirza Sahib taught, has not altered one little bit since it was revealed. Every word, every letter, remains as it was revealed to the Holy Prophet. Not only has the Book not altered in any way, it is incapable of such alteration. Neither the meaning nor the text can undergo any change. There can be neither interpolations nor extrapolations. God Himself is its Protector. He has provided both physical and spiritual means for its protection. Human interference can corrupt neither the text nor the teaching. It is wrong, therefore, to think that any verses or parts of verses have been superseded by any others, or that there has been any change in the Holy Book.

The slightest change is inconceivable. The Holy Quran today is secure in every sense of the word and will remain so in the future. To say that any part of the Holy Quran disappeared is an accusation against God. It means that God sent a perfect book for the guidance of man, but the perfect book could not maintain its perfection. It failed to fulfil its purpose even for a day. To think that the Holy Book is capable of alteration is to make the Holy Book unreliable. If the Holy Quran is subject to alteration, it is necessary that a new prophet and a new book should be sent for the guidance of mankind. It is against all reason to think that mankind should go without divine guidance even for a day.

Hazrat Mirza Sahib also proved that the Holy Quran – in fact, every kind of revelation – is proof against interference by Satan. It is impossible that Satan should mix his speech with the speech of God by overpowering the Prophet's vocal apparatus or by mimicking the Prophet's voice. Hazrat Mirza Sahib cited his own experience in this connection. Though only a humble follower of the Holy Prophet, a mere servant, revelations received even by him were free from doubt. How could any doubt be cast on revelations received by the Master? No doubt could, therefore, be cast on the Holy Quran. The Holy Quran was a guidance for all time. To think that such a revelation was subject to Satanic interference, even if it lasted for only a moment, was fatal.

Hazrat Mirza Sahib stressed the true character and status of the Holy Quran. He pointed out that the promise of divine protection had been fulfilled in most wonderful ways. Even the enemies of Islam had admitted that the Holy Quran had remained intact since its revelation. To try and match the *Hadith* with the Holy Quran was an insult to the Holy Book. It amounted to a rejection of the Holy Book. If there are *Hadith* which contradict the Holy Quran, they cannot be true *Hadith*. Even the Holy Prophet of God cannot go contrary to the Word of God. Nor have the various kinds of *Hadith* been as carefully collected or recorded as they could have been. The *Hadith*, therefore, cannot be equated with the Holy Quran. The *Hadith* has to occupy a place subordinate to the Holy Quran. If ever a contradiction is spotted between a *Hadith* and any part of the Holy Quran, it is the *Hadith* that we must give up. A contradictory *Hadith* is a witting or unwitting fabrication. It was commonly believed that details of religious duties and religious history have come to us through the *Hadith*. Hazrat Mirza Sahib taught that there was a third source of Islamic knowledge; the *Sunna*. By *Sunna* is meant the visible practice of the Holy Prophet, whatever the Holy Prophet did and whatever his Companions saw him do. What they acquired through direct imitation of the Holy Prophet was even more reliable than any alleged utterance of the Holy Prophet; the latter may have been transmitted through a long chain of narrators. The reliability of the *Sunna* rested on secure foundations. Millions of Muslims saw millions of other Muslims do certain things in certain ways and learnt to do those things in those ways. From them the practices were transmitted to other Muslims. Such well-established practices, persisting through generations of Muslims, do not contradict the Holy Quran. *Hadith* records are supposed to be utterances of the Holy Prophet. In the course of reporting, these utterances can become distorted, so that *Hadith* may contradict the Holy Quran. The reliability of *Hadith*, therefore, is open to question. If a *Hadith* contradicts any part of the Holy Quran, it deserves no attention. If, however, it is consistent with it and in accordance with it, it deserves acceptance. It then becomes a part of history, or historical evidence which cannot be dismissed without cause. Important truths would become lost if historical evidence were to be dismissed so easily.

Hazrat Mirza Sahib also demonstrated the futility of the view that the words of the Holy Quran are not divine, that they could be attributed to the Holy Prophet. Hazrat Mirza Sahib proved that the words, the vowels, and vowel points of the text of the Holy Quran are divine. The Holy Prophet himself was a Messenger, a communicator of the Word of God, not the author. It was wrong to think that as human speech entails the use of lips and a vocal apparatus, and as God cannot be said to possess such an apparatus, it is impossible to think of God speaking to man as one man speaks to another. Such thoughts are far-fetched. God is Unique. 'Nothing is like unto Him.' The powers and attributes of God cannot be thought of as being like those of human beings. If speech is impossible without vocal organs, so is the making of a thing impossible without the use of hands. It is crude to attribute to God hands similar to human hands. Must we then deny that God is our Creator? It follows that God can speak to man without the usual vocal apparatus, just as He can create without physical hands. Again, he cited his own experience and said that difficulties of this kind arose because of sheer ignorance. Those who are not strangers to the experience of revelation know what revelation can be. Hazrat Mirza Sahib said that revelations received by him were couched in words. If he could receive verbal revelation, why not the Holy Prophet, the Leader of mankind, the Elect, the Most Favoured of God (on whom be peace and the blessings of God)? Those who have no experience of revelation have no need to speculate about its nature and content. Ignorance is bad enough, but to volunteer opinions about matters about which we are ignorant is worse. It was futile, said he, for strangers to God to speculate about the ways of God.

Hazrat Mirza Sahib also refuted the view that the Word of God cannot be translated. How else could the meaning of the Holy Quran, its beauty and depth, be communicated to those who did not know Arabic? It was wrong to publish only translations of the Holy Book. If only translations were published, people would gradually forget the revealed text. It was even possible that translations made from translations would result in the obliteration of the original text. It was both useful and necessary for the text to accompany the translation. It was necessary also to promote a minimum knowledge of Arabic. Muslims should know Arabic to be able to read the Arabic Quran and receive benefits and blessings which they could receive in no other way. It was necessary to master at least the parts of the Arabic Quran used in the daily prayers.

Hazrat Mirza Sahib also refuted the view that the Holy Quran was a revealed book in general but not in particular, that it taught broad principles on certain matters but was always not to be taken too literally. Hazrat Mirza Sahib stressed the view that the Holy Quran was comprehensive and clear. It had laid down clearly all truths which man needed for his spiritual advancement. As such it had no parallel. But Muslims had ceased to reflect upon the contents of the Holy Book; therefore, they themselves were to blame if the meaning of the Holy Quran did not dawn upon them. The Holy Quran teaches:

لَّا يَمَسُّهُۥٓ إِلَّا ٱلْمُطَهَّرُونَ ۔

'None shall touch it except the clean and pure.'[19]

19 *Al-Waqiah*, 80.

To have access to the deeper meaning of the Holy Quran, it is necessary to be clean and pure. Those who are low of understanding are wont to project their low minds onto the Holy Quran. Hazrat Mirza Sahib showed how religious truths and principles could be derived from the Holy Quran itself. He discussed objections raised by the enemies of Islam against the Holy Book and proved that a clearer and a more comprehensive treatment of the moral, religious, and spiritual difficulties of man could not be found. The Holy Quran economizes on words, but underneath the words are oceans of meaning. A single phrase, a single sentence, can branch out into a number of different meanings. The text of the Holy Quran is miraculous because the same text can meet the changing needs of man. The needs of man change according to the time and the circumstances.

Hazrat Mirza Sahib also refuted the theory of *Taqdim* and *Takhir*. He taught that the words of the Holy Quran are set in the most appropriate places. The places appointed for them in the Holy Text cannot be altered without damaging the meaning. Only the ignorant believe that the words of the Holy Quran are subject to alteration of order. These words are to be read where they are. The place of each word is essential to its meaning. The beauty and variety of meaning depend on the word order adopted in the Holy Quran. By examples Hazrat Mirza Sahib showed that word order is a part of the Holy Text. Ignorance and lack of insight lead people to cast doubts on the subject.

Israelite stories

Hazrat Mirza Sahib also protested against the free use of Israelite stories for an understanding of the Holy Quran. Writers of commentaries had been misled by slender and superficial resemblances between accounts of the Holy Quran and accounts contained in Jewish literature. When accounts in the Holy Quran are different, it is because the Holy Quran does not accept the Jewish version. It is wrong in such cases to force on the Holy Quran accounts invented by others. The Holy Quran is not a book of fiction or even of history. It is not interested in narratives of past events except for their spiritual significance or as pointers to the future. References to past history are warnings that similar events are going to take place in the life of the Holy Prophet or in the subsequent history of Muslims. If accounts given in the Holy Quran of past events are to be construed so as to make them consistent with the elaborate versions of the same events in the books of the Jews, we only ruin the meaning which the Holy Quran wishes to convey. The Holy Quran bears witness against earlier books. The earlier books do not bear witness against the Holy Quran. To understand the meaning of the Holy Quran we need not draw on the evidence contained in the earlier books. To understand its meaning we need to draw on the Holy Quran itself. The meaning of the Quran is in the Quran. No outside help is needed.

Hazrat Mirza Sahib also proved that the Holy Quran was as perfect in *arrangement* – arrangement of chapters, verses, and words – as it was in its thought and its language. The themes of the Holy Book are connected. They do not succeed one another arbitrarily but arise naturally and inevitably out of one another. A perfect arrangement runs through the whole. From the first word of the first chapter to the last word of the last runs a rational arrangement. The Holy Quran has a perfect internal design. Its chapters, verses, and words follow a perfect plan. Those who ever become aware of this design go into ecstasy. When they compare the beauty of internal arrangement which they find in the Holy Quran with the beauty of arrangement in some human book, they find a world of difference. Those who have had no insight into the Holy Book hold the view that the Holy Book is full of disjointed themes or useless narrations. Their view is based on ignorance, or they are too quick to pronounce an opinion. Hazrat Mirza Sahib demonstrated the perfect arrangement running through the Holy Quran by examples. People were surprised.

Hazrat Mirza Sahib also refuted the idea that God does not now speak to man. He cited his own experience and said that the attributes of God are everlasting. Divine attributes do not lapse. If God continues to see and hear as He did in the past, He must also continue to speak. And God need not communicate laws and ordinances only. He also communicates assurances. Assurances of His pleasure, for instance. If such assurances were to cease, we would have no means left of finding out whether God was pleased with us or not. God must continue to speak, therefore. While there are human beings in the world, and while there are those amongst us who strive with sincerity for the realization of His pleasure and act on the teaching of Islam, God must continue to favour men with His verbal assurances. Hazrat Mirza Sahib thus removed the many misconceptions which had grown around revealed books and around the very institution of revelation. These misconceptions taken together had cast serious doubt on the value and validity of revealed books, including the Holy Quran. Hazrat Mirza Sahib rebuilt this part of a Muslim's faith on secure foundations. He disclosed the true nature and greatness of divine revelation and persuaded his followers and others to believe in and become aware of it again. He removed the error which had crept into the minds of both Muslims and others and revealed the truth about revelation. Muslim and non-Muslim alike saw the resplendent light of the Holy Quran. They could not open their eyes for the glare.

Misconceptions about prophets

The fourth fundamental belief taught by Islam is belief in prophets. This belief too had decayed. Lacking rational and spiritual insight, Muslims had corrupted their belief in prophets in many strange ways. Not only had the belief changed, it had become repulsive to Muslims as well as to others. The vile attacks which have been made on the personal character of the Holy Prophet (on whom be peace and the blessings of God) are due to the fantastic views which Muslims in our time had come to hold about prophets in general and about the Holy Prophet in particular. Christians and other critics of Islam draw more on the false traditions included in Muslims' books than on evidence which they themselves fabricate. These false traditions have become part of the everyday beliefs of Muslims. They narrate them in daily conversation and in weekly sermons, to the sorrow of all self-respecting Muslims. Enemies of Islam are seen attacking the person and character of the Holy Prophet by weapons forged foolishly by Muslims themselves. These attacks reveal the hypocrisy of those who fabricated traditions and spread them among Muslims. But they also give non-Muslims a chance to attack the purity of life and character possessed by our Holy Prophet.

Prophets are raised to promote piety and purity among mankind and to guide them back to ends forsaken and forgotten. During the days of their decline Muslims started attributing to prophets moral weaknesses one hesitates to attribute to ordinary decent men. Not a single prophet has escaped their accusations. From Adam to the Holy Prophet all have been charged with transgression against the Laws of God. Noah is said to have prayed for his son when he had been forbidden to do so. Abraham is said to have lied on three different occasions. Jacob is said to have cheated his dying father and to have obtained his blessing by masquerading as his elder brother. Joseph is said to have committed adultery in his mind with the wife of the Egyptian ruler. It is said that Joseph was about to commit adultery and could not be persuaded against it. Then he saw the image of his father, Jacob, became ashamed and restrained himself. It is said also that he committed theft as a child and that he once intrigued to let his brother stay with him. Moses is said to have murdered an innocent person without cause and to have thus committed a major sin. It is said that Moses was not content to murder this man. He also made off with his belongings. David is said to have murdered a man in order to possess his properly wedded wife. He had to be reprimanded by God on marrying the widow of his victim. Solomon is said to have fallen in love with a pagan woman; also to have become possessed by Satan so that Satan began to rule instead of him. Affected by love of riches he became forgetful of his duty to God. Inspecting horses he forgot his time of prayer and did not remember until after sunset.

However, the worst faults have been attributed to the Holy Prophet (on whom be peace and the blessings of God). We men owe so much to the Holy Prophet that in sheer gratitude we must hold our heads bowed before him. It is cruel in the extreme that he to whom we owe most has had the worst faults attributed to him. No aspect of his life has gone untouched. It is said, for instance, that he wanted Ali as his successor, but did not appoint him for fear of other people. It is also said, God forbid, that he became infatuated by Zainab, his cousin. It is said that at last God let him marry Zainab when her divorce from Zaid had received divine sanction. It is also said that he had secret relations with a slave girl in the care of one of his wives. The wife saw them together, whereupon he was full of remorse and promised solemnly not to do it again. He also made his wife promise that she would not tell anybody. It is also said that he wished the teaching of Islam could be softened for the sake of pagan Arabs. He was willing to make concessions out of respect for their feelings. These beliefs about prophets are held by Muslims. They are included in commentaries and histories venerated among Muslims.

A form of thinking current among modernist Muslims cuts at the very root of religion. According to this, prophets were more like diplomats. They loved their people and wished to raise them up the moral and political scale. They found, however, that no moral or political teaching had any chance of success unless it was connected with beliefs relating to the Hereafter, the Day of Judgment, Heaven and Hell, etc. The inculcation of these mysteries was necessary not because they were true, but because without them no people would observe the restraints which civilization entails. Revelation is not a fact. No prophet ever had any revealed knowledge or guidance. The claim was made in order to impress people. But even as diplomats, prophets were deserving of respect and reverence. Their intentions were pure and their influence was wholesome. Such beliefs can be no part of Islam, but they have been held by Muslims in our time.

Hazrat Mirza Ghulam Ahmad (on whom be peace) refuted these among other misconceptions. He stated the correct teaching of Islam on these matters for the benefit of both Muslims and others.

He taught, for instance that the primary reason for the appearance of prophets is to promote a life of piety. They serve as examples to others. If this is not one of their most important functions, why must they come at all? If all that is required is a teaching, a book of beliefs and laws, why not have books and nothing more from God? But we have had prophets as well as books; from which it seems that the great object which the appearance of prophets serves is that practice should go with precept, that men should try and establish in the concrete what revelation teaches, that they should know what revelation really means and should feel heartened and inspired by seeing in the flesh models of virtue and piety, and should solve their difficulties through strength derived from spiritual preceptors who are also spiritual exemplars.

Hazrat Mirza Sahib taught that the many errors current in his time about the moral side of prophets were due to gross misunderstanding. The care needed to understand the revealed Word of God had not been exercised. Conclusions carelessly drawn had been handed down from generation to generation. The Prophets of God are pure, sinless, and models of truth, love and loyalty. They reflect in their characters the noble attributes of God. Their clean and beautiful lives point to the Purity and Holiness of God. They also serve as a mirror in which others can see their own image reflected. Evil men, therefore, often see their own vicious nature in them. What they impute to the prophets really belongs to the evil men themselves. Adam was no sinner. Abraham never lied. Joseph never resolved on any evil deed, nor did he steal or fabricate. Moses committed no murder. David did not seduce anybody's wife. Solomon did not forget his duty to God for the love of a pagan woman or for the sake of his horses. Nor did the Holy Prophet (on whom be peace and the blessings of God) commit any sin, great or small. He was holy, free from the least lapse, incapable of any wrong or transgression. Whosoever points to faults in his conduct or character shows his own faults. The stories told about him are the inventions of hypocrites. They cannot be substantiated by canons of history or biography. They are inconsistent with the rest of his life, thoughts and sentiments. Imputations against him or other prophets are survivals of lies deliberately invented by hypocrites who lived and moved among genuine believers. Or they are the result of failure to understand the meaning of the Texts of the Holy Quran.

Hazrat Mirza Sahib proved from the Holy Quran that all such thoughts are un-Islamic. They crept into Muslim writings through Christian influence. In Christian writings it had been the aim to enumerate the faults of prophets in general. They did this in order to prove the divinity of Jesus. Unless Jesus was absolutely without sin and other prophets were sinners to some extent, Jesus could not be proved superhuman and God-like. This seems to be the reason why, even among Muslims, faults are attributed to all prophets including the Holy Prophet (on whom be peace) while Jesus is absolutely sinless. Not only Jesus, but also Mary, his mother, is regarded as a paragon of sinlessness. This difference in the treatment meted out to Jesus, on the one hand, and to other prophets, on the other, proves that false and repulsive stories found their way into Muslim books through Christians. How this vicious influence came into Islam is another question. It is possible that Muslims accepted the influence unconsciously because of daily contact with Christians. It is also possible that some mischievous Christians outwardly accepted Islam and then spread these false Christian stories among Muslims. In the beginning Muslim historians and collectors of Traditions included these fables with the other Traditions current among Muslims. Their honest regard for historical material demanded nothing less. The distinction between true and false Traditions was maintained for a time. The example and influence of the Holy Prophet became more distant. Writers who came later lost sight of the distinction between true and false. They accepted tales contrary to the spirit and standards of Islam, but rejected Traditions which pointed to the truth about prophets. Had such Traditions remained in these writings, they would have dissolved all doubts and difficulties.

But, thank God, Hazrat Mirza Sahib separated the gold from the dross. The true status of prophets was re-asserted and their honour re-established, especially the honour of the Holy Prophet of Islam (on whom be peace and the blessings of God). The purity of life and character which the Holy Prophet possessed was not only re-asserted but made plain by irrefutable arguments. The worst enemies found themselves silenced.

The Hereafter, Heaven and Hell

The fifth fundamental belief of Islam is belief in the Hereafter, in Heaven and Hell. This belief too had all but disappeared. It certainly disappeared from men's hearts. For had the belief really survived, Muslims would not have turned their backs on the teachings of Islam as they did. Conceptions and constructions current among Muslims on the subject of life after death and Heaven and Hell seemed to bear little relation to the true Islamic conceptions. What was the Paradise of popular Muslim belief, for instance? A place of pleasure, of unremitting sensuality. If this was the Paradise promised to good and godly men, then human existence was to be a life of sensuous delights, of wine, women, and song! There was nothing more that men could aspire to! But the object of human existence, according to the Holy Quran, is very different. It is that men should learn to adore God (51:57). To adore is to obey. To obey is to imitate. To imitate is to absorb, to appropriate and acquire the attributes of God. The object of human existence, therefore, is to promote a godly life. A godly life is the good life. It is impossible that in this life men should try for three score years and ten to learn to live godly lives, but should hereafter enter a life of sensuous pleasures. This conception of the life hereafter bore no relation to the life valued even in this world. Similarly, Hell was thought to be the permanent abode of evil-doers. Those who were condemned to live in Hell were condemned to live there for ever. An uncompromising despot, God would never again forgive His sinners!

Hazrat Mirza Sahib rejected all these conceptions. He employed arguments and showed miracles to restore the correct Islamic belief on each subject. He demonstrated the instability of life in this world, the beauty and value of life hereafter. He created in human hearts conviction and certainty about the life to come and the desire to live and work, and wait for it. The half-truths and sensual images Muslims had come to believe about Paradise were also removed by him. Paradise was no mere metaphor, nor was it a place of physical delights, more stable and on a larger scale than the physical delights of this world. The blessings of Paradise are very different. The physical delights of life hereafter are like the joy one derives from good works in this life. What is mind and spirit in this life, becomes body in the life hereafter. What is mind and spirit in the life hereafter is a more developed and a more advanced form of existence than anything we know in this world. The powers of the spirit in the life hereafter are far more advanced than the powers of the spirit we know in this world. The human sperm has a physical as well as a spiritual side. It consists of both body and spirit. But the man who develops out of the sperm has a spirit far superior to the spirit within the sperm.

Similarly, Hazrat Mirza Sahib proved that the punishment of Hell is not a punishment without end. It is a punishment destined to end sooner or later. It may last a long time but not for ever and ever. It is not punishment without end. A permanent Hell is contradictory to the dignity of a Merciful God. 'My mercy encompasses all things' (7:157). This is the fundamental character of God according to the Holy Quran. Everything is ruled by Divine Mercy.

The Holy Quran describes the rewards of Heaven as rewards 'which shall not be cut off' (11:109), and as 'rewards unending' (95:7). The description used for the punishment of Hell is very different. The difference of description proves that the rewards of Heaven and the punishment of Hell are long-lasting but in very different ways. Why should not readers of the Holy Quran observe and heed this difference?

The Holy Prophet himself said in explanation of the teachings of the Holy Quran about Heaven and Hell:

يَأْتِيْ عَلٰى جَهَنَّمَ يَوْمٌ مَّا فِيْهَا مِنْ بَنِيْ اٰدَمَ اَحَدٌ تُخْفَقُ اَبْوَابُهَا۔

> 'A time will come in Hell when not a single man would be left in it. Its doors and windows will rattle to the blowing wind.'[20]

This is a description of an emptied Hell. The Mercy of God will eventually take out of Hell every one of its inmates, and Hell will become empty. This being the teaching of the Holy Prophet, nobody has any right to teach anything else.

Muslims victims of extremes

Fundamental beliefs apart, great changes had taken place in the everyday life of Muslims. They had become fond of extremes. Some of them advocated complete casualness as far as religious duties and works were concerned. It was quite enough, they thought, that one should profess belief in the *Kalima*: 'There is no god but Allah and Muhammad is His Prophet.' After this profession one was free to do and live as one liked. The Holy Prophet was their intercessor. If there were no sinners, for whom would the Holy Prophet intercede?

Others thought that religious ordinances were only a means to an end, like the boat which carries one to the shore. Those who had found God had no further use for religious ordinances. These were intended for those who had to complete the journey.

Still others thought that religious duties had been ordained as external symbols of internal states. When the Holy Prophet appeared in Arabia, the Arabs were savage and primitive. Their minds and spirits were also savage, primitive, and immature. Therefore an emphasis on external performances – ablutions, prayers, prostrations, fasts, etc. – was necessary. Now mankind had advanced. Their understanding had also advanced, so the external

20 Kanzul Ummal, p. 270.

formalities were no longer necessary. If a man is clean, if he remembers his God, is mindful of the needs of the community, serves the poor, is moderate in eating and drinking, takes part in patriotic activities, and so on, he does as much as he is required to do as a Muslim. His prayers, fasts, *Zakat* and *Hajj* are now the good and prudent things he does.

Other Muslims went to the other extreme. They thought that to attain salvation it was necessary for Muslims to follow the example of the Holy Prophet in the minutest detail. If, for instance, the Holy Prophet used a certain form of dress, it was the duty of Muslims to use the same kind of dress. If the Holy Prophet wore long hair, then long hair had to be worn by Muslims, and so on. Some Muslims thought that the Holy Prophet had no right to teach anything by way of religious duties. The Holy Quran contained everything which God required of man. Anything besides this was false and futile. The Holy Prophet as a human being could not add anything to what God had taught.

Still others placed excessive reliance on certain scholars or doctors of religion. These authorities, they thought, had said the last word on questions of beliefs and works. Our duty was to obey, and obey without question.

These were the larger beliefs and works in which Muslims had deviated from the true teaching of Islam. When we turn to details, we come across even more dangerous digressions into un-Islamic ways. Some Muslims branded as *Kufr* the learning of languages other than Arabic, English for instance. Some thought learning modern science was inimical to true faith. On the other hand, some among Muslims deny some of the clear teachings of the Holy Quran, about the taking of interest for instance. According to the Holy Quran, the taking of interest is like going to war against God (2:280). Yet the taking of interest is said to be lawful and permissible.

In details of prayers, fasts, obligatory charity, rules of inheritance and other matters, irreconcilable differences existed between the various schools. The true teaching of Islam had become completely confused. Sometimes small and minor points were fancied to be fundamental. Those who proposed to think of certain details in a different manner were censured. Should a Muslim raise his index finger while reciting the part in the *Kalima* 'I bear witness', etc., he had to lose that finger. If Muslims said 'Amen' loudly while praying in congregation, they had their mouths filled with dirt and dung. The practical life, like the life of belief, had deteriorated through deviations, disagreements and extremes of various kinds.

Hazrat Mirza Sahib reformed the practical life of Muslims also. He pointed out that indifference to prescribed religious duties was wrong and led to ruin. One could not sin deliberately and expect intercession by the Holy Prophet on the Day of Judgment. The Holy Prophet's intercession was for those who did their utmost to avoid sin. Intercession was to help them over weaknesses and lapses which occurred in spite of an effort to avoid them. Intercession was not for sinners. The privilege of intercession had been awarded to the Holy Prophet to put down sin, not to promote sin.

Abudiyat or *Shariat?*

Thus Hazrat Mirza Sahib demonstrated that the object of human life was *Abudiyat*, absorption of divine attributes or imitation of His character, and not *Shariat*, the observance of prescribed laws or external duties. What God had commanded, we must indeed observe and do. But closeness to God was an infinite process. We could be closer and closer to Him, yet not quite reach Him; so that we could never think that closeness had been achieved, that there was nothing more to be done. The prayer taught in the *Sura Fatiha* – 'Thee only do we worship' and 'Thee only do we ask for guidance to the straight path' – had to be repeated many times a day by every Muslim. It had to be repeated even by the Holy Prophet, who repeated it up to his death. He also repeated other prayers contained in the Holy Quran, such as 'O my Lord, increase me in knowledge' (20:115). Closeness to God and insight into His nature are of infinite dimensions, closer and closer to completion but never quite completed. Not even the Holy Prophet, to say nothing of ordinary believers, could think that praying had become redundant. Those who think so can have no conception of the Infinity of God. God is like a limitless ocean. One can never hope to cross it. To think so is to offend God.

Similarly Hazrat Mirza Sahib pointed out that the object of human life and of human aspirations lay in practising the teachings of Islam. These teachings keep in view the needs of all times and of all levels of culture. The spiritual advance of man necessitated a due observance of the teachings of Islam, of practical ordinances as well as theoretical beliefs. It was wrong to think that they were meant for a bygone age, that their interest now lay in their history. The teachings of Islam had everlasting value. They could not be replaced by anything else.

Hazrat Mirza Sahib also taught that human activities are of two kinds. One kind consists of prescribed acts of worship and of preferred ways of doing things. The other kind consists of modes, methods, or manners favoured by a community or nation. The Holy Prophet (on whom be peace and the blessings of God) displayed in his person and in his example both kinds of activities. He carried out the different forms of worship which were to become part of the daily life of a Muslim. He also demonstrated ways of doing things which he would prefer to other ways. But the Holy Prophet also observed the modes and manners of his time, his community and race. The latter were no part of Islam. Islam could not be conceived in terms of any community, nation, race, or group. It had to be conceived in universal human terms. To compel Muslims to adopt the ways and modes which the Holy Prophet adopted as an Arab or as a Quraish was cruel and un-Islamic. In such matters even the Companions of the Holy Prophet, his devoted contemporaries, did not conform to a single pattern. They observed their individual ways and fashions, but did not accuse one another of being un-Islamic.

Hazrat Mirza Sahib also refuted the idea that as the Holy Prophet was a man like other men, Muslims owed obedience only to God, not to the Holy Prophet. Against this Hazrat Mirza Sahib taught that prophets are endowed with a special understanding of the Word of God. Insight into divine purposes, which prophets have, can be acquired by nobody else. The interpretation of divine purposes is a prerogative of each prophet. Not to recognize this subverts true faith.

Hazrat Mirza Sahib also corrected the belief that any good man can be held up as an authority and as the last word on the subject of religious belief and duty. True, there are men who are incapable of judging for themselves. For their convenience it seems pardonable and even necessary that they should appoint as their leaders men whose personal piety, purity, and insight in religion are superior to their own. But this does not relieve individual Muslims of their responsibility to judge all questions for themselves and to find their own answers to those questions. Muslims who are endowed with knowledge and understanding cannot offer blind, unquestioning obedience to anyone else. Those who are blessed with knowledge are duty-bound to act in accordance with their knowledge and judgment of what the Holy Quran and the *Hadith* have to say on any given subject.

Hazrat Mirza Sahib exposed the absurdity of extending the scope of religious teaching unnecessarily. Religion is concerned with the moral and spiritual advance of man. Its prohibitions and its commands do not apply beyond a given point. A knowledge of languages, for instance, is a useful acquisition. All languages have in some sense been created by God. A language could be acquired or not, according as it serves or does not serve a given purpose. Not only is it not a sin to acquire proficiency in useful languages, it is necessary to do so. Some languages are useful for the propagation of religion. The acquisition of such languages is an act of spiritual merit.

Hazrat Mirza Sahib strongly prohibited the receiving of interest. He taught that this prohibition of Islam was full of wisdom. Muslims could not take it lightly and compromise with it for the sake of small worldly gains.

Hazrat Mirza Sahib also taught that religious teachings are of two kinds. They are either principles or details of principles. Principles have been laid down in the Holy Quran and on them no disagreement is possible. It is open to everybody, however, to try and understand their meaning and their scope. Details of principles, on the other hand, are also of two kinds. The first is details which have been settled by the Holy Prophet himself; maybe he ordered certain things to be done in certain ways and prohibited other ways of doing the same things. In such details, Muslims are bound to act as they have been commanded to do by the Holy Prophet. The second is details which can be understood in different ways. Sometimes we have more than one version of how the Holy Prophet did a certain thing. It may also be that in such details Muslims since the very earliest times have acted in different ways. In such matters the obvious duty of Muslims is tolerance. They can choose their own way of doing those things but must tolerate ways different from their own. Other ways were as well sanctioned by practice as the ways preferred by them. The different ways must be considered right and proper and equally sanctioned. If the different ways had not been sanctioned by the Holy Prophet, how could one section of Companions adopt one way and another section another way of doing the same thing? The truth of the matter is that human individuals are very different from one another. They therefore act in different ways in certain matters. Keeping in view this important fact of human nature, the Holy Prophet permitted a variety of ways of carrying out the same duties. He himself may have adopted different ways for doing the same thing. He did this in order to show that human nature was variable, that not only did different individuals do the same thing in different ways, but that the same individuals did the same thing in different ways on different occasions. Raising the two hands at the time of *Takbir* in the course of the daily prayers had to be understood and tolerated in the light of this fact of human nature. It is known that the Holy Prophet himself sometimes raised and sometimes did not raise his hands at the time of *Takbir*. The same applies to the saying of 'Amen' in a congregation. Some members of the congregation said the 'Amen' loudly, some not. The Holy Prophet accepted both practices. Folding the arms while standing in prayer could also be done in different ways. It seems that the Holy Prophet himself or the Companions folded their arms, now nearer the waist, now higher up. Again, variety was permitted. Within limits one could choose to do as one liked. But someone who chose to do a certain thing in a certain way need not object to another doing the same thing in a different way. The other was free to do the same thing in his own way. By laying down and re-stating all the wise provisions of Islam, Hazrat Mirza Sahib resolved many disagreements between sects and put an end to many controversies among them. These controversies related to details of doing certain things. Rid of these disagreements and controversies, Muslims of our time can go about their religious duties with the dignity and freedom of the Companions of the Holy Prophet.

Why wait for another?

This may give you, dear reader, some idea of the reform which Hazrat Mirza Sahib carried out in the attitudes and beliefs of Muslims. If this reform were to be described as fully as it deserves, it would need a book to itself. Therefore I am content to point only to the main outlines. You can judge even from this short account that Hazrat Mirza Sahib removed the errors which had crept into the belief of Muslims and their conceptions of religious duties. Islam has been presented by him in its true light, so its original charm has begun again to attract its followers and others. Its purifying power has begun to show again.

Now, dear reader, I have described the errors of belief and action from which Muslims had begun to suffer in our time. These errors crept in despite the fact that Muslims are in possession of a Book whose every word and vowel-point has since its revelation been under divine protection. A people possessing a protected holy text like the text of the Holy Quran could not have strayed into errors worse than these. Worse errors of belief and action are conceivable but only in the event, God forbid, of the Holy Quran undergoing a textual alteration. But a textual alteration of the Holy Quran is impossible under divine promise. Therefore Muslims could not have fallen into worse errors.

Now let us think awhile. The errors into which Muslims have fallen have reached the worst possible limits. Yet the time has not arrived for the coming of the Promised Messiah? On the other hand, Hazrat Mirza Sahib has not only come, but has also corrected the errors into which Muslims had fallen and removed the dangers to which Islam had become exposed. Must we still wait for another to come and do the same thing? The tasks appointed for the Promised Messiah have been duly carried out by Hazrat Mirza Sahib. Therefore he must be the Promised Messiah. When the sun is at the zenith, it is futile to deny its existence. In the face of clear arguments, it is futile to deny the truth that Hazrat Mirza Sahib is the Promised Messiah.

Argument 6
Divine Help

This argument, like the others, comprises a large number of sub-arguments. It is the argument of divine help. Without it a Divine Messenger cannot prove his contact with the Divine. Every Divine Messenger or leader is loved by God. His special relation to God cannot be proved unless the hand of God can be seen working behind him. God should stand by him because He stands by those whom He loves. A Messenger may claim special office on behalf of God, but if he does not receive from God the support which God's favourite should receive, he must be dismissed as a pretender and a liar. It is impossible that God should appoint a Messenger or a deputy and show no special regard, interest, or love for him; that He should not help him when help is needed by him. Earthly kings help their deputies and messengers. They take care of them and give whatever help is necessary. The resources of God are infinite. He has knowledge of the unseen. He cannot fail to help his servants and deputies. A claimant to divine messengership who receives help and support from God is a true Messenger, for, it is impossible that God should abandon His true servants. It is as impossible for God to support a pretender and not to hold him answerable for his pretence, as for a liar and pretender to go about misleading God's creatures with success. It is even more against reason and common sense that God should help, and help abundantly, such a liar and pretender. The Holy Quran says:

كَتَبَ اللّٰهُ لَاَغْلِبَنَّ اَنَا وَرُسُلِیْ اِنَّ اللّٰهَ قَوِیٌّ عَزِیْزٌ۔

'Allah has decreed, most surely I will prevail, I and My Messengers, Verily, Allah is Powerful, Mighty.'[1]

1 *Al-Mujadilah*, 22.

God has ordained that He and His prophets shall always prevail against others. This is evidence of His Power over all things. Those who bring messages from God must succeed. God is the Guarantor of their success. If this were not so, men would begin to have doubts about His Power and Dominion.

We read in the Holy Quran:

إِنَّا لَنَنْصُرُ رُسُلَنَا وَالَّذِيْنَ اٰمَنُوْا فِي الْحَيٰوةِ الدُّنْيَا وَيَوْمَ يَقُوْمُ الْاَشْهَادُ ـ

'Most surely We help Our Messengers, and those who believe, in the present life and on the day when witnesses will stand forth'.[2]

And again,

وَلٰكِنَّ اللّٰهَ يُسَلِّطُ رُسُلَهٗ عَلٰى مَنْ يَّشَآءُ وَاللّٰهُ عَلٰى كُلِّ شَيْءٍ قَدِيْرٌ ـ

'But Allah grants to His Messengers power over whomsoever He pleases and Allah has power over all things.'[3]

Help for true Messengers, punishment for pretenders

It is evident from these verses that according to the Holy Quran God grants power and success to His Messengers. He makes them dominate others, possibly in the physical as well as in the spiritual sense, or only in the spiritual.

We also read in the Holy Quran how God deals with pretenders to messengership. We are told that they cannot be left to prosper. They must await divine punishment:

وَلَوْ تَقَوَّلَ عَلَيْنَا بَعْضَ الْاَقَاوِيْلِ ـ لَاَخَذْنَا مِنْهُ بِالْيَمِيْنِ ـ ثُمَّ لَقَطَعْنَا مِنْهُ الْوَتِيْنَ ـ

'And, had he forged (and attributed) any sayings to Us, We would surely have seized him by the right hand, and then surely We would have severed his life-artery.'[4]

2 *Al-Mumin*, 22.
3 *Al-Hashr*, 7.
4 *Al-Haqqah*, 45–7.

The verse is very clear. If a messenger lies deliberately about God, claiming to have had messages from Him, God seizes him by the right hand and cuts asunder his life artery. God's help and support are cut short for him. Instead, he is disgraced.

We also read in the Holy Quran:

وَمَنْ أَظْلَمُ مِمَّنِ افْتَرٰى عَلَى اللّٰهِ كَذِبًا أَوْ كَذَّبَ بِاٰيٰتِهٖ إِنَّهٗ لَا يُفْلِحُ الظّٰلِمُوْنَ ۔

> 'Who is more unjust than he who forges a lie against Allah or gives the lie to His Signs? Surely, the unjust shall not prosper.'[5]

This verse leaves no doubt that the unjust cannot prosper according to the Law of God. How can one who lies about God, one who is spiritually the most unjust, succeed in fabricating false claims?

It appears, therefore, that God works in two ways. Firstly, He helps His Messengers, and gives them power and success. Secondly, if a person deliberately concocts a message and attributes it to God, not only is he refused help by God; he is discomfited, disgraced and destroyed by Him.

What I have said on the basis of common sense is duly supported by verses of the Holy Quran. According to the Quran, this is how God treats true and false Messengers. These are the two Laws of God.

If we consider the claims of Hazrat Mirza Sahib (on whom be peace) in the light of the Laws of God, his authenticity becomes as clear as day. He is proved a Messenger and a deputy of God.

Before I proceed to show the different ways in which God helped him, it seems necessary to recount the circumstances in which he was born, the conditions which could have helped him, and the conditions which stood in his way; also whether his claim was such as could reasonably be expected to succeed under his circumstances and the circumstances of his time.

Unfavourable circumstances and universal opposition

What were the conditions that could have helped him? He belonged

5 *Al-An'am*, 22.

to a respectable family. This has been the fortune of all Messengers of God. They have always been raised out of good families, to make it easy for people to accept and follow them. The family of Hazrat Mirza Sahib, once important, was no longer so. It was now a poor family compared to its former prosperity and influence. Both landed property and political power had all but gone. Political power had been confiscated by the Sikhs, and landed properties had to be ceded to the British, who had succeeded the Sikhs as rulers of the Punjab. Influence and wealth, therefore, did not exist. It could not be said that he owed his large following to his political or social status.

Nor did he hold the traditional rank of a doctor or scholar of religion. His education had been arranged through private tutors, so that it was little or nothing compared with what one could get in the old religious schools of the country. Neither in his district or province, nor outside, was he counted among the doctors of religion or the *Ulema* of Islam. People could not turn to him out of regard for proved scholarship and learning.

His family was not a family of *Pirs* (hereditary saints) or *Sufis*. Nor was he a successor to a saint or *Sufi*. Such status is enjoyed by many religious leaders, so that the following of the elder saint or *Sufi* becomes, on his death, the following of the successor. Hazrat Mirza Sahib had no such status and enjoyed no such advantage.

He held no office in the Government of the day. He could not, therefore, attract anyone by reason of high position in Government.

A man of retiring nature, he preferred to live in solitude and seclusion; even those who lived near him did not know him. He had some visitors, but these were mostly the orphans and the needy. With them he shared his daily meals, often giving his own food to them and going hungry himself. Some of his visitors were interested in religion. Apart from the visitors I have mentioned, there were no others. He did not meet people and the people did not need to meet him.

As for circumstances, conditions, etc., which went against him, we must remember that Hazrat Mirza Sahib claimed to be the Messiah of Muslim Traditions. The first large group bound to resist the claim was the group of the *Ulema*. Acceptance of the claim meant an end of the hold the *Ulema* had enjoyed for hundreds of years over common Muslims. Small wonder the *Ulema* were vehemently opposed to him and his claim. The success of his claim meant defeat and failure for them. If people in general found a Messenger of God, and found him to be genuine, who would look to the *Ulema* for leadership and guidance?

The *Gaddi Nashins* (hereditary or traditional saints) also became his enemies. As the influence of Hazrat Mirza Sahib increased these saints were certain to lose their followers. They could no longer pose as Shaikhs or guides. They had to accept someone else as their Shaikh or guide. Loss of followers meant loss of income. The success of the Promised Messiah as leader and reformer was also to limit the life of licence which the traditional saints enjoyed as their right.

The rich too were against him. Hazrat Mirza Sahib invited them to observe the ordinances of Islam, and the rich were not accustomed to this. The daily obligations of Islam were to them a nuisance. At the same time he taught charity, equality and sympathy; equality between all, charity and sympathy for the poor and the weak. This the rich did not like. They could see that with Hazrat Mirza Sahib's influence the social deprivation of the poor would disappear; the hold which the rich had over the poor would also disappear.

Followers of other religions could only be hostile. All religions other than Islam seemed threatened with defeat. A lamb has an instinctive fear of the tiger. So, all non-Islamic religions felt threatened by him. They did all they could to destroy him and his influence.

The ruling class were also against him. They had ever been afraid of Messiahs and Mahdis. Old tradition had long associated with these names disturbances, lawlessness and rebellion. True, Hazrat Mirza Sahib professed and promised loyalty to any existing government. But this did not satisfy them. Expressions of loyalty they regarded as part of his strategy. They thought that as soon as Mirza Sahib attained power, he would abandon his professions of peace and loyalty and start a rebellion.

The common people were also against him. Firstly, the common people are under the influence of their leaders, the *Ulema*, the saints, the rich, the *pundits*, the *padres*. Secondly, they are ignorant and custom-ridden. They are against any new idea, any change of belief or outlook. The claim of the Promised Messiah was a novelty for them; therefore, partly under the influence of their leaders and partly out of ignorance, they too were against him.

In different ways, from different motives, all classes were hostile to Hazrat Mirza Sahib. They did what they could to destroy him. The *Ulema* prepared *Fatwas* of *Kufr* against him. They went to Mecca and Medina to obtain signatures of approval on them. True to their traditions, they invented strange causes for declaring Hazrat Mirza Sahib a *Kafir* and roused the masses by concocting all sorts of things against him.

The *Sufi* class also set their followers against him. They described his conception of religious merit and religious exercise as being contrary to all established conceptions. At the same time their leaders made exaggerated claims about their own spiritual powers and the closeness of their contact with God. Intimidating their followers and generally prejudicing them against Hazrat Mirza Sahib, they did not hesitate to invent stories about their own miraculous powers and cheat people by fraudulent activities. Some of them told their followers that if Miraz Sahib was genuine the sin of denying him would be borne by them. The followers need have no anxiety. By methods of this kind they kept alive a large part of the opposition.

The rich fought against him with their wealth and influence. Leaders of other religions joined the Muslim opponents of Hazrat Mirza Sahib. The ruling class used their own special influence to set people against him. Those who wished to believe and join him incurred their displeasure. The common people indulged in boycotts, made trouble, and persuaded their leaders against him.

In short, as many circumstances as there could be were against him. Opposed by all classes and by followers of all religions, Muslims and others, he found himself one against all. All joined together in opposing him.

Now, how was his teaching related to current tendencies? If it only promoted current beliefs, current practices, it could be said that his success was not due to divine help or divine intervention, but was due to the tendencies of the time. These tendencies might not have been clearly formulated by anybody, yet it might be said that what Mirza Sahib taught and preached was in accordance with these tendencies and therefore people flocked to him. They found him saying the same things, promoting the same ends, as themselves. Tendencies current at any time can be of two kinds: tendencies of a majority, or tendencies of an intellectual minority, the result of advanced thinking and experimentation. Thoughts and beliefs acceptable to a majority are easily propagated. Thoughts and beliefs acceptable only to an intellectual minority are also easily propagated. The thoughts and beliefs of such a minority meet with some initial hostility, but if founded on reason, experience, and good observation, they are bound to spread sooner or later. Their spread waits for the spread of knowledge.

Teaching contrary to current tendencies

The thoughts and beliefs which Hazrat Mirza Sahib advocated were of neither kind. He invited his generation to accept ideas which the majority of them were not willing to accept. Nor were his thoughts and beliefs acceptable to the intellectuals. His teaching, therefore, was opposed to the thoughts of both the masses and the intellectual classes. He had to struggle against both. He had to fight traditional ideas as well as the ideas of men of knowledge, the votaries of current culture. Those who subscribed to traditional beliefs described him as a non-conformist, a seceder, a non-believer. Those who subscribed to current science described him as an obscurantist, a diehard, a conservative. When he taught against the belief that Jesus was alive, against superstitious miracles, misconceptions about angels, abrogation of parts of the Quran, crudities about Heaven and Hell, and an over-literal meaning of religious ordinances, he offended the common man, When he insisted on the importance of religious observances like the prohibition of interest, the belief in angels, the efficacy of prayer, the truth of Heaven and Hell, the validity of revelation and miracles, he roused the intellectuals against him. He was in agreement neither with the common many nor with the intellectual few. It cannot be said, therefore, that he succeeded because he swam with the current. He was against tendencies which already existed, as well as tendencies which were likely to grow in the immediate future.

There were thus no natural conditions or circumstances which could help in the promotion of his claim. On the other hand, all sorts of circumstances were against him. His personal circumstances could not help his claim. He possessed neither riches nor influence, nor personal or family prestige. Nor could he hope to succeed because of the circumstances of his time. What he taught was not in accord with contemporary tendencies. If he succeeded in spite of this complete lack of natural advantages, the success of his claim has to be attributed to the special help and concern shown by God, not to natural circumstances.

Success under divine help

I now proceed to describe how, in spite of universal hostility and the absence of natural advantages, Hazrat Mirza Sahib succeeded in his claim. I have already pointed out that the Holy Quran lays down as God's law that God does not spare for long those who invent lies about Him. But we find that Hazrat Mirza Sahib published the revelations which he received from God and which addressed him as a reformer. Yet he lived for forty years after the publication of those revelations and during this long time he continued to receive the Help and Grace of God, in small ways and large ones. If an impostor could live so long and prosper so well after the publication of fabricated revelations, then, God forbid, we would have to admit that the criterion laid down in verse 69:45 of the Holy Quran quoted above was false and that even the Holy Prophet (on whom be peace and the blessings of God) could not cite this criterion in proof of his claim. But the criterion laid down by the Holy Quran cannot be false. If it cannot be false, and it is not false, then it should also apply to the claims of Hazrat Mirza Sahib. If he published the revelations received by him, and lived long after their publication, and God did not only spare him but even helped him, then we have to admit that he was a true one sent by God.

At the time when he published his revelations he was not known to many, certainly not to the world at large. After their publication, in spite of untold hostility from all classes, he won the esteem and allegiance of large numbers, so much so that even his enemies were obliged to show regard for him. He began to be called an important Muslim leader. The Government of the day, which at first suspected him, came to trust and respect him as an influence for peace and goodwill. His name spread to many parts of the world, and among his followers could be counted many sincere devotees who would sacrifice their lives for his sake. Even in European countries where people are generally hostile to Islam, he found followers who accepted Islam on hearing his message. They came to feel real and deep love for him. One of them wrote to the present writer saying that he was deep in Hazrat Mirza Sahib's debt. He owed the blessing of Islam to Hazrat Mirza Sahib. Therefore, he wrote, every night on going to bed he prayed for Hazrat Mirza Sahib and added this prayer to the usual prayer for the blessings of God on the Holy Prophet. The devotion, esteem, and affection which Hazrat Mirza Sahib came to inspire, despite universal hostility in the beginning, would have been impossible had he been an impostor.

When Hazrat Mirza Sahib announced his claim, he was alone. Hostility of the worst kind by Maulvis, *Pirs, Gaddi Nashins, pundits, padres,* by rich and poor alike, and (at least in the beginning) by the ruling class, greeted the announcement of his claim. All endeavoured to prevent any attention being paid to it. In spite of this, people began to join him in twos and threes. He found followers among rich and poor, among the *Ulema* as well as *Sufis*. Muslims joined him as well as Hindus and Christians, from his own country and from abroad. His following increased. When he died they could be counted in six figures. The numbers continue to increase. In Afghanistan, they could be found in every province, even after the stoning of several Ahmadis on the orders of Afghan rulers, instigated by the Mullas. Members of the Movement are to be found in Arabia; Iran; Russia; Egypt; West, East, North, and South Africa; Australia; the USA; and Europe. Hazrat Mirza Sahib belonged to a politically subject people; yet he found followers among the free nations of the world. Converts came from religions which for generations had maintained a deep and incurable prejudice against Islam. Success of this kind and on this scale cannot be accounted for without divine help.

His enemies also tried to murder or poison him. He was dragged into the law courts. False accusations were brought against him. Christians, Muslims, Hindus all joined in these attacks. They almost put the Second Messiah on the cross as they had the first. But all attacks failed. He remained safe and, thanks to divine help and grace, went on prospering.

The *raison d'être* of his advent, let us remember, was the revival and propagation of Islam. For these two great objects God gave him a sincere following; also money, so that at present the community works with an annual budget of between four and five hundred thousand rupees. Periodicals devoted to Islam are published in the Punjab, Bengal, Ceylon, Mauritius and America. Hundreds of books have been written in support of him. God inspires people and opens their hearts to his message, so that they turn to him and offer him loyalty and help. Thousands who have joined him have done so because they had visions or revelations or premonitions of some kind in which the truth of Hazrat Mirza Sahib's claim was communicated to them by God. They were against him, yet God put love for him into their hearts.

Hazrat Mirza Sahib met with success in spite of universal hostility, in spite of numerous natural disadvantages and general initial helplessness.

The Law of God is that a true claimant receives divine help and a pretender suffers defeat, disgrace and death. This being the law – and a law more just cannot be laid down – then no doubt is left about the truth of the claim of Hazrat Mirza Sahib. If his claim is still in doubt, the question is; What is the evidence for the truth of other prophets celebrated in religious history?

Points which distinguish Divine Messengers from others

Let me make my point clear. Hazrat Mirza Sahib's claim to spiritual office was genuine not just because he started in poor circumstances and then attained honour and success. Honour and success often come to those who are insignificant at first. Nadir Shah was a shepherd and became famous and important. Napoleon was a poor man but he became a world conqueror. In spite of phenomenal success, they cannot claim to have been appointed by God to do the things they did. They cannot be said to have received the gift of His grace and His love. But Hazrat Mizra Sahib can claim to have been appointed to spiritual office and to have been honoured by the grace of special divine help because:

1 Hazrat Mirza Sahib claimed early on that he had been appointed by God to a spiritual office. If his claim was a pretence, a deliberate lie, he should have met with disgrace and even death. According to the Law of God, this is the end of all false claimants.

2 There were no natural advantages which could have helped him in his claim.

3 Not only was there no natural advantage; he had, in addition, to confront the hostility of every class, every people. He had no friends or followers who could have given the Movement a start.

4 He taught and persuaded people to believe things which were against current trends among the orthodox as well as liberal modernist Muslims.

5 In spite of these difficulties he succeeded and founded a Movement. Beliefs and propositions which his contemporaries hated became accepted. He remained safe from the attacks of his enemies. The help of god descended on him in many different ways.

These five essentials distinguish a true from a false claimant to spiritual office. They can never all be present together in a false claimant. If they are all present in any claimant, he is a true one from God. If even this criterion is doubted, we have no criterion for distinguishing true from false claimants.

This criterion does not apply to persons who make no claim to spiritual office. It does not apply, for instance, to Nadir Shah or Napoleon. Nor does it apply to those who do not claim spiritual office conferred by God, but claim to be God or to share some divine attributes. Nor does the criterion apply to those who are insane, or to those who regard their own speech as the speech of God. The Shaikhiya sect held beliefs of this kind. They thought that at all times in the world there were men who could be said to represent the will of the Mahdi. As the will of the Mahdi is the Will of God, whatever happens to drop from the lips of such men or to emerge from their hearts is from God. Ali Muhammad the Bab, and Bahaullah, the founder of Bahaism, both belonged to this sect. As the sect believe that certain individuals incarnate God, that their speech is His speech, their thoughts His thoughts, they do not incur the penalty laid down in verse 69:45 of the Holy Quran. This verse relates only to claimants who forge lies about God.

A person who achieves some success in his claims cannot claim divine sanction for them if his success can be attributed to one natural advantage or another, say personal influence, party support, a teaching which follows some current tendency; or if he invites men to believe in scientific discoveries that are certain to become, in the course of time, generally accepted knowledge; or if his success can be attributed to lack of general opposition.

Argument 7
Defeat of Enemies

The seventh argument, also a composite of many arguments, argues from the fact that those who chose the way of hostility against Hazrat Mirza Sahib suffered defeat, disgrace, discomfiture, and even death. The argument is rooted in human and divine nature. If we find our dear ones molested, we are roused against the molester, resisting him and, if necessary, punishing him in whatever way we can. If we find our plans hindered, we try to put the hindrance out of the way. Similarly we should expect God to remove the hindrance to His Own plans, to show special regard for the Messengers whom He charges with their execution, to humiliate their enemies, and to defeat those who seek to defeat His Messengers. If God did not do so, His interest in His Messengers and His regard for them would go undemonstrated, unproved. The claims of those Messengers would remain for ever in doubt. Earthly kings and rulers with limited means and powers stand by their deputies. Those who try to disgrace or defeat the deputies are disgraced and defeated by the kings whom the deputies represent.

The Holy Quran and enemies of God's Messengers

It appears from the Holy Quran that what seems so clearly indicated by our own nature and judgment is in full accord with God's Own teaching. Enemies of God's Messengers must suffer for their misdeeds. The Holy Quran says:

وَمَنْ أَظْلَمُ مِمَّنِ افْتَرَىٰ عَلَى اللَّهِ كَذِبًا أَوْ كَذَّبَ بِآيَاتِهِ إِنَّهُ
لَا يُفْلِحُ الظَّالِمُونَ ۔

'And who is more unjust than he who forges a lie against Allah or gives the lie to His Signs? Surely the unjust shall not prosper.'[1]

To forge lies against God is serious; equally serious is deliberate enmity and hostility shown to His true Messengers. Forgers of lies against Allah cannot succeed, according to the Holy Quran. No more can they who choose to oppose and defeat the true Messengers of God.

وَلَقَدِ اسْتُهْزِئَ بِرُسُلٍ مِّنْ قَبْلِكَ فَحَاقَ بِالَّذِيْنَ سَخِرُوْا مِنْهُمْ مَّا كَانُوْا بِهٖ يَسْتَهْزِءُوْنَ - قُلْ سِيْرُوْا فِي الْاَرْضِ ثُمَّ انْظُرُوْا كَيْفَ كَانَ عَاقِبَةُ الْمُكَذِّبِيْنَ -

'And surely have the Messengers been mocked at before thee, but that which they mocked at encompassed those of them who scoffed. Say, "Go about in the earth, and see what was the end of those who treated *the Prophets* as liars".'[2]

Those who scoff at true prophets become victims of their own machinations. God-fearing people must ever remember what happened to those who decried true prophets as impostors.

There are many verses of this kind. The point need not be stressed further. We may accept it as a Law of God that the opponents of His Messengers and Apostles meet with destruction and prove an object-lesson for others.

Hazrat Mirza Sahib had the same assurances on the subject. One of his revelations says: 'I will humiliate him who seeks to humiliate thee.'

This promise revealed to Hazrat Mirza Sahib is in accordance with God's eternal law. The enemies of Hazrat Mirza Sahib suffered defeat and disgrace enough to make everybody think.

Enemies of the Promised Messiah

I have mentioned before a great Maulvi, leader of the Ahl-i-Hadith sect and the companion of Hazrat Mirza Sahib from early child-

1 *Al-An'am*, 22. 2 *Al-An'am*, 11–12.

hood, who wrote a review of Hazrat Mirza Sahib's first big book, the *Barahin-i-Ahmadiyya*. The Maulvi described this work of Hazrat Mirza Sahib as one without a parallel in the history of Islam.

This same Maulvi became angry and turned into a mortal enemy when Hazrat Mirza Sahib announced his claim to be the Promised Messiah. The Maulvi began to think that whatever importance and fame Hazrat Mirza Sahib had attained was due to his review of *Barahin-i-Ahmadiyya*. Mirza Sahib, the Maulvi thought, owed his reputation to this review. The Maulvi's praise had led Hazrat Mirza Sahib to think excessively of himself! So, the Maulvi declared, he would repudiate Hazrat Mirza Sahib by criticizing and exposing him, just as he had raised him to importance by his earlier praise.

With this intention the Maulvi set out to tour all over India. He persuaded scores of *Ulema* to put their signatures to a *Fatwa* of *Kufr* prepared by him. Not only Hazrat Mirza Sahib himself but also his followers were *Kafirs*. Those who did not think them *Kafirs* were *Kafirs* too. This *Fatwa* was printed and published throughout the country. The Maulvi thought he had schemed successfully for the disgrace of Mirza Sahib. However, he did not know that God had decided to dispose of the Maulvi's schemes in His Own way. Angels in heaven were rehearsing the Divine Promise contained in 6:11.

فَحَاقَ بِالَّذِينَ سَخِرُوا مِنْهُمْ مَّا كَانُوا بِهِ يَسْتَهْزِءُونَ ۔

'That which they mocked at encompassed those of them who scoffed.'[3]

They also rehearsed the Divine Promise given to Hazrat Mirza Sahib himself:

اِنِّي مُهِينٌ مَنْ اَرَادَ اِهَانَتَكَ ۔

'I will humiliate him who seeks to humiliate thee.'

It so happened, dear reader, that not long after the publication of this *Fatwa* the popularity of the Maulvi began to decline. Until

3 *Al-An'am*, 11; and *Al-Anbiya*, 42.

now, he had never passed through a street in metropolitan Lahore without shop-keepers and all others standing in their places out of deference and respect for him. Even non-Muslims, Hindus and others, would follow suit and show reverence to him in imitation of Muslims. Wherever he went he was received with demonstrations of reverence. Seeing his hold on the people, the highest in the country's hierarchy, the Provincial Governor, the Governor-General, received him with great courtesy. After the publication of the *Fatwa*, however, for no apparent reason, the great regard he enjoyed among all classes of people began to decline. The decline went on until the members of his own sect decided to abandon him. He was no longer the leader he had once been. I have myself seen him at a railway station carrying his own heavy baggage – packages under his arms, on his back, and in his hands – as he walked, one in a crowd. People around hardly knew who he was. For some reason he lost standing in his own neighbourhood. Tradesmen and shop-keepers refused to sell anything to him on credit. He obtained his groceries through others. His domestic life also became bitter. Relations with his family deteriorated. His wife secured a separation; some of his sons and their wives refused to see him. One of the sons gave up Islam. His last days were most miserable. He lost all respect and importance, and died unhonoured, unsung, his end a moving commentary on the verse:

قُلْ سِيْرُوْا فِي الْاَرْضِ ثُمَّ انْظُرُوْا كَيْفَ كَانَ عَاقِبَةُ الْمُكَذِّبِيْنَ۔

'And go about in the earth to see the end of those who treated the Messengers of God as liars.'[4]

A second example of disgraceful death suffered by an enemy is that of Chiragh Din of Jummu. This man first counted himself a follower of Hazrat Mirza Sahib, but later decided to claim spiritual office for himself. He declared that he had been commanded by God to reform the world. He published pamphlets and articles against Hazrat Mirza Sahib. Not content with this, he decided to pray against him. The prayer was to be printed and published. The prayer said:

4 *Al-An'am*, 12.

اے خدا! تیرا دین اس شخص (یعنی حضرت اقدسؑ) کی وجہ سے فتنے میں ہے اور یہ شخص لوگوں
کو ڈراتا ہے کہ طاعون میرے ہی سبب سے نازل ہوئی ہے اور زلزلے بھی میری ہی تکذیب کا نتیجہ
ہیں۔ تو اس شخص کو جھوٹا کر۔ اور طاعون کو اب اُٹھالے تاکہ اس کا جھوٹا ہونا ثابت ہوجائے اور
حق اور باطل میں تمیز کر دے۔ (رسالہ چراغ دین۔ حقیقۃ الوحی)

'O God, this man [meaning Hazrat Mirza Sahib] is the cause of grave mischief in your religion. He is also frightening people by telling them that the plague has come on account of him and that the earthquakes are the result of a denial of his claims.'

'O God, prove him a liar. Remove the plague, so that the lie becomes evident and truth manifest from falsehood.' (A pamphlet by Chiragh Din, cited in *Haqiqat-ul-Wahy*)

This prayer was sent to the press. But how the Hand of God seized him! The prayer had only been copied by the *katib* and had not yet been pressed on the printing stone when the plague which he knew had been described by Hazrat Mirza Sahib as a Divine Sign, and for the disappearance of which this Maulvi had addressed this prayer to God, seized him and his family. First, his two sons (his only children) died. Then his wife left him and ran away with someone else. Then he himself fell a victim to it and died. While he was dying he said, 'O God even You have abandoned me.'

The death of Chiragh Din of Jummu was eloquent proof that hostility to men of God is no ordinary thing. Sooner or later it involves the offender in divine punishment.

Others besides Chiragh Din addressed the *Dua-i-mubahila* (prayer for a divine decree) and were soon seized by God. One was Maulvi Ghulam Dastgir of Kasur, a scholar of the Hanafi School and a man of great influence in his sect. He also prayed invoking divine punishment for the liar. Within a few months this Maulvi died of plague, an object-lesson to all. Another was Faqir Mirza of Dulmiyal, in the district of Jhelum, who started broadcasting that the Promised Messiah (on whom be peace) was to end life by the 27th of Ramadhan 1321 A.H. He had had a revelation to this effect, he said. He put this claim in writing and handed the writing to local members of the Ahmadiyya Jama'at. It contained accounts of a vision and the definite claim that if Hazrat Mirza Sahib and his

Movement did not come to an end by the 27th of Ramadhan 1321 A.H. he would be willing to accept any punishment. The writing was attested by a large number of signatories. An examination of the document showed that it had been written on the 7th of Ramadhan. The 27th of Ramadhan passed. Nothing happened. The truthful had nothing to fear from the boasts of liars. But the following year, in the month of Ramadhan, plague visited Dulmiyal and claimed his wife. Later he himself fell a victim to it and exactly one year after he had signed away the fateful document, that is, on the 7th of Ramadhan 1322 A.H., he died in racking pain. A few days later his daughter also died.

Examples of deaths invited by hostile deniers as the Judgment of God are many. They run to hundreds or even thousands. Thousands of men defeated in argument and chagrined by defeat addressed desperate prayers to God, asking for the death or discomfiture of Hazrat Mirza Sahib. The result was their own discomfiture or death. The wonderful part of it is that God showed this tragic Sign in characteristically different ways. Those who prayed for the death of the 'liar' in their own lifetime, died in the lifetime of Hazrat Mirza Sahib. Those who said that a longer life was no sign of being truthful (that, in fact liars had longer lives, that Masailma the pretender lived long after the Holy Prophet and so on) lived long and were proved the spiritual kin of Masailma the pretender.

A sign of the latter kind was provided by Maulvi Sana Ullah of Amritsar, editor of the weekly *Ahl-i-Hadith*. The Maulvi exceeded all bounds. Hazrat Mirza Sahib, following the teaching of the Holy Quran, invited the Maulvi to a *Mubahila* (prayer for a divine decree). The verse of the Holy Quran sanctioning this method of invoking decision by God says:

فَمَنْ حَآجَّكَ فِيْهِ مِنْۢ بَعْدِ مَا جَآءَكَ مِنَ الْعِلْمِ فَقُلْ تَعَالَوْا نَدْعُ
اَبْنَآءَنَا وَاَبْنَآءَكُمْ وَنِسَآءَنَا وَنِسَآءَكُمْ وَاَنْفُسَنَا وَاَنْفُسَكُمْ ثُمَّ
نَبْتَهِلْ فَنَجْعَلْ لَّعْنَتَ اللّٰهِ عَلَى الْكٰذِبِيْنَ۔

'Now, who disputes with thee concerning it, after what has come to thee of knowledge, say to him, "Come let us call our sons and your sons, and our women and your women, and our people and your people, and let us pray fervently and invoke the curse of Allah on those who lie".'[5]

The challenge to seek a decision by such a serious prayer frightened the Maulvi. All methods to persuade him to seek a divine decision in this way failed. The Maulvi did not accept the challenge, but did not stop his hostility. Hazrat Mirza Sahib then wrote out a prayer and proposed that the Maulvi should copy and publish it in his paper *Ahl-i-Hadith*. The prayer invoked Almighty God to decide between him and the Maulvi on the criterion that the pretender would die in the lifetime of the other. Even this did not meet with the Maulvi's acceptance. Again and again he wrote, and wrote strongly, that this was no criterion, and that he did not accept it. The Holy Quran, he said, taught that the liar had a longer lease of life. The Law of God proved the same. Masailma lived longer than the Holy Prophet. God convicted the Maulvi by his own criterion. God gave him a long life and made him live after Hazrat Mirza Sahib had died. The Maulvi thus proved himself a Sign of God.

Enemies' disgraceful end

In different ways the enemies of the Promised Messiah met with a disgraceful end. Those who said the criterion was 'short life for the liar' died in his lifetime. Those who said the criterion was 'long life for the liar' lived after him. Abu Jahl and Masailma (examples respectively of a short and a long life, relative to the Holy Prophet's), were reproduced in the history of the Promised Messiah, who was proved true like his prototype, the Holy Prophet (on whom be peace). The dealings of God with the enemies of the Promised Messiah were appropriate to their own professions. Not accidents, but a divine design seemed to determine the end of each. Enemies of the Promised Messiah have suffered in other ways. They have experienced punishments of many different kinds. The afflictions they have seen are without parallel in history. A description of them would take too long and this is not the place for it. Examples of them have been experienced by nearly every country

5 *Al-Imran*, 62.

and every people. Plague, earthquakes, war-fever, famine, wars, have visited different parts of the world and spread ruin.

Individual enemies have suffered in most peculiar ways. Often an enemy met his end through a malady or misfortune he wished on the Promised Messiah. If someone maliciously accused him of suffering from leprosy, then leprosy seized the accuser. If someone gave out that the Promised Messiah had died or was destined to die of plague, then plague claimed the author of the wishful lie. Dr Abdul Hakim Khan of Patiala claimed to prophesy that Hazrat Mirza Sahib would die of lung-disease. The doctor himself died of protracted lung-disease. Hundreds of other examples can be cited. Whatever lie was invented against Hazrat Mirza Sahib claimed the inventor as its victim. Dreadful Signs were shown by God in his support. It is necessary only to contemplate them with an open mind. The power and revenge of God became evident in them. They demonstrated clearly that Hazrat Mirza Sahib was a true servant of God. The tremendous and watchful regard which God showed for him and which He continues to show can mean nothing else.

Argument 8
Adored by Angels

We know from the Holy Quran that God created Adam and commanded the angels to do obeisance to him. The usual method of obeisance is to prostrate oneself. But this sort of self-abasement is shown only to God. To show it to others, however high and mighty, is forbidden. One may not prostrate oneself even to prophets, not even to the Chief of the prophets, Muhammad Mustafa (on whom be peace and the blessings of God). Not only is prostration to anyone other than God forbidden; it is counted among the worst of sins. Whoever is guilty of it loses the favour and grace of God. One may prostrate oneself in a different sense, however; in this sense prostration is not an act of worship.

It cannot be said that prostration was permitted when the human race was young and was forbidden when the race became more mature. Such a thing would be quite wrong. Prostration is a form of *shirk*. It amounts to setting up equals with God and this, according to Islamic conceptions, can never be right. Acts of *shirk* could not have been permitted at any time: God is One and the Oneness of God is a basic conception. If it is said that prostrating oneself to beings other than God was permissible at first, but was forbidden later on, being a species of *shirk*, then Satan would have an important text in his own favour. Satan refused to prostrate himself before man, saying man was not God. This may have offended God at the time, but later even God forbade obeisance to man, and to beings other than God.

When angels prostrate themselves before man

Obeisances and prostrations to beings other than God can never be right. They were not right in the past and they are not right today. When angels were commanded by God to prostrate themselves before man, prostration was not to be an act of worship. This prostration had a different meaning. The Arabic language provides for this meaning: it is complete obedience. *Sajdah* may mean 'worship' or 'obedience'. In the Arabic lexicon *Lisan-ul-Arab* (vol. IV, under *Sajdah*), we have:

> 'He who shows perfect obedience to another may be said to have performed *Sajdah.*'

The command to angels to perform *Sajdah* to Adam was not a command to *worship* Adam, but a command to *obey* him. Obedience to man was to help man in his plans and aspirations. The command to angels to help Adam is repeated in the time of every prophet. A person who claims to have been appointed to spiritual office should expect and receive the help of angels. He should receive such help because he is commissioned by God for such an office.

Help from angels

From the life of the Holy Prophet (on whom be peace and the blessings of God) can be cited a number of incidents which demonstrate the help which the Holy Prophet received from angels in his plans and projects. One such example is the Battle of Badr. In this battle the angels struck the minds of the enemy with inordinate fear. As the Holy Prophet picked up a handful of pebbles and threw them towards the enemy, a swift wind began to blow. Another example was witnessed during the Battle of the Ditch. Muslims were surrounded by the enemy. The siege might have succeeded but for the fact that a fire lit by a chief was extinguished by the wind, and this led to a panic in the enemy camp. Yet another example is the Holy Prophet's miraculous escape from an attempt by the Jews to poison him.

The help of angels usually comes under cover of natural processes and natural events. The first conditions and causes of all natural processes and events are the angels. When a prophet finds himself confronted by enemies and a conflict ensues, angels become busy turning processes of nature to the advantage of the prophet. In spite of the worst natural disadvantages success attended the Holy Prophet, not his enemies. Success which comes thus is proof of a prophet's authenticity.

Help from the angels came to the Promised Messiah also. He experienced the support of angels and their backing. They saved him from all sorts of difficulties; they directed processes of nature in his favour. I quote a well-known example. The Promised Messiah and a group of companions including Hindus, Muslims, and men of other religions were asleep under a roof. Suddenly he woke up and felt that the roof was about to collapse. No signs of an imminent collapse were apparent. A faint sound, perhaps the sound of a worm eating into the wood, could be heard. The Promised Messiah wakened all his companions and said they should all get out. The companions did not heed the advice and went to sleep again. They said that Mirza Sahib was mistaken and that there was no danger. After a little while, Hazrat Mirza Sahib experienced the feeling for a second time. Again he wakened his companions, this time insisting strongly that they should move out of the room. The companions agreed, not without grumbling. They said Hazrat Mirza Sahib had the room vacated because of a delusion. Hazrat Mirza Sahib, on the other hand, felt that the collapse of the room waited on his own exit. He made everybody get out first before he got out himself. He then placed one foot on the staircase and had just lifted the other when the roof came down with a thud. All were filled with amazement and all expressed gratitude to Hazrat Mirza Sahib. Their lives were saved.

It often happened that during serious illness he would have cures told to him. A drug would appear in a dream, sometimes a waking dream. Drugs and the bottles in which they are contained do not move about. Their appearance could only be an act of the angels. The curative and other properties of drugs also are controlled in the last resort by angels, their first causes. Once the Promised Messiah became very ill. He used some drugs, but derived no benefit from them. Then an appearance presented itself and declared, 'I am peppermint.' Peppermint was the treatment and the illness disappeared.

Sometimes it happened that someone would come to murder him. Often the coming of such a man was anticipated by him through a divine premonition. Or the angels would strike the murderer with fear, as in the Battle of Badr. Murderers would change into followers. The sight of the Promised Messiah would convert them; and they would decide to join him instead of wishing to murder him (incidents reminiscent of Hazrat Omar, who became converted in an effort to murder the Holy Prophet).

Household protected from plague

The greatest sign of help by angels appeared at the time of the plague which first came into this part of the world in the lifetime of the Promised Messiah. I shall have more to say about this later. Here I only wish to say that the plague assumed the symbolic appearance of an elephant wreaking havoc in the world. In the symbolic scene, the animal in the premonitory dream became tame and harmless and sat respectfully when it came near the Promised Messiah. The symbolic scene meant that the plague would not harm the Promised Messiah. The angels of God would see to this. In support of this promise of help through angels, the Promised Messiah had other revelations. One said, 'Fire is our slave, nay the slave of slaves.' On receiving such revelations he declared that he and his followers would remain relatively immune from the deadly effects of the plague. Individuals might suffer, but that would not alter the general truth, even as in the time of the Holy Prophet Muslims suffered in encounters with the enemy, but the enemy suffered much more.

He also announced that the town of Qadian would suffer much less than other places; that here the plague would not be so deadly as in other places and that the house in which he lived would remain completely immune. Not a single case of plague was to occur in the house itself. After these declarations the plague made its appearance in the sub-continent and wrought havoc. Every year hundreds of thousands of persons died of it. In spite of the fact that he had forbidden his followers to adopt the preventive inoculation, his followers suffered the fatal effects of the plague much less than others. This went on for several years. Many people were impressed. Thousands joined the fold. In fact the great majority of his followers at that time were the result of this sign.

When the plague visited the country, it seized many of his enemies. His own followers remained largely immune; only stray cases of the plague occurred amongst them. The visible protection which he and his followers enjoyed from the ravages of the plague was a clear Divine Sign. This kind of epidemic had been unknown before. It came after he had announced his prophetic vision about it. The epidemic spared him and his followers. The relative immunity demonstrated the truth of his revelation 'Fire is our slave, even the slave of slaves.' The angels carried out the promise. The germs of the plague acted in his favour and showed him the adoration and obedience which is their duty towards every Messenger of God.

The plague travelled to Qadian as to other places. But it did not stay in Qadian for long, leaving after three years. In other towns it stayed for as long as ten years, or even longer.

The protection which his household enjoyed provides incontrovertible proof of the loyalty and obedience of angels. Cases of the plague and of death from the plague occurred next door. The danger remained for three years. The household of the Promised Messiah consisted of more than a hundred persons, and was unhealthily situated in a depression. Still no death occurred in the house. Not even a rat suffered. (It is well known that when plague visits a place, the first casualties are the rats.) A wonderful sign, which should convince those willing to think. If it was not the angels who worked in his favour, then what was it? What was it which made this tremendous difference? Rulers and kings and men of power could not control forces which worked in his favour. Processes of nature seemed to have turned from their normal course and to have devoted themselves to his service. Doctors who could adopt the usual precautionary measures fell victims. Those who lived in healthy quarters far out of town could not escape it. Those who had themselves inoculated against it had to suffer. But he and the members of his household did not suffer at all. They accepted no treatment, adopted no precautionary measures. They did not go out of the town. Even the rats in his house did not suffer. The household was not a small one. It was large to start with and had become larger because of the many guests who had come to seek shelter from the plague.

If the plague had not visited Qadian, or if after visiting Qadian it had not come and affected his neighbourhood, it could have been said that the immunity which he, his family, and members of his household enjoyed was a matter of accident. But he had proclaimed this fact of immunity long before, a prophecy based on divine communications. Some time after its proclamation, angels devoted themselves to the execution of the prophecy. The plague came to Qadian, but it came as a slave. It did its work, but under definite limitations, as though it were under someone's vigilance. It came to the town, affected his closest neighbours, but did not touch any member of his household. This is evidence of the devotion of angels to him and to his cause. They had been told to obey him and they carried out the command in true spirit. They were appointed to protect him. Forces of nature were enslaved for his sake.

The devotion of natural forces to him and to his cause is proved by many other incidents. But I hope the examples I have given will suffice, and that they will give some idea of the miraculous protection Hazrat Mirza Sahib enjoyed. These examples should make it clear that such consistent and constant divine support could not be earned by a liar and a pretender.

Argument 9
Gift of Special Knowledge

The ninth argument, also composed of many smaller arguments, pertains to the gift of special knowledge. The coming of prophets fulfils one cardinal need, namely, the instruction of mankind in principles without which spiritual life is not possible. Prophets come and guide men to the fountain of spiritual knowledge so that they can slake their spiritual thirst. Now, the ultimate source of all life, and therefore of spiritual life, is the One All-Powerful and All-Knowing God. Prophets come and establish links between men and their God. This results in knowledge of spiritual matters, which results in nearness to God and insight into His nature and attributes. He who would impart this knowledge to a whole generation of human beings must himself possess it in abundance.

Prophets endowed with special knowledge

He who claims to have been appointed to spiritual office cannot make good his claim unless he can show that he himself possesses such knowledge in abundance, and that God Himself imparts this knowledge to him and guides him in its acquisition. To measure the claim of Hazrat Mirza Sahib, therefore, we can draw on the criterion of special knowledge. We can see how far God endowed him with such knowledge. The Holy Quran says:

وَعَلَّمَ اٰدَمَ الْاَسْمَآءَ كُلَّهَا

'And He taught Adam all the names.'[1]

Names here means the attributes of God. Knowledge of these

1 *Al-Baqarah*, 32.

attributes is knowledge of all things. Knowledge of the Divine Being is knowledge of divine attributes, which also comes of observation and experience. But one appointed to a spiritual office is endowed with such knowledge by God. We read of the prophet Lot:

وَلُوطًا اٰتَيْنٰهُ حُكْمًا وَّعِلْمًا

'And to Lot We gave wisdom and knowledge.'[2]

And of David and Solomon:

وَلَقَدْ اٰتَيْنَا دَاوٗدَ وَسُلَيْمٰنَ عِلْمًا

'And We gave knowledge to David and Solomon.'[3]

And of Joseph:

وَلَمَّا بَلَغَ اَشُدَّهٗ اٰتَيْنٰهُ حُكْمًا وَّعِلْمًا

'And when he attained to years of strength, We granted him judgment and knowledge.'[4]

And of Moses:

وَلَمَّا بَلَغَ اَشُدَّهٗ وَاسْتَوٰى اٰتَيْنٰهُ حُكْمًا وَّعِلْمًا وَكَذٰلِكَ نَجْزِى الْمُحْسِنِيْنَ

'And when he reached the years of strength and knowledge, and attained maturity, We gave him wisdom and knowledge; and thus it is We reward those who do good deeds.'[5]

Of the Holy Prophet (on whom be peace and the blessings of God), we read:

وَعَلَّمَكَ مَا لَمْ تَكُنْ تَعْلَمُ وَكَانَ فَضْلُ اللّٰهِ عَلَيْكَ عَظِيْمًا ۔

2 *Al-Anbiya*, 75.
3 *Al-Naml*, 16.
4 *Yusuf*, 23.
5 *Al-Qasas*, 15.

And He has taught thee what thou knewest not and great is Allah's grace on thee.'[6]

All prophets, all those who hold spiritual office from God, are blessed with the gift of divine knowledge. The Holy Prophet was not only endowed with such knowledge; he was promised more and more knowledge. He was taught the prayer:

قُلْ رَّبِّ زِدْنِيْ عِلْمًا۔

'O my Lord, increase my knowledge from more to more.'[7]

One of the special gifts every Messenger of God receives from God, therefore, is the gift of special knowledge. Such knowledge was imparted to the Promised Messiah. The difference between the Promised Messiah and other messengers is that the Promised Messiah enjoyed a special grace and attained special knowledge, because of his devotion to his master and preceptor, the Holy Prophet of Islam. He received the gift in imitation of the Holy Prophet. A special grace of God endowed the Promised Messiah with a special measure of natural and spiritual knowledge. Not only was he endowed with insight into spiritual truths, he was also endowed with the power to express those truths. He challenged his contemporaries in respect of both. Knowledge and the power to communicate knowledge were his as divine gifts.

The Holy Quran, an unchallenged literary miracle

Of the two I shall now describe the second, the power to communicate knowledge. As an example I cite the miracle of language, a spiritual inheritance from his master, the Holy Prophet (on whom be peace and the blessings of God). This miracle was not given to earlier prophets. About the Holy Quran a unique claim was first made:

وَاِنْ كُنْتُمْ فِيْ رَيْبٍ مِّمَّا نَزَّلْنَا عَلٰى عَبْدِنَا فَاْتُوْا بِسُوْرَةٍ مِّنْ
مِّثْلِهٖ ص وَادْعُوْا شُهَدَآءَكُمْ مِّنْ دُوْنِ اللّٰهِ اِنْ كُنْتُمْ صٰدِقِيْنَ۔

6 *Al-Nisa*, 114.

7 *Taha*, 115.

'And if you are in doubts as to what We have sent down to Our servant, then produce a chapter like it and call upon your helpers besides Allah, if you are truthful.'[8]

This challenge of the Holy Quran claims unique merit for the language and contents of the Holy Quran. The challenge is accompanied by the warning that those who deny the Holy Quran will never be able to produce anything like it. The merit of the Holy Quran to which the challenge pertains comprehends everything – its spiritual and moral teaching, its prophecies, its appeal, and not least its language and style. The challenge is addressed to all and sundry. Let them all match their literary productions with the Holy Quran. In one place we read:

كِتَابٌ اُحْكِمَتْ اٰيٰتُهٗ ثُمَّ فُصِّلَتْ مِنْ لَّدُنْ حَكِيْمٍ خَبِيْرٍ۔

'This is a Book whose verses have been made unchangeable and then have been expounded in detail. It is from the One, Wise and Aware.'[9]

Two broad hints are contained in the attributes of wisdom and awareness. The All-Wise God can reveal a book full of wisdom. The All-Aware God was aware that the world was entering an era of intellectual progress. Therefore intellectual miracles were to be shown to convince the world of the power and knowledge of God. Therefore, God made the Holy Quran a miracle of perfect knowledge and perfect expression. The Holy Quran lays down not only claims, but also arguments and evidence. It is its own witness.

The Promised Messiah was a disciple, an imitation of his master the Holy Prophet (on whom be peace and the blessings of God). The gifts of the Promised Messiah, therefore, were a reflection of the gifts of his master. His light was a borrowed light. Small wonder that the Promised Messiah was able to demonstrate the miracle of mastery of language. He had attended no Madrassah. He had private coaches of ordinary ability. He only read parts of some well-known texts with them. He never travelled to Arab countries. Nor did he live in towns where Arabic was in vogue. He lived in a village and his resources were limited.

8 *Al-Baqarah*, 24. 9 *Hud*, 2.

The Promised Messiah's Arabic works

When he announced his claim and turned to the work of reform, his critics first attacked his lack of learning. They described him as a Munshi, that is to say, a half-educated scribe. He was literate; so he was able to write. Some of his writings had attracted attention; so he had come to have a reputation. He was no scholar, knew no Arabic, and did not have the qualifications to pronounce on religious matters. This criticism was raised in every conversation and in every hostile writing. A wall of prejudice was erected against him. It was untrue to say that he knew no Arabic, however. He had read the standard books. But he had certainly not had the benefit of instruction from any great scholar. He had earned no testimonial after study at an old school. He was not one of the leading *Ulema* of the country, nor was he a Maulvi of any status. When this criticism spread far and wide and the Mullas started trumpeting it in and out of season, God granted him special knowledge of the Arabic language. According to him, God endowed him with a vocabulary of 40,000 words in a single night. He was granted miraculous competence in the Arabic language; he was commanded to write Arabic books and promised special help. His first attempt in Arabic prose was a chapter he appended to his book *Aina-i-Kamalat-i-Islam*. This chapter contained a challenge to those who found fault with his lack of Arabic. He asked critics to produce something better. Nobody accepted the challenge. He then wrote book after book in Arabic. The number of his Arabic works amounts to more than twenty. Some of these were accompanied by offers of rewards amounting in some cases to Rs 10,000. (These cash rewards can still be won by anyone who produces something which equals them in beauty and power of language.) Nobody took up the challenge; nobody produced anything in reply. Some of his Arabic books were written as a challenge to Arabs. Even they failed to write in reply, and withdrew from the field. One of his books was addressed to Syed Rashid Riza, the well-known editor of *Al-Manar*. The Syed was invited to write in reply, but he did not. Other Arabs were similarly invited, and they did not.

Maulvis in the Indian sub-continent showed they were beaten when they said that the Arabic works said to have been written by Hazrat Mirza Sahib had really been written by an Arab who worked for him in secret. This criticism made it quite clear that the standard of his Arabic works was really very high; but his critics thought they were written for him by someone else. Hazrat Mirza Sahib met the criticism by suggesting that his adversaries could have the help of as many Arab and Syrian writers as they liked. Repeated efforts were made to attract them to this literary contest but nobody came forward. These Arabic works are still without a reply.

A sermon revealed

Besides these Arabic works, he produced an unpremeditated sermon in Arabic. He was commanded in a revelation to make the attempt, even though he had never before made a public speech in Arabic. The *Id-ul-Azhia* (the festival of sacrifice) was due the following day. In obedience to the revelation he delivered a lengthy sermon in Arabic after the *Id* prayers. This sermon was later published under the title *Khutba-i-ilhamiya* ('A Sermon Revealed'). This sermon is couched in Arabic of a high order. It impresses Arab and non-Arab writers and contains an exposition which enhances the merit of the literary production.

This intellectual feat is one of his most outstanding miracles. Some miracles make a great impression, but only on their immediate witnesses. Others produce an impression which lives long afterwards. This intellectual miracle is of the latter kind. The authenticity of this miracle has been admitted even by his enemies. This miracle imitates the miracle of the Holy Quran. The Holy Quran remains unparalleled as a literary composition. So will the Arabic works of the Promised Messiah. This sign of his authenticity will remain resplendent for ever.

Some who are taken aback by this miracle raise the objection that the claim to show the miracle of language is an insult to the Holy Quran, for it is the Holy Quran which first claimed unparalleled merit for its literary quality. To say that Mirza Sahib has been endowed with a miraculous mastery of language is to claim for his writings equality with the Holy Quran. This objection is based on sheer prejudice. The slightest thought would convince anybody that the miraculous merit of the Arabic writings of the Promised Messiah does not detract from the miraculous merit of the Holy Quran, which is only enhanced by those writings.

Merit is of two kinds: absolute and relative. Absolute merit stands by itself. It needs no comparison with other examples of merit. Relative merit is merit in comparison with others. This conception of absolute and relative merit may be illustrated from the Holy Quran. Says the Holy Quran (addressing Israel):

وَاَنِّيْ فَضَّلْتُكُمْ عَلَى الْعٰلَمِيْنَ ۔

'I exalted you above all peoples.'[10]

Addressing Muslims the Holy Quran uses a similar expression:

كُنْتُمْ خَيْرَ اُمَّةٍ اُخْرِجَتْ لِلنَّاسِ ۔

'You are the best people, raised for the good of mankind.'[11]

The Holy Quran describes both Israelites and Muslims as the best of all peoples. This seems like a contradiction, but if we examine the texts more carefully there is no contradiction at all. The description used for Israelites applies only to a certain time, namely, the time at which the description was used. The description used for Muslims applies to all times, past, present, and future. Similarly, the uniqueness and the miraculous character of the Arabic writings of the Promised Messiah are to be understood in a relative sense, that is relative to other human productions. But the uniqueness of the Holy Quran is absolute. It is superior to any human writing and superior also to other books revealed by God. The writings of the Promised Messiah, including his revealed sermon, possess only relative uniqueness while the Holy Quran possesses absolute uniqueness. Therefore the miracle of language which the Promised Messiah showed does not and cannot detract from the miraculous merit of the Holy Quran.

The Holy Quran proved more unique than ever

I said, however, that the writings of the Promised Messiah have enhanced the merit of the miracle of the Holy Quran. This may be

10 *Al-Baqarah,* 48.

11 *Al-Imran,* 111.

explained as follows. Uniqueness itself is of different kinds. One kind of uniqueness is insignificant. A writing may be unique among all known writings, but the difference in merit between it and the other writings may not be very great. The other writings may be inferior, but not very inferior to it. In a race the winning horse can win even if the difference between it and the second horse is only a few inches. This difference could have been larger. It could have been a difference of one yard or several yards. Similarly, a unique writing can be superior to other writings by a small degree or a very large one. The writings of the Promised Messiah stand between the Holy Quran and other writings. If writings can be found which are superior to human writings but inferior to the Holy Quran, this will show how superior is the literary merit of the Holy Quran. Hazrat Mirza Sahib's writings, therefore, have enhanced the merit of the Holy Quran. Writings which were placed equal with the Holy Quran have now been found inferior even to the writings of the Promised Messiah, and this raises still higher the merit of the Holy Quran. The miracle of the Promised Messiah is subordinate to the miracle of the Holy Quran. It serves only to bring out the uniqueness of the original miracle. It makes more evident than ever before how great is the distance between the Holy Quran and other literary compositions.

Arabic, the mother of all languages

Besides the gift of mastery of Arabic, which the Promised Messiah was granted by God, he also had insight through divine grace, into a unique characteristic of the Arabic language, namely that Arabic is the mother of all languages. This was a great and amazing discovery. European scholars, after laborious investigations, pointed to either Sanskrit or Pahlvi as the mother of languages. Some scholars thought that the original language had vanished altogether and that the earliest known languages, Sanskrit and Pahlvi, were branches of this original but extinct language. Arab scholars were not aware of the unique character of their own language. Even they, in deference to European scholars, looked for the most original language among languages other than their own. While scholars groped for the first human language, the Promised Messiah had divine insight into the subject. He was told that Arabic was the mother of all languages. It was a strange discovery. After reflection on the Holy Quran, however, it soon became clear that the discovery was in accord with the teaching of the Holy Quran, for one good reason: that the Holy Quran is a revelation for the entire world. By rights the language of this revelation should have been the language of all mankind. Only the first language, the original of all the subsequent languages which evolved out of it, could be described as the language of all mankind. The Holy Quran teaches that a prophet is spoken to by God in the language of those whom he has to address. Thus:

وَمَآ أَرْسَلْنَا مِنْ رَّسُوْلٍ إِلَّا بِلِسَانِ قَوْمِهٖ -

'And We have not sent any Messenger except with the language of his people.'[12]

The Holy Prophet (on whom be peace and the blessings of God) was a prophet to all mankind. By rights, therefore, the revealed guidance he received from God should have been in the universal language of man. Only the first language which man spoke could be described as the language of man. As divine revelation descended on the Holy Prophet in Arabic, Arabic must be the first language of man, the mother of all languages.

As proof of the truth of this discovery Hazrat Mirza Sahib, through the special grace of God, laid down general principles by which a relatively original language could be distinguished from a relatively derived one. On the basis of these principles he was able to say that Arabic was the mother of all languages, the language revealed by God to man, the language from which the many languages of the world grew as branches from a stem. No other language satisfies the criteria of ultimate origin. Hazrat Mirza Sahib planned to write a book on the subject. Unfortunately this could not be completed; however, it contains a statement of general principles which can be worked out in detail and the whole subject expounded in a suitable manner. God willing, I have a mind to work on the broad principles and hints which the Promised Messiah's unfinished work contains, and to write a systematic

12 *Ibrahim*, 5.

account of the origin of languages. In my account I should like to provide detailed proof of this important discovery by the Promised Messiah. I should also like to use, with due criticism, the principles laid down by European experts in the science of languages. 'And there is no help except what comes from Allah.' His discovery will, however, remain unparalleled in the history of Arabic studies and will prove a landmark in the new view of Islam which the world is certain to adopt in the future. The discovery will bring added strength to Islam.

Besides these intellectual gifts which the Promised Messiah received so abundantly from God, he also received those spiritual gifts which are the special prerogative of prophets. He invited others to match their intellectual powers with his God-given powers, but nobody accepted the invitation. As I have said, Hazrat Mirza Sahib was a teacher of no new religion or law. In fulfilment of ancient prophecies he came only to serve and propagate the Religion of the Holy Prophet (on whom be peace and the blessings of God). To explain and to extend in the world a knowledge of the Holy Quran was his mission and message. After the Holy Quran no new spiritual knowledge can descend from Heaven. All knowledge which man needs for his moral and spiritual advancement is contained in this, the Last Book of God. After the Holy Prophet (on whom be peace and the blessings of God) there can be no new teacher or instructor for mankind. Whoever rises to teach and to instruct must draw on knowledge already imparted by the Holy Prophet. Such a teacher can be a restorer of forgotten treasures, nothing more. His function is to recover or renew, not to create or invent. A revelation of the Promised Messiah says:

كُلُّ بَرَكَةٍ مِّنْ مُّحَمَّدٍ صَلَّى اللّٰهُ عَلَيْهِ وَسَلَّمَ، فَتَبَارَكَ مَنْ عَلَّمَ وَتَعَلَّمَ

'All blessings are from Muhammad, blessings of God be on him and His peace. Therefore, blessed is he who taught, and blessed is he who learnt.'

The revelation describes the relation between the Holy Prophet and the Promised Messiah, the master and the disciple.

Special knowledge of the Holy Book: Twelve discoveries

As the final word on spiritual truths has been said in the Holy Quran, those who are now appointed to any spiritual office can only have the gift of special knowledge of the Holy Quran itself. They cannot have new knowledge of any other kind. The authenticity and the quality of their contact with God will be judged by the quality of their knowledge of the Holy Quran. Such knowledge will have to have the qualities of divine, not merely human, knowledge. It will have to be distinguished by insight into the nature and character of God and into the nature and character of the many stages of spiritual development. It will have to be very different from the logical deductions of philosophers. We find that the Promised Messiah received an abundance of this kind of knowledge. Indeed, so abundant was and is this knowledge from God that we could say, and say truthfully, that through the Promised Messiah the Holy Quran has been revealed again in our time. To say this would be in accord with a Tradition of the Holy Prophet himself, who said:

لَوْ كَانَ الْاِيْمَانُ مُعَلَّقًا بِالثُّرَيَّا لَنَالَهُ رَجُلٌ مِّنْ فَارِسَ -

'If ever the faith disappears to the skies, a man of Persian origin will restore it back to mankind.'

This Tradition relates to the Promised Messiah, a Persian by descent.

I now proceed to give an account of the special knowledge of the Holy Quran which the Promised Messiah gave to the world. I shall begin with a fundamental aspect of this knowledge – one which proved to be of fundamental importance in his battle with other religions. With this, the victors became the vanquished and the vanquished became the victors. The Holy Quran, thought to be a dead book, became, with the discovery which I will presently describe, a living book again. The enemies of the Holy Book were dispersed.

Before the advent of the Promised Messiah, Muslims in general believed that the truths of the Holy Quran had been explained once and for all by the earlier doctors of Islam and the commentators of the Holy Quran. Nothing new could now be added. To try and add to that knowledge was futile, and even dangerous for the faith. The Promised Messiah, however, was assured by God that the Holy Quran was a world of spiritual knowledge. It was infinite in possible meanings even as the physical world was infinite in properties and attributes. The Holy Quran was as infinite in meaning as nature was in its properties. Science had demonstrated that knowledge of physical nature is boundless. The honey-bee is a minor creation, yet it continues to reveal more and more properties. The secrets contained in the different parts of its body and the functions of those parts seem to have no end. The tiniest blade of grass seems to hide within it an infinity of structure and functions. Why should the Word of God be limited in meaning? Was it to yield all its meaning in one or two generations and nothing in the succeeding generations? No, the Word of God would continue to enrich the world. It would not be like the mine which, once quarried, can be quarried no more. In fact the Word of God would be far more infinite in meaning than the world of external nature is in natural properties. The world of external nature would seem finite in comparison with the infinity of meaning which the Word of God holds within it. If external nature can yield new knowledge from day to day, if philosophy and science can continue to advance, if geology, archaeology, physiology, botany, zoology, astronomy, political science, political economy, sociology, psychology, ethics, and other natural studies can be added to daily, should not the Word of God yield more and more knowledge as we advance from one period of history to another? Why should we think the Word of God so limited or so lifeless that it was destined to display its living power for a time, after which it was to become as good as dead? Should we think that for several hundred years now the Holy Quran has yielded no new knowledge?

The lack of interest in religion and the lack of attachment to God and His teaching which we find today is – directly or indirectly – connected with the progress which science and philosophy have made in our time. If the Holy Quran is the Word of God, His very speech, it is but fitting that we should have derived newer and newer knowledge from it so that spiritual science should have kept pace with natural science. The errors of natural science, its deviations from truth and its exaggerations, should have been corrected, whenever and wherever necessary, by new knowledge drawn from the Holy Quran. When natural knowledge seemed contrary to the teaching of the Holy Quran, tending to cast doubt on its truth, we should have had assurances from the Holy Quran itself that the teaching of the Divine Book is rational and right, and the doubts raised by natural knowledge are due only to lack of reflection.

Prophecies in the Holy Quran about our time

Laying down this general principle Hazrat Mirza Sahib demonstrated by argument that the Holy Quran contains prophecies about our time. It gives not only a general account of the progress we observe today but also an account of some interesting developments which have taken place in our time. The earlier commentators and scholars had no knowledge of the conditions which would arise in our time. Therefore they could not understand the prophetic hints of the Holy Quran which have found fulfilment today. Invariably they interpreted these hints as a description of the Day of Judgment. Not finding it very easy they often distorted the meaning of the Holy Quran.

I quote here twelve signs of our time from the famous chapter *Al-Takwir* (81:2-13) of the Holy Quran:

إِذَا الشَّمْسُ كُوِّرَتْ - وَإِذَا النُّجُومُ انْكَدَرَتْ - وَإِذَا الْجِبَالُ سُيِّرَتْ -
وَإِذَا الْعِشَارُ عُطِّلَتْ - وَإِذَا الْوُحُوشُ حُشِرَتْ - وَإِذَا الْبِحَارُ سُجِّرَتْ -
وَإِذَا النُّفُوسُ زُوِّجَتْ - وَإِذَا الْمَوْءُودَةُ سُئِلَتْ - بِأَيِّ ذَنْبٍ قُتِلَتْ -
وَإِذَا الصُّحُفُ نُشِرَتْ - وَإِذَا السَّمَاءُ كُشِطَتْ - وَإِذَا الْجَحِيمُ سُعِّرَتْ -
وَإِذَا الْجَنَّةُ أُزْلِفَتْ -

When the sun is wrapped up;
And when the stars are obscured;
And when the mountains are made to move;
And the she-camels, ten months pregnant, are abandoned;
And when the beasts are gathered together;
And when the seas are made to flow forth, one into the other;
And when the people are brought together;

And when the girl child buried alive is questioned
About the crime for which she was killed;
And when books are spread far and wide;
And when the heaven is laid bare;
And when the fire is caused to blaze;
And when the garden is brought near.[13]

These verses are a picture of our time. Commentators have been misled by the first lines, 'When the sun is wrapped up/And when the stars are obscured' – two signs generally associated with the Day of Judgment. Therefore, the commentators have thought that the rest of the chapter also applies to Doomsday. This is not true, however, because the rest of the chapter is quite obviously a description of conditions and events of our time. The moving of mountains, for instance, the abandonment of camels as beasts of burden, and the regression of civilized man to the level of beasts, the segregation of primitive tribes (as in Australia, the USA, etc), the splitting of rivers for irrigation purposes, the gathering of people from distant parts of the world, the increased facilities for social and international contacts, the social and legal ban on infanticide, the tremendous increase in the publication of books, periodicals and newspapers, the extraordinary increase in our knowledge of heavenly bodies and (metaphorically) of spiritual truths, the increase in the publication of expositions of the Holy Quran and Islam, the phenomenal advances in sciences of different kinds and the resulting indifference to God, the increase in pleasure-seeking, and, lastly, the drawing near of the garden, or God's Grace to rehabilitate godliness in the world (faith will revive, opportunities for godly actions will increase, men will again be able to earn the pleasure of God and find access to His Paradise). Are not these Signs of the time in which we live?

The wrapping of the sun and the obscuring of the stars are Signs of the Day of Judgment; to say, therefore, that the chapter relates to that day is not correct, because the chapter goes on specifically to say that the time will mark the abandonment of the camel as a means of transport. Can this be a special sign of the Day of Judgment? No, because on that day not only camels but everything

13 *Al-Takwir*, 2–13.

else, animals, human beings, the nearest relations, father, mother, sons, daughters, wife, brothers, sisters, will be abandoned. Of this we have a description in the Holy Quran itself. When disruption on such a vast scale takes place there can be no point in speaking especially of the abandonment of camels. To mention this as an important sign seems ridiculous when the time is one of general and universal disruption. Then the question is What can the gathering of beasts mean as a sign of the Day of Judgment? What can be the meaning of the splitting of waters, the meeting of seas, questioning girl-children? These cannot be signs of the Day of Judgment. Questioning on the subject of girl-children can take place after the Resurrection, not at the time of universal destruction and confusion. The verses which follow the verses already quoted also indicate that the description contained in the chapter is not a description of Doomsday, but of events of this life and of this world. The chapter goes on to say:

وَالَّيْلِ إِذَا عَسْعَسَ - وَالصُّبْحِ إِذَا تَنَفَّسَ -

'And I call to witness the night as it passes away and the dawn as it begins to breathe.'[14]

This is a description of the alternation of night and day. Such alternation is possible in a settled universe in which the sun and the stars run their normal courses in their appointed ways. If the sun is wrapped up, as it will be on the Day of Judgment, how can we have the familiar alternation of night with day? The verses do not apply to Doomsday, as many commentators seem to think. They fairly apply to our own time. They are a description of the increase of sin, material advancement and social evil, and of the coming of the Grace of God and the resulting increase of belief and dissolution of doubt.

This is only one example of the prophecies contained in the Holy Quran about changes and events which were due to take place in our time. The example was cited by Hazrat Mirza Sahib himself, but the subject of prophecies of the Holy Quran has been studied further by his followers. In the literature since produced further descriptions of the tendencies – social, political and religious – of

14 *Al-Takwir*, 18–19.

our time and of the methods of dealing with those tendencies have been deduced from a careful study of the Holy Quran. A study of these descriptions will convince the most hardened disbeliever that the Holy Quran is a Book of God which contains a description of important world events, past, present and future. I might have gone on to give further examples, but that would be to deviate far from the subject.

Discoveries 2 to 10 about the Holy Quran

The *second* fundamental discovery about the Holy Quran which we owe to the Promised Messiah is the very important one that the Holy Quran never makes an assertion unless it also points to the reason for that assertion. This discovery is as important as it is true. It has placed in the hands of the followers of the Book a master-key with which they can open the doors to many other important truths. When the followers of the Promised Messiah proceeded to make a study of the Holy Quran, with this unique feature of the Holy Book in view, they found that thousands of assertions which were thought to be unsupported by rational demonstration, and which devotees of the Holy Quran were supposed to believe on authority as assertions of Almighty God, were found to carry their rational basis with them. This was an important revelation. The advance of science and the general development of scientific methods have promoted in our time the type of mind which accepts nothing on mere authority. It was therefore impossible for people in our time to accept statements in the Holy Quran unless they were accompanied by rational justification. With the Promised Messiah's emphasis on the Holy Quran's method of offering argument and assertion together, those who loved the Holy Quran were amply satisfied. They felt excited over the appropriateness with which the Holy Quran linked assertion with argument throughout its treatment. Readers no longer felt burdened with its teaching. The Holy Quran did not invite its readers to accept anything on mere authority. It invited them to accept beliefs and injunctions which appealed to their intellect and conscience. The Holy Quran was concerned not to enslave but to enlighten. The Promised Messiah also derived from it arguments for the Existence of God, taking them all from the Holy Text. These arguments cannot be rebutted by modern science. Their effect on the educated section of our generation has been enormous. Many who would have ended up as atheists are returning to God and godly ways.

Similarly, objections and difficulties which have been raised about angels were answered by the Promised Messiah out of the Holy Quran. The nature and purpose of the institution of prophets; the criteria of their authenticity; the belief in the Day of Judgment; the purpose of the good life; the value of religious ordinances – imperative, prohibitive and permissive: these and other important subjects were deduced by the Promised Messiah from the Holy Quran. The conceptions and the justification of them were presented with the help of texts drawn from the Holy Book. The Promised Messiah showed convincingly that modern science and philosophy cannot overawe the Holy Quran. They cannot show any contradiction between the Holy Quran and reason. Science was concerned with nature, the handiwork of God. The Quran was the Word of God. Both His handiwork and His Word are His. There can be no contradiction between the two. If ever the Word of God seems to go against facts of nature, it must be because it is not His true word, or if it is it cannot have been properly understood. The real Word of God cannot teach anything against the facts of nature.

The publication of these discoveries about the Holy Quran resulted in a new conviction, a new confidence about the Holy Quran. Followers of the Promised Messiah today are as busy as others in acquiring modern knowledge, knowledge of social sciences and philosophies. But at the same time their convictions about the beliefs and ordinances taught by the Holy Quran are as strong as they were at any time in the history of Islam. These convictions arise not from prejudices or from national or racial feeling, nor from love of tradition, but from reason and deliberation. Followers of the Promised Messiah are ready to prove anything which they believe. Other Muslims find themselves in a strange predicament. To save their belief they either have to remain ignorant of modern science and philosophy, or, against their own better reason and judgment, they have to keep denying and condemning as unbelief whatever modern science and philosophy have to teach. Their religious beliefs flourish in a world of fantasy, or else their minds and judgment are overwhelmed by new knowledge and they have little or no faith left in their hearts.

They profess Islam from fear but harbour doubts in their minds.

A *third* fundamental discovery about the Holy Quran which we owe to Hazrat Mirza Sahib is that where rational reflection gives rise to any doubt or difficulty about a given part of the Holy Quran, the solution to that doubt or difficulty will be found in the Holy Quran itself. Hazrat Mirza Sahib laid great stress on this feature of the Holy Book. Not only did he assert this; he proved it by concrete examples. The scale on which he did this is amazing. Practically all his life he dealt with difficulties raised by Muslims and non-Muslims about the Holy Quran. He derived his replies and his solutions from the Holy Quran itself. He never set assertion against assertion. He never said a thought was hateful because it was contrary to the Holy Quran. He dealt with every difficulty on its merits. He made a proper analysis of everything and then, by arguments drawn from the Holy Quran and acceptable to human reason and judgment, demonstrated the baselessness of those doubts. Few who considered the replies with an unprejudiced mind remained unconvinced or unimpressed.

A *fourth* discovery was the distinctive characteristics which made the Holy Quran superior to other religious books. Before the time of the Promised Messiah, one only heard of the broad claim that in some way and in some sense the Holy Quran was higher in merit than any other book held sacred by any other religion. The Holy Quran was said to be unique, but nobody could say why and in what sense. Hazrat Mirza Sahib provided the answer, again out of the Holy Quran itself. He returned to this important subject again and again. Those who care to follow his writings will not fail to be captivated by the appeal and persuasiveness of the arguments he put forward. One wishes in fact to give one's all for the sake of the Holy Quran and the Holy Prophet through whom mankind received this gift of precious guidance.

A *fifth* discovery was the multi-sidedness of the Holy Text. A given verse can have a variety of meanings, some near the surface, some deeper, some deeper still. Whatever the intellectual level of the reader, his background or experience, he can find in a given verse a meaning which will suit his understanding, and which he will find true and relevant. The same words serve different purposes and different kinds of persons. A man of ordinary understanding will discover in those words a simple and convincing teaching which he does not find hard to understand and which he has no difficulty at all in believing. Another man, endowed with a slightly higher intellect, will find in the same words a meaning appropriate to his understanding and experience. A man of still higher intellect will find in it a higher meaning. The Holy Quran has something important and relevant to impart to men of all intellectual levels. Those of low intellect will not find the Holy Quran beyond their understanding; those of high intellect will not find the Book beneath theirs. Men of all levels will find the Book significant and important and able to effect their intellectual and moral improvement.

A *sixth* discovery was that the Holy Quran imparts knowledge about natural phenomena which is both necessary and sufficient for the spiritual advancement of man. It is not a book of spiritual truths only, for it contains other important truths. Insight into these other truths advances with time. At all times in history, therefore, men can turn to the Holy Quran to quicken their faith in God.

A *seventh* discovery we owe to Hazrat Mirza Sahib is the discovery of principles of interpretation by which we can guard against error in our effort to understand the Holy Quran and to apply it to current difficulties. By observing these principles of interpretation, a reader can also gain insight into truths and facts of which he may have been unaware before. Helped by these principles, a reader of the Holy Quran can experience a new joy every time he turns to a reading of the Holy Book.

The *eighth* discovery we owe to Hazrat Mirza Sahib is that the Holy Quran contains a systematic account of the stages of spiritual advancement of which human beings are capable. This subject had been dealt with before, but only on the basis of general experience and argument. Mistakes were committed in scholarly expositions. Hazrat Mirza Sahib found the whole subject in the Holy Quran itself. Under divine grace he defined the stages in the spiritual advance of man (from the lowest to the highest) presented systematically by the Holy Book. Following this account, a seeker after truth and spiritual progress can enjoy the faith and fruits peculiar to every stage. Knowledge of spiritual stages in this sense did not exist before. People did read the Holy Book, but they were only able to point to different parts of the text which contained partial references to the subject. Nobody was able to put the parts together and present the subject of spiritual advance as a systematic and consistent whole.

A *ninth* discovery we owe to Hazrat Mirza Sahib is the discovery of a perfect sequence throughout the Holy Book. The verses of each chapter and the chapters themselves have a rational sequence. Every chapter, every verse in every chapter, and every word in every verse, is in its ideal place. So perfect is the arrangement of words, verses, and chapters, that the internal arrangement of other books seems as nothing compared with the internal arrangement of the Holy Quran. The arrangement in other books is superficial, mostly turning upon the subject in hand, the theme under discussion. The arrangement of the Holy Quran is deep and manifold. Not only do the words and verses follow an order appropriate to the subject in hand, their arrangement is appropriate from many other points of view. Every passage of the Holy Book holds within it a variety of meaning, each meaning appropriate for a particular purpose or point of view. The arrangement of words and verses in each passage is found appropriate to all sorts of purposes and points of view. Such an arrangement is miraculous. It answers to the needs of the general theme of the passage as well as the special themes which one may find beneath the surface. The beauty of arrangement survives whether we regard the passage from one point of view or another. Such an arrangement cannot be found in any human book.

A *tenth* discovery we owe to Hazrat Mirza Sahib is that the Holy Quran contains a systematic account of the various degrees and stages of good and evil in moral life. The Holy Book tells us what virtues lead to what other virtues, what vices to what other vices. Knowledge of this kind is of inestimable help in the practical promotion of the good life. The good life grows by stages, and each stage can be defined and described. This makes possible progress in virtue which without this would remain impossible. Such knowledge enables a toiler on the moral path to treat each step forward as preparation for the next. He can also save himself from slipping back any further. Hazrat Mirza Sahib described these things from the Holy Quran and presented them as yet another miracle of the Holy Book. The Holy Book points to springs where the spiritually thirsty may slake their thirst and the ditches and dark alleys which the spiritual wayfarer would wish to avoid.

Surah Fatiha, a synopsis of the Holy Quran

An *eleventh* discovery of Hazrat Mirza Sahib was that the *Surah Fatiha*, the opening chapter of the Holy Quran, is a true epitome of the Holy Book, a kind of prologue or prolegomena, the rest being the text and the explanation. Everything that is dealt with in detail in the Holy Book, be it belief or practice or whatever, is presented in essence in the *Surah Fatiha*. He wrote many commentaries on this short chapter, in which he presented interesting and invigorating themes all derived from this one chapter. The exposition of Islam for the benefit of Muslims as well as others has been immeasurably facilitated by this discovery. Many people prefer synopses to detailed expositions. A detailed account is difficult to follow, a synopsis not so difficult. Hazrat Mirza Sahib showed that almost any subject can be deduced from this one short chapter. Attributes of God, important spiritual truths, important stages in spiritual advancement are all to be found in this first chapter.

These discoveries are of a fundamental character. They are discoveries of principles which have proved indispensable in the exposition of Islam today.

But to Hazrat Mirza Sahib we owe a *twelfth* discovery regarding the Holy Quran: the meaning of parts and verses of the Holy Text, interpreted with special relevance to present-day needs. Beauty of deduction and interpretation abounds in his works; examples would fill many volumes. A large range of knowledge such as this only points to the source of his abundant grace, which could be none other than the All-Knowing God Himself. Of Him the Holy Quran teaches:

وَلَا يُحِيطُونَ بِشَيْءٍ مِّنْ عِلْمِهِۦٓ إِلَّا بِمَا شَآءَ ۚ

'And they [men] can encompass nothing of His Knowledge except what He pleases.'[15]

It is not for man to discover knowledge beyond his limits. Such knowledge can only come from God. Small wonder we find in the

15 *Al-Baqarah*, 256.

Holy Book oceans of meaning when we read with the help of guiding principles laid down by the Promised Messiah.

Hazrat Mirza Sahib drew repeated attention to a criterion of truth and purity laid down in the Holy Quran:

لَا يَمَسُّهٗۤ اِلَّا الْمُطَهَّرُوْنَ۔

'Only the pure of heart will reach it' [i.e. the Holy Quran].[16]

Reaching (lit. 'touching') the Holy Book means having access to its inner meaning. No wonder Hazrat Mirza Sahib asked his critics and those who denied him: 'If I be an impostor, why should I be favoured with ever new knowledge of the Holy Book?'

He invited scholars and doctors of his time to come forward and match their understanding of the Holy Book against his. An umpire would draw a passage out of the Holy Book, then hand it to him and whoever should come forward to compete with him in an effort to draw new meanings out of the Holy Text. It would then become clear who received divine grace in an effort to understand the Holy Quran. This invitation was repeated many times. Nobody came forward. And no wonder, because in the understanding of the Holy Quran, others cannot match even the followers of Hazrat Mirza Sahib. I propose to close this argument with a passage from the Persian verse of Hazrat Mirza Sahib commending the beauties of the Holy Quran:

از نورِ پاکِ قرآں صبحِ صفا دمیده   بر غنچہائے دل ہا بادِ صبا وزیده
ایں روشنی و لمعاں شمس الضحیٰ ندارد   ویں دلبری و خوبی کس در قمر ندیده
یُوسف بقعرِ چاہے محبوس ماند تنہا   ویں یُوسفے کہ تن ہا از چاه برکشیده
از مشرقِ معانی صد ہا دقائق آورد   قدِّ ہلالِ نازک زاں نازکی خمیده
کیفیّتِ علومش دانی؟ چہ شان دارد   شہدیست آسمانی از وحیِ حق چکیده
آں نیّرِ صداقت چوں رو بعالم آورد   ہر بُومِ شب پرستے در کُنج خود خزیده
رُوئے یقیں نبیند ہرگز کسے بدُنیا   اِلّا کسے کہ باشد با رویش آرمیده

16 *Al-Waqiah*, 80.

آنکس کہ عالمش شد مخزنِ معارف — واں بے خبر ز عالم کیں عالمے ندیدہ
بارانِ فضلِ رحمٰن آمد بمقدمِ او — بد قسمت آنکہ از وے سوئے دگر دویدہ
میلِ بدی نباشد اِلّا رگے ز شیطاں — آں را بشر بدانم کز ہر شرے رہیدہ
اے کانِ دل رُبائی دانم کہ از کجائی — تو نورِ آں خدائی کیں خلق آفریدہ
میلم نماند باکس محبوبِ من توئی بس — زیراکہ زاں فغاں رس نورت بما رسیدہ

From the pure light of the Quran came the dawn of purity,
And over the buds of hearts blew the morning breeze.

The mid-day sun does not have this light or this lustre,
Even the moon does not show this fascination, this charm.

Joseph remained alone in the bottom of the well,
But this Joseph [the Holy Quran] pulled us all out of the well.

It [the Holy Quran] has derived hundreds of important points from the East of Meanings,
The curve of the crescent has become more curved because of its subtle delicacy.

Knowest thou the glory of the truths [of the Holy Quran]?
Celestial honey drips down with divine inspiration.

When that sun of truth turned to this world,
Every night-loving owl crept into its hollow.

Nobody in this world achieves certainty of belief,
Except he who receives comfort from its face.
He who attained a knowledge of it became a treasure-house of ideas,

He who remained ignorant of it remained ignorant of everything.

The rain of the bounty of the Bounteous God came down for his reception,
Woe to him who turned away from it in another direction.

Nothing tempts anyone to evil except the devil in him,
To me he is a man who avoids all evil.

O mine of beauty, I know from where you have come:
You are the Light of the Lord Who created this world and all.

I love not anyone else, Thou alone art my love,
It is through this love that Thy Light has come to me.

Argument 10
Prophecies

The tenth argument, which is myriad smaller arguments, is that God granted to Hazrat Mirza Sahib abundant knowledge of His secrets and this knowledge is evidence of his truth and of his divine commission. The Holy Quran says:

فَلَا يُظْهِرُ عَلٰى غَيْبِهٖٓ اَحَدًا - اِلَّا مَنِ ارْتَضٰى مِنْ رَّسُوْلٍ

> 'And He [Allah] reveals not His secrets to any except the one whom He chooses, namely, His Messenger.'[1]

An abundance of revealed knowledge about matters inaccessible to human beings is a sign by which Divine Messengers may be distinguished from others. Such Messengers receive crystal-clear *wahy* (revelation) free from all confusion. They are helped by convincing signs and are informed about great events before they happen. They are commissioned by God. To deny them is to deny the Holy Quran. The Holy Quran teaches that knowledge of God's secrets is granted only to God's Messengers. To deny this is to deny all prophets. Prophets have ever presented God-given knowledge of secrets as proof of their authenticity. The Bible teaches that the sign of a false prophet is that he should say something in the name of God and this should not come true. When in the light of this we examine the claim of Hazrat Mirza Sahib, the Promised Messiah (on whom be peace), his truth shines forth like the noonday sun. So abundantly and so constantly was he favoured by knowledge of God's secrets that, excepting the Holy Prophet of Islam (on whom be peace and the blessings of God), the prophecies of other prophets provide no parallel to his. In fact, it would be true to say that if the prophetic signs given to the Promised Messiah were divided

1 *Al-Jinn*, 27–8.

among prophets, they would be enough to prove the prophetic status of many.

Of these prophetic signs I give below an account of twelve principal ones as examples.

The prophecies of the Promised Messiah were of many different kinds. Some related to political changes, some to social developments to cosmic events, some to religious matters, some to intellectual activities, some to the birth of children, some to the cessation of births, some to earthly transformations, some to relations between nations, some to relations between rulers and their subjects, some to the success of his mission, some to the defeat and destruction of his enemies and some to the future shape of things. His prophecies, in short, can be divided into a number of categories. A description of the categories would make a long list.

The twelve prophecies which I wish to describe have already been fulfilled. The first of these relates to Afghanistan.

Prophecy No. 1: Afghan martyrs

The martyrdom of Sahibzada Syed Abdul Latif and Maulvi Abdur Rahman of Afghanistan and the events which followed.

May God give rulers His special protection and save them from the consequences of errors in the commission of which they had no hand! Many years ago, Hazrat Mirza Sahib received a revelation:

شَاتَانِ تُذْبَحَانِ وَكُلٌّ مَنْ عَلَيْهَا فَانٍ ۔

> 'Two goats will be slaughtered; everyone who lives here will meet this end.'

The word *Shatan* (two goats) can be a symbol for 'women' or for 'loyal and obedient subjects', so much is clear from the generally accepted meaning of dream symbols. If we take the word to mean women, then the sentence does not make sense. Women are not slaughtered; it is men who are slaughtered. *Shatan* (goats), therefore, means two men distinguished for their loyalty to their king and for their spirit of service. The revelation says that two loyal and innocent servants of a king, not guilty of any offence against the State and certainly not deserving the death penalty, will be put to death. The second part of the revelation, 'and all those who live on this earth must meet their end', points to death and destruction which will follow the killing of the innocent pair.

The revelation does not mention the country in which the event will take place, but the words used make clear that:

1 the prophecy relates not to a peaceful country but to a country in which law-abiding citizens can be murdered to appease the anger of the excited masses;
2 the murdered persons are the prophet's own followers; otherwise the allusion to two victims in the prophecy has little point;
3 the murders were to be unjust and wrong, not the result of any political crime; and
4 as a result of these unjust murders, general destruction was to overtake the country in which the murders were due to take place.

These four points make the prophecy very different from ordinary prophecies. If the name of the country has been omitted, this does not make the prophecy less clear. The four points which the prophecy entails prove its importance. They cannot synchronize by accident.

For about twenty years after its publication nothing happened, then a series of events began which resulted eventually in a strange fulfilment of the prophecy. It so happened that books by Hazrat Mirza Sahib found their way to Afghanistan and into the hand of an Afghan saint and scholar, Sahibzada Syed Abdul Latif of Khost, who was held in great esteem by all classes in Afghanistan and revered for his piety and purity by devoted friends and followers, among them members of the ruling family. The Syed read the books and decided that Hazrat Mirza Sahib was a true claimant. He sent one of his disciples to Qadian to make further enquiries, authorizing him to take the oath of fealty if he felt so persuaded. This disciple was Maulvi Abdur Rahman. The Maulvi travelled to Qadian and took the oath for himself and on behalf of his leader, Sahibzada Syed Abdul Latif. When he returned to Afghanistan with more books by Hazrat Mirza Sahib, he decided to go first to Kabul so as to acquaint the ruler with this new discovery.

As soon as Maulvi Abdur Rahman reached Kabul, some unpatriotic and unwise individuals moved the Amir Habib Ullah Khan against him. This man had become an apostate, they said. He had gone beyond the pale of Islam and the punishment was death. The Amir was coaxed into signing a *Fatwa* of death. Maulvi Abdur Rahman was put to death most cruelly. He had not yet been to his village. He had decided to go first to his king to tell him that the Promised Messiah and Mahdi had come. He did so out of special regard and devotion for his king. But he was rewarded by death. A mantle was twisted tight round his neck. He was strangled to death. The Hand of God was working. Twenty years before, God had foretold the murder of two innocent and loyal subjects of the Amir. One of the two had been murdered.

One or two years later, Sahibzada Syed Abdul Latif left Afghanistan with the intention of performing Haj. Having already entered into *bai'at* (oath) and joined Hazrat Mirza Sahib, he decided to visit Qadian and from thence the Holy places. At Qadian he met Hazrat Mirza Sahib. The impression he had received from his books was deepened; his pure heart was filled with the Light of God. So absorbed did he become that he decided to perform the Haj later and spend more time at Qadian. After a few months' stay he went back to Afghanistan. He also decided to acquaint his king with what he had seen and found. Reaching Khost, he wrote letters to some courtiers. They and others got to know what had happened and decided to set the Amir Habib Ullah Khan, father of King Amanullah, against the Sahibzada. They made many false statements and persuaded the Amir to have Sahibzada Abdul Latif brought to Kabul under arrest. Orders were sent to Khost and the Sahibzada was brought to Kabul. At Kabul, the Sahibzada was handed over to the Mullas. The Mullas could prove nothing against him. Then some individuals, more selfish than patriotic, excited the Amir Habib Ullah Khan and told him that if the Sahibzada were set free and his influence allowed to spread, people would lose their ardour for Jehad and this would harm the Government of Afghanistan. The Sahibzada was ordered to be stoned. The Amir Habib Ullah Khan, out of feeling for the Sahibzada, asked him to give up his belief and announce his recantation. The Sahibzada replied that he had found the true Islam: should he recant and become a *Kafir*? He was not prepared to give up a truth he had accepted after due deliberation. When it became clear that the Sahibzada would not recant, he was taken out of the capital and stoned in the presence of a large crowd.

A loyal and self-sacrificing subject became the victim of selfish and self-indulgent intriguers. They cheated the Amir when they told him that if the Sahibzada survived, he would be a danger to his country. The truth is that men like the Sahibzada are a shield for their country. For their sake, God repels many disasters to which the country is liable. These cruel advisers told the Amir that the Sahibzada's influence would reduce the desire for Jehad. But they did not tell the Amir that one part of the beliefs which the Sahibzada had accepted was loyalty to the government under which one lives.

This teaching, had it been allowed to spread, would have put an end to internecine quarrels in Afghanistan, and made the country loyal and patriotic, ready to stand by authority in all difficulties. Nor did they tell the Amir that Hazrat Mirza Sahib taught against intrigues, corruption, deceit and hypocrisy. They did not tell the Amir that Hazrat Mirza Sahib not only taught, but also insisted on, the observance of patriotic virtues. If the Sahibzada's influence had been allowed to spread, it could only have ushered in peace and progress. Nor did they tell the Amir that the Jehad which Sahibzada Syed Abdul Latif had learnt to deny was the Jehad which seeks to force Islam on non-Muslims through war and violence. This kind of Jehad was no part of Islam. On the contrary, it was an offence against Islam. The Sahibzada was against this Jehad, not against the Jehad which the Holy Prophet (on whom be peace and the blessings of God) had taught and practised. The Holy Prophet's Jehad was defence against those who attacked Muslims to force them from their faith. Nor was the Sahibzada against legitimate political wars which one people may have to wage against another to preserve their political freedom and independence. What the Sahibzada had learnt to believe under the influence of Hazrat Mirza Sahib was that Islam was against making war on any people in the name of Jehad and in the name of Islam, so long as that people had not interfered with the religion of Islam. To do so was to harm Islam and misrepresent its teachings and its ideals. The political interests of a country were quite another matter. Of such interests each country was its own best judge. If these interests necessitated war, war was justified. But such a war could not be called Jehad. A victory wrongly won in the name of Islam, or won at the expense of the good name of its teaching, was worse than defeat in which the good name of Islam had been safeguarded.

In short, Sahibzada Syed Abdul Latif died a martyr, an end

brought about by cruel and relentless cheating. The revelation 'Two goats will be slaughtered' was fulfilled: two followers of the Promised Messiah, loyal and devoted subjects of their king, were slaughtered. There remained the second part of the prophecy, which foretold general destruction. Not one month after the stoning of the Sahibzada Kabul found itself in the grip of a cholera epidemic. So many people died that the entire population was struck with fear. Everybody felt that the pestilence had come as punishment from God for the foul murder of the innocent Syed. An unconcerned observer, Frank Martin, who was for many years Engineer-in-Chief to the Government of Afghanistan, wrote in his book *Under the Absolute Amir* that this epidemic was quite unexpected. Considering earlier epidemics in Afghanistan and the rate at which they had followed one another, a new epidemic could have been ruled out for years. The sudden appearance of cholera was, therefore, a sign of God. The event had been revealed to His Messenger twenty-eight years before. The wonder of it is that to reinforce the prophecy, as it were, Sahibzada Syed Abdul Latif himself had a premonition of it. The Sahibzada had announced that he could see dangerous days coming after his own martyrdom. The pestilence attacked every home in Kabul. It spared neither the poor nor the rich, nor those wont to take preventive measures taught by medical science. But especially seized were those who had taken a prominent part in the stoning of the late Syed. Some of them died; others lost their near relations.

The revelation took its time but met with literal fulfilment. Awful signs appeared. God proclaimed the authenticity and importance of His Messenger. The far-seeing understood it as a divine sign and believed. Such a prophecy cannot be invented by any mortal. What! could a man foretell that he would soon enlist a large number of followers? Could he say that a time would come when large numbers of people would join him; that his ideas would have travelled from his own country into other countries; and that then in some distant country two of his followers would lose their lives, not because of sedition or unpatriotic activities but because of their belief in their leader? Could he say further that when the innocent pair had been put to death God would send a tremendous affliction into the country and that so great would be the destruction wrought by it that it would die? Such a clear and definite prophecy could not be formulated by any man. If it could, there would be no difference between the Word of God and the word of man.

There is one misunderstanding which I wish to clear up. The prophecy contains the words 'all who live on the earth will meet with destruction'. It may be said that all men in Afghanistan did not die; some died but many were saved. I need only say that *kul* in Arabic may mean 'all' or 'some'. Here, it seems, *kul* means some. In the Holy Quran, we read of God revealing to the bee thus:

كُلِىْ مِنْ كُلِّ الثَّمَرٰتِ

'then eat of *every* kind of fruit.'[2]

Everybody knows that not every bee alights on every kind of fruit. Therefore, *kul* in the prophecy really means some or many. Similarly, we read in the Quran of Queen Saba:

وَاُوْتِيَتْ مِنْ كُلِّ شَىْءٍ

'And she has been given everything.'[3]

The description is of a queen who was the ruler of a small territory. What the verse means is that the queen had a large share of the blessings of this world. It only means that whenever and wherever the word *kul* is used, it means some good quantity or some significant number. The cholera epidemic which appeared in Kabul soon after the stoning of the lamented Sahibzada shows these two important features. It struck terror into the people at large and a good number out of them met their death by it; so much so that a European writer, unaware of its significance for any revelation, mentioned it in his book.

A second difficulty which may be raised about the prophecy is that the prophetic description is *Tuzbahan*, i.e. slaughtered. But this description does not apply to the two martyrs. One was strangled to death, the other was stoned. The revelational description, therefore, does not apply to the deaths. This difficulty arises from lack of thought or insight. The Arabic root *Zibah* (slaughtering) means two things: 'being slaughtered', and 'being put to an end',

2 *Al-Nahl*, 70.

3 *Al-Naml*, 24.

the method of doing so being left undetermined. In the Holy Quran, we have many examples of this use of the word *Zibah*. In the narrative of Moses, we are told that the Egyptians 'slew your sons and spared your women' (2:50). The word used is from the root *Zibah* which, strictly, should mean that the only method of killing the males adopted by the Egyptians was that of slaughtering, or cutting the throat. This is not true. It is known from history that the Egyptians employed many different methods of killing the Israelite males. First, the midwives had orders to kill the male children born in Israelite homes. When the midwvies hesitated, the Egyptian Pharaoh ordered them to be thrown into the river (Exodus 1:22, Acts 7:19, Talmud). Moreover, the Arabic Lexicon *Taj-ul-Urus* (vol. 1, p. 141) says that at least one meaning of *Zibah* is 'to destroy'. It is wrong, therefore, to say that the word *Zibah* can only mean 'to be slaughtered' (as the word can be used for other forms of killing), and wrong to find fault with the prophecy by saying that the Sahibzada was stoned and not slaughtered.

Prophecy No. 2: Revolution in Iran

The second prophecy which, out of many thousands, I now wish to narrate relates to Afghanistan's neighbour Iran. On January 15, 1906, Hazrat Mirza Sahib, the Promised Messiah (on whom be peace) received the revelation: تَزَلْزَل در ایوانِ کسریٰ افتاد۔ i.e. 'Shaking in the palace of Chosroes.'

As was the practice, the revelation was published in all Urdu and English newspapers and periodicals of the Jama'at. At the time of its publication, the then ruler of Iran sat comfortably on his throne. In 1905 he had accepted proposals for popular representation. Government by parliament had been promised and proclaimed. The country rejoiced over this, and the king, Muzaffar-ud-Din Shah, was the popular monarch of a grateful nation. Great satisfaction prevailed because a political revolution had taken place without bloodshed. The rest of the world looked hopefully to Iran because this experiment in democracy was new for the whole of Asia, excepting Japan. But they were unaware of the difficulties it entailed. The people were without sufficient education and without sufficient experience of democratic government. At such a time Hazrat Mirza Sahib published his revelation—'Shaking in the palace of Chosroes.' The revelation seemed strange. Nobody seemed to apprehend the consequences pointed out in the revelation. Iran was happy with its new-found freedom. The king, Muzaffar-ud-Din Shah, was happy with the popularity he had built.

In 1907, at the age of fifty-five, the king died. His son, Mirza Muhammad Ali, ascended the throne. The new king confirmed the constitutional changes which had been inaugurated by his father. The Iranian Parliament, the Majlis, was to continue. Representative government had come to stay. But a few days later ominous signs began to appear which pointed to events foretold in the revelation of the Promised Messiah. A year after the publication of the revelation, one could see signs of rebellion and disorder. A conflict began between the king and the parliament, the Shah and the Majlis. The Majlis put forward demands which the Shah could not accept. At last, on the insistence of the Majlis, he agreed to turn out certain men, leaders of mischief according to the Majlis. At the same time, the king decided to leave Teheran. Grave tension arose between the Nationalists and the Cossacks who formed the king's body-guard. The revelation of the Promised Messiah received partial fulfilment. The Iranian House of Representatives was shelled and destroyed. The king abolished the parliament. General rebellion ensued in many parts of Iran. Laristan, Labudjan, Akbarabad, Bushehr, Shiraz, and practically the whole of Southern Iran were involved. Governors and officers of the old regime were dismissed and the administration assumed by Nationalists and democrats. Iran was in the grip of internecine warfare. The king could see the country's critical condition. He started moving the treasury and his personal effects to Russia, himself staying behind to use all his tact and will to put down the rebellion. The rebellion only grew. By January 1909 it had spread to Isphahan. The Bakhtiari chief also joined the Nationalists. The royal troops suffered ignominious defeat. The king was forced to proclaim his acceptance of parliamentary government. He told the people again and again that the old autocratic order will not be re-established. But God had ordained otherwise. In the palace of Iran anxiety increased from day to day. At last even the Cossacks, the Shah's body-guard, joined the revolutionaries. The Shah and his family left the palace and took refuge in the Russian Embassy. This was on July 15, 1909, two and a half years after the publication of the revelation 'Shaking in the palace of Chosroes'. The revelation was literally fulfilled. Autocracy and reaction disappeared from Iran. Democracy came instead. The months of June and July passed in great anxiety. Only those who have ever lived through such conditions can have an idea of the anxiety, the restlessness and desperation which reigned in the palace of Iran for these two months. We need imagination to think of what must have happened. So much at least is clear, that the prophecy of the Promised Messiah came true. It was a Sign, even though few benefit from such Signs.

Prophecy No. 3: Abdullah Atham

This prophecy relating to Abdullah Atham is a Sign for Christians in general and Indian Christians in particular.

It is one out of a series of prophecies which the Promised Messiah published against a hostile group of Christians. They should serve as a Sign for Christians.

I do not know, dear reader, whether you are aware of the vile attacks which Christian missionaries made in those days on the person and character of the Holy Prophet (on whom be peace and the blessings of God). These attacks used as their excuse beliefs which Muslims falsely attributed to Islam, also some false Traditions which crept into the literature of Islam. At the time of Hazrat Mirza Sahib, these attacks were at their worst. Moved by the boldness of these attacks Hazrat Mirza Sahib decided to attack back. The result at last was that Christians found themselves unable to stand against him. They left the field and abandoned their foul methods. Their present attitude and style of writing against Islam is different. Among vilifiers of the front rank at the time was one Abdullah Atham, a retired civil servant. It so happened that a public debate was arranged between Hazrat Mirza Sahib and Abdullah Atham. The debate was held at Amritsat, and in this debate Abdullah Atham suffered disgrace. He employed devices of various kinds but could make no impression. He sank low in the estimation of both Christians and others. In the debate was raised the subject of miracles. Because of this, it seems, God did not let the debate go without a miracle. Hazrat Mirza Sahib had the revelation:

"اس بحث میں دونوں فریق میں سے جو فریق عمداً جھوٹ کو اختیار کر رہا ہے اور سچے خدا کو چھوڑ رہا ہے اور عاجز انسان کو خدا بنا رہا ہے وہ انہی دنوں مباحثہ کے لحاظ سے فی دن ایک مہینہ لے کر یعنی پندرہ ماہ بیں ہاویہ میں گرایا جائے گا اور اس کو سخت ذلّت پہنچے گی بشرطیکہ حق کی طرف رجُوع نہ کرے۔"

> 'In this debate the party which follows falsehood deliberately, which has abandoned the True God, and which seeks to make God of a mere man will drop in Hell. This will happen within fifteen months, i.e. within a period counted at the rate of one month to every day of this debate, the only condition being that the party should not retreat from its position'.

In his last paper for the debate, Hazrat Mirza Sahib included this prophecy and declared that the prophecy would prove that the Holy Prophet (on whom be peace and the blessings of God), whom Abdullah Atham in his book *Andruna-i-Bible* (lit. 'Inner Nature of the Bible') had described (God forbid) as the Dadjjal, was a true Prophet and Messenger of God.

The prophecy consisted of two important parts: (1) that Abdullah Atham (who sought to prove that Jesus was God) would go to Hell because of his deliberate fault-finding and vilification; (2) that if he should feel repentant and realize his mistake, he would be saved from this punishment. Or, if he did not change his attitude but persisted in hostility and fault-finding, and yet escaped punishment, the prophecy would be untrue; on the other hand, if he should change but still met his death within fifteen months from the conclusion of the debate, even then the prophecy would be untrue. The words of the prophecy clearly indicated that, according to God. Atham was due to live longer than fifteen months, but that he would die within fifteen months if he persisted in his hostility. A little reflection on the words would show that the two steps of the second alternative lent greater grandeur to the prophecy than the two steps of the first alternative. The two steps of the first alternative were that *if* Atham persisted in hostility, *then* he would die within fifteen months. For Atham to persist in hostility and unjust opposition was natural and easy. He was a Christian writer who had written books in support of Christianity and against Islam. He held high social status and enjoyed valuable contacts with Englishmen.

For this public debate between Christians and Muslims, he had been selected as the Christian exponent in preference to other *padres* and preachers. Important Christian missionaries acted as his assistants. Such a man could be expected to continue to hold fast to all his Christian beliefs. Having done so much for the publicity of Christianity and played the role of exponent and advocate, one would not expect that he would, even for a moment, recant his belief in the godhead of Jesus or be impressed by the miraculous power of Islam. To say that in that case he would die within fifteen months seemed a grand prophecy. But Atham was sixty-five and a man as old can be said to have completed his span of life. Were he to die it would not have been so extraordinary. But consider the other alternative. Were Atham to retreat from prejudice and hostility, he would be safe from death for fifteen months. It was far more difficult for Atham to retreat from his confirmed and settled attitude against Islam than to persist in it. And while death can be brought about by human hand, a guarantee of life for fifteen months cannot be given by anybody. The steps of the second alternative were evidently more difficult. The second alternative could make the prophecy more grand and more impressive. It appears that God chose the more difficult alternative. Atham, in spite of his circumstances, his associations, his position and his past, became overawed by God and the prophecy. The first sign of it occurred in the debate when Atham put his fingers over his ears and said that he had not called the Holy Prophet a Dadjjal. After the publication of the prophecy everybody in the country was agog, anxiously awaiting the result. But God did not let fifteen months pass without more signs of Atham's retreat from hostility. Atham stopped all his work in support of Christianity. He stopped speaking and writing. A well-known preacher and author cannot at once retire into silence. The fact that Atham did so, proves that Islam had made some impression upon his mind, that at least he had come to think it wrong to attack, and perhaps even to resist, Islam. But he showed this not by retiring into silence only. He suffered great mental anguish, a sort of hell. Feelings of guilt over his unjust hostility towards Islam mounted. He began to have strange hallucinations and admitted this to his relations and friends. He day-dreamt about snakes, rabid dogs, and armed men ready to attack him. These experiences cannot be produced through human agency. Snakes and dogs cannot be exploited for the purpose, and in India, because of the ban on the free use of weapons, armed men could not be found and paraded. These hallucinations constituted the mental hell into which Atham had fallen. It was the result of remorse, of feelings of guilt over his support of Christianity and hostility to Islam. This mental hell was a substitute for the physical Hell to which he would have had to go had he stuck to his antipathy to Islam. If his faith and trust in Christianity had remained as before, if he had continued to regard Islam as false as he had done before, he would not have suffered the delusions and hallucinations which he did. He would not have suffered from fear of snakes and dogs as he did. If he continued to feel sure that God was not against him, why did these mean animals seem so fearful to him? Why did he abandon all writing and speaking on behalf of Christianity? Why did he go from town to town in dread of something?

In short, God chose to fulfil the second part of the prophecy, the part which predicted Atham's retreat from his excessive attachment to Christianity and excessive hostility to Islam. This part of the prophecy was less likely to be true. Atham began to have doubts about Jesus's divinity. The truth of Islam began to dawn upon his mind. On his retreat God completed the second step of this part of the prophecy. Atham was saved from death even though fear and guilt had driven him very near it. The promise of God came true. He was saved because he had retreated.

This was a grand prophecy fit to open everybody's eyes. But if nothing had been said or done about it after the appointed time was over, critics of Hazrat Mirza Sahib would after a time have gone on to say that Atham had made no retreat whatever, that it was a concoction on the part of Hazrat Mirza Sahib and his followers. To make the truth of the prophecy even more clear, God roused a group of Christians and Muslims to say that the prophecy had proved untrue and that Atham had not died within the appointed time. They were told that the prophecy could be fulfilled in two alternative ways, and it had been fulfilled in the second way. But the critics did not agree and went on to say that Atham had not retreated. At this, Hazrat Mirza Sahib invited Atham to declare on oath that his Christian and Muslim supporters were right and that during this time he had not entertained the least thought of the truth of Islam and the falsehood of Christianity. Atham, however, refused to make any declaration on oath. He made a statement without oath that he still thought Christianity to be true. But thanks to God and His Power over the minds and thoughts of men, in the same statement he declared that his conception of the divinity of Christ was different from the conception of other Christians. This declaration only fulfilled the prophecy. The prophecy had said that the party which sought to make God of mere man would go to Hell. Atham admitted that he did not think Jesus Christ was God. Notwithstanding this declaration, Atham was asked if he would make a declaration on solemn oath that he had entertained no doubts whatever about the truth of his religious beliefs, that the truth of Islam had not made the least impression upon him, and that during all this time he had continued to hold the thoughts and beliefs which he had held before. While inviting Atham to make this declaration on solemn oath, Hazrat Mirza Sahib himself declared that if, in the event of such a declaration on oath, Atham did not meet with divine punishment, he would admit his falsehood. He also promised to offer a cash reward of Rs 1,000 if Atham was able to take the oath. Atham wrote in reply that oath-taking was not permitted by his religion. This was strange because in the New Testament the disciples are said to have taken different kinds of oaths. In Christian states nobody is appointed to high office unless he takes the oath of allegiance. Even the king has to take such an oath. Judges, members of parliament, high civil and military officers have to take an oath. Witnesses in court have to take an oath. Christian courts, in fact, restrict oath-taking to Christian witnesses. Non-Christian witnesses only say, 'I declare before the ever-present and ever-seeing God,' etc. Therefore, if oath-taking, according to Christians, is the special privilege of Christians, Atham could not plead disability because of his religion. His plea was not honest. It was a device to escape the oath and its penalties. Atham had seen fearful scenes and had become convinced that if he took the oath he must die. That Atham refused to take the oath using false excuses becomes clear also from the fact that among Christians no important religious office is given to anybody unless he takes the oath of loyalty. Protestant Christians, and Atham was a Protestant, have to take two oaths, one of loyalty to the Church, the other of loyalty to the State. When these things were explained to Atham, he was completely silenced. The value of the cash reward offered to Atham if he was able to take the oath was raised gradually from Rs 1,000 to Rs 4,000. The condition of a year of waiting was dropped. Atham could claim the cash reward as soon as he had taken the oath. But Atham knew that out of fear of his community he was trying to conceal the state of mind from which he had suffered for fifteen months. Knowing all this he dared not take the oath. He spent the rest of his days in silence. All his writing and speaking against Islam was over. The preaching of Christianity was also over. The truth of Hazrat Mirza Sahib's prophecy became more plain than ever. The retreat of Atham from his belief in the godhead of Christ had, in a way, been admitted by Atham himself. That his earlier thoughts about Islam underwent a change was proved by his refusal to affirm the contrary on solemn oath and by his reply on being challenged to take such an oath. (And yet in one of his papers for the debate at the end of which this prophecy was made, Atham had tried to prove that Christ was God and that he possessed all the attributes of God in his person.)

The greatness and grandeur of this prophecy quickens the faith of every honest person. In it one can see the working of the Hand of God. Here was a sworn enemy of Islam, the leader of an important community and its advocate in controversy with another. He had spent all his life preaching and propagating one religion and propagating against another. This man came to entertain thoughts against his own religion and in favour of the other. This hardened antagonist also had terrifying day-dreams. In consideration of this change of attitude he was saved from the threatened death for full fifteen months. These things are beyond human power and human planning.

Prophecy No. 4: An American impostor

This prophecy relates to the end of Dowie, the American impostor. It is a Sign for Christians in general and for the people of America in particular.

I now proceed to narrate the prophecy which proved a Sign for Christians in general. In addition to being a Sign for Christians, it also proved a Sign for people in the West. Alexander Dowie was well known in America. Australian by birth he had acquired American citizenship. In 1892 he started preaching. He claimed powers of healing and people gathered around him. In 1901 he claimed to be a forerunner of the second coming of Christ, just as

Elijah was a forerunner of his first coming. The second coming of Christ was then a much discussed subject. The signs laid down for it in the scripture had appeared, and people interested in religion were eagerly waiting. The publication of his claim brought Dowie a further increase of followers. He bought some land and founded a town called Zion, declaring that Christ would descend in that town. Many rich people, eager to have the first view of Christ on his second coming, paid large sums of money for land on which to build houses in that town. Dowie began to rule in that town as an uncrowned king. Soon his followers numbered more than 100,000. He sent preachers to different Christian countries. Full of hatred for Islam, he hurled foul abuse against it. In 1902 he published a prophecy that unless Muslims of the world became Christian, they would meet with death and destruction. Hazrat Mirza Sahib, the Promised Messiah, heard of this and wrote a leaflet in reply. In it Hazrat Mirza Sahib enumerated the beauties of Islam and said that it was quite unnecessary for Dowie to predict and proclaim the destruction of the Muslims of the world. He (Hazrat Mirza Sahib) had been sent by God as the Promised Messiah, so Dowie could enter into a prayer contest with him. The result of this contest would enable the whole world to determine the Truth. This leaflet by Hazrat Mirza Sahib was published in September 1902, the publication having been arranged on a very large scale in both Europe and America. From December 1902 to the end of 1903, newspapers in Europe and America kept commenting on this leaflet, and about forty of them sent to Qadian copies of issues containing their comments. Judging from the extent of the publicity it may be estimated that between two and two and a half million people came to know about the proposed prayer contest.

Dowie did not write in reply to this leaflet, but he went on praying for the defeat and destruction of Islam. He also renewed his attacks. On February 14, 1903, he wrote in his paper: 'I pray to God that Islam will soon disappear from the world. O God, accept this prayer of mine. O God, destroy Islam.'

On August 5, 1903, he wrote in his paper: 'The blackspot on the mantle of man [Islam] will meet its end at the hands of Zion.'

Hazrat Mirza Sahib saw that Dowie was in no mood to retreat from his hostility; so he issued another leaflet sometime in 1903. This leaflet was called *Prophecies about Dowie and Piggott*. Piggott was a pretender in England. Hazrat Mirza Sahib wrote in this leaflet that he had been sent by God to re-establish belief in the Oneness of God, to put an end to all attempts to associate others with this One God, and that he had a Sign to show to America. The Sign was that if Dowie entered into a prayer contest with him and he decided, directly or indirectly, to accept his challenge, then in Mirza Sahib's lifetime Dowie would leave the world in great pain and misery. Hazrat Mirza Sahib went on to say that Dowie had been invited to enter this prayer contest before, but had made no reply. He was now allowed seven months more. During this time he could publish his reply. The leaflet ended by saying: 'Be sure, calamity is due to befall Dowie's Zion.'

Then in the end, without waiting for Dowie's reply, he prayed: 'God, ordain that the falsehood of Piggott and Dowie may soon become patent to people.'

This leaflet also was published in the West on a very large scale. Newspapers in Europe and America commented upon it. The *Glasgow Herald* in Britain and the *New York Commercial Advertiser* in America published summaries of it. Millions of persons came to know of it.

When this leaflet was published, Dowie's star was at its zenith. The number of his followers was increasing. They were so rich that every New Year Dowie received presents worth a hundred thousand dollars from them. Dowie owned many industrial establishments. His bank balance amounted to about twenty million dollars. His staff of servants was larger than that of the richest in the land. He was in excellent health: health, he said, was his special miracle, and he claimed the miraculous power of healing by the touch of his hand. Dowie had money, health, followers, influence, everything in abundance.

On the publication of the second leaflet by Hazrat Mirza Sahib, people asked Dowie why he did not reply to the Indian Messiah. Dowie said contemptuously:

> There is a Muhammadan Messiah in India who has repeatedly written to me that Jesus Christ lies buried in Kashmir, and people ask me why I do not answer him. Do you imagine that I shall reply to such gnats and flies? If I were to put down my foot on them I would crush out their lives. I give them a chance to fly away and live.

Foolishly Dowie, who had so far kept out of any contest with

Hazrat Mirza Sahib, had now entered the contest, though he continued to say he had not. He forgot that Hazrat Mirza Sahib had written clearly that even if Dowie entered the contest *indirectly* he would have to leave the world in great pain and misery while Hazrat Mirza Sahib was still alive. Dowie described Hazrat as a worm and said he could kill him with his foot. Thus Dowie had entered the contest and invited the punishment of God.

Dowie's vanity and ostentation increased. Some days later he again described Hazrat Mirza Sahib as the 'foolish Muhammadan Messiah', he also wrote, 'If I am not a messenger of God on this earth, then no one is.' In December 1903 he entered the contest openly. He declared that an angel had told him that he would be victorious over his enemies. The declaration was a counter-prophecy, a prophecy of the death of Hazrat Mirza Sahib. The spiritual contest which had been developing gradually now became patent and open. After this last declaration, the Promised Messiah wrote nothing and in accordance with the Quranic injunction 'And wait as they also wait', he waited for the Judgment of God. God is slow but firm in His grip. The grip of God got hold of the feet with which Dowie wanted to trample down the Messiah of God. Dowie's feet became impaired. Far from being able to trample over the Messiah with them, he could not even rest them on the ground. He had an attack of paralysis. From this, however, he recovered after a few days. But two months later, on December 19, he had a second attack which prostrated him. Completely disabled, he left his work to his secretary and himself went in search of health to an island supposed to possess a climate that cured paralytics. But the Wrath of God followed him. Dowie had described the true Messiah as a worm. Now Dowie himself was to be reduced to the status of a worm. The miraculous powers of which he used to boast began to desert him. After he left home, his followers began to wonder why he who had the power to heal others could not heal himself. And he did not even need to pray but only to give a touch of his hand. Why did he fall ill at all? They began a search of his rooms, which had been inaccessible until now. They found bottles of wine. His wife and son declared that Dowie drank heavily in secret though he had prohibited his followers from drinking or using any intoxicants. He had prohibited even tobacco. His wife declared that she had been loyal and faithful to him even during the days of his poverty, but she had been sorely disappointed to know that in order to marry a rich old woman, Dowie had started saying it was lawful to take more than one wife. In promulgating this law he was finding an excuse for bigamy. Dowie's wife produced letters which this woman had written in reply to Dowie's. His followers became infuriated. They decided to check the accounts of Dowie's organizations. It was found that Dowie had misappropriated about five million rupees (a million and a half dollars). It also appeared that he had given presents worth more than a hundred thousand rupees to young girls in the town. Upon these disclosures Dowie's leading followers decided to depose him. They sent him a telegram which said: 'Unanimously the organization seriously objects to your expensive habits, hypocrisy, mis-statements, exaggerations and ill-temper. Therefore, you are hereby deposed from your office.' Dowie could not refute these charges, and eventually all his followers turned against him. As a last effort he wanted to address them and convert them again to his side. But when he alighted from the train, only a few persons had come to receive him. Hardly anyone paid any attention. He turned to the law courts, but the law courts gave no help in obtaining possession of public funds. He was awarded a miserable maintenance. On the other hand, his paralysis had reduced him to complete helplessness. His Negro servants had to carry him from room to room. He lived in unrelieved misery and pain. A few friends of his continued to visit him during these last days. They advised him to have proper treatment, but Dowie did not agree. He knew he had been advising others against treatment. How could he have any treatment himself? At last out of about a hundred thousand followers, only about two hundred remained with him. He had failed in the law courts. His paralysis had advanced. He could not endure his mounting troubles. His mind became unbalanced and he was practically insane. In this condition he appeared before some of his followers, who saw the once robust, pompous forerunner of Christ swathed all over. Dowie said his name was Jerry! He had been battling with Satan the night before! In the battle his general had been killed! He himself had received injuries! Those who heard this disjointed speech knew what had happened. Dowie had gone mad. The last followers left Dowie. The words of Hazrat Mirza Sahib were fulfilled. Mirza Sahib had said that before his eyes Dowie would leave this mortal world 'in great pain and misery'. On March 9, 1907, Dowie died, abandoned and disgraced. When he died, he had only four men with him and his assets amounted to about thirty rupees!

A worse picture of pain and misery cannot be imagined. Dowie's death was an object-lesson, a Sign for the people of the West. Many newspapers declared that the prophecy of Hazrat Mirza Sahib had been fulfilled. I quote some of the newspapers of those days:

> Ahmad and his adherents may be pardoned for taking some credit for the accuracy with which the prophecy was fulfilled a few months ago. (*Dunville Gazette,* June 7, 1907)

> The Qadian man predicted that if Dowie accepted the challenge, 'he shall leave the world before my eyes with great sorrow and torment.' If Dowie declined, the Mirza said, 'the end would only be deferred; death awaited him just the same, and calamity will soon overtake Zion.' That was the grand prophecy: Zion should fall and Dowie die before Ahmad. It appeared to be a risky step for the Promised Messiah to defy the restored Elijah to an endurance test, for the challenger was by 15 years the older man of the two and probabilities in a land of plagues and famines were against him as a survivor, but he won out. (*Truth Seeker,* June 15, 1907)

It is quite true that Hazrat Mirza Sahib was much older than Dowie. So there were more chances for Dowie to survive Hazrat Mirza Sahib.

> Dowie died with his friends fallen away from him and his fortune dwindled. He suffered from paralysis and insanity. He died a miserable death, with Zion city torn and frayed by internal dissensions. Mirza comes forward frankly and states that he has won his challenge. (*Boston Herald,* June 23, 1907)

These quotations from the American newspapers show that the prophecy made an impression not only on Christians but also on free-thinking editors of the American newspapers. They had been so impressed by the grandeur of the prophecy that they felt obliged to write about it. They were not able to deny its truth or its importance. Whenever the Sign of the death of Dowie is narrated before Western audiences, they will have before them the testimony of scores of newspapers, edited by fellow-countrymen and fellow-believers. Western audiences on hearing about Signs of this kind will be forced to admit that Islam is the true religion. Salvation is not to be found outside Islam. On being convinced, they will give up their prejudices and old beliefs. They will enter Islam and declare their faith in the Holy Prophet (on whom be peace) and in his servant the Promised Messiah (on whom also peace). Coming events cast their shadows before them. In America, several hundred persons have already joined the Ahmadiyya Jama'at.

Prophecy No. 5: Death of Lekh Ram, a sign for the people of India

I now turn to another prophecy, one of many which proved the truth of Islam to the people of India. Their fulfilment moved several hundred thousand persons and convinced them of the truth of Islam and persuaded many of them to declare openly that Islam was the true religion. The effect of the prophecy has continued ever since.

The circumstances of the prophecy are that late in the last century a new Hindu sect called the Arya Samaj came into existence. Seeing the low condition of Islam in our time, this sect conceived a bold plan to convert Muslims to the Hindu religion. To this end Arya Samaj writers began to publish the most scurrilous attacks on Islam. The most daring of these leaders and writers was one Lekh Ram. In the course of several exchanges Hazrat Mirza Sahib tried to explain to this Arya leader the truth of Islam; but to no avail. Lekh Ram stuck to his anti-Islam ideas and schemes. He produced the most distorted translations of passages from the Quran. Common decency found it difficult even to read those translations. He held the most foul views about the Holy Prophet and the Holy Quran. The best of mankind he thought the worst of mankind, the best book in the world the worst. A diseased eye cannot stand the light. This was the case with Lekh Ram. The controversy with him began to mount. Lekh Ram went further and further in his abuse of the Holy Prophet (on whom be peace) and ridicule of Hazrat Mirza Sahib. He also became impatient for a sign. Hazrat Mirza Sahib prayed to God and learnt that this man's end was near. Before publishing this prophecy Hazrat Mirza Sahib offered to withhold publication of the prophecy if Lekh Ram had any objection, but Lekh Ram said he had nothing to fear from such prophecies. The revelations received at first were general. No time limit had been set for Lekh Ram's end. Lekh Ram insisted on a time limit. Hazrat Mirza Sahib therefore withheld publication of the prophecy until he had more knowledge from God. Eventually, he learnt that Lekh Ram was due to meet with a fatal calamity within six years counting from February 20, 1893. On receiving this assurance Hazrat Mirza Sahib published the prophecy. He added to it an Arabic revelation relating to Lekh Ram.

عِجْلٌ جَسَدٌ لَّهٗ خُوَارٌ، لَهٗ نَصَبٌ وَّ عَذَابٌ ۔

'A miserable half-dead calf; nothing awaits it but disgrace and destruction.'

Declaring his prophecy and this revelation, Hazrat Mirza Sahib wrote (addressing all religious parties): 'If within six years from today, February 20, 1893, this man does not meet with punishment from God, which is unusual in its poignancy and tragedy and which impresses all and sundry with the fear of the Lord, then let everybody think that I am not from God.'

A little later, Hazrat Mirza Sahib elaborated the prophecy on the basis of further revelations. He wrote:

وَبَشَّرَنِیْ رَبِّیْ وَ قَالَ مُبَشِّرًا   سَتَعْرِفُ یَوْمَ الْعِیْدِ، وَالْعِیْدُ اَقْرَبُ

'And God gave me the tidings that I will witness a day of *Id,* and this day will be close to the *Id*.'

He went on:

وَ مِنْهَا مَا وَعَدَنِیْ رَبِّیْ وَاسْتَجَابَ دُعَآئِیْ فِیْ رَجُلٍ مُّفْسِدٍ عَدُوِّ اللّٰهِ
وَرَسُوْلِهٖ مُسَمّٰی لِیْکھرَامِ الْفِشَاوَرِیِّ، وَاَخْبَرَنِیْ رَبِّیْ اَنَّهٗ مِنَ
الْهَالِکِیْنَ، اِنَّهٗ کَانَ یَسُبُّ نَبِیَّ اللّٰهِ وَیَتَکَلَّمُ فِیْ شَاْنِهٖ بِکَلِمَاتٍ
خَبِیْثَةٍ، فَدَعَوْتُ عَلَیْهِ فَبَشَّرَنِیْ رَبِّیْ بِمَوْتِهٖ فِیْ سِتِّ سَنَةٍ، اِنَّ
فِیْ ذٰلِکَ لَاٰیَةً لِّلطَّالِبِیْنَ ۔

'And among the graces of God which I have received is this that He has accepted my prayers relating to one Lekh Ram and that

> He has informed me that he will soon receive his just deserts. This man was foul in his abuse of the Holy Prophet. I prayed against him. So my God informed me that this man will die within six years. There are Signs in this for seekers after truth.'

A little later Hazrat Mirza Sahib added further details to the prophecy. These were published as a note inside the front cover of his book *Barakat ul-Dua*. It was headed 'A further prophecy about Lekh Ram of Peshawar'. In the course of it he wrote:

> Today, April 2, 1893 A.D. (Ramadhan 14, 1310 A.H.), early in the morning, in semi-sleep, I saw myself sitting in a large house, some friends with me. Suddenly in front of me I saw a man, fearful looking with blood-shot eyes. As I saw, he seemed a strange creature, of a strange character. Not a human being, I thought, but a dreadful and dangerous angel. He struck terror into those who saw him. As I looked at him, he asked, 'Where is Lekh Ram?' Then he named another and asked me his whereabouts also. I then understood that this person had been appointed to punish Lekh Ram and this other man.

Hazrat Mirza Sahib also referred to Lekh Ram in his Persian verse included in his book *Aina-i-Kamalat-i-Islam*:

الا اے دُشمنِ نادان و بے راہ   بترس از تیغِ بُرّانِ محمّد
الا اے مُنکر از شانِ محمّد   ھم از نورِ نمایانِ محمّد
کرامت گرچہ بے نام و نشان است   بیا بنگر ز غلمانِ محمّد

Foolish and misguided foe,
Fear the sharp sword of Muhammad.

Denier of the greatness of Muhammad,
And of the luminous light of Muhammad!

Miracles may seem a thing of the past,
Come yet and see one through the devotees of Muhammad.

Put together, the prophecies relating to Lekh Ram foretold;

1 that Lekh Ram would meet with a calamity which would prove fatal for him;

2 that this calamity would take place within six years;
3 that it would be on a day close to *Id*, just before or just after;
4 that Lekh Ram would meet with the fate of the Calf of Samri; that is, dismemberment and death and dispersion of his ashes into a river;
5 that this fatal process would be carried out by a ruddy person with blood-shot eyes;
6 that Lekh Ram would be a victim of the sword of Muhammad.

These details are so clear and determinate that nobody can have any doubt about their meaning and content. Five years after the publication of these prophecies, however, people started ridiculing the Promised Messiah. The time limit of the prophecies, they said, was over and nothing had happened! Could Mirza Sahib still be genuine? But the next *Id-ul-Fitr*, which marks the end of Ramadhan, occurred on a Friday. On the day following the *Id*, that is, Saturday, in the afternoon, an unknown person stabbed Lekh Ram in the stomach with a sharp knife. Stabbed on Saturday, Lekh Ram died on Sunday. The Word of God came true in all its grim details. The prophecy had laid down a six-year limit. Lekh Ram died within six years. The prophecy said the fatal event would occur on a day close to the *Id*, and that this day would prove the *Id* of the believers. It happened exactly like this. Lekh Ram was stabbed on the day following the *Id*. The prophecy said that Lekh Ram would meet his end at the hands of a fearful red-looking person. That is exactly what happened. Lekh Ram was to be a victim of the sword of Muhammad; so, he died of a stab wound. The prophecy said that Lekh Ram would meet a fate similar to the fate of the Calf of Samri. This calf was dismembered on a Saturday, burnt to ashes, the ashes dispersed in a river. This is what happened to Lekh Ram. Being a Hindu he was cremated and his ashes thrown into a river.

The story of the murder of Lekh Ram is that some time before, a man with blood-shot eyes had come to him, wishing to be converted from Islam to Hinduism. People tried to dissuade Lekh Ram from entertaining him. But Lekh Ram did not heed. This man became Lekh Ram's trusted companion. Lekh Ram had appointed the fateful Saturday as the day of his conversion. Lekh Ram was busy writing. He asked for some book. This man, pretending to hand Lekh Ram the book slipped a knife into his stomach and turned the knife round and round so as to cut the entrails thoroughly. He then disappeared, according to the statement of Lekh Ram's family. Lekh Ram was on the upper floor of the house. Near the gate, on the ground floor, were many men; but no one saw the murderer come down and escape. Lekh Ram's mother and wife were certain he was still in the house. On a search of the house nobody was found. Where had he disappeared to? Into the earth or the sky? Lekh Ram died in great pain on Sunday. On a Sunday, the Promised Messiah had seen in a vision this red-looking fearful murderer who asked for Lekh Ram. Lekh Ram's end was a Sign of the truth of the Promised Messiah, a divine warning for those who would heap vile abuse on the holy person of the Holy Prophet (on whom be peace and the blessings of God).

Prophecy No. 6: Prince Dalip Singh, a sign for Sikhs

I now pass on to a prophecy which on fulfilment proved a sign for Sikhs and demonstrated to them the truth of Islam and the authenticity of the Promised Messiah.

It so happened that when the British annexed the Punjab they decided for obvious political and psychological reasons to send away to England the young heir to the Sikh throne, Prince Dalip Singh. He was to stay there until British rule became established in the Punjab. After the mutiny of 1857, however, the last vestiges of the Mughal power in Delhi disappeared and everything seemed safe for the British. Raja Dalip Singh expressed a desire to return home and it even began to be rumoured that the Prince was really returning. Hazrat Mirza Sahib, however, had a revelation that the Prince would not return. He informed many people about it, especially Hindus. In one of his leaflets he predicted that a returning Punjab prince was going to encounter trouble. At the time of the publication of this prophecy nobody imagined that the Prince's return home would be stopped; in fact, it was understood that he would soon set foot on his native soil. But just about this time the British Government changed their mind. They decided that the Prince's return would be dangerous for the Government. As the news of his return spread, the Sikhs became more and more restive. Their thoughts turned to the recent past. The British authorities began to fear trouble. The steamer which carried the returning

Prince reached Aden. He was stopped at Aden and ordered back to England. The news of this last-minute change came when everybody was expecting the Prince back home. The Sikhs felt very resentful. The Might of God showed itself. God becomes aware of the thoughts of men before they themselves become aware of their thoughts.

Prophecy No. 7: The plague

I have related prophecies of the Promised Messiah about Afghanistan and her neighbour Iran. I have also described four prophecies which may be said to have completed Islam's argument against three important Indian communities, the Christians, Hindus and Sikhs. I now proceed to narrate a prophecy which completed the argument against all communities of India and eventually against the whole world. This prophecy has proved that God has power over the minutest causes. If He wills He can turn them into the service of his Messenger. Many prophecies of Hazrat Mirza Sahib have been fulfilled already. Many await fulfilment. As an example of such prophecies I present an account of his prophecy regarding the onset of plague. There is an added point of interest in the prophecy, namely, that this pestilence is mentioned in the prophecies of the Holy Prophet who foretold that this deadly disease would appear in the time of the Promised Messiah. When, according to a prophecy of the Holy Prophet, a lunar eclipse occurred on the 13th of Ramadhan and a solar eclipse on the 28th of the same month. Hazrat Mirza Sahib was informed that if people did not heed this important Sign and did not accept him, they would meet with divine punishment on a considerable scale. Hazrat Mirza Sahib wrote:

وَحَاصِلُ الْكَلَامِ اَنَّ الْكَسُوْفَ وَالْخُسُوْفَ اٰيَتَانِ مُخَوِّفَتَانِ وَاِذَا اجْتَمَعَا فَهُوَ تَهْدِيْدٌ شَدِيْدٌ مِّنَ الرَّحْمٰنِ وَاِشَارَةٌ اِلٰى اَنَّ الْعَذَابَ قَدْ تَقَرَّرَ وَ اُكِّدَ مِنَ اللّٰهِ لِاَهْلِ الْعُدْوَانِ ـ

'The lunar and the solar eclipse were two grave warnings from God. Their occurrence in the same month should serve as an admonition and point to the divine punishment which those who persist in hostility must receive.' (*Nur-ul-Haq*, part II)

Soon afterwards, as a step towards the fulfilment of the prophecy, he was moved to pray for a pestilence. Thus in one of his Arabic poems (1894) he said:

فَلَمَّا طَغَى الْفِسْقُ الْمُبِيدُ بِسَيْلِهِ   تَمَنَّيْتُ لَوْ كَانَ الْوَبَآءُ الْمُتَبِّرُ
فَإِنَّ هَلَاكَ النَّاسِ عِنْدَ أُولِي النُّهٰى   أَحَبُّ وَأَوْلٰى مِنْ ضَلَالٍ يُّخَسِّرُ

When iniquity and ungodliness rose to a deadly height; even as flood reaches its dangerous level,

I wished from God that a pestilence should come and destroy; For, according to the wise, it is better for people to die than to become involved in fatal misbelief and misguidance.

Then in 1897, in his book *Siraj-Munir*, he quoted a revelation of his:

يَا مَسِيْحَ الْخَلْقِ عَدْوَانَا۔

'O Messiah for men, rid us of our pestilences.'

Commenting on this he wrote:

دیکھو یہ کس زمانے کی خبریں ہیں اور نہ معلوم یہ کس وقت پوری ہوں گی۔ ایک وہ وقت
ہے جو دُعا سے مرتے ہیں۔ اور دوسرا وہ وقت آتا ہے کہ دُعا سے زندہ ہوں گے۔

'Wait and see how and when these warnings fulfil themselves. There are times when prayers bring death, and times when they bring life.'

When this last prophecy was published, plague had already made an appearance in Bombay. It stayed for a year and disappeared. There was a feeling of relief. Its spread had been prevented by the public health authorities. But a warning from God pointed the other way. When general complacency had been induced by the belief that the disease had come and gone, when the Punjab, except for one or two villages, seemed quite safe, when in Bombay its ravages had been more or less halted, the Promised Messiah issued a statement in which he said:

> I am constrained to write about an important matter and this owing only to overwhelming sympathy. I know that those devoid of spiritual feelings will tend to ridicule my statement. Nevertheless, out of sympathy for them, it is my duty to warn people. The warning is this. Today, February 6, 1898, Monday, I saw in a dream that angels of God were planting black seedlings in different parts of the Punjab. The seedlings are ugly, dangerous looking, black and stunted. I asked some of the angels about them. I was told that they were the seedlings of plague which was about to spread in the country. It did not become quite clear to me whether this was to be next winter or the winter after the next. But the scene and the experience were full of terror. I am reminded also of a revelation of mine about the plague. It said, 'Verily Allah does not change the lot of a people unless they first change their hearts.' It seems that the plague will not disappear unless extreme sin and transgression disappear first.

At the end of this warning the Promised Messiah added some Persian verse:

گر آں چیزے کہ مے بینم عزیزاں نیز دیدندے — ز دنیا توبہ کردندی بچشمِ زار و خونباری

خورِ تاباں سیہ گشت است از بدکاریٔ مردم — زمیں طاعون ہمی آرد پئے تخویف و اندازی

بہ تشویشِ قیامت ماند ایں تشویش گر بینی — علاجے نیست بہرِ دفعِ آں جز حُسنِ کرداری

من از ہمدردیت گفتم تو خود ہم فکر کن باری — خرد از بہر ایں روز است ای دانا و ہشیاری

If my friends could see that which I see,
Tears of blood would they shed and say goodbye to the world.

The bright sun has become dark for the sins of men,
The earth has thrown up the plague to frighten and warn.

If you but knew, you would liken this calamity to the calamity of Doomsday,
There is no cure for it but the cure of good deeds.

I say all this out of sympathy for you: It is for you to think over,
Use then your wisdom today, you wise and alert.

It appears from these prophecies that in 1894 the Promised Messiah prophesied a general calamity. The description of this he himself elaborated into a pestilence. Then, when the plague first made its appearance in India, he issued a special warning to the Punjab against the impending destruction. He described the threatened calamity as the calamity of Doomsday and said that there was to be no escape from it unless there was a change of heart.

What happened subsequently is terrible beyond words. The plague started in Bombay as though its worst effects were to be there, but Bombay recovered and the Punjab became its centre. So deadly and so widespread was it that the death-rate rose to thirty thousand per week and several hundred thousand died in a year. Hundreds of doctors were appointed. Many different kinds of treatment were invented. But to no avail. Every year the plague flared up with added virulence. The Government authorities looked on helplessly. A general feeling arose that this was the consequence of denying the Promised Messiah. Then several hundred thousand persons believed. The epidemic continued to rage until the Promised Messiah was told by God that the plague was over, only fever remained. After this declaration the plague began to decline steadily. However, from some revelations it appears that it may break out again in our own country or in others.

This clear prophecy compels assent by believers and deniers alike. If there are those who still refuse to believe this, they can only have our sympathy. Those who consider the facts with an open mind must agree that:

1 The warning about the plague was given a long time before its occurrence and a long time before medical science was able to predict its appearance anywhere.
2 When the plague made its first appearance people were warned that the attack would be repeated annually.
3 People were also warned that the attack on the Punjab would be the most virulent. It was in the Punjab that it was at its worst and that the largest number of deaths took place.
4 Doctors assured the people again and again that the epidemic had been controlled, but the Promised Messiah declared that the epidemic would not abate until God let it. As everybody knows the devastation continued for full nine years.

5 At last God Himself, out of compassion, promised to reduce its virulence. The Promised Messiah was told that *the plague had disappeared, only fever remained.* After this revelation the worst of the epidemic was over. However, a serious malaria epidemic broke out in the Punjab. Not a single household remained immune from it. Official reports admit that a malaria epidemic had never raged on such a scale.

Prophecy No. 8: A great earthquake

The prophecy I now proceed to narrate proves the Might and Dominion of God in the innermost depths of the earth as over its surface. The prophecy relates to the great earthquake which visited the Punjab on April 4, 1905. The earthquake fulfilled this prophecy and the fulfilment was, for all faiths, a proof of the truth of Islam and of the Promised Messiah. The revelations containing the prophecy said:

زلزلہ کا دھکّہ

'A shock of earthquake'

and

عَفَتِ الدِّيَارُ مَحَلُّهَا وَ مَقَامُهَا۔

'Destruction will come over temporary habitations as well as settled places.'

The revelations were soon published in the Ahmadiyya newspapers. Their literal fulfilment was utterly remote. Many thought they related only to the severity of the plague. But God meant otherwise. God meant the eruption of the volcanic hill at Kangra. This hill was supposed to be dead and inactive. It had a goddess made of stone installed on it to which superstitious Hindus made offerings. Geologists thought the hill had lost all capacity for harm; there was nothing to fear from it. Temples had been built all around, at great cost, and had existed for several hundred years. Devotees lived in these temples. Thousands of pilgrims visited them every year. God commanded the dead volcano to become active again and become a witness of the Truth of God's Messenger.

As the words of the revelation show, the earthquake was to deal particularly severely with *mahalluha* (temporary habitations), residences, camps, hotels, *sarais*, military barracks. It cannot be said that *mahalluha* (temporary hutments) precedes *maqamuha* (settled places) for the sake of rhythm, not for stressing temporary residences as the special target of the earthquake. For rhythm could have been served by some other word. The revelation consisted of a single line, and rhythm could have been secured by a rearrangement of its own words. The arrangement of words in the revelation, therefore, pointed to something significant. It was that the worst effects of the earthquake were to appear over an area full of temporary dwellings. Such dwellings exist only in cantonments, holiday resorts and places of pilgrimage. The earthquake of the prophecy was to visit an area of this kind.

Some time after the publication of these revelations, the dead volcano of Kangra suddenly became active. It was early on April 4, 1905. Morning prayers were hardly over. For miles around Kangra, the earth suffered a severe shaking. Kangra, its temples, and its *sarais* were completely destroyed. Eight miles away was the cantonment of Dharmsala. The military barracks there was razed to the ground. Bungalows built by Englishmen for use during holidays were reduced to rubble. Dwellings at Dalhousie and Bakloh were also destroyed. Towns and villages all around suffered. About twenty thousand persons died. Experts – geologists and others – wondered why the earthquake had come. Little did they know that the earthquake was the result of the denial and derision heaped upon the Promised Messiah. It had come to alert people to the importance of his claim. Experts searched for the cause inside the earth. The cause lay outside. The dead volcano of Kangra had obeyed the behest of its Lord and Creator. The Promised Messiah foretold many other earthquakes, and they came in their time. More may yet come.

Prophecy No. 9: The Great War of 1914–18

The ninth prophecy of the Promised Messiah, which I now proceed to narrate, is one out of many which proved to the whole world that the dominion of God extends over the hearts and minds of rulers and leaders, as it extends over common men and women, and that man, proud and powerful though he be, is as much constrained to obey God as any of His other creatures. This prophecy was published in 1905. The prophecy foretold the Great War of 1914–18, which shook Europe and perplexed the peoples of the world. It swept common men and women off their bearings and its ill-effects survive to this day. Its flames have yet not died out.

The prophecy apparently speaks of an earthquake, but the description of this earthquake indicates that it was to be a world-wide calamity resembling an earthquake. Other revelations on the subject also indicated a calamity other than an earthquake.

I first quote the revelations containing the prophecy.

تازہ نشان۔ تازہ نشان کا دھکّہ

'A fresh sign. Shock of a fresh sign.'

زَلْزَلَةُ السَّاعَةِ، قُوْٓا اَنْفُسَكُمْ، نَزَلْتُ لَكَ، لَكَ نُرِيْ اٰيَاتٍ
وَّنَهْدِمُ مَا يَعْمُرُوْنَ، قُلْ عِنْدِيْ شَهَادَةٌ مِّنَ اللّٰهِ فَهَلْ اَنْتُمْ
مُّؤْمِنُوْنَ۔ كَفَفْتُ عَنْ بَنِيْٓ اِسْرَآءِيْلَ، اِنَّ فِرْعَوْنَ وَهَامَانَ
وَجُنُوْدَهُمَا كَانُوْا خَاطِئِيْنَ۔

'An earthquake resembling Doomsday. Save your lives. I descended for your sake. We will show many Signs for your sake. We will destroy whatever the world is building. Say, "I have God as my witness – will ye believe?" I have saved Israel from detriment. The Pharaoh and Haman, the armies of both, are in the wrong.'

فتح نمایاں ہماری فتح

'Victory resplendent. Our victory.'

اِنِّیْ مَعَ الْاَفْوَاجِ اٰتِيْكَ بَغْتَةً۔

'I will come to thee with the armies and will come suddenly.' (This revelation has been repeated again and again.)

پہاڑ گرا اور زلزلہ آیا۔ آتش فشاں

'A mountain fell; and came an earthquake! A Volcano!'

مَصَالِحُ الْعَرَبِ، مَسِيْرُ الْعَرَبِ

'Avenues useful for Arabs. Arabs set out from their home.'

عَفَتِ الدِّيَارُ كَذِكْرِي، اُرِيْكَ زَلْزَلَةَ السَّاعَةِ، يُرِيْكُمُ اللهُ زَلْزَلَةَ السَّاعَةِ، لِمَنِ الْمُلْكُ الْيَوْمَ، لِلّٰهِ الْوَاحِدِ الْقَهَّارِ۔

'Houses will disappear even as all thought of Me has disappeared. You will see the earthquake of the appointed day. Allah will show you the earthquake of the appointed day. Dominion on that day will be for the One, Relentless God.'

The 'earthquake' of the prophecy was also described by the Promised Messiah in some detail in an Urdu poem. According to this poem:

The earthquake was to bring destruction to human beings, villages and fields. Aman caught naked will not have time to dress. The earthquake will entail special hardship for travellers. Many will stray far from their appointed routes to escape the terrors of the earthquake. Depressions will be produced in the earth. Streams of blood will flow. Streams of water running downhill will become red with blood. The calamity will involve the whole world. All men, great and small, all governments, will break under its impact. Especially will the Czar be reduced to a state of misery. Even birds will suffer. They will lose their sense and forget their sweet songs.

The Promised Messiah had other revelations on the subject. One was 'Boats sail that there may be duels'; another 'Raise the anchor.' Hazrat also wrote that all this was to happen in about sixteen years' time. An earlier revelation said the calamity was to take place in his lifetime. Then he was taught a prayer, 'O God, do not let me see this earthquake.'

So the Great War took place within sixteen years of the publication of the prophecy, but not in his lifetime.

The prophecy speaks of an 'earthquake', but this should not be taken in its literal sense but as a world calamity of some kind, i.e. a world war. For those who do not see this at once, I state my reasons:

Firstly, the word 'earthquake' is often used for war, for a great calamity. We have examples of this in the Holy Quran. Thus:

إِذْ جَآءُوكُم مِّن فَوْقِكُمْ وَمِنْ أَسْفَلَ مِنكُمْ وَإِذْ زَاغَتِ الْأَبْصَارُ
وَبَلَغَتِ الْقُلُوبُ الْحَنَاجِرَ وَتَظُنُّونَ بِاللَّهِ الظُّنُونَا هُنَالِكَ ابْتُلِيَ
الْمُؤْمِنُونَ وَزُلْزِلُوا زِلْزَالًا شَدِيدًا ـ

> 'When they came upon you from above you, and from below you, and when *your* eyes became distracted and *your* hearts leaped into your throats and you thought *diverse* thoughts about Allah, there and then. But the believers were *sorely* tried and they were shaken with a violent shaking.'[4]

The 'shaking' in these verses, the English for the Arabic *Zilzal*, should ordinarily mean an earthquake. But here it means war. The word is capable of such a meaning and the Holy Quran has used it in this sense. Therefore, where a context permits we can take 'earthquake' to mean some other calamity. 'Earthquake' can be a metaphor.

Secondly, when the Promised Messiah published this prophecy, he appended to it a note which said:

> It is possible that the description relates not to a literal earthquake but to some other calamity, grave enough to remind us of the Day of Judgment and unusual enough not to have been known before. This calamity may bring destruction to both life and property. (*Barahin-i-Ahmadiyya,* vol. V, p. 120)

This clearly shows that the Promised Messiah's prophetic description is not necessarily the description of an earthquake. It could be a calamity different from the conventional earthquake. When he published the prophecy, his critics insisted on taking the

4 *Al-Ahzab,* 11, 12.

earthquake of the prophecy for a common earthquake. They asked Hazrat Mirza Sahib not to let 'earthquake' mean anything else. But Hazrat Mirza Sahib said again and again that in the revelations several different metaphors had been used. He could not, therefore, take the descriptions to mean any one thing. The grandeur of the prophecy lay in the many Signs which it foretold, the foretelling of which does not lie in the power of man. The prophecy laid down a time limit. It also said that the events it foretold had not been seen before in the history of man.

Thirdly, the words used in the prophecy make it clear that a literal earthquake could not be meant, but instead probably a calamity of some other kind:

1 The prophecy says that the earthquake will involve the whole world. But everybody knows that earthquakes never do that; they only involve parts of the world.
2 The prophecy says the calamity will prove very hard on travellers, who will lose their way and stray far from their routes. But earthquakes do not trouble travellers. They trouble those staying in houses, in big cities. A calamity which can trouble travellers can only be war. When war starts, travellers cannot follow their normal routes. They have to give them up and adopt devious and difficult routes instead.
3 The prophecy points to the ill-effects of the calamity on farms, fields, etc.; but earthquakes have no ill-effects on farms and fields, which are destroyed only by war. Shelling from both sides destroys them. Sometimes 'scorched-earth' policy destroys them.
4 The prophecy points to the ill-effects of the calamity on birds; they were to lose their 'senses' and their 'songs'. An ordinary earthquake can have no such effects. The vibrations only last for a time. If birds sitting on a tree or a building fly into the air, they experience no ill-effects whatever. A modern war, however, is very hard on birds. Day and night bombing and the destruction of trees is highly detrimental to bird-life. The birds either die or suffer greatly.
5 The prophecy contains the revelation 'I have saved Israel from detriment.' This indicates that the calamity was to result in some advantage for the Jews. Such a thing can have no connection with an ordinary earthquake. (I will explain below the meaning of this

part of the prophecy; and I will show that this prophecy is also contained in the Holy Quran.)

6 The prophecy points to war because, apparently speaking of an earthquake, it goes on to say that the Pharaoh and Haman and their hosts are in the wrong. This is an obvious reference to the German Kaiser, who thought himself God or at least God's Deputy, just as the Pharaoh of Moses thought he was 'God of his people and Mighty'. Haman in the revelation means the Kaiser's ally, the Emperor of Austria, who had little will or personality and was totally obedient to the German warlord. If the prophecy meant a literal earthquake, the words 'Verily Pharaoh and Haman and their hosts are in the wrong' would have little or no meaning.

7 The revelations mention the repeated promise 'I will come suddenly with my armies.' This also points to war rather than earthquake. The revelations speak of a volcano, the eruption of which will entail advantages for the Arab peoples, who will also venture out of their homes. The description cannot apply to an ordinary earthquake. A volcano can only mean the violent expression of political discontent which may be precipitated by some passing event. Some such event was to stimulate the Arabs into some large action by which they were to turn events in their favour.

8 The revelations assert that on that day, God Almighty will be the Universal King. This description also indicates a war in which powerful states were to be involved against one another. The great powers, according to the prophecy, would become weak. The Dominion of God was to be re-asserted by powerful Signs.

9 One revelation says, 'A mountain fell and came an earthquake.' Even schoolchildren know that earthquakes are not the result of falling mountains. In fact, it is the other way about. Mountains may fall as the result of earthquakes. This also shows that the prophecy does not apply to an ordinary earthquake, but is a metaphorical description of some other large calamity involving the nations of the world in mutual warfare.

The fourth reason why the earthquake of the prophecy did not necessarily mean an earthquake but indicated some other calamity is that other revelations of the Promised Messiah received at about the same time point to a great war. One revelation says, 'Raise the anchor.' This points to the entry of different nations into naval encounters against one another. The command 'Raise the anchor' indicates the beginning of naval hostilities. Another revelation says, 'Boats sail that there be duels.' This is a picture of the vessels going in one direction and another in search of naval encounters.

After showing that the earthquake of the prophecy really meant the Great War of 1914–18, I wish to describe in greater detail how the several parts of the prophecy found fulfilment in the events of the Great War.

The first thing we must remember in this connection is that, according to the prophecy, war was to follow upon a certain incident. According to the prophecy, an unfortunate event was to be followed by a world-wide 'earthquake'. The Great War started exactly in this way. The heir-apparent of Austria-Hungry and his wife were assassinated. The assassination resulted in war. This was different from the way wars normally start. Wars are precipitated by differences and disagreements between great powers, but this war was precipitated by the assassination of an archduke and his wife.

A second feature foretold of the calamity was its universality. This feature too was fulfilled in a remarkable manner. Before the Great War, calamities universal in scope were not known. This war was the first world calamity. The countries of Europe entered the war first. Soon Asia became involved and then China, Japan and India were in it. A German battleship attacked Indian shores from the Indian Ocean. Iran was the scene of fighting between British and Turkish forces. Iranians had trouble with the German Consulate. Fighting, and grim fighting, took place in Iraq, Syria, Palestine and Siberia. Fighting took place in the four important parts of Africa. South Africa attacked German West Africa. There were disorders in South Africa itself. German colonies were attacked in East Africa. On the West coast fighting took place in the Cameroons. Fighting occurred on the border between Egypt and Tripoli. A German battleship attacked parts of Australasia before being cornered at last. There was fighting in New Guinea. The British and German navies encountered each other near the American coast. Canada and the United States had to enter. South American states declared war on Germany. In short, no part of the world remained outside or escaped the effects of the war.

A description of the war contained in the prophecy is the breaking of hills and the destruction of cities and cornfields, and this is what happened. Many hills disappeared because of bombing or because of mines which had to be cut through them. Many cities were ruined. Germany had to pay large sums of money for the rehabilitation. She still has to pay a large figure in reparations. The damage done to farms and fields cannot be estimated. Wherever the forces of one country advanced into another, the destruction of farms followed. Towns were destroyed and nothing remained of the green fields and pastures. Artillery lines were spread over thousands of miles. The resulting destruction was beyond calculation.

Another feature of the war was that birds lost their senses. This is what happened. In battle areas bird-life came to an end.

Another sign of the war was depressions and general destruction of the land surface. In France, Serbia and Russia, excessive bombardment produced deep depressions. In places water came out of such depressions. Fighting involved the digging of trenches. Countries which saw the fighting became full of these dug-outs. Nobody who saw them could say that these were countries with settled populations. For what were these lines and lines of dug-outs? Brick-kilns like those in our country? Or caves?

Another sign of the war was that streams of water red with human blood were like streams of blood. This is what happened. So much blood was shed at times that for miles waterways in the locality would turn red. There was so much fighting on the different fronts that streams of blood flowed literally.

Another sign of the war was the difficulties travellers and wayfarers were going to have. Many of them were to lose their way. This is what happened. On the land, because of fighting armies and their movements, normal routes became blocked. On the sea, owing to submarine warfare, boats carrying passengers were constantly in danger. When the war started, several hundred thousand persons were stranded in enemy countries. Many of them had to reach their own countries by circuitous routes. Troops of different countries also had to travel by longer routes, shorter routes having gone into enemy possession. British soldiers serving in France often lost their way. Many unhappy incidents occurred and to prevent this British soldiers were ordered to wear the names of their regiments and their stations round their necks.

Another sign was that 'things' which the world was trying to build would be wiped away. This is what happened, both in the physical and in the metaphorical sense. Many well-known buildings in Europe were destroyed. Destruction was also wrought to the foundations of European life. The old security, the old confidence in continued peace and progress were gone. European nations are trying to rebuild these foundations, but all efforts seem to fail. It seems inevitable that European – and Western – life will have to seek new foundations on which to rebuild. The old foundations have been destroyed, and destroyed for good. The new foundations will have to be more rational and nearer to the teaching of Islam. Something like it seems ordained by God and nothing can stop it.

A very important feature of the war was relief to the people of Israel. This feature of the prophecy received a clear fulfilment. The war was not yet over when, as a consequence of the war itself, Mr (later Lord) Balfour declared that the people of Israel who had been without a 'homeland' would be settled in their ancient 'homeland', Palestine. The Allied nations promised to compensate the people of Israel for injustices done to them in the past. in accordance with these declarations, Palestine was taken from Turkey and declared the national home of the Jews. The administration of Palestine is being shaped so as to make it easy for Jews to make it their homeland. Jews from different countries are being encouraged to settle in Palestine. A very old demand of the Jews, that conditions promoting their national cohesion should be created for them, has been met.

The strangest thing about this part of the prophecy is that references to it exist also in the Holy Quran. Thus in the chapter *Bani-Israil*, we read:

وَقُلْنَا مِنْ بَعْدِهِ لِبَنِيٓ إِسْرَآءِيلَ اسْكُنُوا الْاَرْضَ فَاِذَا جَآءَ
وَعْدُ الْاٰخِرَةِ جِئْنَا بِكُمْ لَفِيفًا

'And after him We said to the children of Israel, "Dwell ye in the land; and when *the time of* the promise of the latter days comes, We shall bring you together *out of various people*.'[5]

5 *Bani-Israil*, 105.

Commentators of the Holy Quran take the land to be Egypt and the promise of the latter days to be the Day of Judgment. But such interpretations are wrong because the Israelites were never ordered to live in Egypt. They were ordered to live in the Holy Land, namely, Palestine, and there they lived. Similarly, 'promise of the latter days' cannot mean the Day of Judgment, because the Day of Judgment has little connection with Israel's having to live in the Holy Land. All that this promise of the latter days means, therefore, is that a time was to come when the Jews would leave the Holy Land, to be gathered into it again at the time of the 'promise of the latter days'. The promise of the latter days relates to the time of the Promised Messiah. The re-gathering of Israel, therefore, was to take place in the time of the Promised Messiah.

In the commentary *Futuh al-Bayan* we are told that 'the time of the promise of the latter days marks the descent of Jesus from heaven'. Also the chapter of the Holy Quran just quoted divides the history of the Jewish people into two great periods (17:5). Of the second period the same chapter goes on to say:

فَإِذَا جَآءَ وَعْدُ الْآخِرَةِ لِيَسُوْٓءُا وُجُوْهَكُمْ وَلِيَدْخُلُوا الْمَسْجِدَ
كَمَا دَخَلُوْهُ أَوَّلَ مَرَّةٍ وَلِيُتَبِّرُوْا مَا عَلَوْا تَتْبِيْرًا -

> 'So when the time for the latter warning came, *We raised a people against you* to cover your faces with grief, and to enter the Mosque as they entered it the first time and to destroy all that they conquered with utter destruction.'[6]

From this it appears that the warning of the latter days relates to the time in Jewish history subsequent to the first coming of Jesus. However, after this warning we know from history that Jews were not gathered; they were dispersed. Therefore in verse 17:105 the warning of the latter days relates to the period after the second coming of Jesus. The words 'shall bring you together' refer to the present influx of Jews into Palestine. Jews from different countries are offered facilities of travel and rehabilitation. The revelation of the Promised Messiah said, 'I will *relieve* the children of Israel.' This indicated a great change in the position of the Jews. It indicated the

6 *Bani-Israil*, 8.

end of the opposition which nations of the world had made for so long to an independent home for the Jews.

An important sign of the war was the time limit of sixteen years, It happened exactly as had been foretold. The revelations about the war were received in 1905; the war started in 1914, i.e. within sixteen years from the date of the prophecy.

Another sign of the war was that naval forces of different nations were to be kept ready. Accordingly, we find that not only combatant nations, but other nations too had to keep their naval forces in readiness. Every nation had to see that no other nation violated her waters. War could be forced upon them at any time. So naval forces had to be ready, even for the protection of neutrality.

One important sign of the war was the movement of ships for sea warfare. The prophecy pointed not merely to preparations and readiness for combat on the sea but also to the movements of vessels. Accordingly, in this war many more sea vessels were used than had been used ever before. Vessels of small size, destroyers, and submarines were used on a scale completely unknown before. The expression used in the revelation is 'boats' which points to a bias for fighting seacraft of small size, and this is true of the Great War of 1914–18.

One sign told of the war was its suddenness. The suddenness with which this war broke out is well known. Statesmen later admitted that though they expected a war sometime, they had no idea that it would come suddenly. The murder of the Austrian archduke proved to be a fuse which touched off a world-wide conflagration.

A sign of the war was the advantages which it was to bring to the Arab nations and the way Arabs were to exploit the opportunities it offered. For a long time Arabs had entertained the idea of Arab independence. When they heard that the Turks had entered the war, they thought the time for their freedom had come. They at once declared themselves against Turkey and entered the war against them. Arabs achieved the goal of their freedom.

Another sign was the destruction of cities and places noted for their godlessness. 'I will obliterate habitations much as they have obliterated My name.' It is generally agreed that Eastern France was the worst part of Europe from the point of view of sensual indulgence. From this part was sent the wine consumed in different countries of Europe. It was also the rendezvous of pleasure-seekers from Western countries. In accordance with the prophecy this part suffered the most. Pleasure resorts crashed and crumbled, and were wiped out as God's name had been wiped out from them.

One sign mentioned in the revelations was 'Our victory'. This clearly indicated that victory was to come to the side which possessed the sympathy of the followers of the Promised Messiah. This is what happened. The Promised Messiah prayed for Britain, and God helped Britain out of this terrible calamity. British statesmen may attribute their victory to their plans, but a careful observation of the crucial phases of the war shows that British forces received miraculous help repeatedly. Again and again accidents went in their favour. This shows that British victory was due to special divine help. It was not due to human planning only.

One sign in the prophecy was of outstanding importance, because this one sign consisted of a number of other signs. This sign was that the war was to reduce the Czar of Russia to a most pitiful condition. Circumstances at the time of the publication of the prophecy gave no such indication; in fact there were indications to the contrary. But the prophecy was fulfilled, and the fulfilment surprised everybody.

The prophetic description of what was to happen to the Czar implies a number of separate prophecies. One was that until the 'calamity' appeared, no harm would come to the Czar. Harm to the Czar was to come as a result of the 'calamity', namely the war. Secondly, the prophecy implied that the harm destined for the Czar was not death or a sudden end. Death or a sudden end does not connote a pitiful condition. The prophetic description, therefore, does not connote the *death* of the Czar. It connotes instead a condition lasting over some time and full of pain and privations of various kinds. The description also implies the end of the Czars as a dynasty. The prophetic description speaks of the *Czar*. It points to the Russian royalty, not to any individual Russian ruler. But see how literally the prophecy was fulfilled! Before the Great War, efforts were made to depose the Czar and to get rid of the Russian royalty, but nothing happened. Then came the war and the time appointed for the end of the Czar. The end came with a suddenness which astonished everybody. It appears that when the revolution of 1917 started, the Czar was not in the capital but at the front inspecting battle lines and positions. When he left for a tour of the battle area there were no signs of a revolution. Then, because of some indiscretion on the part of a governor, people became angry. Such anger is common in organized states; it seldom or never leads to their fall. On this occasion, however, the Hand of God was at work. The Czar, on hearing of this unrest, sent instructions to the Government to put it down with a strong hand. But a strong hand this time produced a contrary effect. It resulted in more unrest. The Czar replaced the governor and himself started back for the capital. On the way, he heard further accounts of the situation. He was advised that unrest was on the increase and that he should not enter the capital. But the Czar did not care. Believing that his presence on the scene would calm down the people, he continued the return journey. He had not gone very far when he learnt that a general revolution had taken place; that the revolutionaries had taken possession of the State Secretariat; and that a popular government had been set up. On March 12, 1917, in the course of a single day, the greatest and most powerful monarch in the world, designated the Czar (literally 'one who rules over all and is ruled by none') was deposed from his mighty throne and reduced to the status of his own people's subject. On March 15, under duress, he signed a declaration that he and his family would never again claim the Russian throne. This was literally in accordance with the prophecy. The family of the Czar fell as a ruling family. But there were other parts to the prophecy. The Czar, Nicholas II, imagined that by surrendering the throne he would save his own life and the lives of the Czarina and their children, and that they would be able to live as private citizens. But this was not to be. He surrendered the throne on March 15. On March 21, he was taken prisoner and sent to Skosilo. On March 22, America declared her recognition of the new revolutionary government. This killed the last hope. The throne had gone. Even physical survival was in doubt. He could see now that the powers on whose help he had relied and who were his allies in the war against Germany did not take much more than a week to recognize a government set up by disloyal subjects. On March 24, England, France, and Italy declared their recognition of the new government. Then the Czar gave up all hope. He could see that friendly powers for whose sake he had been fighting against Germany did not wait much more than a week before recognizing the disloyal revolutionaries. These erstwhile friendly powers did not raise even a feeble voice in his support. But there were other pains for him to endure. To fulfil the prophecy, his condition was to become really pitiful. The Czar was a prisoner, but the reins of government were still in the hands of a member of the royal family, Prince Dilvao. The good offices of this prince assured the Czar's kind treatment in prison. In fact, the Czar and his family had more or less settled into gardening and other occupations appropriate to an ex-king and his family. But in July this prince also had to surrender. The reins of government passed into the hands of Kerensky. The life of the royal prisoners now became harder, but it was still bearable. On November 7, Bolshevik revolutionaries dismissed the Kerensky government, and the condition of the Czar became so pitiful as to make the stoutest heart flinch. The Czar was removed from internment in the Royal Palace and taken from place to place, ultimately to Ekaterinburg. Here he was to have a taste of the tortures he used to inflict on prisoners serving sentences in Siberia. This small town is to the east of the Urals, fourteen hundred miles from Moscow. Here machinery for use in Siberian mines was manufactured. Russian political prisoners had to work in these mines. The scenes around his new prison reminded the Czar of the atrocities perpetrated by him on others.

However, the pitiful condition of the Czar was not to be measured by these tortures only. The Bolshevik government reduced his rations and ordinary comforts. His sick child was beaten by ill-mannered guards. The parents had to watch. His daughters were maltreated. Even these tortures did not satiate the revolutionaries. They invented new penalties and new pains. One day, when the Czarina was present under compulsion, the virgin daughters of the Czar were raped by the soldiers. If the Czarina, unable to bear the sight, turned her face away, the soldiers would compel her to observe the inhuman scene. Witnessing these brutalities and enduring more pains and poignancies than can have been endured by any mortal, the Czar at last met his end. He was shot dead on July 16, 1918, and with him the entire royal family. The prophecy 'Even the Czar at that moment will be in a pitiful condition' was fulfilled literally.

The war was over. The Czar died a pitiful death. The rulers of Germany and Austria had surrendered their crowns. Cities had been laid waste. Hills had disappeared. Millions of men had died. Rivers of blood had flowed and destruction had stalked the land. But alas! the world still asked for signs and arguments to prove the authenticity of the Divine Messenger. God's resources are limitless.

His punishment is as ready to come as His forgiveness. But blessed are they who are willing to understand, who will hasten to make peace with their Lord rather than continue at war with Him. They heed His Signs and do not pass by them as though they did not see them. They draw the Compassion of God, receive His blessings and prove a blessing for the world.

Prophecy No. 10: Expansion of Qadian

So far I have narrated prophecies embodying warnings, or both warnings and promises. Now I wish to narrate three prophecies containing promises of progress, expansion, and general advance.

These three prophecies, like all the others, received full publicity well before their fulfilment. Both friend and foe knew about them. Men of all religious persuasions could be found who would say that they knew of the existence of these prophecies. They have been reproduced repeatedly in the books and journals of the Promised Messiah. The first of these three prophecies relates to the expansion of Qadian. Hazrat Mirza Sahib was informed that the village of Qadian, the birthplace and centre of the Ahmadiyya Movement would grow from year to year and become in time a large city, like Bombay or Calcutta, with a population of a million or so. Eastward it was to expand as far as the river Beas, nine miles from Qadian. When the prophecy was published, the population of Qadian was only about two thousand. Except for a few houses made of baked brick, the whole town had houses made of mud. Rents were extremely low: one could have a house for about four or five annas a month. Land for a house could be had very cheaply. A plot could be had for about ten or twelve rupees. Hardly any shops existed. Ground flour could be bought for only two or three rupees at one time. Men lived as in villages. They ground their own flour to make their own bread. There was only one school, a primary school; its one teacher, on a small extra allowance, also worked as the village postmaster. Mail from outside arrived twice a week. Houses in the village were enclosed within the village wall. No natural conditions existed which could have helped the prophecies. Qadian was eleven miles from the nearest railway station. The road connecting it with the railway was a *kacha* dusty road. Towns grow on railways or other routes, but Qadian was not on any such route.

There was no local industry to attract labour, no official activity, institution or department. Qadian was not a district or sub-district headquarters. It did not have even a police post. It was not a market for any kind of produce or goods. The followers of Hazrat Mirza Sahib did not number more than a few hundred at the time. A town could not have been created by asking devotees to come and live at Qadian.

True, it may be said that a claim to spiritual office had been made. Therefore, Mirza Sahib could expect to have a following of some size, and this following could come to Qadian and make it a large town. But who could say that Hazrat Mirza Sahib would have a large enough following? And how often do followers of a spiritual leader give up their vocations and habitations to live near their leader? Jesus was born in Nazareth and Nazareth is still a village. Great Saints like Shahabal-Din Suhrawardy, Sheikh Ahmad Sirhindi and Bahaud-Din Naqshbandi (mercy of Allah be on them) were born in villages, went to live in villages. But those villages remained villages. They did not grow any more in size, or if they did, it was within economic limits. The founding of towns or cities is not easy. Kings who plan and found towns without regard for economic conditions do not succeed. Such towns are soon abandoned. From the economic standpoint Qadian was very poorly situated from a railway line that its inhabitants could set about promoting it as a centre of some sort, independently of the railway. Nor was Qadian on a river or a canal. Waterways stimulate trade and help the growth of towns. but Qadian did not have even this advantage.

Against all normal and natural conditions, without any of the usual advantages, Qadian was to grow bigger and bigger. After the prophecy had been published, God began to help the Jama'at with an increase in numbers. Members of the Jama'at began to turn to Qadian as a place to settle in. Ahmadis who came to settle attracted others. The complete fulfilment of the prophecy will take time but its partial fulfilment is astonishing. The population of Qadian is now [1920s] about four and a half thousand, already more than twice its original population. The old village wall has disappeared and the town has overflown its boundaries. At the present time houses can be seen at least a mile out of the old village. Some big brick buildings and wide roads have been added, so that what was once a village is now a town. The bazaars too have grown.

Purchases worth thousands may be made at one time. Instead of the old primary school, there are three high schools (they include one for Hindus, one for girls) and a college for religious studies. The post office, which received outside mail only twice a week and which was run by the local schoolmaster, now has a staff of seven or eight. Telegraph facilities are being added. Several newspapers are issued; at present one bi-weekly, two weekly (one Urdu, one English), and one bi-monthly and two monthly journals besides. Five printing presses exist, one of them a machine press. Many books are published every year. The name Qadian is firmly installed on the postal map. Bigger towns may lose their mail, but not Qadian. In short, under inauspicious circumstances, Qadian has grown in an unparalleled manner. Its unusual growth is against normal economic laws and is proof of the truth of God's communication. Those who have known it and knew its situation (whatever their religious attachment) admit that Qadian has expanded and is expanding. They may think it only an unusual coincidence. But woe to them who never ask why all coincidences are ordained for Hazrat Mirza Sahib.

Prophecy No. 11: Financial relief

A second example of prophecies promising progress and prosperity is the prophecy about increasing financial help. This prophecy was attended by the strangest circumstances. In respect of time, it was the Promised Messiah's earliest prophecy. It so happened that his father was taken ill. Hazrat Mirza Sahib had had no experience of revelation until then. One day it seemed that his father had more or less recovered. Only some diarrhoea remained. Yet Hazrat Mirza Sahib had the revelation.

وَالسَّمَآءِ وَالطَّارِقِ

'By the Heaven and by the Night-comer.'

Night-comer (in Arabic, *Tariq*), means 'that which comes at night'. Hazrat Mirza Sahib understood that the revelation foretold the time of his father's death and that it had come as divine condolence over his impending bereavement – the sympathy of

God in the coming grief. Many sources of family income were connected with his father: pension and presents and a part of the family property. On receiving the revelation Hazrat Sahib experienced some anxiety. The pension, the periodical presents, and a part of the property were all to go. But then came a second revelation and this contained a grand prophecy. It said:

أَلَيْسَ اللّٰهُ بِكَافٍ عَبْدَهٗ

'Is not God sufficient unto His servant?'

The revelation conveyed to Hazrat Mirza Sahib the promise that God would look after him and meet all his needs. He mentioned this revelation to Hindu and Muslim friends. One of them, a Hindu (who is still alive), went at his request to Amritsar to have a ring made with the revealed words engraved on the stone. Knowledge of the revelation spread. The importance of it became more evident when, under providence, litigation over family property started within the family. Even what was to remain with Hazrat Mirza Sahib out of the family property seemed likely to slip away from him. His elder brother managed the family affairs. Differences arose between this brother and other relations. Hazrat Mirza Sahib proposed that they should treat the relations with more than ordinary consideration. The brother did not agree. Matters went to court. The brother requested Hazrat Mirza Sahib to pray; he prayed, but was warned that the brother would lose and the relations would win. The warning proved true. More than two-thirds of the family property went to others, very little remained with the brothers. Enough for maintenance, it was not enough for the great work Hazrat Mirza Sahib was about to undertake. He was preparing his magnum opus, *Barahin-i-Ahmadiyya*, a work destined to produce a revolution in the religious world. The publication of this book needed funds. The provision of funds, apparently impossible, became possible through miraculous ways. Men little interested in religion were moved to help and to provide the funds for its publication. Four parts of the book were published. But it was obvious that more and more funds were now required. The published parts confounded the critics of Islam. They stopped their attacks on Islam, but started attacking Hazrat Mirza Sahib. Great excitement arose. Hindu, Christian, and Sikh publicists all joined in. Hazrat Mirza Sahib was ridiculed about his revelations. The object of their propaganda was to alienate the people from his writings on Islam and to save the critics of Islam from a defeat which seemed inevitable. Some Muslims out of jealousy also joined them. The attack on Hazrat Mirza Sahib came from four sides. To repulse the attack more and more funds were required. Attacks by Muslims as well as non-Muslims had to be met and the glory of Islam maintained. Thank God, the means were not long in coming.

And now Hazrat Mirza Sahib advanced into a third period of his life. He began to have revelations that he was the Messiah promised in the old prophecies. The first Messiah was not alive in Heaven, but had died like all mortals. On the publication of this claim many who had attached themselves to him withdrew. Only forty persons accepted the claim and made a solemn affirmation on his hand. Hazrat Mirza Sahib was now at war with the whole world. Many erstwhile friends joined the opponents and started doing their worst. The funds needed began to exceed all estimates. Replies to opponents, publicity of the claim and of arguments for the claim, also the publication of leaflets for the instruction of followers, were heavy liabilities. At the same time the Power of God was due to manifest itself in new ways. Still heavier liabilities were to be incurred by Hazrat Mirza Sahib. God commanded him to start a guest-house at Qadian and invite all and sundry to come and stay as his guests, receive direct instruction in religion, and have their doubts and difficulties removed through personal contact with him. The loss of old friends and helpers, the increase in printing and publishing needs, and now building a guest-house and entertaining a stream of visitors, amounted to a huge liability. It might have disrupted the Movement at its very inception, if Allah had not been ready with His help. A few dozen men who had joined him (and not one rich man among them, most of them in fact very poor) proved equal to the task. God filled the minds of these poor men with extraordinary zeal. They endured hardships and privations, but did not let the interests of faith suffer. Apparently, their sincerity and their sacrifice, but really the Promise of God in the revelation 'Is not Allah sufficient unto His servant?' was at work.

The Ahmadi Jama'at now faced general persecution. Maulvis had issued the *Fatwa* that the punishment for Ahmadis was death. Looting their houses and dispossessing them of their property and marrying their women elsewhere without the formality of a divorce was not only lawful but an act of merit. Ill-motived and criminal-minded men looking for excuses for the display of their lusts had started acting on this *Fatwa*, Ahmadis were being turned out of their houses and dismissed from service or work. They were also being deprived of whatever they possessed. The only salvation from these troubles was migration to Qadian. A steady flow of refugees into Qadian increased the expense of housing and feeding them. The Jama'at now numbered one to two thousand, but every one of them was exposed to hostility and hatred. They lived in continued anxiety: anxiety over their lives, honour, possessions, and property. They also had their daily debates over differences. Yet they found the money required for the propagation of Islam, for the feeding and putting up of visitors, and for an increasing number of refugees. Hundreds of persons had their meals twice a day at the guest-house instituted by Hazrat Mirza Sahib. The very poor among them had to have other needs provided for besides. Individual residents also had to entertain visitors and refugees. Every house in Qadian was open for this purpose. The Promised Messiah's own house always remained full. Every room in the house sheltered some guests, sometimes a whole family. The financial burden, already heavy, became heavier and heavier. New difficulties and new responsibilities were being added every day. But anxieties did not stay. They were driven away by the divine promise – 'Is not Allah sufficient unto His servant?' Circumstances which seemed to threaten the very existence of the Jama'at turned into assets, sources of weakness into sources of strength. Thunderstorms turned into welcome light rain. Every drop echoed back the promise of divine help – 'Is not Allah sufficient unto His servant?' The troubles of those early days can well be imagined. The people of Afghanistan, at one time, had to receive an influx of refugees from India. Afghanistan had an established government ready to entertain them, and many refugees paid their own expenses. The number of hosts was larger than the number of guests. Ten million Afghans had to entertain one or two hundred thousand refugees. Yet difficulties arose. Thus the pressure on the resources of a Jama'at, one or two thousand poor, in feeding several hundred visitors and refugees and financing the propagation of Islam, can well be imagined. And, let us not forget, the small group who bore all this lived not in peace but in perpetual anxiety.

The needs and liabilities of the Movement were not to last for days or months, or even years. They were to last and increase from year to year. But every year God's help came and provided the necessary means. In 1898 Hazrat Mirza Sahib opened a high school for the education of the young members of the Jama'at. The school was to have a proper religious side. Financial liabilities further increased. A little later two monthly journals, one English, one Urdu, were started for the propagation of Islam. Activities of the Jama'at expanded. Means were provided by God. At the present time the Jama'at maintains an English high school, a theological college, and a girls' school at Qadian, plus primary and middle schools in other places. It also maintains a number of preachers for work in India. Missions for the propagation of Islam are maintained in Mauritius, Ceylon, and England, and also an establishment at the headquarters to organize and direct the work of the Jama'at. There are editorial and publishing departments, a department for instruction and education, a department for general administration, a department for settling disputes, a department for determining questions of religious laws, etc., etc. The budget of the Jama'at amounts to about three or four lakhs (three or four hundred thousand) rupees. The rising financial liabilities of the Jama'at are being met by the special Grace of God promised in the revelation 'Is not Allah sufficient unto His servant?'

The Jama'at remains poor. This is in keeping with a law of God which permits only the poor to collect around a divine teacher in the beginning. People hold early followers in contempt:

مَا نَرٰىكَ اتَّبَعَكَ اِلَّا الَّذِيْنَ هُمْ اَرَاذِلُنَا بَادِيَ الرَّاْيِ

'We see that none have followed thee but only the meanest amongst us.'[7]

The wisdom of this law is that the success of a Divine Movement cannot then be attributed to the help and interest of human beings. Neither friend nor foe is able to say such a thing. The fact that a small and poor community is able to bear an increasing financial burden can only be accounted for by divine help. Members of the Jama'at pay the same taxes that other citizens pay. They pay the revenue assessed on their lands. They pay for roads, hospitals,

7 *Hud*, 28.

schools, etc. They have their other normal financial obligations to discharge; but, in addition, they have their voluntary liabilities for the propagation of Islam which they also discharge. They have done this now [1920s] for thirty-five years. True, during this time some relatively well-to-do and socially well-placed persons have also joined the Jama'at, but the liabilities of the Jama'at have increased proportionately. It may seem strange that while others who are richer and more prosperous grumble over their private budgets, Ahmadis year after year not only do not grumble over their private budgets but give away lakhs for the sake of God. Many of them rely so much on the Grace of God that if need arose they would put their all in the way of God. Where did this faith and this spirit come from? Only from God. Only God can provide the stimulus. It was God Who first assured the Promised Messiah, 'Is not Allah sufficient unto His servant?' No power could have held out such a promise and so early. At the time of this revelation the Promised Messiah feared for a mere living. How could he hope to find the large funds needed for the ever-increasing liabilities he had incurred on behalf of Islam? What power could promise such a thing and then fulfil the promise? There are tens of millions (crores) of Muslims in the world. How much do they give for the propagation of Islam? If other Muslims in India were to make financial contributions at the same rate as members of the Ahmadi Jama'at for the propagation of Islam, they could provide about nine or ten crores every year for this purpose. This, if their economic level were the same as that of Ahmadis. But Indian Muslims include many rich men, rulers of native states, and owners of big businesses. If we keep in view the resources of the richer Muslims, Indian Muslims alone could subscribe more than fifteen crores of rupees for the propagation of Islam. But they do not provide even a decent fraction of what this small, poor community is able to provide for this purpose. Why such a difference? Because Ahmadis are sustained by the Divine Promise – 'Is not Allah sufficient unto His servant?'

Prophecy No. 12: Expansion of the Jama'at

This prophecy relates to divine promises about the diffusion of ideas, teaching, and spirit which Hazrat Mirza Sahib was commissioned to impart. These were the ideas and teachings of the Holy Quran, which had been forgotten by both Muslims and others. The prophecy received good publicity. It was issued at a time when not the slightest conditions conducive to its fulfilment existed in the world. I quote the exact words of some of the revelations:

میں تیری تبلیغ کو دُنیا کے کناروں تک پہنچاؤں گا۔

'I will carry thy message to the ends of the earth.'

میں تیرے خالص اور دلی محبوں کا گروہ بھی بڑھاؤں گا اور ان کے نفوس اور اموال میں برکت دُوں گا اور ان میں کثرت بخشوں گا۔

'I will add to the fold of thy sincere and loyal friends. I will add to their progeny and their wealth and increase them manifold.'

اللہ اس گروہِ احمدیاں کو نشوونما دے گا۔ یہاں تک کہ ان کی کثرت اور برکت نظروں میں عجیب ہو جائے گی۔

'He , God, will make the Ahmadiyya group grow, so that their size and their influence begin to seem strange.'

يَأْتُوْنَ مِنْ كُلِّ فَجٍّ عَمِيْقٍ۔

'They [visitors to Qadian] will come in large numbers.'

اِنَّآ اَعْطَيْنٰكَ الْكَوْثَرَ

'Verily We will grant you increase of everything.'

Some revelations came in English. One said: 'I will give you a large party of Islam.'

Another revelation said:

ثُلَّةٌ مِّنَ الْاَوَّلِيْنَ وَ ثُلَّةٌ مِّنَ الْاٰخِرِيْنَ

'A party out of the first and a party out of the latter [peoples].'

This may mean that the members of the Ahmadi Jama'at would

be drawn from the followers of earlier prophets as well as from Muslims.

Another said:

يَا نَبِيَّ اللهِ كُنْتُ لَا أَعْرِفُكَ

'O Prophet of Allah, I knew you not.'

This speech is put into the mouth of the earth, meaning people in general, who would be remorseful at their failure to believe in the Promised Messiah.

Yet another revelation said:

إِنَّا نَرِثُ الْأَرْضَ نَأْكُلُهَا مِنْ أَطْرَافِهَا

'The earth is Our inheritance. We will devour it from all sides.'

Some of these revelations belong to the very earliest days. They were received and published when Hazrat Mirza Sahib did not have a single follower. Others were received later when the Jama'at had grown, but not yet to any size. It was no ordinary thing for Hazrat Mirza Sahib to proclaim that a time would come when he would have a large following; that members of his Jama'at would be found not only in India but also in other countries; and they would be drawn from all communities and sections; and that their numbers would increase and no country would remain inaccessible to his message. To say such a thing is not easy. Human imagination cannot make predictions of this size, not on the basis of ordinary knowledge.

Today science and philosophy predominate. Belief in all religions is on the decline. Beliefs held from early childhood are being abandoned. Christians today are no longer Christians, Hindus no longer Hindus, Jews no longer Jews, and Parsis no longer Parsis. The place of old religious beliefs is being taken by a vague sort of rationalism which tends to become the inner content of all religious beliefs. Only the external forms are still different. In the face of this universal tendency, it seemed futile to expect people to turn to Hazrat Mirza Sahib's teaching and to adopt the beliefs he taught. Followers of earlier prophets, who were turning away from their own prophets and were gradually adopting a kind of natural religion, could not so easily accept the claims of Hazrat Mirza Sahib. At the same time Hazrat Mirza Sahib's power to reach the peoples of the world was severely limited. He knew only Urdu, Arabic, and Persian. He had been born in India, and Indians until quite recent times have been hated in Arabia and Iran. Nobody could imagine that the inhabitants of Arabia, Iran, Afghanistan, Syria, and Egypt would believe in revelational claims made by an Indian. English-educated Indians had come to think divine revelation mere delusion, the Holy Quran not the Speech of God but the speech of Muhammad, the Prophet. How could they believe that divine revelation was a fact and that God really does communicate His Will and Knowledge to His favoured servants, even to those who do not know English? Not knowing English is like a sin in the eyes of the English-educated Indians. Hazrat Mirza Sahib was completely ignorant of European languages, European sciences, European customs and institutions. He had never stepped out of his own province. Only once did he go as far as Aligarh. Nobody would have thought that such a man would address himself to Western countries and win converts. Nobody would have thought that well-trained European minds full of contempt for Asians would pay any attention to the teaching of an Asian, much less accept it. Nobody would have said that people in isolated parts of Africa would accept the teaching of such a man. Nobody in India could use an African language. These insuperable difficulties were challenged by the Word of God, and the Word of God came true. A man walked alone in the small yard of his house and wrote down the revelations of God as he received them. The revelations predicted acceptance of his teaching by the world; this, at a time when his own village did not know him that well. In the face of all difficulties, he arose and thundered like a cloud. Jealous and hostile eyes looked on. But the cloud spread, to their discomfort and dismay. It spread over the whole sky, and it rained. It rained over India, Afghanistan, Arabia, Egypt, Ceylon, Bokhara, East Africa, Mauritius, South Africa, parts of West Africa (Nigeria, the Gold Coast, and Sierra Leone), Australia, England, Germany, parts of Russia, and America.

In every continent of the world, somewhere, followers of the Promised Messiah can be found. There is not a community in the world which has not yielded followers to him. Members of the Ahmadi Jama'at have been drawn from Christians, Buddhists,

Parsis, Sikhs, Jews, and also Europeans, Africans, Americans, and Asians.

If what the Promised Messiah prophesied was not prophesied in the name of God, why was it fulfilled? Why did it come true? It is strange that Europe and America until today treated Islam as their prey, but now thanks to the Promised Messiah, Islam can treat Europe and America as its prey. Several hundred persons in England and several hundred in America have accepted Islam already. Similarly, individuals in Russia, Germany, and Italy have accepted and joined the Jama'at. The Islam which suffered defeat after defeat at the hands of other religions now inflicts defeats on them. The tables have now been turned by the prayers and the spiritual power of the Promised Messiah. Islam is on the march, the enemy in retreat. 'And praised be Allah, the Lord of all the worlds.'

Argument 11
Love of God and the Holy Prophet

After enumerating some of the prophecies of the Promised Messiah (on whom be peace), I proceed to the eleventh argument for his claim.

This argument is based on a well-known verse of the Holy Quran:

وَالَّذِيْنَ جَاهَدُوْا فِيْنَا لَنَهْدِيَنَّهُمْ سُبُلَنَا

'And for those who strive in Our path, We will surely guide them in Our ways,'[1]

and on another verse which says:

قُلْ إِنْ كُنْتُمْ تُحِبُّوْنَ اللّٰهَ فَاتَّبِعُوْنِيْ يُحْبِبْكُمُ اللّٰهُ

'Say, if you love Allah, follow me; Then will Allah love you.'[2]

The verses teach that true and burning love of God and the Holy Prophet results in a meeting between God and man. He who loves God and the Holy Prophet is beloved of God. True love of God, therefore, is a sign of truth and sincerity. When the truth and sincerity of a person are in question, we should ask, 'Does he love God? Does he love the Holy Prophet and obey him?'

The Quran on love

The subject of love is well known. Poets of all countries write about it at length. Different religions hold it up as the real measure

1 *Al-Ankabut,* 70. 2 *Al-Imran,* 32.

of faith and nearness to God. The most comprehensive description of love, however, is to be found in a passage of the Holy Quran:

قُلْ إِنْ كَانَ آبَاؤُكُمْ وَأَبْنَاؤُكُمْ وَإِخْوَانُكُمْ وَأَزْوَاجُكُمْ وَعَشِيرَتُكُمْ
وَأَمْوَالٌ اقْتَرَفْتُمُوهَا وَتِجَارَةٌ تَخْشَوْنَ كَسَادَهَا وَمَسَاكِنُ تَرْضَوْنَهَا
أَحَبَّ إِلَيْكُمْ مِنَ اللَّهِ وَرَسُولِهِ وَجِهَادٍ فِي سَبِيلِهِ فَتَرَبَّصُوا حَتَّىٰ
يَأْتِيَ اللَّهُ بِأَمْرِهِ وَاللَّهُ لَا يَهْدِي الْقَوْمَ الْفَاسِقِينَ ـ

> 'Say, if your fathers, and your sons, and your brothers, and your wives, and your kinsfolk, and the wealth you have acquired, and the trade whose dullness you fear, and the dwellings you love, are dearer to you than Allah and His Messenger and striving in His cause, then wait until Allah comes with His Judgment and Allah guides not the disobedient.'[3]

According to this passage, perfect love of God is willingness to sacrifice everything for His sake. If a man is not prepared to sacrifice everything for the sake of God, then his profession of love is vain, a lip service only. Many would assert that they love God and His Prophet. Certainly no Muslim can be found who would say he does not love God and the Holy Prophet. But the question is, whether the love he professes has any visible expression. Does it influence his daily life, his speech, his conduct, his everyday movements? Many who profess this deep love for the Holy Prophet, who compose or listen devotedly to panegyrics in his praise, pay not the least heed to the things he taught and valued. Love of God is on their lips, but they do nothing at all to please Him and to acquire nearness to Him. When a dear one visits us, we lay aside important tasks for his sake. When there is a chance to meet friends, we are pleased beyond measure. When we receive attention from a ruler, we feel proud and elated. But how do we behave towards God? We profess love for Him, but do not care to join the daily prayers, or do so very casually. If we observe prayers regularly, we go through them with unbecoming speed, the prescribed movements, prostrations, etc., running into one another in unseemly haste. There is no absorption or self-abnegation. The same is true of fasting. The reward of fasting, says the Quran, is

3 *Al-Tauba*, 24.

God Himself; yet those who profess love of God do not seek His nearness through obligatory and other fasts. Many who proclaim their love of God ignore the rights of others, broadcast falsehoods about them, and indulge in backbiting. They love God, but do not care to open the Holy Book, to reflect upon its meaning. The way they treat the Holy Book is not the way they treat messages from friends. Who would leave unopened a letter received from a friend? Who would not read such a letter with care so as to grasp its message and meaning? Profession of love, therefore, is one thing, but practising it quite another. True love must seek expression. It must show itself in sacrifice, for instance. Such an expression of the love of God, and willingness to sacrifice for His sake, are found today in Hazrat Mirza Sahib and his followers.

Distaste for worldly occupations

Evidence of sacrifice is to be found in the life of Hazrat Mirza Sahib. Since his years of discretion, God and the Holy Prophet were the objects of his devotion. Every part of his being was steeped in this love. He observed the law of *Shariat* from his very childhood. He loved solitude and contemplation. After his early education his father wanted him to accept employment of some sort, but he held back, accepting no employment in spite of his father's insistence. Undisturbed remembrance of God he preferred to other occupations. His family had some social prestige. If he had cared to, he could have acquired some position in the Government. His elder brother did hold such a position, but Hazrat Mirza Sahib avoided these things. Not that he did not like hard work: his subsequent life proves that few persons can have worked harder. In spite of a very different religious profession, an old Sikh resident whose family had known the family of Hazrat Mirza Sahib used to relate an incident with tears in his eyes: 'Once the father of Mirza Sahib sent me to him to persuade him to see some high officials for appointment as revenue officer. We found the Mirza Sahib in his cloister, absorbed in study. We mentioned the subject. Did his father, he asked, want him to serve in a Government post? If so, his reply should be conveyed with due respect to his father. The reply was – he had agreed to serve someone else; therefore, he was best left alone.'

In those days he was absorbed in a study of the Holy Quran, the *Hadith,* and the *Masnawi Rumi.* He had his visitors, but they were the poor and the orphans whom he fed with his own daily food. Often, for their sake, he would miss a meal and be content, say, with some roasted gram. Retiring and self-effacing, he was easily forgotten; often, indeed, his brother's family would forget to send him any food.

Once he decided to leave Qadian and escape the distractions his father kept proposing for him. He went to Sialkot and there accepted work in the District Court. He spent all the time he saved from court work in study and meditation. Probably it was here in Sialkot that he realized for the first time that Islam was in a precarious condition and that Christians and others were determined to put an end to it. Sialkot was a centre of Christian activity. *Padres* could be seen preaching Christianity openly in the streets and squares. They attacked Islam and aroused feelings against it. Hazrat Mirza Sahib was surprised to see that nobody came forward to reply. Christianity was the religion of the rulers; so people were afraid to confront Christian preachers in the open. The *Ulema* as a class avoided replying to the *padres.* Some who dared suffered defeat. They had little knowledge of the Holy Quran and were easily defeated in debate. On seeing this, Hazrat Mirza Sahib resolved to meet the *padres* in the open, and later the other adversaries of Islam such as the Aryas. A little later, his father asked him to return to Qadian. Maybe he thought his son had become reconciled to accepting employment with the Government. Therefore he started his persuasion again and asked him to try and accept some respectable Government appointment. The son requested the father to give up such attempts. But he found the father involved in difficulties of various kinds, the worst of them over family litigation. Hazrat Mirza Sahib agreed to relieve his father of the obligation to attend the various courts. During visits to courts, Hazrat Mirza Sahib's absorption in God became more evident. It had become part of his nature. Once he was present in court and the proceedings would not start. The time came for prayers. Others in the court insisted he should stay as the proceedings might start at any time. But Hazrat Mirza Sahib did not stay. The case in which he was interested was taken up while he was away. He was sent for but did not come until he had finished his prayers. By rights the case should have gone against him. The judge ignored Mirza

Sahib's absence and decided the case in his favour; in his father's favour, to be exact. Another incident which shows his absorption in God is related by a life-long friend of his who lived in Lahore. An appeal, which if it had failed was going to involve his father and his family in great loss, was before the highest court of the province. Hazrat Mirza Sahib returned from the court very satisfied and happy. His friend thought the appeal had gone in his favour and proceeded to congratulate him. But, said the Mirza Sahib, it was not true he had won. He felt satisfied because now for some time he would have an uninterrupted opportunity for worship and meditation. He found at last that he could not be occupied thus. After deliberating he wrote to his father requesting him to relieve him of his duties connected with family litigation. The letter, reproduced below, shows the other-worldliness of Hazrat Mirza Sahib even in his youth. He wanted all his time for devotion to God. In accordance with custom the letter was written in Persian:

حضرت والد مخدوم من سلامت! مراسم غلامانہ و قواعد فدویانہ بجا آوردہ، معروض حضرت والا میکند چونکہ دریں ایام برائی العین می بینم و بچشم سر مشاہدہ می کنم کہ در ہمہ ممالک و بلاد ہر سال چناں وبائے می افتد کہ دوستاں را از دوستاں و خویشاں را از خویشاں جدا می کند و ہیچ سالے نمی بینم کہ ایں نائرہ عظیم و چنیں حادثہ الیم در آں سال شور قیامت نیفگند۔ نظر برآں دل از دنیا سرد شدہ است و رو از خوف جان زرد و اکثر ایں دو مصرع شیخ مصلح الدین سعدی شیرازی بیاد می آیند و اشک حسرت ریختہ می شود۔

مکن تکیہ بر عمر ناپائدار   مباش ایمن از بازی روزگار

و نیز ایں دو مصرعہ ثانی از دیوان فرخ قادیانی (حضرت اقدس کا ابتدائی ایام کا تخلص ہے) نمک پاش جراحت دل می شود۔

بدنیائے دوں دل مبند اے جواں   کہ وقت اجل می رسد ناگہاں

لہذا میخواہم کہ بقیہ عمر در گوشہ تنہائی نشینم و دامن از صحبت مردم بچینم و بیاد او سبحانہ مشغول شوم مگر گذشتہ را عذرے و مافات را تدارکے شود۔

عمر بگذشت و نماند است جز از گامے چند   بہ کہ در یاد کسے صبح کنم شامے چند

کہ دنیا را اساسے محکم نیست و زندگی را اعتبارے نے۔ والکیّس من خاف علیٰ نفسہ من آفۃ غیرہ۔

والسلام"

My master and father, Peace!

With tender obeisance and due abasement, I beg to submit that I can see with eyes wide open that every year some calamity overtakes countries and towns which separates friend from friend and relation from relation. Alas, these calamities, these tragedies, produce not the wail and woe they should. Seeing all this, my heart has turned cold towards the world, and my face has become pale with fear. Often do I remember the two lines from Sheikh Muslih-ud-Din Saadi of Shiraz and my tears flow when I do so:

> Depend not on this transient life; think not you are safe from the sport of passing time.

The two lines out of the verse of Farrukh[4] of Qadian also act as salt for my wounded heart:

> Young one, set not thy heart on this mean world:
> The moment of death may come suddenly.

Therefore I desire to spend the rest of my life in solitude, to shun the company of men and remain occupied in the worship of God that this may atone for past neglect and guard against possible disasters.

> Life has run its course and nothing is left except a few steps,
> Better, therefore, that I keep awake a few nights in remembrance of some One.

This world has no firm foundation and life here is not dependable. 'Wise is he who learns from the example of others.' And peace.

When his father died, Hazrat Mirza Sahib withdrew from everything mundane, leading a life of study, prayer, fasting, and sleepless nights. Now and then he would write to newspapers in reply to attacks by the critics of Islam. Contrary to the usual practice, Hazrat Mirza Sahib made over his property interests to his elder brother. He received his daily meals from him; his clothing also was supplied by him. He drew no income from his share of the family property, not did he give any of his time to its maintenance. He spent his time expounding the beauties of Islam and urging people to pray and fast. He ministered to the poor and the needy. With little else to give, he shared his meals with them, himself

4 Nom-de-plume used by the Promised Messiah in his early verse.

living on a few ounces of food every day or on nothing at all. His share of the property was not so small that he could ignore it for bare subsistence. He shared a whole village with his brother and there was additional income from another property.

Moved by the condition of Islam

During this time he was moved by the condition of Islam. He decided to devote himself to prayer, penance, and self-abasement. Following a hint from God he began his great book, *Barahin-i-Ahmadiyya*. In this book he promised to enumerate 300 arguments in proof of the truth of Islam. The book, he said, would prove a sharp weapon in defence of the Islamic conception of God, the truth of the Holy Prophet, and the truth of Islam. Only some parts appeared, but even so the book received unqualified tributes from both friend and foe. Leading *Ulema* of the time said the book had not had an equal for the last thirteen hundred years. Islam has had its authors and writers; therefore, bearing in mind the distinguished tradition, the praise given to the *Barahin-i-Ahmadiyya* speaks for itself. Hazrat Mirza Sahib looked for other opportunities to write and publish on behalf of Islam. If there was a periodical or a newspaper for which he could write, he would hasten to write and reply to the enemies of Islam. As he became known, hostility against him grew also. But he remained constant in his service of Islam.

Ulema fiddling

At this time foul attacks were being made on the life and character of the Holy Prophet (peace and the blessings of God be upon him). Christian writers and Arya Samaj propagandists were in the forefront of this campaign of abuse and vilification. But the *Ulema* of Hindustan were busy imputing *Kufr* to one another. Islam stood threatened with destruction and the *Ulema* were fiddling. They debated over silly questions: Was it lawful to raise the two hands with *Takbir* as a worshipper went from one part to another of the prescribed prayers? Exactly where were the folded arms to rest while standing in prayers? Should the congregation of worshippers say 'Amen' aloud or in silence? These and other questions of this kind were their principal occupation. Only the Promised Messiah was concerned with defending Islam against its enemies. Only he thought of impressing upon Muslims the importance of good works. Only he steered clear of sectarian controversy. The important thing was not who was right, *Hanafis* or the *Ahli-Hadith*. The important thing was sincere service based on beliefs sincerely held. What they needed was avoidance of irreligious ways and general inaction, and instead devotion to God and His Laws. Among Arya-Samajists against whom Hazrat Mirza Sahib entered the lists was the founder, Pundit Dayanand; also Lekh Ram, Jiwan Das, Murli Dhar, and Inder Mun. With one and all Hazrat Mirza Sahib joined in public debate. He pursued them till they withdrew from the field or met their end. Among Christian missionaries whom Hazrat Mirza Sahib fought were Fateh Masih, Atham, Martin Clarke, Howell, Talib Masih. Writing did not satisfy him. He would write, have his writing translated into English, print several hundred thousand copies, and circulate them in Europe and America. If ever he heard of someone who was interested in Islam, he would write and invite him to accept the truth. The famous American convert, Alexander Russell Webb, was a fruit of his efforts. Webb was a highly esteemed American. He had served his country as ambassador. Hazrat Mirza Sahib wrote to him. Eventually, good Alexander Webb accepted Islam, surrendered his position, and became a Muslim preacher. Hazrat Mirza Sahib was dominated by two great passions: the Oneness of God and the truth of the Holy Prophet. He was always ready to prove and to explain the two Islamic ideas. His mind was occupied with nothing else. Later, after the announcement of his claim, he became more and more completely absorbed in them. Was there an enemy of Islam anywhere? If so, Hazrat Mirza Sahib was ready to fight. If ever anybody thought of attacking Islam, Hazrat Mirza Sahib was ready to meet the attack. Dowie, the American impostor, has been mentioned. As soon as he heard of him, Hazrat Mirza Sahib decided to fight him even from across the seas. Similarly, he challenged Piggott, a false prophet in England. If there was an enemy of Islam anywhere in the world, he had to confront Hazrat Mirza Sahib. Then the fight would go on until the enemy retreated or met his end. Hazrat Mirza Sahib lived to the age of seventy-four. Day and night throughout this long life he remained a devoted servant of

Islam. Often he would set himself to complete a special writing and become so engrossed that nobody could say whether he was having any sleep. His devotion to God and the Holy Prophet was total. Serving Islam seemed like serving himself or his dear ones. If he had any help in his work, he felt very grateful. Night after night, he would go without the usual minimum of sleep and remain at work. If anybody helped, say, in comparing or correcting proofs, or sat up with him for a night or two, he would thank him as he would for a personal favour. He would not care that Islam was as much other people's concern. Service to Islam he thought was service to himself. In spite of continual sickness and physical weakness, he wrote more than eighty books and several hundred leaflets and must have made hundreds of speeches. In addition, he had his daily visitors whom he received and addressed on Islam, on its beauties and the subjects connected with it. His doctors would order him to rest, but rest for him, he would say, was to go on explaining the meaning and purpose of Islam and fighting its enemies. Even the day he died he was busy with this, his life work. He died one morning. The evening before he had been busy completing a book inviting Hindus to an understanding of Islam. From this, one can measure the quality of his passion and the depth of his devotion to God and the Holy Prophet. He had but one desire and this was to make manifest to all and sundry the living might of God and the truth of His Holy Prophet.

Poems of devotion to the Holy Prophet

The quality of love, as I have said, is not to be judged by the loudness of its professions. Here was a man who proved his love to the utmost. He proved it in his smallest deeds, his most insignificant movements. The professions of such a man are of a different order from those of ordinary men. They are a true representation of his innermost thoughts and feelings. True love is measured by acts of devotion. It is measured also by those innermost thoughts and feelings which rise to find beautiful expression on the lips of the lover. Being the cries of a truthful person, they pierce the hearts of others. I make no apology for reproducing two poems of the Promised Messiah, one written in love of God, the other in love of the Holy Prophet:

قربان تست جانِ من اے یارِ محسنم
با من کدام فرق تو کردی کہ من کنم

ہر مطلب و مراد کہ می خواستم زِ غیب
ہر آرزو کہ بود بخاطر معیّنم

از جود دادۂ ہمہ آں مدّعائے من
وز لُطف کردۂ گذرِ خود بمسکنم

ہیچ آگہی نبُود ز عشق و وفا مرا
خود ریختی متاعِ محبّت بدامنم

ایں خاکِ تیرہ را تو خود اکسیر کردۂ
بُود آں جمال تو کہ نمود است احسنم

ایں صیقلِ دلم نہ بہ زہد و تعبّد است
خود کردۂ بلطف و عنایات روشنم

صد منّتِ تو ہست بریں مُشتِ خاکِ من
جانم رہینِ لطفِ عمیمِ تو ہم تنم

سہل است ترکِ ہر دو جہاں گر رضائے تو
آید بدست ای پناہ و کہف و مامنم

فصلِ بہار و موسمِ گل نایدم بکار
کاندر خیالِ رُوئے تو ہر دم بگلشنم

چُوں حاجتے بود بہ ادیبِ دگر مرا
من تربیت پذیر ز ربِّ مہیمنم

زاں ساں عنایتِ ازلی شد قریبِ من
کامد ندائے یار ز ہر کوئے برزنم

یارب مرا بہر قدمم استوار دار
واں روز خود مباد کہ عہدِ تو بشکنم

در کوئے تو اگر سرِ عشّاق را زنند
اوّل کسیکہ لافِ تعشّق زند منم

My Beneficent Lord, my life is but an humble offering to Thee,
What hast Thou grudged me that I should grudge Thee anything?

Every desire and every wish for which I prayed to the Invisible,
Every longing that my heart determined to ask

Has been achieved through Thy Magnanimity, Indeed Thou
hast honoured this humble dwelling with Thy Gracious visit.

Nothing did I know of love or loyalty,
It is Thou Who hast filled my bosom with the wealth of Thy love.

Thou Who hast turned this base clay into gold,
It was Thy Beauty that lent beauty and grace to me.

The refulgence of my heart is not due to my piety or penance,
It is Thou Who hast illumined me with Thy favours and Thy gifts.

Hundreds of Thy favours have been showered on this mortal frame of clay,
My soul and my body owe gratitude to Thy unfailing kindness.

Easier is it to renounce the two worlds if Thy pleasure
Can be had by me, O my refuge, my shelter, my peace!

What avail are the spring and flowers to me?
I am ever in the garden contemplating Thy Face.

Would I care for anyone who can teach?
I have received tuition from my Lord and Protector.

The eternal benevolence has drawn so near to me,
That the Voice of the Lord reaches me from the farthest nook and corner.

O God, make me firm at every step.
May the day never dawn when I should fail in my bond to Thee!

If Thy lovers have to lose their heads for daring in Thy name,
Then I would be the first one to proclaim his love for Thee.

There is light miraculous in the soul of Muhammad,
There is a ruby rare in the mine of Muhammad.

The heart is cleared of all darkness,
If it but becomes one of the lovers of Muhammad.

I wonder at the wisdom of those fools
Who turn away from the feast abundant of Muhammad.

No man in the two worlds do I know
Who shares the greatness and glory of Muhammad.

A hundred times disgusted is God with him
Who harbours hostility to Muhammad.

God Himself consumes in fire the contemptible worm
Who chooses to be one of the enemies of Muhammad.

If you want to shake off the intoxication of the baser self,
Then come and sit among the devotees of Muhammad.

If you wish that God Himself should sing your praises,
Then sing sincerely the praises of Muhammad.

عجب نوریست در جانِ محمدؐ
عجب لعلیست در کانِ محمدؐ

زظلمت ہا دلے آنگہ شود صاف
کہ گردد از محبانِ محمدؐ

عجب دارم دلِ آں ناکساں را
کہ رُو تابند از خوانِ محمدؐ

ندانم ہیچ نفسے در دو عالم
کہ دارد شوکت و شانِ محمدؐ

خُدا زاں سینہ بیزار است صد بار
کہ ہست از کینہ دارانِ محمدؐ

خُدا خود سوزد آں کرمِ دنی را
کہ باشد از عدوّانِ محمدؐ

اگر خواہی نجات از مستیٔ نفس
بیا در ذیلِ مستانِ محمدؐ

اگر خواہی کہ حق گوید ثنایت
بشو از دل ثنا خوانِ محمدؐ

اگر خواہی دلیلے عاشقش باش
محمدؐ ہست بُرہانِ محمدؐ

سرے دارم فدائے خاکِ احمدؐ
دلم ہر وقت قربانِ محمدؐ

بگیسوئے رسول اللہ کہ ہستم
نثارِ رُوئے تابانِ محمدؐ

دریں راہ گر کشندم ور بسوزند
نتابم رُو ز ایوانِ محمدؐ

بکارِ دیں نترسم از جہانے
کہ دارم رنگِ ایمانِ محمدؐ

بسے سہل است از دُنیا بُریدن
بیادِ حُسن و احسانِ محمدؐ

فِدا شُد در رہش ہر ذرّۂ من
کہ دیدم حُسنِ پنہانِ محمدؐ

دگر اُستاد را نامے ندانم
کہ خواندم در دبستانِ محمدؐ

بدیگر دلبرے کارے ندارم
کہ ہستم کشتۂ آنِ محمدؐ

مرا آں گوشۂ چشمے بباید
نخواہم جز گلستانِ محمدؐ

دلِ زارم بہ پہلوئم مجوئید
کہ بستیمش بدامانِ محمدؐ

من آں خوش مُرغ از مُرغانِ قدسم
کہ دارد جا بہ بُستانِ محمدؐ

تو جانِ ما منوّر کردی از عشق
فدایت جانم اے جانِ محمدؐ

دریغا گر دہم صد جاں دریں راہ
نباشد نیز شایانِ محمدؐ

چہ ہیبت ہا بدادند ایں جواں را
کہ ناید کس بمیدانِ محمدؐ

الا اے دشمنِ نادان و بے راہ
بترس از تیغِ بُرّانِ محمدؐ

رہِ مولیٰ کہ گُم کردند مردم
بجو در آل و اعوانِ محمدؐ

الا اے مُنکر از شانِ محمدؐ
ہم از نورِ نمایانِ محمدؐ

کرامت گرچہ بے نام و نشان است
بیا بنگر ز غلمانِ محمدؐ

Lookest thou for proof for his truth? Then his lover be,
For Muhammad himself is the proof of Muhammad.

A head have I to offer at the altar of Ahmad,
And a heart ready to be sacrificed for Muhammad.

By the tresses of the Messenger of God,
It is true, I am infatuated by the resplendent face of Muhammad.

Whether I am killed or burnt in this path,
Never will I turn away from the court of Muhammad.

In matters of faith I fear not even the whole world,
For I am dyed in the faith of Muhammad.

Easy it is to be carried away from the world,
In the memory of the charms and graces of Muhammad.

Every atom of mine is sacrificed in his path,
For I have peeped into the hidden beauty of Muhammad.

I know not the name of another teacher,
For I have been to the school of Muhammad.

I am not interested in another beloved,
For I have been captivated by the comeliness of Muhammad.

Only a favour need I from the eye of Muhammad,
All I seek is access to the garden of Muhammad.

Do not look for my stricken heart in my side,
For I have tied it to the robe of Muhammad.

I am a sweet bird out of the sacred flock
Which has its nest in the grove of Muhammad.

Thou hast illumined my soul with thy love,
May I be a sacrifice to thee, soul of Muhammad.

Even were I to offer a hundred lives in this path,
It would still fail to match the worth of Muhammad.

What terror does this young one [Muhammad] strike
That no one can meet him in his arena!

Beware, O foolish and misguided enemy,
Fear the sharp sword of Muhammad.

The path of God from which men have strayed far,
You can still find with the followers and friends of Muhammad.

Listen, O thou who denieth the greatness of Muhammad,
And the luminous light of Muhammad!

Though miracles seem a thing of the past,
Come thou yet and see them with the servants of Muhammad.

Here, therefore, was a man who spent literally every moment of his life in devotion to God, expounding the message of His Prophet and nurturing his love for him and his teaching. This man suffered at the hands of his own people and others for the sake of his devotion to God, his regard for the name and honour of His Prophet. Every atom of his being, his body, mind, and spirit, was consecrated to this service. Could such a man be misguided, a rebel, a Dadjjal? If all he did and said and felt constitute rebellion, if this kind of love connotes unbelief or *Kufr*, if this kind of devotion is irreligion, then we can only say:

یہ گمرہی خدا مجھے ساری کرے نصیب   یہ کفر مجھ کو بخش دے سارے جہان کا

Such misguidance may God grant me in full!
May He bestow upon me this unmitigated *Kufr*!

And now, God, His Word, His Prophet, and human reason are witnesses that such a man could not be a pretender. He could not be misguided. If a man could love and obey God and His Prophet to this degree, and devote himself so completely to the duty of propagating the truths taught by them, if he could show more regard for these things than any other man living or dead, and still be branded an impostor and a Dadjjal, then we must say, there has never lived, and never will live, a man deserving the grace of guidance by God.

Argument 12
Life-giving Powers

As my twelfth argument for the authenticity of Hazrat Mirza Sahib I wish to cite his life-giving powers. This argument also, like all the others, is made up of a thousand and one smaller arguments. Today Muslims, like Christians, believe that Jesus Christ (on whom be peace) possessed the power to restore the dead to life. This belief, as I have shown already, is contrary to the teachings of the Holy Quran. It amounts to *shirk*, or setting up equals with God. It is subversive of faith in the One and Only God. In one sense, however, Jesus did restore the dead to life, and in this sense all prophets perform this miracle. The word of God testifies to this, and to deny this is to deny the Word of God. It is the spiritual not the physical dead whom prophets restore to life. In fact, to replace spiritual death (and disease) by spiritual life (and health) is the *raison d'être* of the coming of prophets. No prophet has, therefore, ever come who has not restored the dead to life in this sense. From Adam down to the Holy Prophet of Islam (on whom be peace and the blessings of God), all prophets have been raised for this purpose. One criterion by which the claims of great prophets may be judged is whether or not they bring life to those who are spiritually dead. If a claimant to prophetic office is unable to show this miracle, his claim must be held in great doubt. If, on the other hand, he is able to demonstrate his life-giving powers, he must be a man of God. No man can have life-giving powers except with the sanction and support of God; and one who earns divine sanction and support must be genuine.

A time of spiritual death

Now, dear reader, this sign in the case of Hazrat Mirza Sahib has been so clear and frequent that a parallel to it cannot be found in the case of any other prophet excepting, of course, the Holy Prophet of

Islam. God knows best; but Hazrat Mirza Sahib came at a time when spiritual death had overtaken the whole world. Not only death but disintegration and decomposition had set in. So sad and so certain was this death that we find all the earlier prophets warning us of it. The Holy Prophet (on whom be peace and the blessings of God) said:

إِنَّهُ لَمْ يَكُنْ نَبِيٌّ بَعْدَ نُوحٍ إِلَّا قَدْ أَنْذَرَ الدَّجَّالَ قَوْمَهُ وَإِنِّيْ أُنْذِرُكُمُوهُ۔

'Every prophet after Noah has warned his people of the menace of the Dadjjal. I also warn you against him.'[1]

The death and destruction associated with our time was to be spread by the Dadjjal. Human beings could not be more dead than they are today. To restore them to life was a most difficult task. Yet this task has been accomplished by Hazrat Mirza Sahib. He has restored to life many hundreds of thousands of spiritually dead human beings. He has created a following which has no parallel among prophets other than the Holy Prophet of Islam. Moses was a political and a spiritual leader. Many of his followers professed only outward loyalty to him. They supported and followed him out of political considerations, not out of spiritual conviction. On this we have the testimony of the Holy Quran:

فَمَآ اٰمَنَ لِمُوْسٰٓى اِلَّا ذُرِّيَّةٌ مِّنْ قَوْمِهٖ

'Only some young men obeyed Moses.'[2]

This was the situation in Egypt. After Moses had moved out of Egypt, a majority of his people were still unconverted at heart. Politically, they were with him. For this also we have the authority of the Holy Quran. Some time after the Exodus, a section of the people told Moses:

يٰمُوْسٰى لَنْ نُّؤْمِنَ لَكَ حَتّٰى نَرَى اللّٰهَ جَهْرَةً فَاَخَذَتْكُمُ الصّٰعِقَةُ وَاَنْتُمْ تَنْظُرُوْنَ ۔

1 Tirmizi, Abwabul Fitan. 2 *Yunus*, 84.

> 'O Moses, certainly we will not believe thee until we see Allah face to face; then the thunderbolt overtook you while you gazed on.'[3]

From the Holy Quran and the New Testament and from history it appears that very few people believed in Jesus Christ. Of this small number those who were sincere and had found a true spiritual life were even fewer. But Hazrat Mirza Sahib was a disciple of the Holy Prophet of Islam. He came into the world to demonstrate the spiritual graces of his master and to spread the blessings of his master's influence and his example. He was the Messiah of the line of Muhammad, not of the line of Moses. Through Hazrat Mirza Sahib God restored many a dead person to life, and the dead he restored to life were so dead that, but for the water of life borrowed from the Fountain of Muhammad, there was no hope whatever of instilling any life into them again.

The Promised Messiah's life-giving powers, a reflection of the powers of the Holy Prophet

It is amazing how great is the spiritual change effected by Hazrat Mirza Sahib. What did he find when he came? Human inventions and superstitions masquerading as divine religion; devotion to worldly ends; a general revolt against spiritual life, hatred of godly ways, of revealed knowledge and of revealed law; insensitiveness to moral distinctions; casualness in prayer and lack of reverence for religious teachers. This was what he found. And what did he achieve? A following, as well educated as any, who yet believed in God and His Prophet, in angels, in prayer, miracles, revelation, the Hereafter, the Day of Judgment, and Heaven and Hell: a following which observes the religious duties prescribed by Islam. Few among his followers can be found who are lacking in the observance of daily prayers and so on. Even such lack as may be found can be attributed to the weakness of early days and may be trusted to disappear before long. It is commonly known that college-educated young men and women and those who have acquired any degree of modern education acquire a perfect hatred for religion. If

3 *Al-Baqarah*, 56.

they value religion it is for its political benefits. Yet Hazrat Mirza Sahib has created a modern educated following, a following steadily growing in size, whose members are at the same time devoted to God and His religion. Their tears flow as they prostrate themselves in prayer. Their bosoms are filled with tender fervour when they entreat their God. They hold the interests of Islam and their duty to propagate it above their worldly interests. They sacrifice their time, money, and other opportunities for the sake of Islam. They are moved by the plight in which the religion of God finds itself today. They have become impressed by the need for an organized exposition of Islam, an intellectual Jehad: Jehad by argument. Many among them could have achieved outstanding success in worldly careers, but they have surrendered their careers for the sake of religion. They prefer poverty to plenty, starvation to satiety. On their lips are the names of God and the Holy Prophet; in their hearts love of both. Their actions glorify God and the Holy Prophet and their faces are suffused with the spirit of devotion. They live in the same world as others. They know the attractions of carefree living. They have the normal egoism and love of self. They too would live their own lives. They too read and hear what others read and hear. But they have decided to submit themselves to discipline and direction for the sake of Islam. Islam they find, needs discipline more than liberty. The harm done by the Dadjjal today has been done through world-wide organized propaganda. The effort on behalf of Islam needs a similar organization. It requires Muslims to come together under one flag. It requires the high and the low among them, the rich and the poor, the learned and the not-so-learned, to pool their efforts and organize themselves under one leader. Dissensions and disagreements among Muslims hamper Islam and help its enemies. To promote a united and organized effort on behalf of Islam, followers of Hazrat Mirza Sahib have determined to put the interests of Islam above their own interests, the Call of God above their personal predilections. They have turned away from all current influences and have entered into a pact of voluntary obedience to their Imam. It is for the Imam to point out where and when they must go to serve the interests of Islam. It is for them to obey, and obey without hesitation, without demur. No sacrifices are too heavy and no difficulties too great for them. They perform what they profess. At this time many of them can be found far from their homes and families working not for personal gain but for Islam. In spite of physical and financial privations, under the behest of their leader, the Khalifa of the Promised Messiah, many are already in the field, and many wait for their turn. They care little for their earthly life. They have left their homes and relations for the Glory of God. 'There are some among them who have fulfilled their vow and some who wait' (33:24).

Spiritual sight sharpened

They are threatened and beaten. Sometimes they are driven out of their homes. Invariably they are derided and abused. But they take it all for the sake of God. Their spiritual sight has been sharpened. They have come to see what others do not or cannot see. They are treated with contempt. They meet with physical violence and injury and with personal humiliation. But these things to them are as nothing. They bear them easily for they live and work for Islam.

If there is a solitary individual without money or means who may be working for Islam, say in the USA, then he is a follower of Hazrat Mirza Sahib. He may be as a drop in the ocean, but he is not down-hearted and he does not fear the future. He was a dead man who has been quickened to life by a touch of the hand from the Messiah. He is alone but can dare to invite the continent of America to study, examine, and accept Islam. He can do this because he knows that one living man is superior to a million dead.

If there are any men in England trying to spread Islam among Englishmen, they are again the dead who have been quickened to life by the Muhammadan Messiah. Physically England was able to subjugate India, but followers of the Messiah know that spiritually England is dead and has strayed far from God. They have carried to England the water of life which the Messiah gave them and which will now give life to the dead of other countries. The might and wealth of England do not frighten them, for they know that they are alive and England is dead. The living have nothing to fear from the dead.

Now, look at the West Coast of Africa. Christian missionaries went to this part of the world long ago and started working for Christianity. Millions of West Africans became Christians. They began to worship a mere human being as God. Did anybody go to this region to tell them of the One and Only God? Did anybody go out to face the superstitious and pagan beliefs and practices of this people? Yes, the followers of the Promised Messiah, quickened to life by his breath, went there to espouse the cause of Islam when Islam had been given up as dead, when its decline had become apparent.

Did anybody think of Mauritius, a forgotten island, or of Ceylon, where much history has been made, or of Russia or Afghanistan? Yes, the followers of the Promised Messiah, the erstwhile dead brought to life by the Messiah's touch.

Signs of life

Who can mistake these signs of life? Of four or five hundred million Muslims not one has left his home in order to tell others of Islam, to preach to them the message of the Holy Prophet. But hundreds of Ahmadis can be named who have left their homes and gone to live and work in other countries. The number of Ahmadis in the whole world cannot be more than a few hundred thousand. Yet they are making Muslims of men who would hate even to hear of Islam. If the followers of the Messiah have no life in them, how did they manage to change the map of the world? How did they dare to confront countries and continents? Whence did they gather this courage, this confidence? What was it that persuaded them to leave their own countries and go to strange lands, and for what? They have their near and dear ones, their relations, their families, and friends. They have their interests and occupations. What leads them to forsake the world and turn to religion? It is the gift of life they have received from the Messiah. They can see the difference between the living and the dead. It is not difficult for them to give up the dead and turn to God, the Source of all life. He has entered into them and they into Him. And blessed is Allah, the Best of Creators.

The life-giving power of the Promised Messiah has been inherited by his followers. Life creates more life: this indeed is its best evidence. It is not life alone that Hazrat Mirza Sahib gave to his followers. He gave them the power to give life, the power to raise the dead. If Mirza Sahib had not done this, his own power to raise the dead through the Grace of God would have remained in doubt. It would then have been said that his powers, his special knowledge, his warnings, his prayers, were a gift of nature, a special talent or attribute or quality of mind, not evidence of the Grace of God. But such doubts cannot hold. The life-giving powers which the Promised Messiah displayed have not been confined to him; they have not vanished with him. They have been inherited by his true followers. In different degrees and according to their deserts, the same powers are displayed by them. In proportion to their regard for him and the degree of their spiritual contact they also possess the gift of spiritual knowledge. Many among his followers can discourse on the beauties of the Holy Quran. Their eloquence is unbounded, their speech persuasive, as they start speaking on the subject. It melts away doubts and difficulties. No religion or philosophical system or thought which chooses to challenge Islam can overawe us. We can deal with it with the help of the Holy Quran. No objection or difficulty has ever been raised about any single verse of the Holy Quran, the reply to which has not been disclosed to us by the special Grace of God.

Spiritual experience – that is, experience of divine revelation, or of true visions – has also passed on from Hazrat Mirza Sahib to his followers, who have experienced a sort of re-birth through his influence and example, and have received the gift of this experience from God. They receive revelations from God and true visions from Him. Their fulfilment brings an increase of faith and certainty of conviction to them and their friends. The Living God speaks and discloses His Will to them. They discover the ways which lead to His pleasure. They tread these ways and this brings them courage and strength of mind and spirit.

Spiritual experiences continue

Acceptance of prayers and the gift of special divine help also continue, thanks to the beneficent influence of Hazrat Mirza Sahib. Those who have found life through him experience the sign of this life in themselves. Their prayers are heard more than the prayers of others. They experience the help of God more often than others. Their enemies suffer disgrace and defeat, while their efforts and sacrifices are rewarded manifold. They are never left alone. God is with them and guards them, their interests, and their honour.

In short, not only did Hazrat Mirza Sahib himself raise the dead to life. He raised followers who could do the same. This power and this influence is the special prerogative of prophets, the favoured ones of God. This special gift he owes to his Master, the Holy Prophet (on whom be peace and the blessings of God). The Promised Messiah carries forward the work of the Holy Prophet. His gifts are the gifts he has received from the Master. A revelation of the Promised Messiah says:

كُلُّ بَرَكَةٍ مِّنْ مُّحَمَّدٍ صَلَّى اللّٰهُ عَلَيْهِ
وَسَلَّمَ فَتَبَارَكَ مَنْ عَلَّمَ وَتَعَلَّمَ

> 'Every grace comes from Muhammad, peace and blessings of Allah be on him. Blessed, therefore, is he who taught and he who learnt.'

Part III

Invitation

The Messiah Has Come

The twelve arguments which I have presented are enough to prove the truth of the claim of Hazrat Mirza Sahib (on whom be peace). Anybody who is prepared to deliberate upon them with the intention of finding out the truth will not only perceive the truth but will be convinced of it. Hazrat Mirza Sahib is the Messiah promised and commissioned by God for our time; he is His Messenger. To wait for anyone else is pointless. A person who gains this conviction will hasten to declare his belief, as one who is thirsty will run to a spring. He will not hang back for a moment, but will at once enter the Messiah's fold and will think it his salvation.

Testimony of God and His Prophet

What can be more convincing for a Muslim than the testimony of God and His Prophet? For Hazrat Mirza Sahib we have the testimony of both, and furthermore, the testimony of other prophets. Our own judgment and reason point to the present time as the time for a reformer. The Signs which the Holy Prophet (on whom be peace and the blessings of God) enumerated as Signs of the Messiah and Mahdi have become visible. The purity of Hazrat Mirza Sahib's personal life testifies to the truth of his claim. The enemies of Islam whom the Promised Messiah had to defeat have been defeated. The internal dangers from which Muslims suffer have reached their utmost limit. In the presence of the Holy Quran these dangers could not be worse than they are. The Promised Messiah has re-stated Muslim beliefs and removed the dangerous distortions Islam was undergoing from within. Throughout his life he enjoyed the help and love of God, as prophets and favourites of God have always done. He was granted victory after victory. He was protected from intrigues and attacks. His enemies suffered disgrace and death, as enemies of the prophets and the messengers of God have done in the past. The processes of nature pressed themselves into the service of his cause and heaven and earth moved in his favour. A special knowledge of the Holy Quran was bestowed on him, also special means for its diffusion. He invited all and sundry, including the most learned, to test his claim to miraculous and intellectual gifts, but nobody dared do so. His miraculous Arabic works and his special knowledge of the meaning of the Holy Quran remained unchallenged. And why? Had not God Himself promised that 'only the pure in heart will have access to the Holy Book' (56:80)? He was granted also a knowledge of the unseen. Several thousand examples of this knowledge were shown by him with the special help of God. His prophecies came true and afforded visible evidence of the Might and Power of God. This accorded with God's own law, for God only grants an abundance of such knowledge to His Messengers. Throughout his life he remained a devotee of God and His Prophet, and such devotees are not driven by God out of His Grace. He left behind followers sincere in word and deed. A number of them enjoy special contact with God. They are able to quicken the spiritually dead and to resolve spiritual difficulties. They are devoted to caring for religion, indifferent to worldly interests and worldly contacts. They long for the glory and triumph of Islam and care about nothing else. These facts bear witness to the authenticity of Hazrat Mirza Sahib. To refuse to believe in him, therefore, cannot be right, or pleasing to God. Muslims who love Islam and the Holy Prophet, who are prepared to place the interests of Islam above their personal interests, will not hesitate to accept the truth after that truth has become so clear. If the arguments which I have enumerated above fail to prove the truth of his claim, then the question is: What better arguments were ever adduced in support of earlier prophets? What better proofs prompted belief in their authenticity? The arguments in support of Hazrat Mirza Sahib are more numerous and more cogent than the arguments in support of earlier prophets, excepting, of course, the Holy Prophet (on whom be peace and the blessings of God). Why then believe in the earlier prophets but not in the Promised Messiah? True belief is not belief inherited from parents or accepted as a tradition. True belief is assent after deliberation. If this is not true belief, then we have to deny the authenticity of earlier prophets. If we cannot deny their authenticity, we have to accept that of Hazrat Mirza Sahib, the Promised Messiah (on whom be peace). An understanding and intelligent person will adopt the second alternative. He will accept the Promised Messiah rather than deny the earlier prophets. He will not hesitate to accept one who has come to proclaim the truth of the Holy Prophet of Islam, to lead Islam to triumph again and to make Muslims Muslims once more. To accept the Will of God and to subscribe to His Plan yields His blessings. To resist His plan and His Will can yield no blessings.

The condition of Islam today stirs our pity. Nobody who loves Islam can view this condition with equanimity. Every lover of Islam will do all he can to save Islam from the dangers which seem to threaten its very existence. He will wish to see it live and prosper again. The enemies of Islam have become so hardened that they can see evil but no good in it. The friends of Islam are disappointed and disgusted, or if not disgusted with it they are at least indifferent to its interests. They profess loyalty to it, but the profession does not travel beyond their lips. True, they care for the political prosperity of Islam. If a Muslim country loses its freedom, they are stricken and raise an alarm. But if hundreds and thousands of Muslims give up Islam and become Christians or Hindus, they are moved not at all. They can raise volunteers for political programmes, but not for the exposition and propagation of Islam. A denial of the Turkish Sultan as Khalifa infuriates them, but a denial of the Holy Prophet does not even move them. The political outlook is on the increase. Little interest is taken in Islam as such. Muslims are interested in their political fortunes. The promotion of Islamic Tabligh among non-Muslims is a far cry. They do not like even to repel the unrestrained attacks which non-Muslims constantly hurl against Islam. To do so seems inexpedient or impolite. For Islam as such they have no use. Only the name is retained for political purposes. There is only one way to rescue Islam from this abject state, and that is to accept the Promised Messiah and to enter his fold. Islam cannot advance now except under his leadership. Jehad by the sword cannot help Islam. The desideratum is true faith in Islam, a true conception of its teachings, and a united effort on its behalf. Without this Islam cannot rise again. The Holy Prophet of Islam, say the enemies of Islam, used the sword for its propagation. But for the sword, Islam would not have spread at all. Islam, according to them, could cite no reason or argument in its support. Wittingly or unwittingly Muslims themselves have supported this attack. God today has ordained that this vile attack on His Beloved Prophet should be repulsed and proved false. He has, therefore, sent one of the followers of the Holy Prophet to defeat the enemies of Islam and to lead Islam to triumph again, not by physical force but by argument and persuasion. Only thus will the world be convinced that what the servant can achieve, the master could achieve many times over. For Muslims today, this is the only way. God wants even the enemies of the Holy Prophet to join him as his followers and servants. To make this possible there is only one way, and that is to present to the world the true Islam, the Islam described anew by the Promised Messiah, by methods taught by him and with the faith re-created by him. This is the way to guide lost mankind back to the true path. If, in the knowledge of God, other avenues existed by which Islam could be helped, why did He close these avenues for us? To remain aloof from the Promised Messiah is to hinder the advance of Islam and to help its enemies. Not to join the Promised Messiah is to embolden the critics of Islam, to re-inforce their attacks on the Holy Prophet, his teaching, his example and his honour. The Holy Prophet (on whom be peace and the blessings of God) said:

كَيْفَ تَهْلِكُ أُمَّةٌ أَنَا فِي أَوَّلِهَا وَالْمَسِيحُ ابْنُ مَرْيَمَ فِي آخِرِهَا

> 'That *Umma* can never die which has me at one end, and the Messiah, son of Mary, at the other.'[1]

From this it seems that belief requires two stone walls for safety. He who rejects the Promised Messiah is outside the bounds of safety. He who hinders the Promised Messiah is an enemy of Islam. He is not happy at the advance of Islam. If this is not so, why should he oppose the raising of a wall which ensures safety for Islam? His hostility invites the anger of God. It would be better if he had not done so.

1 Kitab Ibn Majah – Babul etisam Bil Sunnat.

Great promises

All the great promises made by God for our time are linked with the coming of the Promised Messiah. Islam is to have a new lease of life through him. A tree which begins to die of drought becomes green again if rain comes in time. Even so is the dead and dry tree of Islam certain to become green again with the coming of the Promised Messiah. A new power and a new spirit will be granted to those who join the Promised Messiah. God has long borne with patience what He has seen. He has remained a silent Witness, but He will remain so no longer. He can no longer permit that a mere man, a creature of His, should be made an associate with Him; that those who take Jesus for a son of God or believe him to be alive in Heaven, or think he was able to raise the physically dead to life or that he could create, should continue to do so. True, God is Merciful, but He is also Jealous of His Own Uniqueness and Oneness. He waited and waited for men to turn to His Holy Book, but they only turned away from it. They became interested in other things and paid little attention to the Book of God. They forgot the warning contained in the Holy Book itself:

يَا رَبِّ إِنَّ قَوْمِي اتَّخَذُوْا هٰذَا الْقُرْاٰنَ مَهْجُوْرًا۔

> 'O my Lord, my people indeed treated this Quran as [a thing] abandoned.'[2]

They abandoned the Book of God and turned to other things. Small wonder that God abandoned them and turned away from them. He will not turn to them now until they declare, putting their hand in the hand of the Promised Messiah, that they will no longer treat the Holy Book with inattention and indifference, but will make up for past neglect and past mistakes. They loved the world but did not love God; God wrested the world from them and humiliated them. They professed to be Muslims, yet they buried the last Beloved of God underground and raised the Messiah of Nazareth alive to Heaven. God made them low on the earth and set Christians as rulers over them. Their condition now will not

2 *Al-Furqan*, 31.

change unless they agree to reform. Political schemes and plans can avail but little. The degradation of Muslims is the result of the anger of God. Unless Muslims make their peace with God they will only go under. Blessed, therefore, is he who hastens to make his peace with God. He will be saved from humiliation and disgrace. The Help of God will be with him and the Hand of God will steer him out of difficulties.

A great event

The coming of the Promised Messiah is no ordinary event: it is a great event. Did not the Holy Prophet send him greetings? Did he not warn his followers and say that they must go and join the Promised Messiah even if it entailed the hardest toil and trouble? Prophecies about the Promised Messiah exist in all religions. No prophet has failed to mention the coming of the Promised Messiah. Great must be the man who fulfils the prophecies of so many prophets, and for whose coming they all asked their peoples to wait. Blessed are those who witness the Promised Messiah or his time and receive the benefits promised at his hands. The coming of messengers is rare, especially of great messengers like the Promised Messiah. The Holy Prophet (on whom be peace and the blessings of God) stressed the coming of the Promised Messiah more than the coming of anyone else. A greater man among Muslims may not arise. He is the Seal of spiritual leaders (*Khatam al-Khuḷafa*) who will hereafter arise among the followers of the Holy Prophet. After him we only wait for the Day of Judgment. Every day in our time is therefore precious, infinitely more precious than the most precious possession of this world. Lucky is he who knows the value of the present and decides to join the Promised Messiah, and so earns the approval and pleasure of God. Such a man will find the goal of his life and capture the secret of being truly human.

Future of Ahmadiyyat

When a Messenger of God comes and raises a Jama'at, the first people to join are generally the poor. But the Jama'at does not remain poor for all time. It begins to prosper and ultimately even kings enter its fold. It takes root in a centre, then spreads over the area for which the Messenger was intended. Nobody need think, therefore, that our Jama'at is poor and will remain poor. It will grow by leaps and bounds. Let powerful countries join together and try to stop its growth; they will not succeed. A day will come when this Jama'at will beat all other groups and movements in the race. Revelations of Hazrat Mirza Sahib promise that his followers will be dominant over those who deny him until the Day of Judgment; also that the number of those who remain outside his fold will go on declining, and ultimately kings will join this Jama'at.

The Jama'at-i-Ahmadiyya, therefore, will not remain as poor and insignificant as it seems today, but will increase in numbers and influence and begin to surpass others. It will not remain weak but will become strong and victorious. A revelation of the Promised Messiah says:

بادشاہ تیرے کپڑوں سے برکت ڈھونڈیں گے۔

'Kings will seek blessings from thy garments'.

The value of great events or good actions depends upon the time chosen for them. A thing done at a certain time is very great, but at another time the same thing may be much less great. Those who were the first to believe in the Holy Prophet remain to this day the spiritual leaders of the world. Those who believed when Islam had become a power in the world attained little fame or honour. Therefore those who join the Ahmadiyya Jama'at now, when it is thought to be weak and insignificant, will attain the honour of early believers. They will inherit special rewards and blessings. Much time has gone by already, but the door to honour is still open; to earn nearness to God is still easy. I invite you, dear reader, to consider how precious is your opportunity. It is for you to say like all believers:

رَبَّنَا إِنَّنَا سَمِعْنَا مُنَادِيًا يُّنَادِي لِلْإِيْمَانِ أَنْ آمِنُوا بِرَبِّكُمْ فَآمَنَّا

> 'Our Lord, we heard a Crier call unto faith, "Believe ye in your Lord," and we have believed'.[3]

It is for you to say 'yea' to him who cries in the name of God. It is for you to become a dearly beloved of God.

I say truly that nobody can find God today outside Ahmadiyyat. Everybody outside the fold, if he searches his heart, will admit that he does not have that certainty of belief in God and His promises which one should have in indubitable realities. Equally will he fail to find in his heart the light by which he can see the Face of God. This certainty, this conviction, and this light you will not find outside the Jama'at of the Promised Messiah. The divine design is to unite mankind again. He who knows that death is certain cannot accept a life remote from God, a life devoid of His Light. Hasten, therefore, to the Light and to the certainty of conviction which you will find today in Ahmadiyyat alone, and without which life can have no attraction or charm. Lead others in your declaration so that you are remembered with honour and respect, that believers who come after you may pray for you to the end of days.

Sacrifices not a burden

True, those who join a Divine Movement have to carry a heavy load of sacrifices and responsibilities, but not every load is a burden. Does the peasant who carries on his back the produce of his hard work think his load a burden? Or the mother who carries her baby in her arms think the baby a burden? Service of a divine movement and effort on its behalf, therefore, is no burden for believers. Others may think it a burden, but for believers it is joy and hope. Do not be overawed, therefore, by the responsibilities you will incur by accepting the truth. Think, instead, of the gratitude you owe to God, of the mercy and grace mankind has received from Muhammad, the Prophet (on whom be peace and the blessings of God). Do not hesitate to lend your shoulder to the burden which it is the duty of every Muslim to carry. You may be high-placed or low, a leader or a common man; in the Sight of God you and other humans are all equal. The service of Islam is your duty as well as theirs. To believe

3 *Al-Imran*, 194.

in the Messengers of God is your obligation as well as theirs. Receive, therefore, the Command of God and His scheme of duties and rewards. Enter the Divine Movement and reap the rewards ordained for its entrants. The meanest reward that comes from God is better and more precious than a kingdom.

The Holy Prophet (on whom be peace) has said:

مَنْ فَارَقَ الْجَمَاعَةَ شِبْرًا فَلَيْسَ مِنَّا

> 'He who keeps away from a divine Jama'at by so much as a step is not one of us.'

To stay out of a Jama'at raised by God, therefore, is a serious matter. It is especially serious for those whose responsibility is twofold: towards themselves, and towards those who follow their lead. Men follow their leaders even in matters of religion. In the Sight of God, the mistakes they make are the mistakes of their leaders. The Holy Prophet (on whom be peace and the blessings of God) expressed this thought when he wrote to the Roman Emperor:

فَإِنْ تَوَلَّيْتَ فَعَلَيْكَ إِثْمُ الْأَرِيسِيِّينَ

> 'If you deny, the sin of your subjects will also be upon you.'

Therefore, dear reader, believe, that if you have friends or followers they may have no difficulty in believing too; so that you may not keep others from believing. Share rather the reward of their belief and of the good deeds which will come from believing.

In the Presence of God

Life here is limited. Nobody knows how long each of us may last. Sooner or later all must be ready to go and stand in the Presence of Almighty God. Nothing will then avail but true beliefs and good works. All of us, rich or poor, go from here empty-handed. Neither rich nor poor take away anything with them when they go from here to the Hereafter. We all carry only our faith and our good works with us. Believe, therefore, in the Messenger of God, that God may grant you peace. Answer the call of Islam that you may become accepted of God. The duty that was mine has been done. I have delivered to you the message. It is for you to accept or not. The least I hope and expect is that you will read this message with care, and that if you find it right and true you will not hesitate to believe. May God make it so! And our last words are:

وَاٰخِرُ دَعْوٰنَآ اَنِ الْحَمْدُ لِلّٰهِ رَبِّ الْعٰلَمِيْنَ -

'All praise for Allah, the Lord of the Worlds.'